MW00467011

The Real World Reader

The Real World Reader

A Rhetorical Reader for Writers

James Miller
University of Wisconsin-Whitewater

New York   Oxford
Oxford University Press

Oxford University Press is a department of the University of Oxford.
It furthers the University's objective of excellence in research,
scholarship, and education by publishing worldwide.

Oxford   New York
Auckland   Cape Town   Dar es Salaam   Hong Kong   Karachi
Kuala Lumpur   Madrid   Melbourne   Mexico City   Nairobi
New Delhi   Shanghai   Taipei   Toronto

With offices in
Argentina   Austria   Brazil   Chile   Czech Republic   France   Greece
Guatemala   Hungary   Italy   Japan   Poland   Portugal   Singapore
South Korea   Switzerland   Thailand   Turkey   Ukraine   Vietnam

For titles covered by Section 112 of the US Higher Education
Opportunity Act, please visit www.oup.com/us/he for the
latest information about pricing and alternate formats.

Published by Oxford University Press
198 Madison Avenue, New York, New York 10016
http://www.oup.com

Oxford is a registered trademark of Oxford University Press

Library of Congress Cataloging-in-Publication Data
Miller, James S., 1966-
   The real world reader / James S. Miller, University of Wisconsin-Whitewater.
      pages cm
   Includes index.
   ISBN 978-0-19-932989-2 -- ISBN 978-0-19-932990-8 (instructor's edition)
1. College readers. 2. English language--Rhetoric--Problems, exercises etc.
3. Report writing--Problems, exercises, etc. I. Title.
   PE1417.M486 2015
   808'.0472--dc23
                                                                    2014034140

Printing number: 9 8 7 6 5 4 3 2 1

Printed in the United States of America
on acid-free paper

Contents

Chapter 3: Thinking Rhetorically About the Revision and Editing Process   37

Chapter 4: Thinking Rhetorically About Different Modes of Writing   48

Rhetorical Table of Contents

Thematic Table of Contents

RELIGION

TECHNOLOGY

VIOLENCE

Preface

Reading and Writing in the Real World

In our increasingly fast-paced and interconnected age, we have never before enjoyed so many different opportunities to play the role of reader and writer. From email to text messages, blogs to Facebook, magazines articles to Wikipedia posts, we have at our disposal an unprecedented array of tools for communicating what's on our minds. But are we using these new opportunities to their full advantage? True, it's never been easier to exchange ideas, information, and points of view. But are we developing the skills to understand and respond to them fully? For all the benefits they confer, these new opportunities also confront us with some fundamental challenges. In a world where it can sometimes feel as if reading and writing are all that we do, it couldn't be more important to undertake these activities in the most thoughtful, critical, and purposeful ways.

This is the goal *The Real World Reader* sets about to accomplish. Bringing together a wide and diverse collection of writing from the real world—from websites to magazine articles, op-eds to advertisements, essays to news stories, book chapters to blogs—the book creates a comprehensive framework that allows students to identify and analyze the different rhetorical considerations that determine what a piece of writing looks like and how it works. It accomplishes this goal by dividing the process of rhetorical analysis into a set of logically sequenced steps, each of which focuses on a key concept or concern: purpose, audience, argument, voice, and credibility. Bringing together a representative sampling of writing from the real world, each chapter walks students through a step-by-step process in which they learn how to analyze these texts rhetorically and then use this analysis to undertake writing of their own.

About *The Real World Reader*

Starting With What Students Know

One of the major benefits of a reader that focuses on real world writing is that it meets students where they are. Focusing on the kinds of writing they already know and do in their own daily lives, *The Real World Reader* conveys a powerful message about the role that writing plays. Rather than treat it as a set of abstract skills to be mastered, this book instead presents writing as an empowering tool that allows students to speak about—and speak back to—the larger world of which they are a part.

Using a Rhetorical Framework to Teach Writing

Unlike other readers, *The Real World Reader* organizes its approach to writing around the rhetorical process itself. Rather than examine different modes of writing in isolation, this book teaches students to find the rhetorical concerns that *all* writing shares in common. What, it asks, are the core questions (about audience or purpose, argument or voice) that all writers have to address? And how can students use these same questions as the foundation for analyzing and creating such writing themselves?

Teaching Writing in an Accessible and Hands-On Way

Rather than present rhetorical modes and terms simply as abstract concepts, *The Real World Reader* shows how these concepts shape the choices and decisions actual writers make. Whatever the rhetorical concept under examination, students will consistently learn by thinking like writers themselves.

Integrating Patterns of Development

Rather than treat rhetorical modes as separate, stand-alone categories, this book presents a variety of writing examples that show students how these patterns intersect and interact in the real world. In doing so, it not only helps students better perceive the ways different rhetorical modes work together but also encourages them to consider the rhetorical factors that motivate writers to employ different modes to achieve different goals.

Connecting Rhetorical Analysis to Cultural Analysis

Each of the book's rhetorical chapters supplements its real world writing instruction by joining its informal reading selections to a second set of formal reading selections that focus on the broader cultural issues these rhetorical concepts raise—from debates about multiculturalism to discussions about online privacy, critiques of modern political campaigning to analyses of modern consumerism.

Scaffolding Instruction by Presenting a Diversity of Selections

The Real World Reader creates a scaffold for its reading and writing instruction by moving students through a step-by-step engagement with four distinct types of selections: informal selections, formal selections, academic selections, and a sample student essay. Each rhetorical chapter begins by presenting students with a set of informal selections, using this kind of accessible, popular writing as a model for how to undertake rhetorical analysis. Each chapter then walks students through a rhetorical analysis of more formal and academic types of writing. Each chapter concludes by presenting a sample student essay, an example that shows students how this same rhetorical approach can be used to create successful college writing.

Providing an Intuitive and Flexible Organization

The Real World Reader is divided into three main parts. Part One consists of four chapters that provide students with a rhetorical framework for reflecting upon and mastering the process of critical reading and writing. The first three of these chapters teach students how to use a set of rhetorical terms to become more thoughtful, proficient readers and writers. The final chapter in Part One rounds out this instruction by showing students how to apply this same rhetorical approach to the most common patterns or modes of writing we encounter in daily life—including narration, description, cause and effect, and analysis.

Part Two consists of five chapters, each of which is organized around a key rhetorical concept: purpose, audience, argument, voice, and credibility. Each of these rhetorical chapters includes:

- An introductory essay that invites students to reflect upon the particular rhetorical concept at hand. Each of these essays also includes an example of real world writing and uses it as a model or template for how to conduct rhetorical analysis.
- A set of informal writing selections accompanied by a set of discussion and writing prompts (entitled *Thinking Rhetorically About . . .*) that ask students to analyze these selections in relation to the rhetorical concept at hand. To facilitate this work, the first selection also includes a sample or model of what this analysis looks like.
- A set of formal selections that explore some of the broader social or cultural questions related to the rhetorical concept at hand. Like their informal counterparts, these selections are also accompanied by their own set of discussion and writing prompts.
- A set of academic selections that model some of the more traditional ways writing is presented and taught within the college classroom. Like the formal and informal readings, these selections are accompanied by their own set of discussion and writing prompts.
- A group work writing assignment that asks students to collaborate in analyzing one of the chapter's selections along rhetorical lines.
- A writing assignment that asks students to address a given topic from both a formal and an informal venue to prompt reflection on some of the rhetorical differences between formal and informal writing.
- A writing activity (entitled *Speaking For Yourself*) that invites students to use the rhetorical analysis modeled within the chapter to create a real world writing example of their own.

Part Three consists of two chapters that use the book's rhetorical framework to examine each stage of the research process. These two chapters cover:

- Finding, evaluating, and documenting sources
- Creating and revising a research paper draft

What follows is an outline of *The Real World Reader*, with a summary of each chapter:

Introduction
Presents an overview of the book's framework, outlining the pedagogy for analyzing and creating different types of real world writing.

Part One—The Reading and Writing Process
Chapter 1: Thinking Rhetorically About the Reading Process
Presents step-by-step instructions for analyzing writing in rhetorical terms.

Chapter 2: Thinking Rhetorically About the Writing Process
Presents step-by-step instructions for approaching the invention and arrangement
stages of the writing process in rhetorical terms.

Chapter 3: Thinking Rhetorically About the Revision and Editing Process
Presents step-by-step instructions for approaching the editing and revision stages of
the writing process in rhetorical terms.

Chapter 4: Thinking Rhetorically About Different Modes of Writing
Presents step-by-step instructions for analyzing the different patterns or modes of
writing in rhetorical terms.

Part Two—Rhetorical Readings
Chapter 5: Purpose
Brings together a collection of real world writing that foregrounds rhetorical considerations of *purpose*. Creates a set of discussion and writing prompts that call on you
to address such questions as: What goals does this writer seem to have in mind?
Where in the text do we see evidence of this? And how do such goals influence the
way this writing is put together?

Chapter 6: Audience
Brings together a collection of real world writing that foregrounds the considerations of *audience*. Creates a set of discussion and writing prompts that call on
you to consider such questions as: Who is the ideal reader for this type of writing? How does the choice of audience influence the other, rhetorical choices the
writer makes?

Chapter 7: Argument
Brings together a collection of real world writing that foregrounds the issues of *argumentation*. Creates a set of discussion and writing prompts that call on you to consider such questions as: What is the main point this writer is trying to get across?
What message or idea is the writer trying to get the reader to accept?

Chapter 8: Voice
Brings together a collection of real world writing that foregrounds the question of
writerly *voice*. Creates a set of discussion and writing prompts that call on you to
consider the particular decisions a writer makes regarding tone, style, and/or word
choice.

Chapter 9: Credibility
Brings together a collection of real world writing that foregrounds the strategies
and dynamics of *credibility*. Creates a set of discussion and writing prompts that

call on you to consider such questions as: What evidence or proof does this writer offer in support of the claims that are made? On what basis does this writer ask to be believed?

Part Three—The Research Process
Chapter 10: Finding and Evaluating Sources
Demonstrates how to think about the research process in rhetorical terms. Discusses the preliminary stages of the research process, including how to generate a viable research topic, how to create a formal research proposal, and how to identify and evaluate research sources.

Chapter 11: Creating and Revising a Research Draft
Focuses on the work involved in creating and revising a draft of a research essay. Discusses the key strategies, including creating a research outline; integrating research sources into a first draft; quoting, paraphrasing, and summarizing source material; identifying and avoiding plagiarism; and documenting sources in MLA format.

Practical Resources

Student resources for *The Real World Reader*, including worksheets, links to digital compositions, grammar tips and quizzes, dictionaries and thesauruses, and online self-tests, are available at www.oup.com/us/miller. An eBook version of *The Real World Reader* is also available through CourseSmart.com.

Instructor resources for *The Real World Reader* are also provided digitally for your convenience at www.oup.com/us/miller. By clicking on "Instructor Resources," you will be directed to a page for creating an instructor's account with Oxford University Press. Content cartridges for the most common course management systems can be created for you or your institution by contacting your local OUP representative or by calling Customer Service at 1-800-280-0280.

Acknowledgements

The Real World Reader has followed a long and circuitous path on its journey from informal vision to full-fledged book. But like many such odysseys, it has proven well worth the effort. Along the way, the book has benefited immeasurably from the input and assistance provided by countless friends, students, and colleagues.

First of all, I'd like to extend my thanks to my colleagues and students at the University of Wisconsin–Whitewater. I could have found no better sounding board for my ideas about writing and teaching than my fellow instructors in the Department of Languages and Literature, nor a more rigorous proving ground than the classrooms where I have tried to put these ideas into practice. I would also like to express my affection and gratitude to the crew at EVP Coffee in Madison. Truly, there is no more congenial environment for writing a book.

The Oxford University Press editors and I also extend our deepest thanks to the many academics across the country whose insights, critiques, and shared experiences helped to shape this rhetoric/reader that you hold in your hands: Wade Bradford, Moorpark College; Jerry C. Blanton, Miami Dade College; Susannah Clements, Regent University; Gretchen M. Cohenour, Averett University; Monica L. Dimauro, Florida State College at Jacksonville; Africa Fine, Palm Beach State College; Selena Flowers, Houston Community College; Tia Gafford Williams, Fort Valley State University; Kim Haimes-Korn, Southern Polytechnic State University; Michael Heumann, Imperial Valley College; Anne Homan, State Fair Community College; Schahara Hudelson, South Plains College; Nancy Kerr, Dallas County Community College; Alice Knox Eaton, Springfield College; Amberyl Malkovich, Concord University; Karl Martin, Point Loma Nazarene University; Annie S. Perkins, Norfolk State University; Stephen A. Raynie, Gordon State College; Guy Shebat, Youngstown State University; Yvonne Sims, South Carolina State University; Michael D. Sollars, Texas Southern University; Mark Stevens, Southern Polytechnic State University; Marjorie Stewart, Glenville State College; Regina Van Epps, Atlantic Cape Community College; and Michelle Veenstra, Francis Marion University.

Of course, *The Real World Reader* would never have reached the publication stage if not for the concerted efforts of my editor, Frederick Speers. Fred's clear-eyed vision of what a book like this truly needs, and his unstinting willingness to share this vision with me, ensured that the full promise of this project was fulfilled. And finally, to Emily Hall, whose love and commitment makes this—and everything else—worthwhile. My love and thanks.

Introduction

Writing in the Real World

How much time over the last couple of days did you spend writing? As a student, perhaps you found yourself working through the first draft of an essay for English class or putting the finishing touches on a chemistry lab report. Outside of class, you may have tweeted your friends about a recent concert, composed a memo for your supervisor at work, posted a response to an online review, or emailed your family about plans for an upcoming visit. Whatever the case, when you tally it all up it's entirely possible that you dedicated more time to writing than to any other single activity.

And yet despite this fact, it's likely that you didn't spend nearly as much time reflecting on *why* or *how* you wrote. In our fast-paced, 24/7 world, we are often simply too busy to pause and take stock of all the considerations and calculations that go into what we write. This is especially true for all the writing we do outside the classroom—out there in what is often called the "real world." Indeed, we tend to treat such writing as precisely the kind of thing we *don't* have to think about: writing so straightforward and obvious that no serious reflection is required.

But while this notion may reflect popular stereotype, it doesn't come close to capturing the truth. In fact, when we take a closer look at all the writing we do in the real world, it becomes clear that a good deal more forethought and planning go into this work than first meets the eye. True, we rarely spend time worrying whether we've properly footnoted our latest Facebook post, and no, we don't grade each others' emails based on the quality of their topic sentences, but this doesn't mean we aren't considering a range of important questions every time we sit down to write. Questions like: What point I am trying to get across? Who are my intended readers, and what effect on them do I want to have? What kind of tone should I strike or language should I employ? And how will these choices make my writing more effective?

Questions like these are important because they shed light on all the different goals we use our writing in the real world to accomplish. We use such writing to express our feelings and air our opinions, to tell our stories and register our complaints, to convey information and connect with others. Indeed, it's not going too far to say that the real world is where we come to most appreciate the power of writing itself. It is the setting in which we come to see most clearly the difference writing can make in our lives: the connections it can help us to forge, the ideas it allows us to exchange, and the larger change in the world it enables us to bring about.

What Does This Book Ask You to Do?

The goal of *The Real World Reader* is to help you develop exactly this kind of understanding. What happens, it asks, when we look more closely and critically at the many different types of writing found in the real world? And how do we master the skills to better understand how such writing actually works? To answer these questions, the book brings together a diverse, wide-ranging collection of writing from the real world (i.e., op-eds, blog posts, essays, and book excerpts), using them as models for teaching you to identify and analyze the rhetorical issues and considerations that underlie them. *Rhetoric*, in the most basic sense, refers to the choices writers consider to make their writing more effective. Among the key rhetorical concepts this book asks you to consider are **purpose** (what is the writer's goal?), **audience** (who is the intended or target reader?), **argument** (what larger point or message is being conveyed?), **voice** (what tone or language is employed?), and **credibility** (what makes this writer believable?).

Because the goal here is to make you a more effective reader *and* writer, the book is organized around chapters that are designed to teach you the concrete skills of both *analysis* and *composition*. Part One, which consists of the first four chapters, uses the book's rhetorical framework to help you master the twin processes of critical reading and critical writing. The five chapters that follow in Part Two build upon this work by focusing on a different key rhetorical concept: purpose in Chapter 5, audience in Chapter 6, argument in Chapter 7, voice in Chapter 8, and credibility in Chapter 9.

Why Should You Do It?

As noted above, *The Real World Reader* is motivated by the belief that we learn valuable lessons about the power of writing when we look more closely at the most familiar and everyday forms writing can take. This belief carries with it two very important ideas. First, it reminds us that—contrary to popular opinion—everyday or real world writing has genuine value. It is not what we do merely to distract or entertain ourselves; very often, such writing serves as the vehicle through which we attempt to figure out the issues, questions, and ideas that matter most to us. Second, and equally important, real world writing throws a spotlight on the role that rhetorical thinking plays in our writing lives. It reminds us that rhetoric is more than an abstract concept, that it is a set of practical tools for making our way through—and making sense of—the world of which we are a part.

How Do You Get It Done?

The success of this approach depends on our seeing how these rhetorical concepts can be used to pose specific and practical questions about the writing we see and do every day. Included below is an outline that translates the rhetorical concepts into useful questions:

- *Purpose*: What is the writer trying to say? Why does the writer want to say it?
- *Audience*: What kind of reader is the writer trying to reach?
- *Argument*: What is the writer's main point?
- *Voice*: What language or word choice does the writer use?
- *Credibility*: What makes the writer believable?

Thinking Rhetorically About Real World Writing: A Step-by-Step Guide

To begin applying these rhetorical concepts in a more developed and detailed way, let's take a look at an example. Imagine yourself in the following real world scenario: You are a football fan who is engaged in an extended online dialogue with others on a website that monitors and rates the performance of your favorite team. Some taking part in this conversation see the team's losing record as evidence of poor coaching or play-calling; others see it as a reflection of poor motivation among the players; still others blame the team's owners for refusing to spend enough money to attract top talent. You have your own views on the matter and are eager to join the conversation. How do you decide exactly what you want to say? How do you figure out how to convince others to share your view? To answer these questions, let's start by looking at how you might go about making your case:

> We've been hearing a lot of complaints about our beloved Eagles, and I totally understand the frustration. I don't think we should go off the deep end and fire the whole coaching staff, though. There's reason to be optimistic about the future, if certain changes are made. The key issue has to do with the players more than the coach. The ownership needs to get serious about spending money to attract quality players. In today's competitive environment, the team can't afford to economize when it comes to the skill positions. Look, for example, at their division rivals, the X. Over the last three years, they have spent twice as much money on their skill players and have finished at the top of the division. If we don't make this commitment, we're going to have to resign ourselves to being just a mediocre team. This is something we really can't afford.

At first glance, it may seem that joining this conversation is a simple or straightforward proposition. But when we begin to examine this passage from a rhetorical perspective, it becomes clear that more is going on under the surface here than first seems apparent. Notice how many different rhetorical questions you have to answer as you begin to put this response together. For starters, you have questions related to your larger **goal** or **purpose**. Do you want simply to convey facts and figures, to inform? Or is your intent to persuade your readers to your own point of view? Do you want simply to air your personal feelings or make a more logical argument? Next is the question of **audience**. Who are the principal participants in this debate? What are their respective backgrounds and levels of expertise? What are they looking for out of this discussion? Following these questions are those related to the specific **argument** you want to make. Are you going to make an argument in which you assign blame for the team's woes? Make recommendations for how the coaching staff should be revamped? Vent your frustration at the unfair criticism being expressed by other fans? Questions like these, in turn, might lead you to consider the particular **voice** you want to adopt. Should you strike an aggressive or adversarial tone, advocating forcefully for your own point of view? Or does it seem wiser to employ more neutral or even conciliatory language in the hopes of finding common ground? And finally, you might want to think about how all of these preceding questions help you figure out your overall **credibility**. Why should somebody accept what you are saying? What evidence or proof can you provide to make your response persuasive and believable?

Now that we've seen the rhetorical questions you might confront here, let's take a closer look at the specific ways you might go about answering them:

Step One: *Determining Purpose*

- *What you are saying*: "We've been hearing a lot of complaints about our beloved Eagles, and I totally understand the frustration. I don't think we should go off the deep end and fire the whole coaching staff, though. There's reason to be optimistic about the future, if certain changes are made."

- *What you are thinking*: This is a website that encourages fans to spout off without really thinking through their points. Given this, I want to steer the conversation in a more reasonable direction so that people can really think about the points they're trying to make. I want to do this, though, without seeming to criticize them too much.

Step Two: *Defining Audience*

- *What you are saying*: "The key issue has to do with the players more than the coach. The ownership needs to get serious about spending money to attract quality players. In today's competitive environment, the team can't afford to economize when it comes to the skill positions."

- *What you are thinking*: Most of the posts I've read seem to come from fans who don't know all of the facts about this situation, and these readers don't seem to know as much about the quality of the coaching as they do about the talent of the players. Therefore, I need to create a new framework for the discussion so that everyone doesn't keep mistaking coaching for the real problem.

Step Three: *Identifying Argument*

- *What you are saying*: "If we don't make this commitment, we're going to have to resign ourselves to being just a mediocre team. This is something we really can't afford."

- *What you are thinking*: This is really my main point. I want my readers to understand the importance of coaching to the overall success of the team.

Step Four: *Developing Voice*

- *What you are saying*: "I don't think we should go off the deep end and fire the whole coaching staff, though."

- *What you are thinking*: I wonder if I'm striking the right tone here. Am I being too aggressive in my point? Too alarmist? Is this going to turn off too many of my readers? And I wonder, too, about my use of the term "we," which seems to imply that fans like us are part of the team. Should I change this?

Step Five: *Defending Credibility*

○ *What you are saying*: "Look, for example, at their division rivals, the X. Over the last three years, they have spent twice as much money on their skill players and have finished at the top of the division."

○ *What you are thinking*: Hopefully, people will see connection between player salary and team performance. This is a connection I'm assuming my readers will grasp, but I don't know for sure. Should I provide more support for this? I wonder if others will disagree or argue that this other team's success is due to other factors? Should I respond to this point, or just say nothing?

> Just saying this, though, is probably not going to be enough. Are people going to agree with this point just because I say it is so? What proof should I provide?

Using These Rhetorical Steps to Analyze Real World Writing

Now, let's take a look at how these steps can be used to analyze an actual example of real world writing. Read the selection below closely. As you do, take note of the comments included in the margins of the text. Designed to model the way a typical reader might respond, they focus our attention on some of the most basic features of this piece (i.e., introductory and concluding paragraphs, topic sentences, and transitions), and they establish a foundation for beginning to think about this piece in rhetorical terms. Once you've finished reading over the essay and its comments, take a look at the accompanying step-by-step outline, which demonstrates how this essay can be analyzed using the book's five key rhetorical terms.

"Column Degrading, Rather Than Empowering"

In many ways, this excerpt from a recent letter to the editor at the campus newspaper for DePauw University represents the type of writing we might easily encounter ourselves.

Dear X,

You wrote that you thought DePauw women to be very beautiful when you first arrived on campus and implied that if their weight increased, their beauty decreased. We are saddened that you have been conditioned to believe that a woman's attractiveness is based on her body size.

Writer's use of the word "saddened" seems significant. It suggests that the larger goal here is to critique certain campus attitudes toward women and women's bodies.

5

It seems ironic that you claim to retain a fit body despite what you eat and yet deem yourself qualified to give eating and exercise advice to overweight individuals. This leads us to believe that you retain an "exceptionally slender figure" due to genetics, despite activity and eating habits. As you supposedly have had no personal experience exercising and eating specific-ally to lose weight your column has little to no credibil-ity because you do not need to pay attention to eating and exercise to stay slim.

A shift toward a more satirical tone. Is this an effective strategy? Or does it risk undermining the writer's credibility?

You imply that size is the key factor in determining a person's health, and gaining weight and maintaining health inversely correlate. According to the Centers for Disease Control and Prevention, vast ranges of healthy weight exist for women of every height. For example, the healthy weight for a 5'4" woman ranges from 114 to 151 pounds. A healthy first year girl who weighed 114 in September could gain 15 pounds or even 30 and still be in that healthy range. Rather than empowering students to embrace a healthier lifestyle, you are endorsing societal standards that beauty is determined by the size of a girl's apple bottom jeans— standards that can drive people to take drastic and unnecessary weight loss measures.

Use of objective data is an effective strategy. Statistical proof is harder to refute than personal opinion.

Your column offends us. As healthy DePauw women, we have more important things to do than obsess over our self-images. We would appreciate if you could refrain from making outrageous and insulting gener-alizations in future columns, and instead utilize your voice to legitimately empower, rather than degrade, your fellow students.

Writer using powerful word choice to conclude: "offends," "outrageous," "insulting." Seems as if the writer's goal is to leave readers with a sense of outrage and anger.

Source: The DePauw, April 13, 2010

Step One: *Determining Purpose*

This letter is clearly intended as a persuasive piece of writing. Its goal is not just to inform readers about the existence of "societal standards" of beauty but to con-vince them to view these "standards" as degrading and dangerous. The objective here is to convince the audience to reject the notion that female "beauty" should be seen largely as a matter of "weight loss."

Step Two: *Defining Audience*

The intended audience seems to be the wider community of students and faculty at the university. This letter is clearly a response to an earlier op-ed in which the writer made certain claims about "weight loss," "societal standards" of beauty, and their overall effect on female students at DePauw. Given the intended audience, it seems as if the writer of the letter is motivated by a desire to change attitudes on campus toward women. The goal here is clearly to challenge what this writer sees as a dangerous and potentially widespread tendency to define women in terms of their physical appearance.

Step Three: *Identifying Argument*

The writer makes several points. The first point is that it is inaccurate and unfair to connect "attractiveness" to "body size." This connection, the writer argues, reduces the question of attractiveness to a narrow and unobtainable standard. The writer's second point is that the "societal standard" promoting this connection does real harm to those women who attempt to live up to it. The writer concludes by making a third point: that there are far more important issues for women to concern themselves with other than "body image."

Step Four: *Developing Voice*

The tone the writer adopts seems to be a mixture of outrage and urgency. We see this clearly in relation to the specific language used to convey this critique: "outrageous," "insulting," "offends." These terms serve to reinforce not only the writer's anger but also a sense of how important a social issue this is.

Step Five: *Defending Credibility*

The writer attempts to establish credibility in a number of ways. The first strategy involves the use of medical statistics. Quoting from the Centers for Disease Control and Prevention, the writer not only provides support for the view that "societal standards" of beauty are dangerous but also for the corollary notion that these standards should be viewed as a medical crisis. In addition, the writer deploys a second strategy, which involves using a hypothetical example of a "healthy weight" woman to further challenge conventional beauty standards. These tactics are effective in part because—as more factual and objective evidence—they supplement the more subjective and opinion-based features of the argument.

Putting It Into Writing

The step-by-step outline above provides a model for analyzing the different choices the letter writer makes in rhetorical terms. Once this analysis is complete, we can then turn our attention to the ways such an analysis can be organized into a more conventional written form. The essay below offers one such example. As you look it over, note how the comments included in the margins serve as a guide for identifying the features and conventions this kind of formal writing typically includes.

"Dangerous Images"

Throughout American history, women have struggled against sexist stereotypes promoted by the larger society. And among these stereotypes, none are more commonplace than those dealing with women's bodies. For centuries, women have been told that in order to be considered "beautiful" or even "acceptable," their bodies had to fit a very narrow standard.

Introduction: Designed to provide background/context for main points to follow.

In the short piece "Column Degrading, Rather Than Empowering," the writer takes direct aim at these stereotypes, arguing that a societal emphasis on female body types, and more specifically weight loss, leads to harmful consequences. The writer does this within the essay by speaking back to those fellow students who have expressed sexist attitudes about women and women's bodies. Calling out these attitudes as "outrageous" and "insulting," the writer makes a spirited argument about both the physical and the psychological damage these kinds of stereotypes can inflict.

Topic sentence: Introduces focus for the first main paragraph.

Overall, this essay presents readers with a powerful critique of our society's misguided and hypocritical "beauty standards," highlighting not only the social and medical dangers they pose, but also the flawed logic that underlies them. The place in the essay where we most clearly see evidence of this critique is the section where the writer offers statistics detailing the "healthy range" for female weight gain. These data, coming from so reputable a source as the "Centers for Disease Control," serves as a powerful counterpoint to the cultural stereotypes about women's bodies the writer wants to challenge. In response to these stereotypes, the writer presents objective, factual data—a contrast that underscores how subjective, even superstitious, these stereotypes actually are.

Topic sentence for second main paragraph that also presents the writer's main point or thesis.

Evidence offered in support of writer's main point or thesis.

Statistical evidence like this provides an effective framework for the writer to advance another key point: namely, that these stereotypes stem primarily from ignorance. This is clearly the message the writer intends to convey in statements such as "DePauw women, we have more important things to do than obsess over our self-images." For the writer here, the problem with these cultural stereotypes is precisely that they emphasize

Topic sentence for third main paragraph that also serves as a transition to the writer's second main point.

unthinking obsession over rational thought. And what results from this ignorance, the writer contends, are attitudes about bodies and gender that are "degrading" rather than "empowering."

Conclusion: Writer summarizing main points and connecting them to quotations from the essay being discussed. 45

Analyzing Rhetorical Modes

As you become more experienced conducting this kind of rhetorical analysis, you'll become more aware that much of the writing we encounter in the real world follows certain patterns. These patterns are called **rhetorical modes**: writing that shares a common feature or adheres to a common format to achieve a specific goal. Among the most commonplace modes are those that tell a story (narrative mode); describe a person, situation, or event (descriptive mode); show how two things are alike or different (compare-and-contrast mode); or explain why something happens (cause-and-effect mode). These and other rhetorical modes can be found in virtually every kind of real world writing—from journal essays to blog entries, newspaper editorials to Facebook posts, workplace memos to Twitter feeds—helping writers accomplish a range of different goals.

Given this, another of the book's objectives is to help you understand and analyze how rhetorical modes work. Traditional approaches have tended to study rhetorical modes by viewing them more or less in isolation: as abstract or stand-alone categories, divorced from the larger context in which they are found and examined separately from the other modes with which they interact. *The Real World Reader*, on the other hand, takes a very different approach. True to its title, this book examines rhetorical modes within the countless real world contexts in which they exist and operate, showing how they serve as tools for different writers to accomplish specific rhetorical tasks. Organized around the the same five key concepts (i.e., purpose, audience, argument, voice, and credibility) employed elsewhere, this approach makes clear that modes, like every other aspect of writing in the real world, are the result of actual writers making specific decisions in the real world. Chapter 4 outlines this approach in the most detailed and comprehensive form. But opportunities for thinking about modes in explicitly rhetorical terms can be found within each of the major chapters in the book.

Looking Forward, Getting Started

Now that you've gotten a sense of the rhetorical analysis the book asks you to undertake, it's time to begin doing this analysis yourself. As you make your way through the chapters that follow, you will be invited to use the same models and guidelines presented here to undertake this kind of analysis and writing. Remember that the ultimate goal is to help you to become more engaged, critical, and skilled readers and writers. To help you achieve this goal, *The Real World Reader* aims to meet you where you are. Introducing you to the kinds of writing you already know and do in the "real world," this book supplies you with the tools to become more thoughtful, proficient, and empowered writers yourselves.

1 Thinking Rhetorically About the Reading Process

These days, it can often feel like we are swimming in a sea of other people's writing. From podcasts to public service announcements, campus flyers to political speeches, texts to tweets, there's a good chance you spend a healthy portion of your day sampling, sifting through, and trying to make sense of other people's writing. To illustrate, consider the examples included below. Taken together, they offer a small sampling of the range and diversity of the writing we come across in our daily lives.

Planet Green Recycle, "The Bike Revolution"

Planet Green Recycle is a website dedicated to providing nonprofit organizations with information and guidelines about recycling. This piece was posted in 2013.

Think back to when you were young. Real young. What was one of the best gifts you remember receiving as a child? Was it a Barbie Doll? Maybe your first baseball glove? There are numerous things you can look back on when thinking about staples of your childhood, and bicycle riding has a good possibility of being one of them. Who would have thought that learning to ride a bike with your oversized helmet and training wheels would revolutionize into something that's being talked about daily by some of the most important people all over the world as ways to increase the quality of life?

FIGURE 1.1

Source: Photo by Arne Hückelheim.
http://planetgreenrecycle.com/blog/

"Editorial: To Eliminate Fraternity Hazing, Pledging Must End"

The Cornell Sun *is the weekly campus newspaper for Cornell University. This article appeared in the paper's op-ed section in 2012.*

Over the course of our time at Cornell, we have seen a full evolution of Cornell's policy toward fraternities and sororities. While we have previously expressed concern about the overly heavy-handed nature of the University's response to the Greek system, recent events have made clear to us that the Greek system is incapable of making broad cultural changes on its own.

In the last month, three fraternities were suspended, including one that was accused of holding a hazing event in which two students were hospitalized. It is disturbing that these incidents come only one year after a Cornell sophomore died in a hazing ritual. It is difficult to assign blame when the entire fraternity culture is responsible.

Source: The Cornell Daily Sun, November 29, 2012.
http://cornellsun.com/node/54508

Visual Rhetoric: Joel Pett, "Unemployment Line"

Published in 2012, this political cartoon was created by Joel Pett for the Lexington Herald-Leader.

FIGURE 1.3

Source: http://politicalhumor.about.com/od/politicalcartoons/ig/Political-Cartoons/
Unemployment-Line.-u2h.htm

These three readings—and, indeed, all such writing—share one thing in common: a desire to reach and influence *you*. Advertisements work hard to make you desire different products; news articles strive to make you better informed; op-eds do their utmost to sway your opinion; social activist blogs try to spur your involvement in different causes; social media posts stir your interest in the daily goings-on of family and friends; Twitter feeds lure you into a conversation about the latest cultural trend or controversy. Whether it seeks to argue or inform, educate or entertain, persuade or distract, all writing is motivated by a desire to shape how you think, feel, or act.

The implications of this fact are hard to overstate. After all, if effective writing is measured by how successfully it influences our thoughts, feelings, or behavior, it seems worth our while to know how writers themselves go about trying to make this happen. A useful place to start is to focus on a writer's plans and goals. What does this writer want from me? What larger idea or message is the writer trying to get across? Why does the writer employ this type of language or adopt this particular tone? Questions like these are called *rhetorical*. Rhetoric, in the most basic sense, refers to the strategies writers use to make their writing more coherent, effective, or persuasive. As readers, posing rhetorical questions is a useful strategy because it helps us appreciate in a more hands-on way how different kinds of writing work. Among the key rhetorical questions we can ask are those about **purpose** (what does the writer want to say and why?), **audience** (to whom does the writer want to say it?), **argument** (what is the main idea or message the writer wants to get across?), **voice** (what style or tone does the writer adopt?), and **credibility** (how does the writer make the writing convincing or believable?).

To see what this kind of rhetorical analysis looks like in practice, let's take a closer look at one of the examples above. If you happened to come across the public service announcement about bicycles, for instance, there are a number of questions you could ask to get a better handle on this writer's objectives and agenda. For starters, you might notice that this post comes from the official blog of Planet Green Recycling, an organization dedicated to providing recycling and fund-raising advice to nonprofit organizations. What does this context suggest about the writer's larger goals here? Answering this initial question might lead you next to focus on some of the more specific elements in the rest of the text. Why does the writer choose the title, "The Bike Revolution"? What kind of "revolutionary" change is the writer suggesting bike riding can achieve? And why, furthermore, does the writer then urge readers to "think back" on their own childhoods? How does this nostalgic invitation relate to the idea of a "bike revolution"? Following this, you might then turn your attention to the comparison drawn between bicycles, Barbie dolls, and baseball gloves. What point about bikes and bike riding is the writer using this comparison to make?

Obviously, it takes practice to answer these sorts of questions thoroughly and effectively. You're not going to completely master this kind of rhetorical analysis the very first time you attempt it. But as you make your way through this book, you will find yourself gaining more and more confidence in your ability to do precisely this type of work. And as you do, you will find yourself becoming an ever more thoughtful, reflective, and critical reader. To get this process underway, take a look at the outline below. Breaking the work of rhetorical analysis into its key components, it models the kinds of questions you can pose to put yourself into more direct dialogue with the writing you encounter:

Step One: *Reading for Purpose*

- º What is the writer's goal?

- º What is the writer's perspective? How does it compare with your own?

- º Do you detect any biases in the writer's perspective?

Step Two: *Considering Audience*

- º Who is the writer's target audience? Whom does the writer seem to be addressing?

- º What assumptions does the author make about the target audience?

Step Three: *Identifying Argument*

- º What is the writer's main point? What larger idea is the writer trying to get across?

- º How does the writer explain and/or support the main points?

Step Four: *Assessing Voice*

- º What is the writer's style or tone?

- º What particular words or phrases stand out?

- º How is the writing organized? What form, structure, and syntax does the writer use?

Step Five: *Determining Credibility*

- º What makes this writer believable or convincing?

- º What gives this writer the authority to speak on this topic?

Posing these kinds of rhetorical questions is an essential first step, but to answer such questions fully, it's also important to have a set of practical tools for addressing the specific elements within a given piece of writing. The activities outlined below provide you with just such tools. Each one describes a specific strategy you can use to begin organizing your own rhetorical analysis. As you review each set of instructions, think about how you might put them into practice yourself:

- *Highlighting*: To highlight a text is to mark it up with the notations (e.g., arrows, underlinings, circles, question marks, or exclamation points) that provide a written record of your initial thoughts and reactions. As a written record of your first impression, highlights are especially important because they lay the foundation for the more focused analysis to come. Here is a quick summary of the kinds of questions you can use highlighting to address:

○ What words or phrases stand out as most noticeable or important?

○ What sentence or section captures the writer's main point?

○ What ideas or claims do you find most interesting or important?

• *Annotating*: To annotate a text is to move from recording your initial impressions to conducting a more focused and detailed analysis of its main points. Annotation is where you begin to bring your own perspective, your own views on the topic, to bear. You might use annotation to pose questions about the text, reflect upon the significance of a given statement put these statements into your own words, challenge or disagree with a point the writer makes, or propose an alternative argument or viewpoint. Here is a quick overview of the kinds of questions you can use annotating to address:

○ What is the main subject being explored?

○ Why does the writer consider this subject important? Do I agree?

○ What point is the writer trying to make?

○ Are there weaknesses or gaps in the how the writer presents this point?

• *Outlining*: Outlining is where you move from highlighting and annotating the text itself to creating a more organized, developed, and detailed analysis of the text's rhetorical features. Generally written as something stand-alone and separate from the text, the outline is where you use your annotations to address the five rhetorical concepts presented above:

○ Purpose

○ Audience

○ Argument

○ Voice

○ Credibility

Now, let's look more closely at the ways these questions and strategies can be used to analyze a specific piece of writing. As you read the selection below, start by noting the highlights and annotations included. What words, phrases, and/or sentences within the essay are circle, underlined, or otherwise called out? What questions or observations accompany these notations? Next, turn your attention to the step-by-step discussion that follows. How does this outline use the highlights and annotations within the essay to offer a preliminary rhetorical analysis of the writer's choices, strategies, and goals?

Sherry Turkle, "The Flight From Conversation"

Sherry Turkle, a psychologist and professor at the Massachusetts Institute of Technology, writes extensively about the role that technology plays in modern life. In this piece, she examines the effect that social media tools like texting and Facebook are having on our ability to engage in meaningful conversation.

We live in a technological universe in which we are always communicating. And yet we have sacrificed conversation for mere connection.

What's the difference? Why "mere connection"?

5　At home, families sit together, texting and reading e-mail. At work, executives text during board meetings. We text (and shop and go on Facebook) during classes and when we're on dates. My students tell me about an important new skill: it involves maintaining eye contact with someone while you text someone 10　else; it's hard, but it can be done.

Writer establishing context. All the different places we text and email. Any others?

Over the past 15 years, I've studied technologies of mobile connection and talked to hundreds of people of all ages and circumstances about their plugged-in lives. I've learned that the little devices most of us 15　carry around are so powerful that they change not only what we do, but also who we are.*

Author's main point?

We've become accustomed to a new way of being "alone together." Technology-enabled, we are able to be with one another, and also elsewhere, connected 20　to wherever we want to be. We want to customize our lives. We want to move in and out of where we are because the thing we value most is control over where we focus our attention. We have gotten used to the idea of being in a tribe of one, loyal to our own party.

Families, executives, students are all "alone together"?

25　Our colleagues want to go to that board meeting but pay attention only to what interests them. To some this seems like a good idea, but we can end up hiding from one another, even as we are constantly connected to one another.

30　A businessman laments that he no longer has colleagues at work. He doesn't stop by to talk; he doesn't call. He says that he doesn't want to interrupt them. He says they're "too busy on their e-mail." But then he pauses and corrects himself. "I'm not telling the truth. 35　I'm the one who doesn't want to be interrupted. I think I should. But I'd rather just do things on my BlackBerry."

Evidence/Support

A 16-year-old boy who relies on texting for almost everything says almost wistfully, "Someday, someday, but certainly not now, I'd like to learn how to have a conversation."

In today's workplace, young people who have grown up fearing conversation show up on the job wearing earphones. Walking through a college library or the campus of a high-tech start-up, one sees the same thing: we are together, but each of us is in our own bubble, furiously connected to keyboards and tiny touch screens. A senior partner at a Boston law firm describes a scene in his office. Young associates lay out their suite of technologies: laptops, iPods and multiple phones. And then they put their earphones on.

"Big ones. Like pilots. They turn their desks into cockpits." With the young lawyers in their cockpits, the office is quiet, a quiet that does not ask to be broken.

Funny! Makes being plugged in sound ridiculous. Author's goal?

In the silence of connection, people are comforted by being in touch with a lot of people—carefully kept at bay. We can't get enough of one another if we can use technology to keep one another at distances we can control: not too close, not too far, just right. I think of it as a Goldilocks effect.

Such a bad thing?

I don't remember this story. Who is the author talking to here?

Texting and e-mail and posting let us present the self we want to be. This means we can edit. And if we wish to, we can delete. Or retouch: the voice, the flesh, the face, the body. Not too much, not too little—just right.

Human relationships are rich; they're messy and demanding. We have learned the habit of cleaning them up with technology. And the move from conversation to connection is part of this. But it's a process in which we shortchange ourselves. Worse, it seems that over time we stop caring, we forget that there is a difference.

Is this true? Do I do this?

We are tempted to think that our little "sips" of online connection add up to a big gulp of real conversation. But they don't. E-mail, Twitter, Facebook, all of these have their places—in politics, commerce, romance and friendship. But no matter how valuable, they do not substitute for conversation.

Connection vs. Conversation

Connecting in sips may work for gathering discrete bits of information or for saying, "I am thinking about you." Or even for saying, "I love you." But connecting

80 in sips doesn't work as well when it comes to understanding and knowing one another. In conversation we
tend to one another. (The word itself is kinetic; it's derived from words that mean to move, together.) We
can attend to tone and nuance. In conversation, we are
85 called upon to see things from another's point of view.

Face-to-face conversation unfolds slowly. It teaches
patience. When we communicate on our digital devices, we learn different habits. As we ramp up the
volume and velocity of online connections, we start to
90 expect faster answers. To get these, we ask one another simpler questions; we dumb down our communications, even on the most important matters. It is as
though we have all put ourselves on cable news.
Shakespeare might have said, "We are consum'd with
95 that which we were nourish'd by."

And we use conversation with others to learn to converse with ourselves. So our flight from conversation
can mean diminished chances to learn skills of self-
reflection. These days, social media continually asks us
100 what's "on our mind," but we have little motivation to
say something truly self-reflective. Self-reflection in
conversation requires trust. It's hard to do anything
with 3,000 Facebook friends except connect.

As we get used to being shortchanged on conversa-
105 tion and to getting by with less, we seem almost willing to dispense with people altogether. Serious
people muse about the future of computer programs
as psychiatrists. A high school sophomore confides to
me that he wishes he could talk to an artificial intelli-
110 gence program instead of his dad about dating; he
says the A.I. would have so much more in its database.
Indeed, many people tell me they hope that as Siri, the
digital assistant on Apple's iPhone, becomes more advanced, "she" will be more and more like a best
115 friend—one who will listen when others won't.

During the years I have spent researching people
and their relationships with technology, I have often
heard the sentiment "No one is listening to me." I believe this feeling helps explain why it is so appealing to
110 have a Facebook page or a Twitter feed—each provides so many automatic listeners. And it helps explain why—against all reason—so many of us are

Not true? Re: my Facebook exchange last night.

Key Point 2

Speed

Shakespeare reference—why?

Title!

Plausible or paranoid?

Author shifting perspective to herself.

willing to talk to machines that seem to care about us. Researchers around the world are busy inventing (sociable robots), designed to be companions to the elderly, to children, to all of us.

Contradiction in terms? 115

One of the most haunting experiences during my research came when I brought one of these robots, designed in the shape of a baby seal, to an elder-care facility, and an older woman began to talk to it about the loss of her child. The robot seemed to be looking into her eyes. It seemed to be following the conversation. The woman was comforted.

120

And so many people found this amazing. Like the sophomore who wants advice about dating from artificial intelligence and those who look forward to computer psychiatry, this enthusiasm speaks to how much we have confused conversation with connection and collectively seem to have embraced a new kind of delusion that accepts the simulation of compassion as sufficient unto the day. And why would we want to talk about love and loss with a machine that has no experience of the arc of human life? Have we so lost confidence that we will be there for one another?

125

130

(We) expect more from technology and less from one another and seem increasingly drawn to technologies that provide the illusion of companionship without the demands of relationship. Always-on/always-on-you devices provide three powerful fantasies: that we will always be heard; that we can put our attention wherever we want it to be; and that we never have to be alone. Indeed our new devices have turned being alone into a problem that can be solved.

"We"? Is it all of us? 135

140

When people are alone, even for a few moments, they fidget and reach for a device. Here connection works like a symptom, not a cure, and our constant, reflexive impulse to connect shapes a new way of being.

I've done this! 145

Think of it as "I share, therefore I am." We use technology to define ourselves by sharing our thoughts and feelings as we're having them. We used to think, "I have a feeling; I want to make a call." (Now our impulse is, "I want to have a feeling; I need to send a text.")

150

So, in order to feel more, and to feel more like ourselves, we connect. But in our rush to connect, we flee from solitude, our ability to be separate and gather

Connection and escape—contradiction? 155

ourselves. Lacking the capacity for solitude, we turn to other people but don't experience them as they are. It is as though we use them, need them as spare parts to support our increasingly fragile selves.

160   We think constant connection will make us feel less lonely. The opposite is true. If we are unable to be alone, we are far more likely to be lonely. If we don't teach our children to be alone, they will know only how to be lonely.

Trying to scare reader. Fair?

165   I am a partisan for conversation. To make room for it, I see some first, deliberate steps. At home, we can create sacred spaces: the kitchen, the dining room. We can make our cars "device-free zones." We can demonstrate the value of conversation to our chil-

My internship last summer

170   dren. And we can do the same thing at work. There we are so busy communicating that we often don't have time to talk to one another about what really matters. Employees asked for casual Fridays; perhaps managers should introduce conversational Thursdays.

My internship last summer

175   Most of all, we need to remember—in between texts and e-mails and Facebook posts—to listen to one another, even to the boring bits, because it is often in unedited moments, moments in which we hesitate and stutter and go silent, that we reveal ourselves to

180   one another.

I spend the summers at a cottage on Cape Cod, and for decades I walked the same dunes that Thoreau once walked. Not too long ago, people walked with their heads up, looking at the water, the sky, the

185   sand and at one another, talking. Now they often walk with their heads down, typing. Even when they are with friends, partners, children, everyone is on their own devices.*

Powerful image

So I say, look up, look at one another, and let's start

190   the conversation.

Source: The New York Times, April 21, 2012. http://www.nytimes.com/2012/04/22/opinion/ sunday/the-flight-from-conversation.html?pagewanted=all&_r=0

As you can see, many of the highlights and annotations included here are designed to clarify what the author is trying to say: the language she uses, the references she makes, the points she raises. Other notations, though, help the reader begin to analyze and respond to the essay. Several of the comments, for example, take the form of thoughts, questions, and observations which lay the groundwork for the more extensive rhetorical analysis to follow. This kind of analysis is modeled in the outline below:

Step One: *Reading for Purpose*

What is the writer's goal?

In general terms, the writer's goal here is to comment on the effect of social media on the way we communicate. More specifically, she wants her audience to adopt a critical, even worried, perspective on these changes. Highlighting the downsides of our "plugged in" lifestyle, she seems to hope that readers will consider alternative ways to converse with each other.

What is the writer's perspective? How does it compare with your own?

The author addresses this issue from the perspective of someone who has studied media and technology over a long period of time. She uses her own extensive research as support for her view that the changes caused by social media are troubling and extremely widespread. While I am far less of an expert, I do have extensive personal experience with social media.

Do you detect any biases in the writer's perspective?

The author is worried about the effect that modern communication technologies are having on our capacity to connect. In expressing this worry, she makes clear her preference for the conversational habits of an older era in which face-to-face contact was more valued. At the same time, it is also clear that the writer doesn't want to reject modern technology altogether. Rather, she seems to want to balance her critique with a desire to make social media better serve our needs.

Step Two: *Considering Audience*

Who is the writer's target audience? Whom does the writer seem to be addressing?

While the author is addressing a general audience, she definitely makes certain assumptions about how familiar her readers are with social media. This is made evident through her consistent use of "we" to describe the behaviors and habits she criticizes. The writer assumes that her readers don't need to be told what activities like Facebook, email, and texting involve because they use these tools in their own daily lives.

What assumptions does the author make about her audience?

While the author assumes an audience experienced with social media, she doesn't address this group as a readership with any special expertise in this area. Indeed, her critique of "connection" suggests that the author views her readers as a group who needs to be educated about the implications of our dependence on social media.

Step Three: *Identifying Argument*

What is the writer's main point?

The essay's main point can be found in the opening paragraph: "we have sacrificed conversation for mere connection." In the author's estimation, social media's emphasis on "connection" has led us to overlook the importance of engaging each other face-to-face. In developing this view, the author makes a series of follow-up points: that this "flight from conversation" has undermined our capacity for self-reflection; that it has diminished the depth and meaning of our social relationships; that it has made us more lonely and detached.

Can you identify any major themes or issues?
The major theme in this essay is the role of technology, and more specifically our growing dependence upon technological tools to perform tasks we should be doing ourselves. The author is particularly interested in understanding the growing role that machines play in meeting our emotional needs, a trend she finds especially worrisome.

How does the writer explain and/or support the main points?
Much of the essay is organized around a series of stories about people dealing with social media, each of which is designed to illustrate one of the author's central points. Drawn from her own research, these anecdotes are meant to stand as individual examples of more widespread trends. The personal detail in each serves to present the issues around technology in more immediate and human terms.

Step Four: *Assessing Voice*

What is the writer's style or tone?
The writer adopts a tone that in many ways is appropriate to a formal essay, one that conveys her points clearly and logically. And yet, while the author emphasizes the logic behind her argument, she also employs language that makes equally clear her strong, personal feelings on this issue. The result is a tone that seems intended to present the author's personal feelings as logically sound and objectively reasonable.

What specific language does the writer use? What word choice and syntax?
We can see the writer's attempt to combine the formal and the personal in such statements as "we have sacrificed conversation for mere connection." While it looks at first to be a simple declaration of fact, the writer's use of such terms as "sacrificed" or "mere connection" reveal her own personal bias, her belief that these communication technologies carry costs and dangers as well.

Step Five: *Determining Credibility*

What makes this writer believable or convincing?
The writer's status as a respected academic gives her discussion a good deal of authority. The references she makes to her research into digital and robotic technology reinforce this authority, bolstering the credibility of the argument she is making. The writer supplements these references with a series of anecdotes about people struggling with the difficulty to "connect," which serves as additional support for her points. Reinforcing her credibility even further, the writer

also regularly uses the more inclusive term "we" in describing the "problem of connection"—a strategy that encourages readers to accept her perspective on this issue as their own.

Multimedia Writing in the Real World

Of course, not all writing these days follows the format of a conventional essay. More and more frequently, the writing we encounter comes in forms that extend well beyond the written word. From news photos to cartoons, blogs to YouTube videos, advertisements to magazine covers, writing in the real world increasingly combines multiple elements—textual, visual (still and video), graphic, and audio—to accomplish its goals. Consider, for example, the screenshot below. As you look over the various features of this multimedia text, start once again by focusing on the highlights and annotations that are included. Then, turn your attention to the rhetorical analysis that follows. How do the observations and questions included set the stage for a deeper examination into the questions about purpose, audience, and the like?

Visual Rhetoric: "D!straction.Gov"

D!straction.gov is a US Department of Transportation website devoted to promoting safer driving habits.

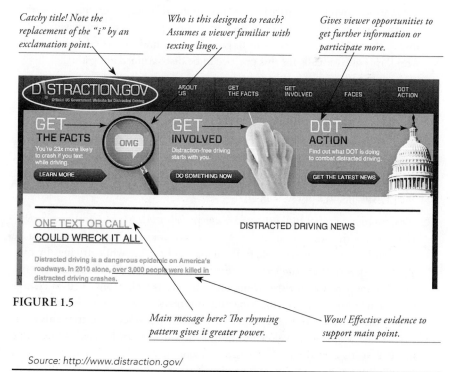

Catchy title! Note the replacement of the "i" by an exclamation point.

Who is this designed to reach? Assumes a viewer familiar with texting lingo.

Gives viewer opportunities to get further information or participate more.

FIGURE 1.5

Main message here? The rhyming pattern gives it greater power.

Wow! Effective evidence to support main point.

Source: http://www.distraction.gov/

Step One: *Reading for Purpose*

What is the writer's goal?
The overall objective is to raise public awareness about the dangers of texting
while driving. The author clearly hopes that being given enough information
about the risks of this practice will motivate readers to change their personal
driving behavior. This goal is also reflected in how interactive the website is. By
including links that invite readers to "Get Involved" and "Do Something Now,"
the writer not only aims to help readers become more actively involved in this
issue but also encourages them to feel a more direct sense of personal responsibility for it.

What is the writer's perspective? How does it compare with your own?
This website promotes the idea that safety should be the paramount concern
when it comes to drivers and driving. This is an attitude I share. While the pros-
pect of multitasking while driving sounds convenient, I know from personal experience that it can be risky to do things like check your phone while you're
behind the wheel. And the statistics about the number of automobile crashes the
website provides only serves to reinforce this belief.

Do you detect any biases in the writer's perspective?
The writer clearly believes that safety is more important than convenience when
it comes to driving. Arguing for attentive over "distracted" driving, the writer
seems to be implying that there is no way to use digital devices safely while driving. Rather than issue suggestions or guidelines for how to text safely behind the
wheel, this website calls for this practice to be discontinued altogether.

Step Two: *Considering Audience*

Who is the writer's target audience? Whom does the writer seem to be addressing?
The website seems to be directing its message toward younger drivers who have
the most extensive experience with social media but who may not be inclined to
worry as much about driving safety. By using text acronyms like "OMG," the
website shows that it is trying to reach a younger demographic, those who are
most fluent in this kind of language.

What assumptions does the author make about the audience?
The writer addresses this audience as a group of young drivers who may not be
sufficiently aware of or sensitive to the dangers of texting while driving. By calling on readers to "Get The Facts," the writer implies that this is a readership not
yet fully informed about this issue, one who needs to be convinced to change
their views. And by supplementing this information with stark warnings like
"One Text Or Call Could Wreck It All," the writer also seems to treat this audience as one who is skeptical or resistant to this idea, one who might need to be
shocked or frightened into adopting a different view.

Step Three: *Identifying Argument*

What is the writer's main point?

The main point here has to do with the risks posed by texting while driving. At the same time, though, the writer is also making a broader argument about the dangers of "distracted" behavior, about the need to cultivate the skills of focus and concentration in everyday life. This larger point is evident in the terminology the writer uses to makes the case against texting, which is regularly referred to as "distracted driving." This emphasis on focus and concentration is further reinforced by the format of the website itself. Readers need to focus closely on the features and links in this text if they want access to all the information it includes.

Can you identify any major themes or issues?

In making its case about the dangers of texting while driving, the writer touches on a number of related themes. Among them: personal responsibility, the importance of focus over distraction, and the need to be fully informed.

How does the writer explain and/or support the main points?

The writer supports the argument about the dangers of texting and driving by supplying statistical data that illustrate these dangers. The writer promotes the message about personal responsibility in part by using the second person ("you") to address the audience. This decision conveys to readers the message that this issue affects them personally and that the solution to this problem depends upon their own decision to change. The website conveys its message about the value of being fully informed largely through the links it includes, each of which gives readers a glimpse of the data on texting and driving (i.e., "You're 23x more likely to crash if you text while driving.") and then invites them to click on the link to get further information.

Step Four: *Assessing Voice*

What is the writer's style or tone?

As befits the topic, the writer adopts a serious tone. Addressing readers in a direct and candid way, the website clearly intends for the information it provides to come across as clear and convincing proof. At the same time, this text also uses language that stresses the urgency of this issue, including statements about the dangers of texting that are clearly meant as personal warnings to readers.

What specific language does the writer use? What word choice and syntax?

Clearly, the statistical data cited here about the rate of text-related accidents or the number of text-related fatalities convey the seriousness of this issue. But this urgency is also reinforced through the decision to include more emotionally loaded language such as "One Text Or Call Could Wreck It All."

Step Five: *Determining Credibility*

What makes this writer believable or convincing?
As noted above, the authority of the writer is established in part through the statistical data the website provides. But this authority is also reinforced by such visuals elements as the picture of the US Capitol, an image designed to associate this no-texting initiative with the authority of the federal government.

Activities for Putting Rhetorical Analysis into Practice

ACTIVITY 1: DOING YOUR OWN HIGHLIGHTING AND ANNOTATIONS

Choose an example of real world writing with which you're familiar (e.g., blog, social network post, tweet, email, magazine or newspaper article). Then, use the guidelines modeled in this chapter to conduct your own highlighting and annotations. Start by focusing on the key details or features in the text. What words, phrases, or sentences stand out as most important? How are they supplemented by or related to other elements (e.g., visual)? Next, annotate these details with questions, observations, or reflections that help you figure out the writer's larger point or purpose.

ACTIVITY 2: ANALYZING YOUR OWN REAL WORLD SELECTION IN RHETORICAL TERMS

Using your highlights and annotations as a foundation, analyze this same selection according to the rhetorical categories modeled above. What seems to be the writer's overall goal or objective (reading for purpose)? What kind of reader does the writer seem to be targeting (considering audience)? What message or main point is the writer trying to get across (identifying argument)? What tone or style does the writer employ (assessing voice)? What does or does not make the writer's presentation effective or believable (determining credibility)?

ACTIVITY 3: COMPARING YOUR RHETORICAL ANALYSIS

Once you have completed your rhetorical analysis, exchange your findings with another member of the class. First, have your classmate re-read the selection these new findings examine. Then, discuss as a group how helpful and/or effective you find this analysis. Do you agree with the conclusions about argument this analysis draws? Do you evaluate the role of argument in different or similar ways? Finally, summarize your key findings in a paragraph. Be prepared to share this written assessment with the rest of the class.

ACTIVITY 4: WORKSHOPPING A REAL WORLD SELECTION

Your group should select one of the real world selections included in this chapter. First, prepare for your group work by re-reading the selection your group has been assigned. Then, with your group, use the step-by-step guidelines modeled above to analyze such writing in rhetorical terms. Here is a quick recap of these steps:

- *Step 1*: Reading for Purpose
- *Step 2*: Considering Audience
- *Step 3*: Identifying Argument
- *Step 4*: Assessing Voice
- *Step 5*: Determining Credibility

Once you have completed this work, exchange your findings with another group. First, have your group re-read the selection these new findings examine. Then, discuss how helpful and/or effective you find this analysis. Do you agree with the conclusion this analysis draws? Why or why not? Finally, summarize your key findings in a paragraph. Be prepared to share this written assessment with the rest of the class.

2 Thinking Rhetorically About the Writing Process

In the real world, we are constantly called on to play the role of both reader *and* writer. And just like the reading process we examined last chapter, the process of writing—of determining what we want to say and how we want to say it—can be approached in rhetorical terms. As we learned in the last chapter, reading a text rhetorically involves looking more closely at the considerations, calculations, and choices that underlie it. This chapter invites you to turn the same rhetorical lens on the work you do as a writer. It does so by returning to the same five rhetorical terms (purpose, audience, argument, voice, and credibility) and by using them to create a step-by-step guide for mastering the four stages of the writing process (invention, arrangement, drafting and revising, and editing and proofreading).

Invention

Invention refers to the early or preliminary stages of the writing process, where we think through the goals we have for a particular piece of writing and formulate a provisional plan for achieving them. Sometimes referred to as prewriting, invention encompasses all the work we undertake before actually beginning a first draft, and it includes such questions as: What topic do I want to write about? What viewpoint or idea do I want to advance? What kind of audience do I want to reach? What effect on this audience do I want to have? Questions like these are called invention because they create (i.e., invent) a plan for a writer to then put into action. Here is an outline that organizes the invention stage of the writing process along rhetorical lines.

Determining Your Purpose

As we learned in the last chapter, *purpose* refers to the goals a writer wants a given piece of writing to accomplish. For writers, thinking about purpose is a crucial first step, helping to determine the rhetorical choices they make throughout the rest of the writing process. The discussion below breaks the work of thinking about purpose into several different categories.

UNDERSTANDING THE OCCASION

Occasion refers to the circumstances that lead someone to write about a given topic. The occasion for posting a political blog, for example, might be a current political debate. The occasion for an essay in your college composition class is likely to be the assignment and instructions issued by the instructor. The occasion for a letter to your college newspaper might be a controversial campus event. Whatever the case, knowing the occasion for your writing helps you think more strategically about the goal you want it to accomplish.

To illustrate, consider the following hypothetical scenario: Spurred by campus demonstrations protesting the wages paid to the custodial and support staff at your school, imagine that you find yourself interested in exploring the broader, national debate over the minimum wage. Motivated by this occasion, you realize that you haven't given much thought to the wages and working conditions of the people you see on campus every day, and you begin to feel that you should. Thinking more about the occasion, you determine that you hold a generally sympathetic view of the protesters' calls for higher wages for campus staff, and consequently, you expect to find yourself in sympathy with the idea of raising the minimum wage nationally.

ASSESSING YOUR KNOWLEDGE

When considering what to write about a given topic, it's important to have a clear and honest understanding of your own knowledge base. What do you know about this particular topic? How does this knowledge qualify you to write about it? What, conversely, do you *not* know about this topic? And how do these gaps in your knowledge set limits around what you should say?

To illustrate, let's return once again to our hypothetical example. Taking stock of what you already know about this topic, you first recall that you have actually held several minimum wage jobs yourself over the years. This first-hand experience has given you a direct understanding of how challenging it is to support yourself on such low wages. At the same time, however, you realize that this personal knowledge is not matched by any broader understanding of the facts or statistics about minimum wage work nationally. How many people, you wonder, actually work for the minimum wage? What are some of the typical difficulties these kinds of workers face? On what basis do employers who pay this wage justify keeping it so low?

THINKING ABOUT THE FORMAT

The goals you have for a given piece of writing also depend on the particular form you want this writing to take. Are you writing a 10-page essay or a 140-character tweet? A journal entry or a job application? Depending on the form you choose, the topic, tone, and purpose will look very different.

The importance of format is also evident if we focus on our hypothetical example. Recall that you were asked to imagine that your interest in the minimum wage issue was spurred by the fact that so many of your fellow students were already engaged with this topic. In light of this fact, it would not be unreasonable for you to decide that the best format for writing about this issue is one that would allow you to reach the greatest number of students. This decision, in turn, might lead you to narrow your choice to such options as writing an op-ed for your college newspaper or posting to a website devoted to work-related issues.

SPECULATING ABOUT YOUR EFFECT

Another question to consider when thinking about your purpose as a writer is the effect you want your writing to have on your readers. Do you want to elicit strong feelings in your audience (expressive writing)? To make your audience better informed (informative writing)? To persuade your audience to adopt a particular point of view (persuasive writing)?

For our hypothetical example, these kinds of questions might lead you to discover that your primary goal is to raise reader awareness about the importance of the minimum wage issue, or perhaps even to motivate readers to support a particular change in minimum wage policy. To increase the likelihood of this outcome, you might decide that your discussion needs the kind of concrete data or statistics that would help readers understand the need for action on this issue.

Activities for Thinking Rhetorically About Purpose

Now that you've seen what this kind of work looks like, try putting it into practice yourself. Included below are some activities designed to give you hands-on experience thinking in rhetorical terms about purpose.

ACTIVITY 1: IDENTIFYING THE OCCASION FOR YOUR WRITING

Make a list of topics you have written about recently. For each, describe the occasion that led you to write about this particular topic. What were the circumstances in which you undertook this writing? How did these circumstances prompt you to write about this topic? Can you imagine another occasion prompting you to write about this topic differently?

ACTIVITY 2: CONNECTING YOUR PURPOSE TO CHOICES ABOUT FORMAT

Consider each of the following formats you could use to write about a particular topic:

- Academic essay
- Blog
- Letter to the editor
- Facebook post

Choose a topic, and discuss the way your choice of format would affect the choices you make as a writer.

ACTIVITY 3: EVALUATING YOUR TOPIC

Here is a list of possible topics you might write about:

- High cost of college education
- Credit card debt
- Video game violence
- Government surveillance

Choose one of these topics. Then, write a quick explanation of why you chose this particular topic. What do you find interesting or important about it? What goal or objective do you want to accomplish by writing about it? Next, write a quick description of the *occasion* for this topic, the background *knowledge* you have about it, the particular *format* in which you would choose to present your writing, and the specific *effect* on your audience you would like to have.

Understanding Your Audience
DEFINING YOUR INTENDED READER
Part of figuring out your larger purpose involves thinking about the specific audience you are trying to reach. What type of reader is best suited to the topic you are raising or the larger point you are trying to make? What specific goal do you have in mind for this audience? What effect on this audience do you want to have?

To demonstrate how this process unfolds, let's return to our hypothetical example about the minimum wage. Given the decisions you've made about your purpose, you might decide that the type of reader you really want to target here is one who is generally familiar with the topic of the minimum wage but who doesn't have any special knowledge or expertise in this area. In light of your goal to inform and motivate your audience, it occurs to you that the reader you most want to reach is someone much like yourself: a college-age person who may have some degree of personal experience working minimum wage jobs but who doesn't know much about the broader, national debate over this issue.

ASSESSING YOUR INTENDED READER
Just as important as defining your audience is evaluating your audience. What do your target readers know about this topic, and what do they need to know? Where do they stand on this topic, and which attitudes about it are you trying to address?

Having determined that your ideal audience is a reader much like yourself, you might next decide that your primary goal in this essay is to be persuasive. Imagining this reader as someone unacquainted with the facts about minimum wage work, you resolve to involve the reader more directly in this issue.

Activities for Thinking Rhetorically About Audience
Now try doing some of this work yourself. Included below are some activities that invite you to think in rhetorical terms about audience.

ACTIVITY 1: DEFINING YOUR INTENDED AUDIENCE
Choose a topic that interests you, one you can imagine yourself writing about. Then, create a list of all the different audiences toward whom you might direct this writing (e.g., a friend, family member, co-worker, supervisor, or professor). Make sure to be as comprehensive as possible in putting this list together. Next, write a brief description of how each choice of audience might affect the way you write about this topic.

In each case, how do considerations about audience influence your decisions regarding what to say and how to say it?

....

ACTIVITY 2: CREATING AN AUDIENCE PROFILE

Here is another list of topics you might write about:

• Doping in professional sports
• Your favorite television show
• Your local community's recycling laws
• The popularity of organic food

For each topic, write a quick profile of who you think the ideal reader would be. What kind of background defines this reader? What interests? How much knowledge about this topic? What attitudes and assumptions about it?

Building Your Argument

NARROWING YOUR TOPIC

Very often, you will begin the writing process by addressing a broad or general subject. In these cases, you need to take steps to turn your subject into a more narrowly focused topic, one better tailored to the particular goals you have in mind. Some of the key questions that help you accomplish this goal are:

• What happened? When did it happen?
• What does it look like? What are its chief characteristics?
• Why did it happen? What caused it?
• What makes it work?
• How is it similar to or different from other things?
• How can it be defined?

Depending on the topic you've chosen, some of these questions will prove more useful than others.

To see how these kinds of questions can be put to use, let's return once again to our hypothetical example about the minimum wage. To narrow your focus on this topic, you might ask yourself questions like: How am I defining minimum wage work? What types of jobs does such work include? What types of workers typically perform these jobs? Is the minimum wage fair? Should it be raised? What individuals or groups would be most affected by this change?

FINDING YOUR FOCUS

Once you've established some boundaries around your topic, the next step is to pose questions that help you figure out *why* you find it important. For instance: I care about this topic because it raises basic questions regarding fairness and economic inequality in America. Or: I want my readers to better understand the scope of this problem—the number of American workers performing minimum wage work and the basic economic challenges this wage imposes on these workers. Or: I want to make the point that minimum wage work is a major social and economic crisis that needs to be addressed. Here are some questions to help you get this process underway:

- Why do I care about this topic?
- What do I want others to know about this topic?
- How do I want others to feel about this topic?
- What larger point am I trying to make?

DEVELOPING YOUR THESIS

Once you've addressed these questions, you are in a position to begin figuring out your message or main point: the idea you want to get across or the point of view you want your audience to accept. In academic writing, this is known as the **thesis**. Try writing out your thesis in a single sentence. For the minimum wage topic, your thesis statement might read: The federal government needs to increase the minimum wage to ensure that such workers are paid a living wage.

SUPPORTING YOUR THESIS

The support for your thesis includes the additional ideas that help you develop, extend, and strengthen your main point. Once you've identified your thesis, start thinking about related ideas and/or points that help you best make your case. To support your thesis about the minimum wage, for example, you would need to convincingly show that the current minimum wage raises basic questions about fairness and economic inequality. You would need to provide solid reasons why 1) minimum wage workers are entitled to a higher wage, 2) it is the responsibility of the federal government to ensure this, and 3) taking this action will actually lead to an improvement in these workers' lives.

Activities for Thinking Rhetorically About Argument

Included below are some activities to give you hands-on practice with thinking in rhetorical terms about argument.

ACTIVITY 1: TURNING A TOPIC INTO AN ARGUABLE ISSUE

Consider the following list of general topics:

- Online education
- Climate change
- Childhood obesity
- Reality television

Turn each of these general topics into a more focused, arguable issue. Then, choose one of these issues, and create a thesis statement for it.

ACTIVITY 2: DEVELOPING SUPPORT FOR YOUR THESIS

Consider the following thesis statements:

- Social media encourage people to be rude to each other.
- The inherent bias in standardized tests like the SAT should be eliminated.
- Universal health coverage is a right, not a privilege.

For each thesis statement listed, describe the support you would present to make it more effective. What reasons or explanation would you offer? What evidence of proof would you cite?

Example: Thinking Rhetorically About Invention

Now that you've walked through the rhetorical steps necessary to think about invention, let's turn our attention to what a finished example of such writing looks like. Read the selection below carefully. Then, take a closer look at the sample discussion that follows. How do these rhetorical categories help you understand the invention process the writer followed to create this writing?

Editorial Staff, "A Big Change, But Not the End"

The 2013 editorial from The Spectator, *the newspaper for Hamilton College, addresses the controversial issue of Greek life on campus.*

As is true for most American colleges, Greek life has been a cornerstone of Hamilton's life for generations. While various reforms have weakened the presence of fraternities and sororities on campus—most nota-
5 bly the removal of Greek housing in 1995—these societies still represent a sizeable percentage of students: Twenty-six percent of men are in fraternities and 17 percent of women are in sororities. More-   *Statistics given to support thesis.*
over, non-Greek students often benefit from the all-
10 campus parties held by the Greeks throughout the school year.

Even so, for all the benefits that Greek societies de-   *Author's purpose is previewed here.*
liver to the campus community, there are also obvious drawbacks to their existence. Besides the exclusive
15 nature of such societies—an exclusivity that serves to divide the campus rather than unite it—there have been growing concerns that pledging and rushing are harming the first-year experience. Do freshmen   *These questions narrow author's focus.*
truly have enough time to settle in, form friendships
20 and explore athletic and extracurricular opportunities

when the rush process begins in the fall semester? January-admits, in particular, are faced with an immediate choice about pledging, giving them no chance to fulfill the aforementioned aspects of the freshman Hamilton experience.

Hence, last spring, the Committee on Greek Recruitment—a committee consisting of administrators, faculty, alumni, Greek students and non-Greek students—issued their recommendations that rush season should be delayed until the spring and that pledging should commence in the fall of a pledge's sophomore year. At this week's Student Assembly meeting, Dean of Students Nancy Thompson and Senior Associate Dean of Students Meredith Harper Bonham outlined these changes to the class representatives and reiterated that they are effective immediately.

What does this information suggest about the target audience?

The Spectator welcomes any and all attempts to promote a "healthier environment around Greek life and student life in general," as the Committee's report puts it. For the most part, these reforms are fair and, ultimately, they may become more effective than Greeks anticipate. After all, pledging takes place sophomore year at Colgate and they have a higher level of Greek participation than Hamilton does. Most would also agree that, in retrospect, the housing reforms of '95 struck a reasonable balance between maintaining the tradition of the Greeks and respecting the voices of those who felt the houses promoted excessive exclusivity.

The present administration, however, must be careful to maintain that balance. The recent reforms should aim to improve Greek life, not abolish it. Some of the bureaucratic requirements in the Committee's recommendations—having societies submit "detailed schedules of pledging activities," for example—have the potential to go overboard. But just as the housing reforms eventually became the status quo for Hamilton culture, we are confident that this decision will follow the same pattern, and most likely, not for the worse.

Key point. Author's thesis?

Source: The Spectator, September 16, 2013 http://students.hamilton.edu/spectator/editorial/p/a-big-change-but-not-the-end/view

25
30
35
40
45
50
55
60

Determining Your Purpose

- *Occasion*: This op-ed is spurred by a campus debate over the role played by fraternities and sororities on campus.

- *Knowledge*: The author provides a good deal of background information about the history of the Greek system on campus as well as the specific policies formulated to oversee and regulate this system.

- *Format*: This essay is presented as an editorial in the campus newspaper.

- *Effect*: The author clearly wants this piece to prompt a deeper reflection about the proper role that fraternities and sororities should play. More specifically, the essay seems designed to persuade readers to accept the efforts to reform the Greek system currently underway.

Understanding Your Audience

- *Defining Your Reader*: This editorial is aimed at a general campus audience: students who are currently enrolled at Hamilton, who may or may not be considering participation in the Greek system.

- *Assessing Your Reader*: While addressing an audience clearly familiar with the debate over the Greek system, the author also speaks to this audience as a group that needs to be educated about this system's recent history on campus.

Building Your Argument

- *Narrowing Your Topic*: While it raises questions about the Greek system in general, this essay narrows its focus to issues that are specific to this particular campus: the effect of fraternities and sororities on the "first-year experience" at Hamilton; the validity of the recommendations by the "Committee on Greek Recruitment."

- *Finding Your Focus*: In many ways, the essay seems motivated by a fear that the effort to reform the Greek system on campus will end up abolishing fraternities and sororities altogether. This is an outcome the author clearly opposes, urging readers to consider the value of keeping the Greek system alive at Hamilton.

- *Developing Your Thesis*: The basic thesis of this essay is: The Greek system at Hamilton should be reformed to better meet the needs of students, but it should not be abolished altogether.

- *Supporting Your Thesis:* The author supports this thesis by highlighting and defending key recommendations for reform: delaying rush season until the spring and requiring that pledging begin in the sophomore year.

Rhetorical Strategies for Invention

If you were to write about the topic explored in the essay above, what would you do? How would you go about figuring out your larger purpose, your target audience, and your main point? The activities listed below provide a starting place for answering these questions. Each one describes a practical, hands-on strategy you can use to begin thinking about your own invention process as a writer. Start by looking over each of these descriptions. Then, turn your attention to the example that accompanies it. To what extent do these examples provide a model for doing this kind of work yourself?

FREEWRITING

This activity involves writing for a short, fixed period, without stopping, in response to a particular question related to your purpose. So, for example, you might do a 10-minute freewrite about what you do and do not know about your topic and how this knowledge influences the kind of writing you want to do. Or, you might freewrite about the format you plan to follow and the effect this choice might have on your audience. Whatever the case, the goal is to get down on paper as many of your own ideas, insights, or reflections as possible. Freewriting is highly informal, and it should be undertaken without concerns for the more formal, polished aspects of more finished writing: grammar, punctuation, and organization. Instead, the goal is to set the basic parameters around how you are going to think about your purpose.

If you were writing about the topic in the essay presented above, you might start by doing a freewrite in which you try to get down on paper as many of your thoughts, feelings, experiences, and associations related to the Greek system. Here is an example:

> Ok, fraternities and sororities. What do I want to say about this topic? Not sure what the big deal is here. These groups have been around forever—part of the never-changing traditions of the school . . . wait, maybe that's the point. Maybe I should write about why this tradition should be challenged or changed. Do I think that? I remember when my freshman roommate went through the rush process—seemed kind of like a waste of time to me. Not really proof that the whole system needs to be changed, though . . . although, it did have a pretty negative impact on her grades. Never had any time for classwork, always tired. That seems like kind of an important issue. Maybe that's what I should write about—the danger fraternities and sororities pose to students' performance. How could I make this argument? Would I need proof?

BRAINSTORMING

Similar to freewriting, brainstorming involves writing for a fixed period of time with the goal of getting down on paper any thoughts, impressions, facts, or recollections that you think are in some way related to your topic. This can include phrases, statements, questions, bulleted or numbered lists, even visuals—anything that feels relevant to your topic. The point behind this exercise is to consider as many perspectives on your topic as possible. It is used most often to help figure out questions related to purpose and audience.

CLUSTERING IDEAS

This strategy involves arranging the main ideas you want to explore in your writing in visual form. Start by writing down your topic in the center of a piece of paper. Then, using such annotation strategies as circling and underlining, sketch out the connection between your topic and the other ideas related to it. This activity is especially useful when you reach the point of identifying and supporting your thesis.

CREATING AN OUTLINE

Outlining helps you put some of the ideas raised in the freewriting, brainstorming, and clustering activities into a more organized form. Outlines don't need to include every detail and element of your final writing. Instead, they can list the major points you want to raise in the rough order you plan to present them.

Here is an example of an outline you might create as a guide to the first draft of an essay you might write about the Greek system:

- *Introduction*: Introduce topic. Provide brief background. Identify key issue or question.
- *Body Paragraph 1*: First major point to support thesis.
- *Body Paragraph 2*: Second major point to support thesis.
- *Body Paragraph 3*: Third major point to support thesis.
- *Conclusion*: Recap main argument and points of support.

CREATING A THESIS STATEMENT

Your thesis is the heart of your argument: the main point you want to get across or the main idea you want to convey. As this description suggests, a thesis is by its very nature subjective and debatable. Not everyone is going to agree with your thesis (if they did, it wouldn't be a thesis). By definition, a thesis involves a claim about which reasonable people will disagree. This means that a thesis needs to be more than a neutral description or a simple statement of fact. To state that the voting age in the United States is 18 is not to offer a thesis because this is a statement for which there exists an objective, right or wrong answer. To present a thesis, conversely, is to advance a view on an issue in the full knowledge that other, competing views also exist. Here are some steps you can use to create a viable thesis statement:

- Find your main idea or central point.
- Describe how you want to get this point across.
- Explain why this point is important or worthwhile.
- Write out your point in a single sentence.

Here is how you might use these steps to create a thesis statement for the topic of the Greek system:

- *Main idea*: The Greek system holds enormous benefits and poses real problems for campus life.
- *How to get this point across*: I need to describe the specific ways policies regarding the Greek system can be changed to better align it with the values and mission of the college.
- *Why this is important*: It is crucial that all campus-sponsored organizations reflect and operate according to the key values of the college. When this doesn't happen, the entire mission of the school is undermined.
- *Write your view as a single sentence*: Because it is crucial that all campus organizations reflect the values of the college, the policies regulating the admission and rush practices of fraternities and sororities on campus need to be reformed.

Arrangement

Once you have done the preliminary work of formulating a plan, the next stage involves putting this plan into practice. This stage is known as *arrangement* because it concerns the specific, concrete choices writers make to create (i.e., arrange) a piece of writing. And like invention, arrangement involves questions and choices that lend themselves to an analysis in rhetorical terms—in this case, voice and credibility. Voice encompasses the decisions you make as a writer about organization and language, including: How should this writing be structured? What type of introduction, body, and conclusion should I include? How do I connect one section of this writing to the others? What specific word choice should I employ? What tone should I strike? Credibility, on the other hand, concerns those questions you address after you've put your first draft together in order to refine your focus, tighten your organization, and enhance your effectiveness. These revision questions include: Is my thesis clear? Do I need to add, subtract, or amend anything in my introduction and conclusion? Do my body paragraphs include the right type of support?

As you consider these kinds of questions, it's important to bear in mind that arrangement is not always a straight, linear process. Very often, moving from a preliminary plan to a completed essay draft requires us to rethink and revise our initial choices. It is not uncommon, in fact, for writers to work through multiple drafts of individual sentences, paragraphs, or sections before reaching a point where they are ready to begin editing and polishing an essay into its finished form. As you look more closely at examples below, think about the ways you might choose to continue revising them.

Creating Your Own Voice
THE INTRODUCTION
True to its name, the Introduction introduces your readers to the subject you are going to discuss. Introductions are important because they set the boundaries within

which the topic is to be explored. Included below are some of the more useful strategies you can use to construct your introduction:

- *Begin with background information or statistics*: If you want to establish your own knowledge or expertise, one strategy is to include information, statistics, or other specialized data particular to your topic. If, for example, you were writing a letter to City Hall advocating for more public parking, you might begin by citing statistics about car use, available parking spaces, etc.
- *Begin with a definition*: Another way to begin is to provide your readers with a definition of the topic under discussion. This strategy helps you control the terms around how your topic will be discussed, to set limits around what is and is not relevant. For example, a writer engaging the debate over government surveillance might begin by offering a definition of "privacy."
- *Begin with an anecdote or story*: A short anecdote or story not only sets boundaries around the discussion to follow but also engages audience interest in the topic as well.
- *Preview your thesis*: Sometimes writers use their openings to introduce readers to the main idea or argument they want to get across.

THE BODY PARAGRAPHS

As a general rule, the body of your writing is where you develop, extend, and support the main ideas presented in your introduction. If, for example, your introduction makes a general claim in favor of stricter gun control laws, you might devote the paragraphs that follow to outlining the specific reasons you favor this plan. Your body paragraphs can also be used to provide additional explanation of or evidence for the point you raise in the Introduction. This kind of support can take a number of different forms:

- Reasons
- Facts/statistics
- Personal experience
- Expert opinion

TOPIC SENTENCES

Every paragraph you write should begin with a sentence that announces the general points you are going to explore in it. By offering an overview or preview of the discussion to come, a topic sentence helps your reader track the focus of your discussion.

TRANSITIONS

In addition to topic sentences, you need to include words, phrases, or sentences that highlight the connection between one paragraph and another. This strategy enables your reader keep track of the different points you are raising as well as how they fit together.

THE CONCLUSION

Regardless of the topic, every piece of writing needs to conclude in some way that recaps or reinforces the main points you are trying to make. Generally, a conclusion consists of a final paragraph in which you restate your overall thesis, review the key points raised in your body paragraphs, pose a final question for your readers to consider, or recommend a particular course of action.

Example: Thinking Rhetorically About Arrangement

To see how these strategies of arrangement can be put into practice, let's return one last time to our hypothetical scenario about the minimum wage. Building on the analysis of purpose, audience, and argument modeled here, the discussion below outlines the strategies for developing, organizing, and revising this discussion from an initial to a more complete draft.

THE INTRODUCTION

BACKGROUND As noted above, the Introduction often frames the discussion of a given topic by presenting background information or statistics. If you were creating an introduction on the topic of the minimum wage, you might begin by presenting information, statistics, or other data that provides the background for the topic of minimum wage:

> In the wake of the recent economic recession, millions of American workers are struggling to make ends meet. In fact, the most recent studies show that over 40 million workers currently live below the poverty line. Given this situation, it is imperative to work toward raising the minimum wage.

DEFINITION You could also begin by providing your readers with a definition of the terms that help frame the discussion of this issue:

> The poverty line describes the boundary separating those who are able to maintain a basic, subsistence standard of living from those who are not. While many experts debate exactly where this boundary should be set, few dispute the fact that many minimum wage workers find themselves on the wrong side of this divide.

ANECDOTE OR STORY You could also decide to begin your essay by relating an anecdote that highlights the key question or idea you want to raise:

> Last summer, I worked as a housepainter, being paid a minimum wage. I vividly recall how arduous this job was: the long hours, the physically demanding work. But even more vividly, I remember those co-workers who didn't have the option of leaving their job at the end of the summer. I had an up-close and personal view on the daily struggles these laborers faced: to support themselves and their families on wages that made this task virtually impossible.

THE BODY PARAGRAPHS

REASONS The body paragraphs typically lay out the reasons you use to develop your main point. Here is an example:

> Many people feel that minimum wage policy involves questions that are purely abstract and economic in nature. In truth, however, the question of what low-wage workers should be paid is a profoundly moral question. It speaks to the values by which we, as a nation, are going to live. And most important among these values is what we should do, collectively, about the needs of those who have the least in our society.

FACTS/STATISTICS You could also support and develop your main point by providing citing statistical evidence or expert opinion:

> According to a recent study by the US Department of Labor, over 80% of households in which the chief breadwinner earns the minimum wage include children under the age of 5. This statistic alone should cause us to re-examine our current minimum wage policy.

PERSONAL EXPERIENCE You can support and develop your main point by using your own experience as evidence or support:

> According to the Bureau of Labor Statistics, over half of the households headed by minimum wage earners experience "chronic hunger." While I have never had the misfortune of suffering from "chronic hunger," I have, at times, found myself temporarily lacking in resources to feed myself adequately. Few experiences are more difficult than going hungry. In my own limited experience, going without adequate food undermined my ability to perform almost all of my other daily tasks. I can only imagine how much greater these difficulties are for those confronting hunger on a more "chronic" basis.

TOPIC SENTENCES Every paragraph in the body of your essay needs to contain a topic sentence that previews the discussion to follow. Here are the topic sentences for the body paragraphs above:

- *Reasons*: In truth, however, the question of what low-wage workers should be paid is a profoundly moral question.
- *Facts/Statistics*: According to a recent study by the US Department of Labor, over 80% of households in which the chief breadwinner earns the minimum wage include children under the age of 5.
- *Personal Experience*: While I have never had the misfortune of suffering from "chronic hunger," I have, at times, found myself temporarily lacking in resources to feed myself adequately.

TRANSITIONS Each body paragraph also needs to include transitions: words, phrases, or sentences that connect one idea, paragraph, or section of your essay to another. Here are some examples of how you might highlight the connection between the body paragraphs above:

- *Reason paragraph to Facts/Statistics paragraph*: According to a recent study by the US Department of Labor, *additionally*, over 80% of households in which the chief breadwinner earns the minimum wage include children under the age of 5.
- *Facts/Statistics paragraph to Personal Experience paragraph*: *Moreover*, according to the Bureau of Labor Statistics, over half of the households headed by minimum wage earners experience "chronic hunger."

THE CONCLUSION

This is where you summarize, reiterate, or reinforce the main points you have covered in the essay overall. To recap the main points made here, you might write the following conclusion:

> It is important to support raising the federal minimum wage for a number of reasons, both economic and ethical. Even a cursory examination of the data makes clear that too many American workers are struggling even to survive, a shameful statistic that should prompt us to treat the minimum wage as one of the most urgent moral issues of our time.

You might also write a conclusion that poses a question for your readers to consider:

> In many ways, the minimum wage debate comes down to a very basic question: Do we want to live in a country that ignores the struggles and suffering of its most vulnerable citizens? Or do we want to live in a country that treats the basic welfare of all its citizens as a central responsibility?

You could also use your conclusion to recommend a specific course of action:

> Given the scope of challenges confronting the working poor, Congress should immediately begin discussing legislation to raise the federal minimum wage.

Activities for Thinking Rhetorically About Arrangement

Included below are some activities to give you hands-on practice thinking about arrangement in rhetorical terms.

ACTIVITY 1: CONSTRUCTING A FORMAL OUTLINE

Choose one of the topics listed below:

- Government surveillance
- Plagiarism among college students
- Genetically modified food
- Kids and violent video games
- The popularity of reality television shows

First, narrow this topic to a more arguable issue, and write out a thesis that expresses your view. Then, create a formal outline that lays out how you would draft an introduction, supporting body paragraphs, and a conclusion.

ACTIVITY 2: PEER EDITING

Exchange the formal outline you created in Activity 1 with someone else in your class. Then, use the questions outlined below to conduct a peer editing review:

- What is the writer's thesis? Is it clear?
- How effectively does the Introduction present the thesis?
- How well do the supporting paragraphs support the thesis?
- Is the essay logically organized? Are there clear transitions?
- Does the Conclusion reinforce or extend the thesis?

3 Thinking Rhetorically About the Revision and Editing Process

Once you have worked through the process of arranging the different elements of an essay, you are ready to undertake the kinds of revision and editing that will help turn a preliminary version of it into a more polished and finished draft. Or, to state the matter in rhetorical terms, you are in a position to begin thinking in a more focused way about *credibility*. As you recall from our earlier discussion, credibility is the rhetorical concept through which we address the central question: What makes me believable as a writer? Defined this way, it could be said that credibility is actually a key concern at every stage of the writing process. But this is especially true when we reach the revision and editing stage, where writers begin to make the final choices to ensure that their key goals are fulfilled, their main points come across persuasively, and their voices are clearly heard. Establishing your credibility through revision is more than a matter of following a set of predetermined guidelines. It requires that you think critically, creatively, and above all, rhetorically about your essay's many different elements and how they are put together.

The discussion below provides a framework for doing just this. More specifically, it organizes the revision and editing process around the book's other key concepts, posing questions about the ways revision decisions are connected to a broader rhetorical consideration of purpose, audience, argument, and voice.

Revision

Revision is an ongoing process in which we reflect upon what we have written and consider different strategies to make this writing even better. Thoughtful revising makes us more credible as writers because it gives us an opportunity to review and reflect upon the decisions we have made in the invention and arrangement stages, amending these decisions to ensure that our finished draft truly reflects our actual intentions and best effort. It is sometimes tempting to think of revision as a synonym for editing: checking for grammatical and punctuation errors or changing a word or two for style. In fact, revision is a far more involved—and far more rhetorical— undertaking. As the term suggests, revision is a process of *seeing* our writing differently, approaching it from a fresh vantage to determine how it can best accomplish our goal, reach and affect our target audience, and capture and convey our main point. Revision, in this sense, is less about writing per se than about *re*writing: reviewing work we have already done to enhance its rhetorical effectiveness.

Included below are two sets of prompts designed to get this work underway. The first presents a list of the specific features of an essay that warrant the closest attention for revision. The second poses a set of rhetorical questions about these features that suggests the specific ways each might be revised. Look them over. Then, turn your attention to the example and example revision that follow. To what extent does this work provide a model for utilizing these prompts to undertake your own revision?

Specific Elements of an Essay to Consider When Revising

- o *Thesis*: the sentence in an essay where the writer's main point or main idea gets presented.

- o *Body Paragraphs*: the separate sections within an essay, generally consisting of four to six sentences, that discuss and develop a specific point or idea.

- o *Transitions*: the sentences at the beginning or end of a paragraph that connect one of the essay's main points to another.

- o *Introduction and Conclusion*: the opening and concluding paragraphs in an essay.

Rhetorical Questions to Help Revise These Elements and Enhance a Writer's Credibility

- o *Thesis*

  - › Purpose: How does the essay's main point reflect the writer's overall goal? What changes in the way this point is presented would make this goal even clearer? Is the main point expressed in a clear, specific thesis statement? Does this statement logically relate to the support provided in the body paragraphs?

  - › Audience: What type of reader would find this main point most appealing? What revisions to the thesis would help appeal to such a reader even more?

  - › Argument: How clearly, coherently, and completely is the writer's main point expressed? What revisions would convey this point even more effectively?

  - › Voice: What specific word choice would most enhance the effectiveness of the writer's main point?

- o *Body Paragraphs*

  - › Purpose: How does each paragraph reflect or reinforce the writer's overall goal? What revisions to each paragraph would help this come through more effectively?

› Audience: How does each paragraph appeal specifically to the writer's target or intended reader? What revisions to each paragraph would enhance this?

› Argument: How does each paragraph help refine, reinforce, or extend the writer's main point? What revisions to each paragraph would better help accomplish this goal?

› Voice: What words need to be added, amended, or removed from each paragraph?

○ *Transitions*

› Purpose: How do the transitions organize the essay's key ideas? What revisions would help this organizational scheme better reflect the writer's overall goal?

› Audience: Does the overall organization of the essay suit the target reader? What revisions to the transitions would help enhance this?

› Argument: How do the transitions connect the points within a paragraph to those in other paragraphs? Do the transitions make clear how these individual points are related to the writer's larger thesis?

› Voice: Does the essay include words or sentences that highlight the connections between these paragraphs? What revisions would highlight these connections more?

○ *Introduction and Conclusion*

› Purpose: What goals are the Introduction and the Conclusion designed to accomplish? How do these goals relate to the writer's overall purpose?

› Audience: Does the Introduction present the topic in a way that makes it especially appealing to the target audience? Does the Conclusion summarize or reinforce the essay's main points about this topic in a way that especially appeals to the target audience?

› Argument: Does the Introduction effectively preview the essay's larger thesis? Does the Conclusion effectively recap or reinforce the larger thesis?

› Voice: Does the Introduction use language that is attention-grabbing and/ or highlights the most important aspects of the topic? Does the Conclusion use language that summarizes or reinforces the important aspects of this topic?

To see how the above framework can serve as the basis for a specific revision plan, let's use the previous chapter's essay about the minimum wage debate as an example. In that chapter, as you recall, we tracked the rhetorical steps by which a writer might move through the invention and arrangement stages of the writing process: the choices the writer might make in reflecting upon goal or purpose, speculating about audience, formulating an argument, and establishing a clear voice. The first draft that resulted from this work is reproduced below. Read it over, and then look at the sample discussion that follows, in which the revised sentences are highlighted in italic. In what ways do the questions and comments here provide a model pursuing a revision plan yourself?

The Minimum Wage Debate

(Introduction): In the wake of the recent economic recession, millions of American workers are struggling to make ends meet. In fact, the most recent studies show that over 40 million workers currently live below the poverty line. Given this situation, it is imperative to work toward raising the minimum wage. The poverty line describes the boundary
5   separating those who are able to maintain a basic, subsistence standard of living from those who are not. While many experts debate exactly where this boundary should be set, few dispute the fact that many minimum wage workers find themselves on the wrong side of this divide.

(Body Paragraph 1): Many people feel that minimum wage policy involves questions
10   that are purely abstract and economic in nature. In truth, however, the question of what low-wage workers should be paid is a profoundly moral question. It speaks to the values by which we, as a nation, are going to live. And most important among these values is what we should do, collectively, about the needs of those who have the least in our society.

(Body Paragraph 2): According to a recent study by the US Department of Labor, over
15   80% of households in which the chief breadwinner earns the minimum wage include children under the age of 5. According to the Bureau of Labor Statistics, over half of the households headed by minimum wage earners experience "chronic hunger." Few experiences are more difficult than going hungry. In my own limited experience, going without adequate food undermined my ability to perform almost all of my other daily tasks. I can only im-
20   agine how much greater these difficulties are for those confronting hunger on a more "chronic" basis.

(Body Paragraph 3): While I have never had the misfortune of suffering from "chronic hunger," I have, at times, found myself temporarily lacking in resources to feed myself adequately. Last summer, I worked as a housepainter, being paid a minimum wage. I viv-
25   idly recall how arduous this job was: the long hours, the physically demanding work. But even more vividly, I remember those co-workers who didn't have the option of leaving their job at the end of the summer. I had an up-close and personal view on the daily struggles these laborers faced; they worked to support themselves and their families on wages that made this task virtually impossible.

30   (Conclusion): It is important to support raising the federal minimum wage for a number of reasons, both economic and ethical. Even a cursory examination of the data makes clear that too many American workers are struggling even to survive, a shameful statistic that should prompt us to treat the minimum wage as one of the most urgent moral issues of our time. In many ways, the minimum wage debate comes down to a very basic question: Do we

want to live in a country that ignores the needs, struggles, and suffering of its most vul- 35
nerable citizens? Or do we want to live in a country that treats the basic welfare of all its
citizens as a central responsibility? Given the scope of challenges confronting the working poor, Congress should immediately begin discussing legislation to raise the federal
minimum wage.

Now, let's take a look at how the writer might go about revising this essay:

- Thesis: This draft leaves me thinking about whether I'm clear in presenting my
  main point. I need to bear in mind that I'm directing my argument toward a
  reader who isn't fully acquainted with the facts about the minimum wage and
  poverty and who right now may not even care that much about this topic.
- Audience: Looking it over, I raise a lot of different points, but I'm not sure I
  ever summarize my main argument in a single sentence. Right now, I seem to
  have two main points: 1) that too many people find themselves burdened with
  the struggles of living on the minimum wage, and 2) that the government
  should work to raise the minimum wage.
- Argument: In truth, my main goal in this essay is to show how these two points
  are connected.
- Purpose: Since each of these points seems to be part of my larger argument, I
  think I need to do a couple things. First, I need to provide a fuller explanation
  of how the minimum wage relates to the poverty line. Then, I need to use this
  explanation as a way to present a more fully developed thesis statement.
- Voice:

  > In the wake of the recent economic recession, millions of American workers are
  > struggling to make ends meet. In fact, the most recent studies show that over
  > 40 million workers currently live below the poverty line. *The poverty line is sup-*
  > *posed to describe the boundary separating those who are able to maintain a basic,*
  > *subsistence standard of living from those who are not, but too many minimum wage*
  > *workers still find themselves on the wrong side of this divide. Because the minimum*
  > *wage is insufficient to keep such workers out of poverty, imposing burdens on them and*
  > *their families that are too hard to bear, it is imperative that policy makers work toward*
  > *raising the federal minimum wage.* While many experts debate exactly where this
  > boundary should be set, few dispute the fact that many minimum wage workers
  > find themselves on the wrong side of this divide.

- Body Paragraphs: In the essay overall, I am clearly speaking to an audience that
  doesn't have a lot of first-hand experience with poverty.
- Audience: In fact, one of my main goals here is to give such readers a more
  direct sense of what it feels like for those people who do live in poverty.
- Purpose: For this point to be credible, I think I need to rearrange the points I
  make in the first body paragraph. Because my thesis emphasizes the struggles
  experienced by people living in poverty, I should start this paragraph with my
  point about the need to help those who have the least.

- Voice: I need to develop the point I am making here about the fact that the minimum wage debate is an important discussion because it raises questions about our values as a society. This isn't clear yet.
- Argument:

> *The most important value in society involves what we should do, collectively, to help those who have the least. This is the issue at the heart of the minimum wage debate. While many treat this debate as a purely abstract, economic discussion, the reality is that it's a debate over basic fairness. What does it say about us as a society if we allow so large a percentage of our fellow citizens to live in poverty? A key component of citizenship is to take responsibility for the welfare of others. For this reason we need to regard the question of what low-wage workers should be paid as a profoundly moral question, one that speaks to the values by which we, as a nation, are going to live.*

If I want the statistics included in this second body paragraph to carry as much authority as possible, I should consider moving the reference to "experts" from the Introduction to here.

- Voice: This could bolster my own credibility by highlighting the similarity between the "expert's" views on this issue and my own.
- Purpose: Making this revision would also help to draw a clearer connection between the statistics on poverty presented here and the point about fairness I make earlier.
- Argument:

> *While many experts debate exactly where this boundary should be set, few dispute the fact that many minimum wage workers find themselves on the wrong side of this divide.* According to a recent study by the US Department of Labor, over 80% of households in which the chief breadwinner earns the minimum wage include children under the age of 5. According to the Bureau of Labor Statistics, over half of the households headed by minimum wage earners experience "chronic hunger." *These statistics provide an objective basis for my earlier claim about inequality and fairness. In a country as wealthy as our own, are we prepared to accept that nothing can be done to eradicate "chronic hunger"? Do we find it acceptable as a society that a disproportionate number of those burdened by the effects of poverty are children?*

Now that I've used statistics and outside "experts" to establish my own credibility, I'm in a position to relate this issue to my own personal experiences in the third body paragraph. I think readers would find this kind of personal discussion a lot less persuasive if it weren't preceded by references and information that carry greater objective authority.

- Audience:

> *Few experiences are more difficult than going hungry. In my own limited experience, going without adequate food undermined my ability to perform almost all of my other daily tasks. I can only imagine how much greater these difficulties are for those confronting*

hunger on a more "chronic" basis. While I have never had the misfortune of suffering from "chronic hunger," I have, at times, found myself temporarily lacking in resources to feed myself adequately. Last summer, I worked as a housepainter, being paid a minimum wage. I vividly recall how arduous this job was: the long hours, the physically demanding work. But even more vividly, I remember those co-workers who didn't have the option of leaving their job at the end of the summer. I had an up-close and personal view on the daily struggles these laborers faced; they worked to support themselves and their families on wages that made this task virtually impossible.

Transitions

One of my goals is to raise awareness about the importance of the minimum wage debate among readers who may not know much about it.

- Purpose and Audience: Given this, I want to make sure the transitions connecting one paragraph to another reinforce the core idea that the minimum wage debate is about social and moral values.
- Argument:

   (Body Paragraph 1): *As this brief summary suggests, the minimum wage debate challenges us to figure out what, as a society, our core values are.* The most important value in society involves what we should do, collectively, to help those who have the least.

   (Body Paragraph 2): *The idea that the minimum wage debate raises questions about core values is also supported by hard economic facts.* While many experts debate exactly where this boundary should be set, few dispute the fact that many minimum wage workers find themselves on the wrong side of this divide.

   (Body Paragraph 3): *We can't lose track of the fact that statistics like these have human stories, human faces, behind them.* Few experiences are more difficult or more debilitating than going hungry.

Conclusion

While I want to raise awareness about this issue, I don't want to come across as if I know all the answers.

- Purpose: Therefore, I want my conclusion to leave readers with questions that will prompt them to think further about this issue.
- Audience: And I think the best way to do this may be to pose a series of questions at the end.
- Voice:

   As I noted above, the minimum wage debate comes down to a very basic question: Do we want to live in a country that ignores the needs, struggles, and suffering of its most vulnerable citizens? Or do we want to live in a country that treats the basic welfare of all its citizens as a central responsibility? We can answer this question by addressing our current policy around the minimum wage. These statistics provide an objective basis for my earlier claim about inequality and fairness. In a country as wealthy as our own, are we prepared to accept that nothing can be done to eradicate "chronic hunger"? Even a cursory examination of the data makes clear that too many American workers are struggling even to survive, a shameful statistical that should prompt us to treat the minimum wage as one of the most urgent moral issues of our time. Given the scope of challenges confronting the working poor, Congress should immediately begin discussing legislation to raise the federal minimum wage.

Activities for Thinking Rhetorically About Revision

Now that you've seen what this kind of work looks like, try putting it into practice yourself. Included below are some activities designed to give you hands-on experience in thinking in rhetorical terms about revision.

ACTIVITY 1: USING REVISION TO EVALUATE CREDIBILITY

Choose an essay. Identify and analyze the choices by which the writer put together this finished draft. Then, evaluate it on the basis of credibility. Based on this finished draft, do you find the writer believable or persuasive? What specific aspects of the essay make you feel so? What changes would you suggest in order to make the writer seem even more credible?

ACTIVITY 2: CONDUCTING REVISION OF YOUR OWN

Use the questions outlined in Activity 1 above to revise an essay of your own.

Rhetorical Strategies for Revising

Here is a list of practical, hands-on activities you can use to begin doing this revision work yourself:

- *Peer Editing*: This activity involves getting feedback from readers. This feedback can take the form of general impressions; questions about the topic, focus, or argument; or suggestions about what specific aspects of your writing to change. This feedback can be given verbally or be conveyed in more formal, written form.
- *Reverse Outline*: A handy way to figure out what revision work is necessary is to create what is called a reverse outline. This strategy involves looking over a first draft and creating an outline of your essay as it currently stands. This type of outline provides you with an overview of where your draft currently stands as well as the further revision it might still require.

Editing

The final step in ensuring your credibility involves editing: looking over your essay for any remaining stylistic, grammatical, and/or punctuation issues. While such issues may strike you as being relatively minor, they can play a significant role in determining the overall credibility of your essay. An essay that contains a number of grammatical or punctuation errors, for example, might easily lead an audience to doubt your authority to write about this topic. Here are some questions to consider as you undertake the editing phase of the writing process:

- Are all of my sentences complete?
- Do I include quotation marks correctly?
- Do I use commas and semicolons correctly?
- Are all of my verb tenses accurate?
- Are my subjects and verbs in agreement?
- Have I followed the correct formatting guidelines, including proscribed spacing and font requirements?
- Are my sources adequately documented?

Strategies for Editing

Now, let's take a look at some hands-on strategies for addressing these questions.

VERIFY SUBJECT-VERB AGREEMENT

When you write, you need to make sure that a singular subject takes a singular verb and a plural subject takes a plural verb. Here is an example taken from our hypothetical essay about the minimum wage above:

> Few experiences are [subject-verb] more difficult than going hungry.

WRITE COMPLETE SENTENCES

Another common mistake in writing is to create fragments: sentences that are incomplete by virtue of missing a subject, a verb, or both. Here is how a sentence from our minimum wage essay might be rewritten as a fragment:

> I vividly recall how arduous this job was: the long hours, the physically demanding work. [complete sentence]

> I vividly recall how arduous this job was. [complete sentence] The long hours, the physically demanding work. [fragment]

AVOID RUN-ONS

The flip side to fragments are run-ons: sentences that contain more than one complete statement. Here, again, is how a sentence from our minimum wage essay could be rewritten as a run-on:

These statistics provide an objective basis for my earlier claim about inequality and fairness. [complete sentence] In a country as wealthy as our own, are we prepared to accept that nothing can be done to eradicate "chronic hunger"? [complete sentence]

These statistics provide an objective basis for my earlier claim about inequality and fairness, reminding us how wealthy a country we live in and that we shouldn't be prepared to accept that there's nothing we can do to eradicate "chronic hunger." [run-on sentence]

USE COMMAS AND SEMICOLONS CORRECTLY
Commas are used to separate elements within a sentence. Often this involves separating a dependent clause within a sentence:

Even a cursory examination of the data makes clear that too many American workers are struggling even to survive, [independent clause] a shameful statistical that should prompt us to treat the minimum wage as one of the most urgent moral issues of our time [dependent clause].

Sometimes this involves separating a dependent clause that serves as the introductory phrase to a sentence:

While many treat this debate as a purely abstract, economic discussion, [dependent clause as introduction] the reality is that it's a debate over economic equality and basic fairness [independent clause following the comma].

Semicolons also separate elements within a sentence. But unlike commas, semicolons are used to separate two related but independent clauses:

I had an up-close and personal view on the daily struggles these laborers faced; [independent clause] they worked to support themselves and their families on wages that made this task virtually impossible [independent clause].

USE QUOTATION MARKS CORRECTLY
Quotation marks are used to identify an excerpt from someone else's writing you are including and/or making reference to. Commas and periods are always placed before quotation marks:

While I have never had the misfortune of suffering from "chronic hunger," I have, at times, found myself temporarily lacking in resources to feed myself adequately.

According to the Bureau of Labor Statistics, over half of the households headed by minimum wage earners experience "chronic hunger."

CONDUCT A FINAL PROOFREAD
Once you've completed your edits, proofread your finished draft to make sure you've avoided such surface errors as:

• Misspellings
• Faulty capitalization
• Typographical errors

Activities for Editing

Included below are some activities to help you put these editing strategies into practice.

....

ACTIVITY 1: CORRECTING FOR GRAMMATICAL MISTAKES

Find an example of everyday writing (e.g., an email, blog post, or academic essay) that in your view contains some mechanical flaws. Then, use the questions outlined below to edit this piece along grammatical and/or punctuation lines:

• Are all of the verb tenses accurate?
• Are the subjects and verbs in agreement?
• Are all of the sentences complete?
• Are quotations included correctly?
• Are commas and semicolons used correctly?

....

ACTIVITY 2: PEER EDITING

Exchange a writing assignment you are currently working on with one of your class-mates. Then, use the categories listed below to edit this writing for grammar and punctuation:

• Subject-verb agreement
• Complete sentences
• Run-ons and fragments
• Commas and semicolons

4 Thinking Rhetorically About Different Modes of Writing

As you become more experienced analyzing the diversity of writing that circulates within our day-to-day world, you may begin to notice—across a range of different settings, genres, and topics—certain patterns emerge. Indeed, within forms as distinct from each other as an academic essay, a blog entry, a newspaper editorial, and a Facebook post, you could well find yourself face-to-face with writing that seeks to do essentially the same thing. Perhaps the writer in each case is attempting to describe a situation or an event, or tell a story, or make an argument, or provide a set of instructions, or offer some kind of comparison.

These patterns found in writing are called **rhetorical modes**. In the most basic sense, a rhetorical mode is any type of writing that shares a common feature or follows a common format to accomplish a specific rhetorical goal. Some of the most familiar, recognizable modes include:

- *Narration*: writing that tells a story.
- *Definition*: writing that explains what a term or a concept means.
- *Exemplification*: writing that uses multiple examples to illustrate a general point.
- *Compare and Contrast*: writing that shows how two things are alike and/or different.
- *Cause and Effect*: writing that analyzes why something happens.
- *Proposal*: writing that seeks to persuade others to adopt a particular point of view.

In the real world, examples of rhetorical modes are easy to find. A teacher, for instance, may assign you an essay with instructions for the specific thesis you need to include. A potential employer may require you to submit a job letter listing your professional qualifications according to a particular organizational scheme. An online movie review may employ a compare-and-contrast format to draw distinctions between one film and others like it. An instructional manual for a new computer software program may present its information by walking you through a familiar, step-by-step guide. It is not uncommon, in fact, for a single piece of writing to deploy more than one rhetorical mode. An environmentalist trying to make a point about the dangers of global warming (proposal) may well decide that including a personal anecdote (narration) helps to get across the larger message. A political scientist seeking an explanation for low voter turnout in recent elections (cause and effect) may spend part of the time assessing two different sets of data (compare and contrast).

It's one thing to describe the various forms that rhetorical modes take or identify the places where they can be found, but it's quite another to figure out how they actually work. How, exactly, are different modes put together? What factors and considerations drive a writer to select one particular mode over another? What specific goals do different kinds of modes help writers accomplish? And under what particular circumstances are these goals most likely to be met?

To answer these questions, this chapter provides a framework that shows in clear, direct ways how different modes function rhetorically. It does so by inviting you to examine modes through the lens of the book's five key rhetorical terms: purpose, audience, argument, voice, and credibility. For example, what happens when you examine a writer's decision to employ a particular mode in light of that writer's broader thinking about rhetorical purpose, assumptions about audience, or concerns over credibility? How might the choice of mode influence the specific tone this writer chooses to adopt or the larger message this writer decides to convey?

Of course, answers to these questions hinge upon *choices* an individual writer makes. Choosing a mode that is appropriate to the occasion is neither easy nor self-evident. Deciding when, where, and how to deploy a given rhetorical mode requires a good deal of deliberation. To do it well, a writer needs to ask and answer a number of key questions. Among them:

• Will employing this mode enhance or undermine my intended purpose?
• Will it influence or alienate my target readers?
• Will it clarify or complicate my larger message or main point?

In the sections that follow, you will take a closer look at some of the most common patterns found in writing today. In each case, you will learn how to use the key concepts of purpose, audience, argument, voice, and credibility to explore how and why different writers elect to employ different modes. You will also learn how to use these key concepts as a guide for creating your own types of mode-based writing. Whether analyzing such writing or composing it yourself, the ultimate objective here is to approach modes not as static or premade rhetorical forms but as a diverse and dynamic set of tools for accomplishing different goals.

Narration

Narration tells a story by presenting events in an orderly, logical sequence. But depending on the topic the writer is exploring, the audience being addressed, and the broader context in which this is happening, what fits the definition of orderly and logical is liable to look quite different. Under what circumstances does it make the most sense to present your writing in storytelling form? And how do considerations about purpose, audience, or voice affect the details such storytelling includes or the sequence it follows?

The selection below provides you with an opportunity to begin answering these questions. As you read through this piece, think about the different ways the writer chooses to organize her story as well as the rhetorical considerations that seem to motivate these choices. When you're done, read through the sample analysis that follows.

Suleika Jaouad, "Life, Interrupted: Five Days of Chemo"

Suleika Jaouad's column "Life, Interrupted" chronicles her experiences as a young adult with cancer.

Day 1

No matter what I do—skip breakfast, set multiple alarms or go to sleep early the night before—I always seem to arrive at the hospital exactly 30 minutes late for my appointments. Today is Monday, and it's the first of five straight days I'll go to the hospital to receive outpatient chemotherapy injections. Then I get three weeks off. Then another week of
5   chemo. And so on. My doctors say this will be my routine for the next year.

My 30-minute lateness buffer has become so consistent, I'm almost proud of it. I am on time, but it's my time. Maybe I'm secretly hoping that if I show up late enough I'll just be let off the hook, told I can take the day off. I set out for the hospital by cab; it's the only way I can travel, for now, because with my weak immune system, public transportation is still
10   off limits.

"Your eyes look red," Abby says when I finally arrive. She's one of my favorite nurses.

I'm just tired, I begin to tell her, which is true. I haven't been sleeping so well lately, a mix of restlessness and staying up late watching movies. Then all of a sudden I find myself tearing up. Then full-on crying.
15   The crying surprises me, but I've been feeling down ever since I learned I would need to start chemotherapy again. Even though my recent biopsy results show no cancerous cells, my doctors say new research shows that for patients with high-risk leukemia, preventive chemo may be beneficial after a bone marrow transplant.

An attendant comes to the room to tell me that they are ready for me in the infusion
20   suite. "I'm sorry," I tell Abby as I start to cry again. "I'm just really tired."

Day 2

I'm standing on a street corner outside my apartment on the Lower East Side of Manhattan. I'm not feeling the effects of yesterday's chemo, but I have a sore throat coming on. The sun is pounding down on my head. I'm feeling a little dizzy from the brightness outside, and I wish I had brought some sunglasses. I'm glad I remembered my fedora, which covers
25   my nearly bald head. (This week I have about a quarter-inch of new hair, evenly growing in.) It's just past 9 a.m., and someone's trying to hail a cab on each corner of the street. Welcome to New York City. I sit down on the curb to rest. Finally I get a cab. The driver seems nice, an older man with a slight Jamaican accent.

As we speed up Franklin D. Roosevelt Drive, the highway that runs along the eastern
30   edge of Manhattan, I catch a glimpse of a young woman cycling on a bike path along the

East River. She's about my age, tan, her blond ponytail moving in the wind. Someday I'll ride a bike, too. When I'm well enough. But for some reason I find myself thinking about how silly I would look in a bike helmet. A sick, skinny girl with bony elbows and peach fuzz for hair—and a ridiculous oversize helmet.

"Hel-lo, anyone there?" the taxi driver says. We've arrived, and I have been lost in my 35 thoughts. "Anyone home?" he repeats. I have this running joke in my head that when strangers ask me how I'm doing, I'll unload a monologue about my latest cytogenetic report. But the driver is just trying to be nice. I know he doesn't actually want me to tell him about how chemo can make a person fuzzy and scatterbrained. Or that I've become quasi-narcoleptic in public. "I'm just tired," I say. 40

Day 3

It's my third day of "Chemo Week." When I say that to myself, it makes me think of "Shark Week" on the Discovery Channel, especially considering that a film crew is following me. But I'm honestly more afraid of sharks.

I'm dragging a little today, but I have something to look forward to: There's going to be a television crew filming my appointment for a project about young cancer patients. It was 45 fun getting dressed and doing my makeup in the morning—though it wasn't lost on me how odd it was to doll up for a chemo date.

It's a strange thought to consider how you may look on camera when you're receiving an injection. My arms are sore from the previous days' injections, but I don't want to ask to have the injection in my stomach because I feel self-conscious about baring my midriff on 50 camera.

Having a film crew in the infusion suite is a self-conscious affair. The crew members are careful to respect the confidentiality of the setting, but I'm worried I'm creating a scene in a place where there are usually no cameras. At least there's hope the project will be real and raw and tell true stories. One thing they'll never relay to the audience, though, is the un- 55 mistakable smell of the hospital.

I feel the sharp pinch of the needle in the fleshy part of my left underarm. It burns for a few minutes, and then the stinging sensation is gone. I'm free to go home.

Day 4

I wake up feeling as if I've been hit by a truck. My sore throat is worse, and now I have a runny nose and a cough. The delayed effects of chemo are setting in. As someone with a 60 compromised immune system, I go through a priority checklist in my head whenever I notice any symptoms. Not all symptoms are an emergency, but none can be dismissed outright. A fever higher than 100.4 is an instant ticket to urgent care, so I'm checking my temperature regularly now.

At the hospital, my nurse notices that my breathing is labored, and I'm sent downstairs 65 for a chest X-ray. It could be a problem with my lungs, a possible side effect of chemo, but it also could be nothing. I change into the robe they give me. The last time I had to wear one of these, I was in a hospital bed in the bone marrow transplant unit in April. I am not fond of robes.

70   In the X-ray waiting room, the TVs are blasting "The View." There is a skinny boy, no older than 7, sitting across from me. A man who must be his father sits next to him. You can't always tell the patients from the caregivers in a hospital. He looks like a relatively healthy boy. Then I see a small scar on his head, almost unnoticeable beneath short hair. He's sticking his tongue out at his father. I hope it's nothing too serious, but still, not a fun
75   place for a boy to be on a sunny summer day.

    "Ja . . . Ja . . . Ja-odd?" a nurse calls out from behind the desk, struggling to pronounce my last name.

Day 5

For whatever reason, the waiting room is packed today. I recognize a handful of the pa-tients from previous visits, but you never know everyone at the hospital. There are always
80   new faces. One girl, about my age, I've seen before. She is a fellow transplant patient with the same form of leukemia. I am shocked by how much her appearance has changed since I saw her last. Her face is gaunt, and she looks weak. She tells me she has just learned that her disease may have returned. She's waiting to find out more.

    We both say the F-word at almost the same time. I don't swear very often, but it just
85   comes out. There's a pause, and then we both break into a burst of laughter at the strange harmony of this.

    My name is called, and the girl offers to accompany me to the infusion suite down the hall. My injection is over in a few minutes, but as I'm getting up to leave I notice that she's still seated, and that the nurse is setting her up for her treatment. I offer to stay, but she insists that she
90   prefers to be alone. We exchange phone numbers. As I'm leaving the hospital, I kick myself for not insisting on staying with her. I wanted to give her a hug, at the very least. But there's an un-spoken no-contact rule between recent transplant patients for fear of getting each other sick.

    After five days of appointments, I'm ready to climb into bed.

*Source: The New York Times, August 30, 2012, © 2012 The New York Times.
http://well.blogs.nytimes.com/2012/08/30/life-interrupted-five-days-of-chemo/?_
php=true&_type=blogs&_r=0*

Analyzing Narration in Rhetorical Terms

Included below is an outline that models how to use the book's five rhetorical con-cepts to analyze the ways the narrative mode operates in this piece of writing. As you look over this analysis, think about the considerations and calculations that seem to underlie the writer's decision to employ this mode in the particular ways she does here. What specific goals does she use narration to accomplish? What ideas or main points does she decide to convey in storytelling form, and why? And where in this essay do we see specific evidence of this?

Purpose: *What larger goals does the writer use this story to accomplish?*

o *Conveying the Personal Impact*: One of the author's primary goals is to give readers an immediate sense of the toll (both physical and emotional) that chemotherapy exacts. This strategy is evident from the earliest moments of the essay, where she draws readers' attention to such side effects as "full-on crying," "sore throat," and "feeling a little dizzy," or where she describes herself as "feeling as if I've been hit by a truck." The same goal informs her subsequent description of the medical treatment itself, a portrait that evokes this experience in such sensory terms as the "unmistakable smell of the hospital" and "the sharp pinch of the needle."

○ *Highlighting the Social Cost*: The writer also emphasizes the way the experience of being in treatment can alienate you from the larger world. The story includes several moments that showcase the author's awareness of how different from others her cancer treatment makes her feel. For example: her glimpse of the blond girl about her age whose tan complexion and ponytail painfully contrast with the writer's own pale skin and bald head. Or her brief interaction with the cab driver who "doesn't actually want me to tell him about how chemo can make a person fuzzy and scatterbrained."

○ *Establishing Common Ground*: In contrast to these experiences of feeling alienated are other moments where the writer describes feeling connected to her fellow cancer patients. She speaks about the recognition she feels in the company of a patient with leukemia, for example, calling out the moment when they both laugh in unison.

○ *Creating Audience Identification*: The goal behind this strategy is to help readers see the world of cancer treatment from the eyes of someone personally experiencing it. This goal is evident in the way the writer chooses to organize her story: as a chronological, day-by-day account of life as a chemo patient.

Audience: *Who is the target reader? What effect does the writer aim to have?*

○ *Addressing Readers Less Experienced With This Issue*: The author is clearly addressing an audience with little or no direct experience in the world of cancer treatment, but one she hopes can be educated about what this treatment involves. Her goal is to generate audience sympathy by creating a sense among her readers that they are sharing in the difficult experiences she is describing.

○ *Building a Connection*: The author builds this connection with her audience in part by combining her portrait of cancer treatment with small moments to which readers can easily relate: finding oneself late for appointments, hailing a cab, and exchanging phone numbers with an acquaintance. These relatable moments serve as a bridge, connecting the details of the writer's very different experiences to the more mundane experiences all readers can recognize.

º *Helping Readers "See" Cancer*: Because her story so often emphasizes the visual aspects of her chemotherapy experiences, the writer's goal could be described as an attempt to give her readers a different way to *see* cancer. In fact, she includes a number of anecdotes that describe the ways people with cancer are viewed by others: standing on the street corner musing about how others may be regarding her appearance, sitting in the waiting room as she discreetly sizes up a young cancer patient, and discussing how it feels to find her treatment the subject of a television documentary.

Argument: *What larger point or message does this story aim to get across?*

º *Conveying Cancer's Multiple Effects*: The writer tells her story in a way designed to convey how cancer affects a person on multiple levels: physically, psychologically, emotionally, and socially.

º *Highlighting the Alienation*: The writer also makes the point that having cancer—particularly as a young person—creates barriers to connecting and communicating with the larger world of nonsick people around you. We see this message conveyed, for example, in the scene depicting a moment of failed communication between the writer and her cab driver, or the nurse's struggle to pronounce her name ("Ja. . . Ja. . . Ja-odd?"), or the moment when she muses about the spectacle she must seem in the eyes of other people: "I find myself thinking about how silly I would look in a bike helmet. A sick, skinny girl with bony elbows and peach fuzz for hair— and a ridiculous oversize helmet."

º *Emphasizing the Importance of Connection*: Another key point concerns how important, but fragile, genuine human connection can be. This idea is conveyed in the story's concluding scene, in which the writer reflects on the intimacy of her interaction with a fellow patient while simultaneously wondering why she didn't do more to reach out and show the real extent of her sympathy.

Voice: *What specific perspective, tone, and word choice does this story employ?*

º *Moving Between Irony and Seriousness*: The writer employs a voice that alternates between dark irony and deadpan seriousness. Examples of the ironic voice include the story's opening lines: "No matter what I do—skip breakfast, set multiple alarms or go to sleep early the night before—I always seem to arrive at the hospital exactly 30 minutes late for my appointments"; "It's just past 9 a.m., and someone's trying to hail a cab on each corner of the street. Welcome to New York City"; "It's my third day of 'Chemo Week.' When I say that to myself, it makes me think of 'Shark Week' on the

Discovery Channel, especially considering that a film crew is following me. But I'm honestly more afraid of sharks." It quickly becomes clear, though, that this irony is being used as a vehicle for making more serious observations about life as a cancer patient.

Credibility: *What makes this story believable, powerful, or persuasive?*

◦ *Power of the First-Person Perspective*: The power of this story derives from the first-person vantage on the world of cancer treatment it offers. The author's credibility is tied directly to her status as a cancer patient, a role in which she is both witness and participant. Because she has experienced the costs of cancer treatment personally, the writer speaks from a position of unique authority.

◦ *Limits of the First-Person Perspective*: At the same time, the first-person perspective also sets certain boundaries around the credibility of the essay's argument. Because it tells the story of just one person's experiences, readers might legitimately wonder how many of the writer's observations and insights apply to the experiences of others.

Using Narration to Create Your Own Writing

The outline below provides you with the tools for creating narrative writing yourself. Using the book's five rhetorical concepts as a framework, it walks you through the questions and considerations essential to using this particular mode most effectively in your own writing. Take a closer look at each of the steps. Then, think about the ways you could use them to put this mode into practice in your own writing.

Step One: *Think About Your Purpose*

◦ Why do I want to include narration in this essay?

◦ What is my goal? To inform? Entertain? Instruct?

◦ What specific aspects of my story do I want to emphasize? Why?

Step Two: *Think About Your Audience*

◦ What kind of reader am I trying to reach with my story?

◦ What kind of reader will best respond?

◦ What particular reaction do I want to elicit from my audience through this story?

Step Three: *Think About Your Argument*

◦ What larger message or main point do I want my story to get across?

◦ What questions do I want my story to raise?

Step Four: *Think About Your Voice*

○ What tone do I want to adopt in telling my story?

○ What language do I want to employ?

○ How do I want to arrange the details of my story?

Step Five: *Think About Your Credibility*

○ How do I make my story plausible or believable?

○ What aspects of my story should I emphasize to accomplish this?

Description

In the most general terms, description tells readers about the characteristics of a person, place, thing, or experience. In the real world, however, it's rare to discover a piece of writing that simply describes something and does nothing else. More often, description comprises one element of a text that utilizes other modes as well. This raises important rhetorical questions: At what moments is it most effective to integrate description into a larger piece of writing? And in what ways can this mode be used to support or enhance the appeal of, say, an argument or a story?

The passage below demonstrates some of the rhetorical purposes to which description can be put as well as the rhetorical considerations that can lead a writer to adopt description as a strategy. As you read it, think about the ways the writer's description of her own experiences helps to advance her larger argument. Then, look closely at how the analysis that follows answers these questions.

Sheryl Sandberg, from *Lean In*

In this excerpt from her 2013 best-selling book Lean In, *Facebook Chief Financial Officer Sheryl Sandberg makes several points about the challenges confronting women in the professional workplace.*

One of my favorite posters on the walls at Facebook declares in big red letters, **done is better than perfect**. I have tried to embrace this motto and let go of unattainable standards. My first six months at Facebook were really hard. A lot of my colleagues followed Mark Zuckerberg's lead and worked night-owl engineering hours. I worried that leaving
5   too early would make me stand out like a sore—and old—thumb. I missed dinner after dinner with my kids. I realized that if I didn't take control of the situation, my new job would prove unsustainable. I started forcing myself to leave the office at 5:30. Every competitive, type-A fiber of my being was screaming at me to stay, but unless I had a critical meeting, I walked out that door. And once I did it, I learned that I could.
10   I do not have the answers on how to make the right choices for myself, much less for anyone else. I do know that I can too easily spend time focusing on what I am not doing. When I remember that no one can do it all and identify my real priorities at home and at

work, I feel better—and I am more productive in the office and probably a better mother as well. Instead of perfect, we should aim for sustainable and fulfilling.

Source: From Lean In: Women, Work, and the Will to Lead *(Knopf, 2013)*

Analyzing Description in Rhetorical Terms

Included below is an outline that models how to use the book's five rhetorical concepts to analyze the ways the descriptive mode operates in this piece of writing. Think about what motivates this writer to employ description in the ways she does. What specifically is she trying to describe? What larger message does such description help her get across? And what specific moments from this essay best illustrate this?

Purpose: *What larger goals does the writer use this description to accomplish?*

º *Highlighting the Challenges*: One of the writer's main goals is to present readers with a snapshot of the challenges she faced trying to balance the needs of work and home as an executive at Facebook. Toward this end, her description focuses on her struggle to combat her "competitive, type-A" impulses and set let limits around the amount of time spent at the office.

º *Posing Broader Questions*: At the same time, the writer also uses this portrait of work life to pose broader questions about "unattainable standards" that countless professional women are expected to achieve. From this perspective, the writer's description of the workplace environment at Facebook serves as a vehicle for getting the reader to consider how other professional women should navigate the work/home divide.

º *Offering Herself as a Model*: While acknowledging that she doesn't have all the answers, the writer does present this description of her own workplace experiences as a model for readers to follow. "I am more productive in the office," she relates, "and probably a better mother as well."

Audience: *Who is the target reader? What effect on the reader is this description supposed have?*

º *Addressing Professional Women*: The essay seems to be targeted toward a readership of professional women who face the same kinds of workplace challenges the writer describes here. More specifically, it looks as if the writer is attempting to reach an audience most like herself: young, ambitious, and upwardly mobile women with young children.

º *Assuming a Shared Set of Experiences*: By offering herself as a role model, the writer makes certain assumptions about the ways her own experiences relate to those of her audience. In the passage where she describes the effort to fight her "competitive, type-A" impulses and "walk out the door" every day at 5:30, for example, she presumes that her target readers have the same competitive attitude and enjoy a comparable prerogative to determine their own hours. For readers who do not fit this model, this description might have a different effect.

Argument: *What larger point or message does this description help get across?*

- º *Critiquing Unfair Standards*: The writer alerts her readers to the larger point she wants to get across from the very beginning: "One of my favorite posters on the walls at Facebook," she writes, "declares in big red letters, **done is better than perfect**. I have tried to embrace this motto and let go of unattainable standards." By opening with this particular description, the writer signals that her argument involves questioning the "unattainable standards" imposed upon women in the workplace and that the solution to this dilemma involves challenging the expectations about perfection that keep these standards in place. As the writer's description of life at Facebook unfolds, this argument is elaborated and expanded. The perfectionist standards that prevail in the modern workplace, we are told, are not only "unattainable" but also "unsustainable," placing working mothers in an impossible bind.

- º *Proposing a Solution*: Having presented the outlines of her workplace critique, the writer then pivots to the second key aspect of her argument: making recommendations about how this problem can be solved. "I walked out that door," she declares. "And once I did it, I learned that I could." In this description, we see another of the essay's key points: that challenging unfair workplace rules depends as much on changing one's attitude as it does on changing the rules themselves.

Voice: *What language and/or tone does the writer employ?*

- º *Adopting an Informal Tone*: Overall, the writer adopts an informal tone to reach her audience. This can be seen perhaps most clearly in her decision to use the first-person address ("I") throughout. This strategy not only personalizes her description of the modern workplace, it also encourages readers to identify with this description in more relatable ways. We can see this strategy at work, for example, in the essay's concluding lines, where the writer shifts from first-person ("I") to third-person ("we") address, a decision designed to emphasize the common ground she shares with her readers.

- º *Using Informality to Establish a Connection*: The writer reinforces this sense of identification by using language that is largely informal. She captures the psychological toll of the modern workplace, for example, by describing her own worries in direct, accessible terms: "[L]eaving too early would make me stand out like a sore—and old—thumb."

Credibility: *How does description make the writer more believable or persuasive?*

○ *Invoking Personal Experience*: The writer bases her authority to speak about this topic largely on her own personal experience. Even as she reminds her readers that she doesn't "have the answers on how to make the right choices for myself, much less for anyone else," the writer clearly intends her own experiences to stand as a model for others.

○ *Relying on Professional Reputation*: The writer's credibility is also aided by the prominent position she holds as a top executive at Facebook. The prestige and success this position signifies gives the writer's insights an additional layer of legitimacy.

Using Description to Create Your Own Writing

The outline below shows you how to use the book's five rhetorical concepts as guides for creating your own descriptive writing. Take a look at each of these steps. Then, think about the ways you could use them to put this mode into practice yourself.

Step One: *Think About Your Purpose*

○ What specifically do I want to describe?

○ What aspects of this description do I want to emphasize? Why?

○ Is my goal simply to describe something, or am I using description in conjunction with other modes?

Step Two: *Think About Your Audience*

○ What kind of reader would be most interested in this description?

○ What specific information is this reader looking for from my description?

Step Three: *Think About Your Argument*

○ Am I using my description to make a larger point or raise a broader question?

○ If so, how can I use my description to set up a discussion of a larger point or question?

Step Four: *Think About Your Voice*

○ Does my description need to sound neutral and objective or opinionated and subjective?

○ How do I want to organize my description? What details should I foreground?

Step Five: *Think About Your Credibility*

○ Is my description accurate?

○ Is my description comprehensive?

○ Does my description include all the information a reader needs to understand what is being described?

Compare and Contrast

Compare-and-contrast writing shows how two or more things are like and/or unlike each other. But under what circumstances is this kind of writing especially useful? The selection below gives us an opportunity to answer this question. Look at how this op-ed presents its argument by walking readers through a point-by-point comparison of public and charter schools. What aspects of each educational model are examined? And on what basis does the writer argue for the superiority of the public option?

The New York Times, "More Lessons About Charter Schools"

Published by The New York Times *in 2013, this op-ed makes a spirited case for changing the tone of our current debate over education.*

The charter school movement gained a foothold in American education two decades ago partly by asserting that independently run, publicly financed schools would outperform traditional public schools if they were exempted from onerous regulations. The charter advocates also promised that unlike traditional schools, which were allowed to fail with-
5   out consequence, charter schools would be rigorously reviewed and shut down when they failed to perform.

With thousands of charter schools now operating in 40 states, and more coming online every day, neither of these promises has been kept. Despite a growing number of studies showing that charter schools are generally no better—and often are worse—than their
10   traditional counterparts, the state and local agencies and organizations that grant the charters have been increasingly hesitant to shut down schools, even those that continue to perform abysmally for years on end.

If the movement is to maintain its credibility, the charter authorizers must shut down failed schools quickly and limit new charters to the most credible applicants, including
15   operators who have a demonstrated record of success.

That is the clear message of continuing analysis from the Center for Research on Education Outcomes at Stanford University, which tracks student performance in 25 states. In 2009, its large-scale study showed that only 17 percent of charter schools provided a better education than traditional schools, and 37 percent actually offered children a worse
20   education.

A study released this week by the center suggests that the standards used by the charter authorizers to judge school performance are terribly weak.

It debunked the common notion that it takes a long time to tell whether a new school can improve student learning. In fact, the study notes, it is pretty clear after just three years which schools are going to be high performers and which of them will be mediocre. By that time, the charter authorizers should be putting troubled schools on notice that they might soon be closed. As the study notes: "For the majority of schools, poor first year performance will give way to poor second year performance. Once this has happened, the future is predictable and extremely bleak. For the students enrolled in these schools, this is a tragedy that must not be dismissed."

The same principles should apply to decisions to allow charter school operators to expand into charter management organizations, which manage several schools under a single organizational umbrella. Permission to expand should be granted only if the schools can demonstrate that they can actually improve student performance.

The study found that minority students and those from poor families fared better in charter management organizations. For example, the Kipp super-network and the Uncommon Schools, two large, established networks, have seen "strong and positive learning gains" for their students.

The study does not explain why these schools perform so well. But the answer is likely that they closely replicate a successful learning program and they keep the level of teaching uniformly high. In any case, the researchers and policy makers need to pay closer attention to how these schools function. For according to the study, Kipp and the Uncommon Schools have actually managed to eliminate the learning gap between poor and higher-income students.

Currently, only 6 percent of all schools are charter schools, and charter networks account for only about one-fifth of that total. States that are in a hurry to expand charter schools should proceed carefully. The evidence of success is not all that ample.

Source: The New York Times, February 1, 2013, © 2013 The New York Times. http://www.nytimes.com/2013/02/02/opinion/more-lessons-about-charter-schools. html?pagewanted=print

Analyzing Compare and Contrast in Rhetorical Terms

Included below is an outline that models how to use the book's five rhetorical concepts to analyze the ways the compare-and-contrast mode operates in this piece of writing. Again, think about the choices and calculations that underlie the way this mode is presented. What specifically is being compared here? And how does the editorial use this comparison to advance a larger argument?

Purpose: *What larger goals does the writer use the compare-and-contrast mode to accomplish?*

  ° *Comparing Charter and Traditional Schools:* The first objective here is to outline the key similarities and differences in educational outcomes between charter schools and traditional public schools.

  ° *Challenging the Superiority of Charter Schools:* The second objective is to challenge the belief "that independently run, publicly financed schools would outperform traditional public schools if they were exempted from onerous regulations." This objective is made clear from the outset, as the writer previews the compare-and-contrast mode to come by announcing an intention to expose the misconceptions surrounding the much-touted promise of the charter school model.

Audience: *Who is the target reader? What effect on the reader is this compare-and-contrast mode supposed have?*

○ *Addressing Both Parents and Education Policy Makers*: While addressing itself to a general audience, the essay does seem designed to reach a more specific readership of people who fall into two basic categories: parents of school-age children trying to figure out the educational options and those educational professionals and policy makers who have long been a part of the debate over charter schools.

○ *Making Parents Better Informed*: The essay offers its comparison and contrast in an effort to help parents make more accurate, informed choices about the school options for their children. More specifically, the essay uses this mode to challenge the myth that student performance scores vary widely between charter and public schools.

○ *Encouraging Policy Revision*: The essay also uses the compare-and-contrast mode as a way to invite educational professionals and policy makers to revise the ways they have traditionally conducted the debate over charter schools. This objective becomes clear near the end of the essay, when the writer declares that "researchers and policy makers need to pay closer attention to how these schools function."

Argument: *What larger points does the writer use the compare-and-contrast mode to get across?*

○ *Questioning Claims About Oversight*: Citing statistics that show no difference in public and charter school performance, the writer uses this comparison to call for stricter accountability: "Despite a growing number of studies showing that charter schools are generally no better—and often are worse—than their traditional counterparts, the state and local agencies and organizations that grant the charters have been increasingly hesitant to shut down schools, even those that continue to perform abysmally for years on end."

○ *Challenging Charter School Standards*: The essay also uses data from this same study to make a point about the standards used to evaluate student performance at charter schools. Quoting this study, the editorial notes that "[f]or the majority of schools, poor first year performance will give way to poor second year performance" and uses this comparative data to indict the standards themselves as "terribly weak."

Voice: *What tone does the writer use in offering this comparison? What specific word choice?*

○ *Combining Objective and Subjective Tones*: This editorial shifts between two distinct but complementary tones: the first more subjective and opinion-based and the second more objective and data-driven. These contrasting tones work together to advance the editorial's larger message about the need to rethink and reform how charter schools are run.

○ *Utilizing Opinionated Language*: Much of the most opinionated language revolves around the criticism of charter schools this editorial makes. Early on, we see words like "abysmally" and "terribly weak" used to assess the relative performance of charter schools and the standards used to judge that performance.

○ *Deploying Abstract Language*: At other points, the essay employs the more abstract, neutral tone of social science, citing statistics that lay out in objective, straightforward terms the ways charter schools have fallen short of their initial promise: "In 2009, its large-scale study showed that only 17 percent of charter schools provided a better education than traditional schools, and 37 percent actually offered children a worse education."

Credibility: *Does this comparison seem accurate or fair? Does it enhance or diminish the writer's authority?*

○ *Relying on Statistical Data*: Much of this editorial's credibility rests upon the data it assembles to bolster its key points. This kind of statistical information provides additional proof that the writer's views are valid because these views are supported by the facts.

○ *Pointing to Credible Sources*: The credibility of this editorial is further enhanced by virtue of the particular types of sources it cites. By putting the findings from the Stanford study at the center of the discussion, for example, the writer lays claim to the authority such prestigious institutions traditionally enjoy.

Using Compare and Contrast to Create Your Own Writing

The outline below shows you how to use the book's five rhetorical concepts as guides for creating your own compare-and-contrast writing. Take a look at each of these steps. Then, think about the ways you could use them to put this mode into practice yourself.

Step One: *Think About Your Purpose*

○ What is my larger goal in comparing/contrasting these two things?

○ Do I want to emphasize similarities or differences?

o Do I want my comparison to be neutral, or do I want to highlight the benefits or superiority of one thing over another?

Step Two: *Think About Your Audience*

o Who would find this kind of comparison most relevant or interesting?

o What attitude toward the things being compared do I want my readers to have?

o What kind of decision or choice will this comparison help my readers make?

Step Three: *Think About Your Argument*

o Do I want to simply describe the similarities and differences here, or do I want to make a larger point about how they compare?

o If the latter, what kind of statement do I want to make?

Step Four: *Think About Your Voice*

o How narrow or broad do I want this comparison to be?

o Is it better to sound neutral, or should I convey my own personal opinion?

Step Five: *Think About Your Credibility*

o Is there a valid basis for this comparison?

o Am I describing each thing under examination fairly and accurately?

Exemplification

Exemplification focuses on an individual example to make a more general point or to illustrate a broader concept. This mode is often used in writing where authors want to use their own experiences or the experiences of others to illustrate a larger issue. As with other modes, the use of exemplification raises certain rhetorical questions: What strategies does the writer use to convince readers that the experiences related are truly representative? What details about these experiences get emphasized? And how does the writer connect these details and the larger issue they are designed to illustrate?

The selection below offers a case in point. As you look it over, think about the larger point or principle the writer is using his own experiences to illustrate. In your view, do the details of his life exemplify the broader problem with immigration policy the writer highlights?

Anonymous, "I Am an Undocumented Immigrant at Stanford University"

Written for **The Guardian** *in 2013 by an anonymous Stanford undergraduate, this essay relates the experience of a young college student forced to navigate the challenges and pitfalls of being labeled an "undocumented immigrant."*

The United States Senate is currently debating a proposal for immigration reform, an issue that affects me personally. Now that I have the chance, it's time for me to speak up and add my story to the mix of perspectives.

I am an undocumented student at Stanford University. I was born in Mexico, but moved to the United States at the age of three after a Mexican construction firm sponsored an E2 investor visa for my father. I began elementary school at age four; by kindergarten, I had started calling Texas home, and by first grade I was fluent in English. My family adjusted well to life in southern Texas, where waves of immigration had made the region predominantly Hispanic, very much like Mexico, and the ideal place to, of all things, build lots of houses. My father's job and the promise of opportunity were secure for the time.

But in 2001, as I was entering second grade, my family's circumstances changed dramatically. My father was suddenly fired from his job as construction manager, after a disagreement over the independent construction projects he was carrying out to supplement his low wage. My father turned in panic to lawyers, but all he learned was that we had to leave the country immediately.

I do not know what eventually pushed my parents to stay. Perhaps it had something to do with the upheaval that turning back our hard-earned progress would cause. How could they take me away from the gifted and talented program I had just been accepted to, or tell my sister that she wasn't going to finish elementary school with her friends? From then on, my family and I became visa "overstays."

I did not understand what it means to be undocumented until I began high school. It was then that I discovered the limits of my circumstances, missing marching band competitions, track meets and summer camps. With further exposure, I began to see what it means to lack health insurance and not have a driver's license like my peers. But I had reason to hope. I was doing well academically and convinced my parents to allow me to change schools after my sophomore year. I entered a public International Baccalaureate school, which would let me take a greater number of rigorous courses.

My idealism and ambition expanded so rapidly that I soon hit the limits of my undocumented status. My senior year of high school, I was arrested at an airport for trying to go visit Texas' largest public university, which I knew accepted undocumented students like me. Twelve hours in an underground Customs and Border Patrol detention facility showed me too clearly the limits of my idealism. With my release, however, everything changed.

The release document that summoned me to see an immigration judge also granted me the ability to travel within the US mainland. All of a sudden, I was able to actually travel to and perhaps even attend the universities I had only dreamed of applying to until then. That small concession renewed my spirit at a time when I was ready to give up.

I graduated from high school a few months later as the class salutatorian, breaking my city's record for International Baccalaureate scores while also achieving the honor of AP scholar with distinction. In what was for me a validation of my hard work, I was accepted to some great schools and decided to attend Stanford University.

Thankfully, now that I have been granted Deferred Action status, I have fewer reasons to fear deportation. Under Deferred Action, I am also able to work, and even obtain a driver's license. But this two-year measure will likely end after one renewal with

President Obama's presidency, as it represents only a temporary exercise of discretion-
45   ary executive power.

Already the same barriers are confronting me. I am again missing out on summer opportunities, missing out on many research and internship opportunities available only to
US citizens. Although I am part of Stanford's solar car team, I will not be going to Australia
this upcoming fall, because I still cannot travel outside the country.

50   Without immigration reform I will be left jobless and exposed after I graduate, unless I
can receive financial aid to pursue a graduate degree somewhere. And what do I do after
that? The reality of my legal circumstances continues to haunt me, and mocks the dreams
that Stanford is helping inspire.

I'm a mechanical engineering major, a field the US wants to grow and promote more
55   students to study. I want to first work as an engineer on green advancements in energy and
transportation, and later in my career use this knowledge to advise policy. I sometimes
also dream of running for public office in southern Texas to help the public education
system that helped me. I'm passionate about what I do at Stanford, and driven to effect
change with what I have learned and hope to achieve. But my wings are cut right now.

60   I have seen the many sides of immigration, from the numerous visa denials my father
experienced before finally receiving an E2 visa, to the often-sad reality of undocumented
workers and families in southern Texas. I have seen deportations and raids occur in my
neighborhoods, and have myself been detained. Now at Stanford, I can see the immigration debate raging in Congress, and just down the street from me at the many Silicon
65   Valley firms that have suddenly become supporters of reform.

I may be without wings because of my undocumented status, but I still have a voice that
I hope will be heard in the midst of all the arguments.

Source: The Guardian, May 16, 2013, copyright Guardian News & Media Ltd 2013.
http://www.guardian.co.uk/commentisfree/2013/may/16/immigration-reform-real-lives-at-stake

Analyzing Exemplification in Rhetorical Terms

Included below is an outline that models how to use the book's five rhetorical concepts to analyze the ways the exemplification mode operates in this piece of writing.
Examine the specific uses to which the author puts this particular mode. What larger
idea or issue does he use the examples cited here to exemplify? How effective do you
find this strategy to be?

Purpose: *What goals does the writer hope to accomplish by relating his
own experiences?*

○ *Using Personal Experiences as an Example*: One of the writer's goals is to present his own experiences growing up "undocumented" in America as an example of the challenges facing thousands of other young people like himself.
"Now that I have the chance," he declares, "it's time for me to speak up and
add my story to the mix of perspectives."

○ *Adding Voice to the Immigration Debate*: Building on this first goal, the
writer also wants to use his personal story as a platform for joining the larger

public debate over immigration reform: "I may be without wings because of my undocumented status, but I still have a voice that I hope will be heard in the midst of all the arguments."

○ *Offering First-Hand Testimony*: The writer tells his own story to serve as a witness to others about what is truly at stake in the immigration debate. This is evident in his repeated use of the phrase "I have seen" in the essay's concluding passage: "I have seen the many sides of immigration, from the numerous visa denials my father experienced before finally receiving an E2 visa, to the often-sad reality of undocumented workers and families in southern Texas. I have seen deportations and raids occur in my neighborhoods, and have myself been detained."

Audience: *What specific readership does the writer hope to reach? What response is he trying to elicit from them?*

○ *Addressing Readers Unfamiliar With the Challenges of the Undocumented*: The essay seems directed toward readers who do not have a personal or direct connection to the experiences of undocumented people in the United States. First and foremost, the writer wants his own example to fill the gap in public awareness and understanding of the plight these people face. By relating the story of his upbringing in the United States with such detail, it's as if the writer is inviting readers to more personally relate to experiences they otherwise would not know, to give them a sense of what the experience of being "undocumented" actually feels like.

○ *Addressing Readers Undecided About the Issue*: This piece is also directed toward readers whose views on the political question of immigration reform may not yet be settled. The writer relates his own experiences not simply as an example of the challenges faced by undocumented people but also as a case study that exemplifies the concerns the broader public should keep in mind as they evaluate our nation's current immigration policy.

Argument: *What larger point or message does the writer use his own experiences to get across?*

○ *Highlighting the Role of Circumstances*: In addition to telling the story of growing up "undocumented" in the United States, the writer is also making an argument about the role that "circumstances" can play in limiting individual opportunity. The unspoken message behind passages where the writer describes his father's sudden job loss or his own exclusion from such activities as "marching band competitions, track meets and summer camps" is that individual drive or initiative is sometimes not enough to ensure that undocumented immigrants will succeed. As the writer notes, he sometimes felt his "idealism and ambition" bump up against "the limits of [his] undocumented status."

○ *Emphasizing the Importance of Individual Initiative*: At the same time, the writer also uses his own story to demonstrate how crucial it is to maintain individual drive and initiative, even in an environment where "circumstances" limits one's opportunities. Throughout his personal account, the writer repeatedly returns to the themes of perseverance and hard work, highlighting examples and anecdotes that illustrate the importance of not giving up.

○ *Itemizing the Benefits of Reform*: Another key point concerns the benefits (social, economic, and professional) that would come from reforming the current immigration system. We see this message, for example, in those moments where the writer talks about his own plans for the future—plans, he suggests, that will improve not only his personal fortunes but also the fortunes of the broader nation as well: "I'm a mechanical engineering major, a field the US wants to grow and promote more students to study. I want to first work as an engineer on green advancements in energy and transportation, and later in my career use this knowledge to advise policy."

Voice: *What specific tone and word choice does the writer use to relate his experiences?*

○ *Employing Direct Personal Address*: As befits a story filled with so much autobiographical detail, the dominant tone of this piece is both direct and personal. The writer's decision to frame the essay as an extended reflection on what he has "seen" during his years living in the United States as an undocumented immigrant personalizes this issue in a way that a more formal discussion would not.

Credibility: *What specific elements or details give the writer the authority to speak on this topic?*

○ *Relying on Retrospective Viewpoint*: The fact that this piece presents a writer reflecting on his past struggles is critical to the essay's overall credibility. The writer informs his readers at the outset that he is currently enrolled at Stanford University, one of the most competitive and prestigious schools in the country. This achievement not only validates the writer as someone whose views should be taken seriously, it also confirms him as an immigrant success story. We are more inclined to respect the writer's point of view, to consider the points he raises and the recommendations he offers, because we know the success he has achieved.

Using Exemplification to Create Your Own Writing

The outline below shows you how to use the book's five rhetorical concepts as guides for creating your own exemplification writing. Take a look at each of these steps.

Then, think about the ways you could use them to put this mode into practice yourself.

Step One: *Think About Your Purpose*

- ° What makes my example exemplary?

- ° What larger question, issue, or idea do I want my example to illustrate?

- ° What is useful or important about offering this illustration? Why does it matter?

Step Two: *Think About Your Audience*

- ° What kind of reader is interested in the question, issue, or idea being illustrated?

- ° What specific things do I want my readers to learn?

- ° What information or details do I need to provide to accomplish this?

Step Three: *Think About Your Argument*

- ° What larger claim am I making about my example?

- ° How do I explain, defend, and support this claim?

Step Four: *Think About Your Voice*

- ° What tone and word choice do I want to employ?

- ° What specific elements or aspects of my example do I want to emphasize?

Step Five: *Think About Your Credibility*

- ° Is my example truly representative?

- ° What specific aspects of my discussion make it so?

Cause and Effect

Cause-and-effect writing analyzes why something happens and/or predicts the effects something will have. The spectrum of issues that cause-and-effect writing encompasses is quite broad, covering such diverse domains as pop culture, politics, and science. Why are reality television shows so popular? What accounts for so few Americans voting in elections? What would happen to the rate of global warming if more hybrid vehicles were put on the road?

The selection below offers an example of one such issue. How do you respond to the cause-and-effect connection the writer draws here? In your view, does she make a credible case that the rise of social media is leading to the demise of personal privacy?

Julia Angwin, "Why I'm Unfriending You on Facebook"

Written by journalist Julia Angwin, this blog post outlines her concerns over the effect that social media sites like Facebook are having on her ability to protect her own privacy.

I have 666 friends on Facebook. By next week, I hope to have none.

I am going to spend this week "unfriending" all of my Facebook friends because I have come to believe that Facebook cannot provide me the level of privacy that I need. And yet, I am not quitting entirely because I believe that as an author and a journalist, it is impor-
5   tant to have a Facebook presence.

My specific concern with Facebook is what NYU Professor Helen Nissenbaum calls a lack of "contextual integrity"—which is a fancy way of saying that when I share informa-tion with a certain group or friend on Facebook, I am often surprised by where the data ends up.

10   Professor Nissenbaum argues that many online services—of which Facebook is simply the most prominent example—share information in ways that violate the social norms established in offline human relationships.

For example: In real life, even if I am friends with someone, I don't necessarily want to join their book group or cooking group etc. But on Facebook, my friends can join me to a
15   group without my permission, and my membership in that group is automatically made public.

This is no small thing: This exact feature is what caused two University of Texas stu-dents to be outed to their parents, when the president of the Queer Chorus joined them to a Facebook group.

20   Although I am not worried about being outed, I am a journalist who needs to protect my sources, my relationships and my affiliations from public scrutiny. I am also, quite simply, a human who doesn't want to be shocked by information about myself that I cannot con-trol. And so, I plan to spend this week unfriending all my Facebook friends.

I did not come to this conclusion easily. I have long struggled with the right approach to
25   Facebook.

I joined Facebook on June 26, 2006, back when it was still only available to people with university e-mail addresses. In fact, I signed up for an alumni address from my college just for the purpose of joining Facebook.

My motivation was primarily journalistic: I was researching a book about the social
30   network MySpace and needed to understand the social networking landscape. But I also enjoyed the thrill of reconnecting with friends from high school and college.

But like many Facebook users, I felt burned when in December, 2009, Facebook unilat-erally changed all users' default privacy settings to encourage sharing information to the entire world instead of just "friends." My list of friends was automatically made public—
35   which is a terrible problem for journalists who may have befriended sources that could be betrayed by disclosure of the relationship.

Outraged, I wrote a column declaring that Facebook had betrayed the confidential nature of friending, and that I was going to treat it as a public forum like Twitter. I opened up my profile entirely; I began accepting all friend requests (even really creepy ones) and scrubbed my profile clean of any personal details. (Facebook later agreed to settle charges brought by the Federal Trade Commission, which alleged that Facebook's actions were unfair and deceptive).

The technical name for my approach to Facebook was "privacy by obscurity." By burying good data (my actual relationships) amidst bad data (people I didn't know), I aimed to shield my relationships from unwanted scrutiny.

However, privacy by obscurity made Facebook almost unusable. My news feed was cluttered with updates from people I didn't know. Many of my new "friends" were joining me to groups and sending me spam. Slowly but surely, I started using Facebook less and less. Last year, I didn't post a single update all year.

Now I am researching and writing a book about online privacy, *Tracked*, to be published next year. In my book, I aim to answer two questions: why does privacy matter? And what should we do about it? To answer the second question, I've been trying out several privacy-protecting measures, such as blocking Web tracking technology and setting up new online identities.

But I've been struggling to figure out what to do about my long-neglected Facebook account. My privacy by obscurity approach had only netted spammers and made Facebook annoying to use.

I considered trimming my friends list to a bare minimum (as Fred Wilson successfully did), but I realized that I don't actually keep up with my closest friends and family on Facebook (we use e-mail, texting and phone).

I considered giving up on privacy by obscurity and actually using Facebook to keep up with people I know. But that would require me to trust Facebook to protect my list of friends. I dug around on Facebook's privacy settings, and found that it still doesn't allow you to completely protect your list of friends. If you share a friend with someone, your mutual friend will be displayed to both of you.

For a journalist, even that amount of disclosure is too much: Imagine a low-level employee of an institution who befriends a journalist to share information. If an official spokesman for that same organization notices that he or she shares a "mutual friend" with a journalist, that disclosure amounts to outing the employee as a source. So that argued against reducing my list of friends to people with whom I actually have relationships.

I considered just deleting my profile. But I realized I was going to miss three things about Facebook: 1) I like being able to be send private messages to people through Facebook when I don't have their latest contact information; 2) I like being notified when I'm tagged in a photo or in a post (usually so I can request being untagged); and 3) As a journalist and author, I would like to be "found" by people who want to read my writing.

And so I've decided to unfriend everyone and keep a bare-bones profile for the simple purposes of messaging, untagging and being found by people who might want to find me.

For those who I am unfriending, apologies in advance. As bizarre as it sounds, I am actually trying to protect the contextual integrity of our relationship.

Source: JuliaAngwin.com, February 12, 2013
http://juliaangwin.com/why-im-unfriending-you-on-facebook/

Analyzing Cause and Effect in Rhetorical Terms

Included below is an outline that models how to use the book's five rhetorical concepts to analyze the ways the cause-and-effect mode operates in this piece of writing. As you look it over, consider the particular cause-and-effect relationship being proposed as well as the broader rhetorical purposes to which it is being put.

Purpose: *What goals does the writer hope to accomplish by outlining this cause-and-effect relationship?*

   ° *Explaining Her Personal Choice*: The author's most immediate goal is to explain her decision to withdraw from her network of friends on Facebook. As she puts it in the opening lines of her piece: "I have 666 friends on Facebook. By next week, I hope to have none."

   ° *Offering a Broader Warning About Social Media*: On a deeper level, her objective is to alert readers to the threat social media sites like Facebook pose to personal privacy. Walking readers through her decision to "unfriend" Facebook, the writer clearly aims to present her own example as a model for others to follow.

Audience: *What type of reader is most likely to respond to this cause-and-effect writing?*

   ° *Speaking to a Social Media Savvy Audience*: This essay addresses itself to a readership experienced in using social media. But beyond this general definition, the piece could also be said to target readers whose personal or professional circumstances have forced them to make difficult decisions about when, where, and how to protect their own privacy. Overall, it is clear that the writer assumes her audience is not only aware of the privacy issues associated with Facebook but directly concerned about them as well.

Argument: *What larger point or message does the writer use her own experiences to get across?*

   ° *Highlighting the Threat to Privacy*: The central premise of this piece is that Facebook poses a threat to the personal privacy of its users. To advance this argument, the writer relies on a more extended cause-and-effect explanation that focuses on the ways that the rules and policies of sites like Facebook coerce users into sharing personal information too widely: "In real life, even if I am friends with someone, I don't necessarily want to join their book group or cooking group etc. But on Facebook, my friends can join me to a group without my permission, and my membership in that group is automatically made public."

   ° *Dissecting the Dangers of "Friending"*: A good deal of the argument here revolves around the author's examination of "friending," a practice she holds particularly responsible for the erosion of personal privacy: "[L]ike many Facebook users, I felt burned when in December, 2009, Facebook unilaterally changed all users' default privacy settings to encourage sharing information to the entire world instead of just 'friends.' My list of friends was automatically made public—which is a terrible problem for journalists who may have befriended sources that could be betrayed by disclosure of the relationship." As the quotation makes clear, the author uses Facebook's policies around "friending" as evidence to support the cause-and-effect thesis (about social media and privacy) that the essay is advancing overall.

○ *Focusing on Social Norms*: A related point concerns the power of online technologies to affect and/or alter established or traditional social norms. Quoting New York University Professor Helen Nissenbaum, the writer criticizes Facebook for "shar[ing] information in ways that violate the social norms established in offline human relationships."

Voice: *What specific tone and/or language does the writer use to present this cause-and-effect connection?*

○ *Employing First-Person Address*: This is another piece in which the writer utilizes a direct, first-person form of address. In general terms, the effect of this strategy is to make the topic she raises more immediately relevant and relatable. By addressing the broader issue of Internet privacy within the context of the writer's personal story, the essay implies that first-person experience constitutes the most effective proof of this connection.

Credibility: *What specific elements or details make these experiences more or less representative?*

○ *Relying on Personal Experience*: Part of the writer's credibility here derives from her own personal experience as a Facebook user. Another part of her credibility stems from her professional status as a journalist "researching a book" about social networks and digital culture.

Using Cause and Effect to Create Your Own Writing

The outline below shows you how to use the book's five rhetorical concepts as guides for creating your own cause-and-effect writing. Take a look at each of these steps. Then, think about the ways you could use them to put this mode into practice yourself.

Step One: *Think About Your Purpose*

○ What type of cause-and-effect relationship am I trying to illustrate?

○ Am I trying to explain why something happened or predict what effect something will have?

Step Two: *Think About Your Audience*

- º What type of reader would care most about, or be most affected by, this cause-and-effect relationship?

- º What information or explanation would be most important to this reader?

Step Three: *Think About Your Argument*

- º What larger point am I trying to make about how this cause-and-effect relationship works?

- º What reasons or evidence can I provide to help get this point across most clearly?

Step Four: *Think About Your Voice*

- º What language and/or tone are most appropriate to this cause-and-effect example?

- º How general or detailed do I want my discussion to be?

Step Five: *Think About Your Credibility*

- º Is the cause-and-effect connection I present logical?

- º Is the example I've chosen truly representative?

Process

Process writing explains how to do something or how something occurs, presenting readers with a set of instructions in a form that generally follows a series of steps or stages. Because the goal is to make the explanation as understandable as possible, process writing tends to present its steps in clear, chronological order, from start to finish.

The selection below offers a case in point. As you look over this essay, think about the rhetorical purposes to which the process mode is being put here. How does the writer use this step-by-step organization as a framework for exploring some of the broader questions (social, economic, and political) that a practice like dumpster diving raises?

Leah Koenig, "The Classy Dive: The Dos and Don'ts of Dumpster Diving"

Written by journalist Leah Koenig, this article walks readers through the steps necessary for executing what she characterizes as a "classy" dumpster dive.

"What is she doing?" I ask aloud, nearly spilling my coffee. My friends turn around just in time to watch the Starbucks barista dump an entire case of sandwiches into a plastic trash bag. At 4 p.m., nearly two-dozen delicious, fresh sandwiches are headed for the Dumpster.

My first instinct is to ask if I can take them home—but then I remember Ralph Reese, the Whole Foods employee who got fired for "stealing" a day-old tuna fish sandwich. I should just head out back to the Dumpster.

In a country where fresh food is viewed as disposable, it is no surprise that some citizens have taken it into their hands to "reclaim the waste" by Dumpster diving. These "divers" literally wade through trash bins and bags to recover still-edible food that has been thrown away.

Sound a bit disgusting? So do the facts on food waste in America.

According to a USDA report, in 1995, 5.4 billion pounds of food were "lost" at the retail level (supermarkets, health food stores, etc.), and 91 billion additional pounds were wasted by consumers and the food service industry (restaurants, delis, coffee shops, etc.). Food organizations like City Harvest in New York help redistribute some of that food, but most of it ends up in the landfill.

Critics of Dumpster diving point out the potential dangers (glass, rodents, expired food) of rooting through the trash—and they are right. It is definitely not the safest or most sanitary way to acquire food. But to the committed, Dumpster diving is an important tactic in the fight against America's food waste problem—not to mention a quick, adventure-filled way to get a potentially delicious free meal.

For the curious Dumpster diver novices out there, here are some useful tips to help keep your diving safe, respectful and bountiful.

Look Before You Dive

Scout out your options before heading out on your first dive—take a walk, bike ride or drive around your neighborhood. Note which stores, bakeries and co-ops seem like good places to stop, what time and where those stores put out their extras, and the best times to head there (hours with low customer traffic, just after close). If you are feeling extra organized, plot out a Google map of the stores or neighborhoods you plan to visit.

Keep an Open Mind

Dumpster diving feels very different than a traditional trip to the grocery or department store. (For starters, you avoid the front door completely!) If you head out hoping to bring home three pears, a dozen eggs and a kitchen table to eat them on, you will likely be disappointed. But if you view your dives as treasure hunts—for *free* stuff, mind you—everything you find will feel like a small victory.

Come Equipped

Like any adventure, having proper gear is crucial. At minimum, be sure to pack a flashlight, rubber gloves and bags to hold your loot. A change of clothes is also a good idea (especially if you are heading somewhere after your dive), and a cooler stocked with ice packs will keep vegetables and other foods cold until you get home.

Don't Arrive with a Crowd

There's safety (and fun) in numbers, but Dumpster diving in a pack draws too much negative attention to the scene, which can lead to unnecessary problems. Find one or two

40   trusted friends to dive with, and make an agreement beforehand to be discreet, quick and
     respectful to the stores you visit.

Trust Your Instincts—and Your Nose

     Like the Starbucks sandwiches mentioned above, much of food thrown away by restau-
     rants and grocery stores is fresh and safe. Still, according to the National Dairy Council,
     perishable foods (dairy, meat, etc.) that are allowed to come to room temperature—
45   between 41 and 140 degrees—can start to grow harmful bacteria. Unless you know for
     certain that perishable foods have been out of the fridge for less than one hour (30 minutes,
     to be on the safe side), avoid them. Of course, foods that have any sort of "off" smell also
     should be left behind.
     Foods that tend to be particularly safe include bread/bagels/baked goods, packaged
50   products (chips, cookies), boxed juices, canned goods (avoid bulging or dented cans) and
     fresh fruits and vegetables.
     When diving for furniture, avoid mattresses at all costs (the potential bed bugs just are
     not worth it) and take special care to inspect upholstered items like chairs and couches for
     stains or dampness. Consider getting upholstered items professionally cleaned before
55   bringing them into your house.

Don't Dig Too Deeply

     Dumpster diving requires a certain mind shift, including the understanding that just be-
     cause something is put into a trash bag does not mean it is garbage. Still, Dumpsters can
     get a little gross. Decide in advance how far you are willing to go for that bag of organic
     black bean chips and respect those boundaries.
60   Meanwhile, if accessing a particular Dumpster requires breaking a lock, jumping a fence
     or otherwise "breaking and entering," head elsewhere.

Learn to Preserve

     Learning basic preserving techniques (baking, pickling, making jam, freezing) will help
     you enjoy your bounty even longer and rescue less-than-perfect produce from the landfill.
     Turn slightly-too-old bananas into delicious bread or not-quite-crisp cucumbers into
65   quick pickles, and freeze that pallet of strawberries to use in smoothies throughout
     the year.

Take Only What You Can Use

     The thrill of "getting stuff for free" can be intoxicating—and just like going to a buffet,
     your eyes can sometimes be bigger than your stomach. But before you haul off four bags
     filled with bagels and scones, think about your freezer space and re-evaluate. In the end,
70   take only what you are reasonably certain you, your neighbors or a nearby soup kitchen
     can use.
     Also, always share the wealth. In Eugene, Ore. (the home of my own first "dives"), there
     was one food co-op that generously and deliberately laid out its extra organic produce and
     natural food products at the end of the day. Within 15 minutes, the community's homeless
75   and less fortunate members would arrive to look through the leftovers. When they left,

the people who dove for sport or principle (rather than need) would come and take anything that still remained. It was a beautiful arrangement—and a good model for other divers to follow.

Seek Out Your Community

Are you a newbie diver looking for tips? Can't convince your friends to go with you on your treasure hunts? The Internet is an ideal place to seek advice and connect with the divers in 80 your community. The website Freegan.info collected a great list of blogs, community boards, e-mail lists and other resources for divers. The site also includes directories that provide invaluable insiders' tips for diving at stores in different cities. For example, are you diving in Seattle? You might like to know that 10:30–11:30 p.m. is the best time to hit the Trader Joe's in the University District. 85

Source: Mother Nature Network, *January 5, 2010*
http://www.mnn.com/lifestyle/recycling/stories/the-classy-dive-the-dos-and-donts-of-dumpster-diving

---

Analyzing Process in Rhetorical Terms

Included below is an outline that models how to use the book's five rhetorical concepts to analyze the ways the process mode operates in this piece of writing. As you read through this piece, try to track the particular steps the writer outlines for her readers. Are they clear, coherent, and logical?

Purpose: *What goals does the writer hope to accomplish by breaking dumpster diving into a step-by-step process?*

○ *Providing an Intimate Glimpse of Dumpster Diving:* The most immediate goal here is to provide an intimate and detailed a glimpse of what dumpster diving actually involves. The instructions presented, which the writer uses the process mode to divide into separate steps, are designed to give readers a sense of what it actually feels (and smells) like to engage in this activity.

○ *Offering a Critique of Excess and Waste:* The essay also uses its advice about dumpster diving as a vehicle for presenting a broader critique of excess and waste in America. The writer makes this goal explicit from the outset: "These 'divers' literally wade through trash bins and bags to recover still-edible food that has been thrown away. Sound a bit disgusting? So do the facts on food waste in America."

Audience: *Toward what specific readership does the writer direct her "advice"?*

○ *Addressing a Novice Audience:* Clearly, the writer imagines herself addressing a readership largely unacquainted both with the realities of dumpster diving and with the conditions of struggle and scarcity that make this option necessary for so many.

º *Educating Her Readers*: We get this sense not simply through the specific
advice the writer presents (e.g., "Don't dig too deeply"; "Take only what you
can use"), which is clearly pitched to a novice audience, but also through
the data regarding Americans and food consumption and food waste:
"According to a USDA report, in 1995, 5.4 billion pounds of food were 'lost'
at the retail level (supermarkets, health food stores, etc.), and 91 billion additional pounds were wasted by consumers and the food service industry
(restaurants, delis, coffee shops, etc.)." In passages like this, we see confirmation that the writer imagines her readership as a group not yet acquainted
with the key facts.

Argument: *What larger points does the writer use these step-by-step
instructions to get across?*

º *Illustrating the Dangers of Waste*: From the first lines, it is evident that the
writer is using the "dos and don'ts" framework here to make a larger point
about food, waste, and inequality in America. Take, for example, the anecdote with which the essay begins: "'What is she doing?' I ask aloud, nearly
spilling my coffee. My friends turn around just in time to watch the Starbucks
barista dump an entire case of sandwiches into a plastic trash bag. At 4 p.m.,
nearly two-dozen delicious, fresh sandwiches are headed for the Dumpster."
This opening story does more than set the stage for the dumpster diving
advice to come. Because it highlights the surprising and unnecessary
wastefulness that makes such diving possible in the first place ("What is she
doing?"), it also alerts readers to the fact that the writer is making a social
critique.

º *Making an Argument About Privilege*: The same is true for the different steps
the essay outlines. In encouraging her readers to "[t]rust your instincts—and
your nose," for example, the writer is not only offering practical safety tips;
she is also forcing her readers to confront some of the more unpleasant (and
hazardous) realities for those not fortunate enough to be able to buy food for
themselves. The unspoken message in moments like this seems to be: Those
who are more fortunate have an obligation to "dig into" and learn about the
reality of our fellow citizens who have less.

º *Advocating Greater Conservation*: The message about obligation and responsibility gets developed throughout the essay's step-by-step instruction. Like
the example cited above, the writer's injunction to "[l]earn to preserve,"
"[t]ake only what you can use," or "share the wealth" can be read both as a
practical advice for would-be dumpster divers but also as an argument
about the need to curb our societal tendencies toward excess, waste, and
overconsumption.

Voice: *What tone and/or language does the writer use to present her advice?*

○ *Adopting a Genial, Inviting Tone*: Even though she offers a pointed political argument, the writer strikes a tone that is genial and free of judgment. Using an informal and accessible diction, she conveys her advice more in the voice of a friendly neighbor than an angry scold. Here are a couple of examples: "The thrill of 'getting stuff for free' can be intoxicating—and just like going to a buffet, your eyes can sometimes be bigger than your stomach." And: "Dumpsters can get a little gross. Decide in advance how far you are willing to go for that bag of organic black bean chips and respect those boundaries."

Credibility: *What gives this writer the authority to offer these instructions?*

○ *Offering Relatable Advice*: To a large extent, the essay derives its credibility from the organizational scheme it follows. By shaping her discussion around a specific set of suggestions to readers, the writer is positioning herself as a competent, knowledgeable guide whose advice should be followed. In an effort to deliver on this claim, the writer supplements her personal observations about dumpster diving with statistical data about the food consumption and food waste in America. This strategy enhances the writer's credibility by placing her own experiences and perspective within a broader statistical context, thereby providing a more objective basis for suggestions that might otherwise come across to readers as "mere" personal opinion.

Using Process to Create Your Own Writing

The outline below shows you how to use the book's five rhetorical concepts as guides for creating your own process writing. Take a look at each of these steps. Then, think about the ways you could use them to put this mode into practice yourself.

Step One: *Think About Your Purpose*

○ What specific information am I trying to get across?

○ What do I want my readers to learn? Why?

Step Two: *Think About Your Audience*

○ What kind of reader would most want or need to learn these instructions?

○ How much prior experience or knowledge would such readers bring?

Step Three: *Think About Your Argument*

○ What makes these instructions useful or important?

○ What larger question or idea am I using these instructions to get across?

Step Four: *Think About Your Voice*

 o What tone and/or language best helps me convey this information?

 o In what order or sequence should I arrange these steps?

Step Five: *Think About Your Credibility*

 o Is it possible for a reader to follow these steps?

 o Will following these steps truly lead to the intended outcome?

Definition

Definition writing provides readers with an explanation of what a given term means. As this broad description suggests, the range of terms included within the mode is extremely wide: from writing that defines an object or person to writing that defines an experience or concept. Whatever the case, the basic goal remains the same: to identify the key qualities or characteristics that define something's individual nature.

The article below provides an example. As you look it over, think about the different ways the subject is being defined: physically, visually, culturally, and historically. Then, use the accompanying analysis to speculate about the different rhetorical purposes to which this definition is being put.

Beth Teitel, "Why Do We Loathe Mullets?"

In this article, Beth Teitel offers a tongue-in-cheek twist on using the definition mode to better understand the widespread public disdain for a much-reviled hairstyle: the mullet.

At this point, it's fair to say that the mullet is as reviled as a hairstyle can possibly be. Any doubt was erased last week, when Iran's move to ban the 'do earned the member of the Axis of Evil not its usual international condemnation but a PR boost.

As New York comedian Ophira Eisenberg observed: "I am not a fan of any government
5   giving guidelines on how people can look, but when I read that Iran banned the mullet I thought, finally, they are doing something right."

The mullet and a number of other styles got snipped for being "decadent," but with all due respect to Iran's culture ministry, that's not the hairstyle's only problem. Why does the mullet elicit such loathing? Perhaps it's the haircut's creepy, suggestive slogan: Business in
10   front, party in the back. *Heh, heh, heh.* Or the in-your-face attitude of its devotees.

Short on top, long in the back, the mullet has been worn by beloved pop culture figures from the Sphinx to Paul McCartney to Florence Henderson. A style staple throughout history, it exploded in popularity in the 1980s, sucking in everyone from Bono to Steve Perry of Journey to ninth grade boys across the US. The mullet is not without practical uses: It
15   allows nice visibility under, say, a helmet, while shading the neck from the sun. Nevertheless, the mullet years ago turned into the red rubber nose of the coiffure world.

"It's not a haircut," Eisenberg quips, "it's a lifestyle."

And not an appealing one, according to Tom Connolly, an English professor at Suffolk University and a pop culture commentator. "There is such an aggressive/humble arrogance that goes with it: 'I'm just a country boy—do you want to go out with me?'" 20

Like others asked to ponder the mullet's infamy, he could have gone on forever: "There is kind of a shirt open to the waist, coiffed chest hair that goes with it," he said, gleefully. "Even someone crawling out from under a double-wide is going to toss his head if he's got a mullet and grin at you through gray teeth."

So bad is the mullet's rap that the word has turned into an all-purpose insult that goes 25 beyond hair. "Fear the Mullet," read a recent *New York Daily News* headline about the horror of the asymmetrical dresses that are currently popular among red-carpet starlets.

But perhaps the mullet's negatives have less to do with the style itself than who it hangs out with. Newbury Street stylist Patrice Vinci says the fault lies not with the mullet, but with the associations it conjures. "It just reminds people of the bad hair in the '80s," 30 she said.

Whether or not the mullet deserves to be an object of ridicule, one thing is clear: Life is different for the mulleted and the regularly coiffed person.

Jake Nyberg, an artsy advertising guy from Minneapolis, spent 10 months rocking a mullet that he grew essentially out of "total boredom," and then turned into a sociology 35 experiment (and, of course, a website, MulletLikeMe.com). "I was ignored at a totally empty J. Crew with four employees," he said. Business meetings, which he'd attend in a dress shirt, sport coat, and his auburn mullet, were also challenging. "The mullet was the elephant in the room." When either he or his business partner would reveal that the mullet was a joke, Nyberg said, "there'd be three or four chuckles and this nervous relief of what- 40 ever tension there was."

Nyberg cut off the mullet for his 30th birthday, and in its place he's got a more open frame of mind. "I used to work in a music store and we'd mock people's hairstyles behind their backs," he said, "but now I realize, you don't know what that guy's story is."

He also has a new appreciation for the mullet: "It's bad, but at the same time it sort of 45 makes you smile."

Emphasis on "sort of." Pats QB Tom Brady has been wearing a carefully cultivated mullet in recent months. Its expertly tousled fringe makes him look like he spends his days on a surfboard rather than shopping for furniture for his sprawling new LA home with wife Gisele Bundchen. 50

But it's still a mullet.

If there's one person in America who loves the mullet in a non-ironic way, it's Dean Mellen, stylist to the stars and local fashionistas. "I think it's misunderstood," his ode began. A nice mullet can flatter a short neck, create the illusion of high cheekbones, lift the eyes. "A mullet can save the day," he cooed. "There's a mullet for everyone." 55

Consider yourself warned.

Source: Boston Globe, *July 15, 2010*
http://www.boston.com/lifestyle/fashion/articles/2010/07/15/why_do_we_loathe_mullets/

Analyzing Definition in Rhetorical Terms

Included below is an outline that models how to use the book's five rhetorical concepts to analyze the ways the definition mode operates in this piece of writing. As you
read through this piece, think about the particular definition being presented. Is it
clear? Does it seem accurate? And how does this definition help the writer convey a
larger point?

Purpose: *What goals does the writer have? How does she use definition
writing to accomplish them?*

○ *Addressing Our Cultural Loathing About Mullets*: The central goal is to
answer the question of why we loathe mullets, to explain for readers the
roots behind our culture's long-standing hostility toward this particular
hairstyle.

○ *Defining Different Types*: Definition forms a crucial element of this overall
strategy. Before she can offer readers a convincing cultural analysis, the
writer first needs to define exactly what a "mullet" is. She accomplishes this
goal in a passage near the outset that defines this hairstyle in visual, historical, and pop culture terms: "Short on top, long in the back, the mullet has
been worn by beloved pop culture figures from the Sphinx to Paul
McCartney to Florence Henderson. A style staple throughout history,
it exploded in popularity in the 1980s, sucking in everyone from Bono
to Steve Perry of Journey to ninth grade boys across the US."

○ *Reviewing Cultural Attitudes*: A second goal is to define not just the mullet
itself but also the range of public opinions and reactions this hairstyle has
evoked over the years. We can see this goal at work in passages such as this,
where the writer directly addresses the cultural stereotypes historically associated with the mullet: "So bad is the mullet's rap that the word has turned
into an all-purpose insult that goes beyond hair. 'Fear the Mullet,' read a
recent *New York Daily News* headline about the horror of the asymmetrical
dresses that are currently popular among red-carpet starlets."

Audience: *Toward whom is this essay directed? What audience is best
positioned to care about and respond to the definition this
essay presents?*

○ *Addressing a Culturally Hip Audience*: Filled with references to celebrities and
fashion trends, this essay is clearly directed toward readers with a strong interest in pop culture. Indeed, the very attempt to provide an overview of attitudes toward the mullet presumes an audience already interested in the
ways that pop culture trends influence our personal lives.

○ *Assuming an Open-Minded Audience*: Although the title addresses the audience as a collective "we," it's not entirely certain the writer assumes all of her

readers feel a common "loathing" toward mullets. Rather than presume everyone automatically shares this attitude, the writer engages the topic in ways that invite a more open-minded examination, asking "[w]hether or not the mullet deserves to be an object of ridicule."

Argument: *What larger point or message does the writer use her definition to get across?*

○ *Highlighting the Mullet's Lowly Status*: The essay begins by making the basic point that the mullet has long endured a comical reputation: "[T]he mullet years ago turned into the red rubber nose of the coiffure world."

○ *Explaining the Mullet's Lowly Status*: The essay goes on to offer a more in-depth argument that seeks to explain some of the root causes behind this reputation. Much of this, the writer suggests, derives from the mullet's status as a symbol or stand-in for stereotypes of working-class life. This is the argument that can be glimpsed in the essay's reference to double-wide trailers or the story about the mullet-wearing customer being ignored by salespeople at the local J. Crew.

○ *Critiquing Cultural Stereotypes*: The writer uses examples like these to make one final point: that the cultural stereotypes surrounding the mullet are neither fair nor set in stone. Quoting the same J. Crew customer, she emphasizes the possibility of cultivating "a more open frame of mind" because you "don't know what that [mullet-wearing] guy's story is."

Voice: *What specific tone and/or language does the writer use in presenting this definition?*

○ *Mixing Critical and Ironic Voices*: In her effort to define the mullet physically, culturally, and historically, the writer employs a tone that is a mix of critical and ironic. In the opening lines, for example, she addresses the mullet's lowly status in the more distanced, formal diction of the cultural critic: "At this point, it's fair to say that the mullet is as reviled as a hairstyle can possibly be." Or: "So bad is the mullet's rap that the word has turned into an all-purpose insult that goes beyond hair." We might wonder whether the ironic tone the writer sometimes strikes here is at odds with the larger argument she is attempting to make. If her main point has to do with the possibility, of keeping an open mind and rethinking the cultural stereotypes surrounding the mullet, this may be undermined by a tone that seems to echo rather than challenge precisely such stereotypical thinking.

Credibility: *What makes this definition persuasive or believable?*

○ *Showcasing a Range of Cultural Attitudes*: A good deal of the writer's credibility stems from the inclusion of a wide range of perspectives on this topic. Rather than devote the entire essay to airing her own personal opinions, the writer spends an equal amount of time presenting the views of others—views that offer a range of different takes on the meaning of the mullet. As a result, the writer comes across as a fair-minded and even-handed arbiter rather than an opinionated partisan, which in turn validates the discussion overall as reliably objective.

Using Definition to Create Your Own Writing

The outline below shows you how to use the book's five rhetorical concepts as guides for creating your own definition writing. Take a look at each of these steps. Then, think about the ways you could use them to put this mode into practice yourself.

Step One: *Think About Your Purpose*

- What am I trying to define?

- What does this definition include and exclude?

- What makes this definition interesting or important?

Step Two: *Think About Your Audience*

- Who would find this definition useful or important?

- What specific information do such readers need to have?

Step Three: *Think About Your Argument*

- What larger point am I using this definition to make?

- What element of this definition conveys this point most effectively?

Step Four: *Think About Your Voice*

- How should I arrange the different elements in this definition?

- Do I want to present a neutral definition, or do I want to offer my opinion?

Step Five: *Think About Your Credibility*

- Is my definition accurate? Is it fair?

- Are there alternative ways to define this same thing? Should I consider using them?

Proposal

Proposal writing takes a stand and presents support designed to convince other people to accept this position. As this definition suggests, the primary goal of a proposal is to persuade readers to consider and/or share the writer's point of view. One of the most widely used modes, proposals come in all shapes and sizes, from a 20-page research essay to a 140-character tweet. When you analyze a poem for literature class, you are engaging in proposal writing. The same is true when you exchange text messages with classmates about who is the best professor to take next semester or when you post comments to a political blog in support of a candidate for office.

Because its primary purpose is to persuade, this mode requires writers to think long and hard about the particular goals they wish to accomplish as well as the rhetorical strategies that will most likely fulfill them. The selection below offers a case in point. The writer here holds very strong views about recent efforts in New York to ban the sale of sugary drinks. How does he attempt to get these views across to his readers? What key claim does he present? And what specific choices does he make to persuade readers to accept it?

Lawrence Gostin, "Banning Large Sodas Is Legal and Smart"

Lawrence Gostin is the Director of the World Health Organization's Center on Public Health Law and Human Rights.

A state trial judge on Monday blocked New York City's plan for a maximum 16 ounce size for a high-sugar beverage. The ban would have included sodas, energy drinks, fruit drinks and sweetened teas. But it would have excluded alcoholic beverages and drinks that are more than 50% milk, such as lattes. The ban would have applied to restaurants, movie theaters, stadiums and mobile food carts. But it would not have applied to supermarkets   5
and convenience stores, such as 7-Eleven.

Mayor Michael Bloomberg's proposal was met with fierce opposition by the industry and public outrage at the loss of "liberty," the so-called "nanny state" run amok. Beyond all the hype, the industry's vociferous arguments, now adopted by a trial court, are badly flawed. In fact, the Board of Health has the power, indeed the responsibility, to regulate   10
sugary drinks for the sake of city residents, particularly the poor.

Would the Ban Work?

Nearly six out of 10 New York City residents are overweight or obese, as are nearly four out of 10 schoolchildren. This cannot be acceptable to our society, knowing that obesity is such a powerful risk factor for diabetes, cancer and heart disease. No one would disagree that government should act, but how? There is no single solution, but many ideas that would   15
work in combination. One of those solutions is to control portion size and sugar consumption. Why?

First, the ever-expanding portions (think "supersized") are one of the major causes of obesity. When portion sizes are smaller, individuals eat less but feel full. This works, even if a person can take an additional portion. (Most won't because they are satiated,   20
and it at least makes them think about what they are consuming.) Second, sugar is high in calories, promotes fat storage in the body and is addictive, so people want more. The so-called "war on sugar" is not a culture war, it is a public health imperative backed by science.

25 So, there is good reason to believe New York's portion control would work. But why does the city have to prove that it works beyond any doubt? Those who cry "nanny state" in response to almost any modern public health measure (think food, alcohol, firearms, distracted driving) demand a standard of proof that lawmakers don't have to meet in any other field.

30 When a law is passed to increase jobs, spur the economy or subsidize a corporate sector (oil, for example), we don't insist that lawmakers prove it works. At least public health officials rely on science and try to craft rules that have a chance of working—if not in isolation, then in combination with other obesity control measures such as food labeling, calorie disclosures, trans fat restrictions and access to affordable fruits and vegetables in 35 schools and poor neighborhoods.

Is the Ban Consistent?

The industry stoked the fires of public discontent with its campaign against the "inconsistencies" in the soda ban. Why doesn't the ban apply to milky drinks, why can 7-Eleven sell large sugary drinks, and why not ban refills? Justice Milton Tingling, Jr., bought both industry arguments: It won't work and it is inconsistent. He went so far as to call the ban 40 "fraught with arbitrary and capricious consequences" and filled with loopholes. Again, we find a double standard.

Bloomberg did what every other politician does: balance public health and safety with realpolitik. Consider one of the judge's major arguments: balancing public health and economic considerations is "impermissible." This judicial reasoning makes no sense. If policy 45 makers could not balance economic consequences, virtually every law in America would be flawed. There is another huge problem with this argument. It assumes that unless public health does everything, it can do nothing. The whole art of politics is compromise. The mayor gets a lot of what he seeks to fight obesity, but not everything.

Does the Board of Health Have the Power?

Admittedly, the soda ban would have been better coming from the city's elected legisla-
50 ture, the City Council. But the Board of Health has authority to act in cases where there is an imminent threat to health. Doesn't the epidemic of obesity count as an imminent threat, with its devastating impact on health, quality of life and mortality? In any event, the Board of Health has authority over the food supply and chronic disease, which is exactly what it has used in this case.

55 Members of the Board of Health, moreover, are experts in public health, entitled to a degree of deference. The fact that the proposal originated in the mayor's office does not diminish the board's authority and duty to protect the public's health. Many health proposals arise from the executive branch, notably the Affordable Care Act.

Should Industry Have an Outsized Influence on Public Health Policy?

The fingerprints of the food and restaurant industries, with their clear economic conflicts
60 of interest, are all over the public and judicial campaign to block the soda ban. Industry undertook a multimillion-dollar campaign, flying banners over the city and plastering ads over the subways. They immediately filed suit and hired the most elite law firms.

Rather than recognize the public health effects of large sugary drinks, they chose to fight, reminiscent of Big Tobacco. What is worse, the public (and now a judge) fell for the industry's manipulations. Most New Yorkers oppose the portion ban, while politicians in other states are scrambling to show their disapproval. Mississippi is about to pass a law forbidding portion control. Imagine that in a state with the highest obesity rate in America! 65

We are used to fierce lobbying for personal gain in America, but that doesn't mean we should be duped by industry propaganda. Is a portion limit really such an assault on freedom? It doesn't stop anyone from buying soda. If consumers really want, they can buy several smaller drinks. It doesn't stop companies from giving refills. 70

There is really no great burden posed on individuals, only a little nudge in the right direction. At the same time, it could make meaningful changes in the drinking habits of New Yorkers. Why is the industry fighting this so fiercely? Because when it is shown to be successful in New York, it will be emulated in major cities in America and worldwide. Isn't that exactly what we need to stem the tide of obesity? 75

Source: CNN.com, March 13, 2013, © 2013 Cable News Network, Inc.
http://www.cnn.com/2013/03/13/opinion/gostin-soda-ban/

Analyzing Proposal in Rhetorical Terms

Included below is an outline that models how to use the book's five rhetorical concepts to analyze the ways the proposal mode operates in this piece of writing. As you read through this piece, think about the larger point this writer is trying to make and what reasons and evidence he presents to support it.

Purpose: *What goals does the writer have? What does he want his readers to see about this issue?*

○ *Arguing in Favor of the Ban*: The central goal here is to argue in favor of efforts by New York City officials to ban the sale of large sugary drinks. More specifically, the writer wants to highlight both the legality and the health benefits of this policy.

○ *Mobilizing Support*: By making this argument, the writer hopes to spur his readers not simply to support the soda ban but also to oppose those efforts to repeal it.

Audience: *Toward whom is this proposal directed? What readership would be most interested or invested in the claims being made?*

○ *Directly Addressing a Local Audience*: On one level, this proposal seems to be directed toward those with the most immediate stake in this issue: people who live or work in New York or those who might soon be visiting. This can be seen in the specifically local references the writer makes to former mayor Michael Bloomberg or the New York City Board of Health.

○ *Indirectly Addressing a National Audience*: On another level, the writer also
seems to be directing his proposal to a more broadly national audience.
For this writer, New York's soda ban is an issue of importance to readers
nationwide.

Argument: *What specific claims does the writer make?*
How are these claims supported or defended?

○ *Protecting the Public Welfare*: A central point concerns the effect the proposed ban would have on public health. This can be seen in such statements
as: "Nearly six out of 10 New York City residents are overweight or obese, as
are nearly four out of 10 schoolchildren. This cannot be acceptable to our
society, knowing that obesity is such a powerful risk factor for diabetes,
cancer and heart disease."

○ *Defending the Ban's Workability*: The writer also makes the point that beyond
being beneficial to public health, the proposed ban is also a sensible, workable plan: "At least public health officials rely on science and try to craft
rules that have a chance of working—if not in isolation, then in combination with other obesity control measures such as food labeling, calorie disclosures, trans fat restrictions and access to affordable fruits and vegetables
in schools and poor neighborhoods."

○ *Defending the Ban's Legality*: Another key point concerns the assertion that
the effort to regulate soda and sugar consumption is entirely within the
boundaries of the law: "[T]he Board of Health has authority to act in cases
where there is an imminent threat to health. Doesn't the epidemic of obesity
count as an imminent threat, with its devastating impact on health, quality
of life and mortality?"

Voice: *What specific tone and/or language does the writer use*
to advance his proposal?

○ *Employing Emotional Language*: The writer employs emotionally loaded language throughout to advance his key claims. We can see this strategy at
work in such moments as when he warns readers against being "duped by
industry propaganda" arguing against the ban and objects to "the industry's
manipulations."

Credibility: *What specific elements make this proposal more or less*
effective?

○ *Invoking Scientific Credentials*: Much of the strength of the writer's argument
rests on his status as the Director of the World Health Organization's Center
on Public Health Law and Human Rights. This position gives him considerable authority to speak on issues of public health.

Using Proposal to Create Your Own Writing

The outline below shows you how to use the book's five rhetorical concepts as guides for creating your own proposal-based writing. Take a look at each of these steps. Then, think about the ways you could use them to put this mode into practice yourself.

Step One: *Think About Your Purpose*

- Why do I want to get this main point or message across?

- What makes it important?

Step Two: *Think About Your Audience*

- What kind of reader cares most about the issue I am addressing?

- What explanation or reasoning will most likely persuade this reader to share my view?

Step Three: *Think About Your Argument*

- What claim do I want to make?

- How should I explain and/or support this claim?

- What evidence do I need to provide?

Step Four: *Think About Your Voice*

- What tone and/or language will help me be most persuasive?

- How forceful or direct do I want to be in presenting my own opinion?

Step Five: *Think About Your Credibility*

- What makes my point of view on this issue plausible or believable?

- What makes my viewpoint more valid than others?

PART TWO
Rhetorical Readings

5 Purpose

Every time you sit down to write, it may feel as if you're starting from a blank slate. Where do I begin? How do I decide what to say? And how should I say it? But the truth is that every time you set about to write something—whether an academic report or a grocery list, an email or a text—you do so with at least some basic idea of what you hope to accomplish already in mind. Whether you are fully aware of it or not, behind every act of writing lies some sort of objective, some goal for what you want your writing to do.

In the world of academic writing, this is called *purpose.* The purpose behind a lab report may be to evaluate certain scientific findings; the objective of a history paper may be to interpret the social or political significance of a given event; the point of an English assignment may be to summarize the key points in a particular novel or poem. Whatever the case, you know from long experience that academic assignments require you to think long and hard about what your ultimate goal needs to be.

The same thing also holds true for the writing we do outside the classroom. Think, for instance, about the last Facebook comment you posted or email you sent. To be sure, you probably didn't devote a lot of time worrying over *why* you wrote what you did. But just because you didn't consciously reflect upon your goals doesn't mean they didn't play an important role in shaping how and what you wrote. Writing in a real world environment as fast-paced as our own, we don't always take the time to pause and figure out exactly what our objectives are. But once we take the time to look more closely at the goals behind our writing, we discover that we have much more control over our writing than before.

What Goal Do I Want to Achieve?

To illustrate, imagine that you are participating in an email conversation with a group of classmates where you are all sharing impressions of a particular professor. Some of the responses are glowing testimonials of this professor's demeanor and style, praising the energy and enthusiasm he brings to his interactions with students. Other responses, however, are far less complimentary, laced with complaints about how unfocused this teacher's instruction seems and how little time he devotes to explaining key assignments or clarifying core concepts.

If you were to jump into this discussion without any forethought, you might assume that your only option is to choose one of these two responses: either praise the professor for his personality or criticize him for his organization. But if you were to slow down this process and reflect a bit more about what you actually want to say, you might decide upon a different plan of action. You might discover, for instance, that your goal isn't to choose between these two rival assessments of your professor ("great personality" or "lack of organization") but rather to offer an assessment that reflects a more nuanced perspective. Think about the ways this revised goal might affect other decisions you make here. Instead of adopting a strident or opinionated voice, you might decide it's better to strike a tone that is more open and curious. Rather than offer a long list compliments or complaints about your professor, you might decide to pose questions about the value or point of crowdsourcing an evaluation of your teacher in the first place. By thinking more intentionally about your purpose, in other words, you will gain a greater understanding of and control over the writing process itself.

How to Analyze Purpose in Real World Writing

While hypothetical, this example illustrates what can happen when we begin to think about purpose in a more explicit and thoughtful way. To do this, however, we need a systematic approach that allows us to analyze the issue of purpose in rhetorical terms. The outline below provides a step-by-step guide for doing precisely this. Dividing the rhetorical analysis into a series of discrete steps, it presents a map for understanding the role that purpose plays both in your own writing and in the writing of others.

Thinking Rhetorically About Purpose

- *Step 1: Planning for Purpose*: What is the writer's basic goal here? What points does the writer want to get across? What effect upon the reader does the writer hope to have?
- *Step 2: Acting Upon Purpose*: How do these goals affect the way the writer decides to organize this writing? How do these goals influence the writer's choice of tone and/or language?
- *Step 3: Rethinking Purpose*: How do readers respond to the writer's choices? Are these reactions in line with the writer's goals?
- *Step 4: Refining Purpose*: How do these reader responses affect or alter the writer's overall purpose? What aspects of this writing do these responses indicate might need to be changed?
- *Step 5: Putting It Into Writing*: How do I summarize these findings in writing?

To see how these guidelines can be put into practice, let's turn to a specific example. As you look over the points the author raises in the excerpt below, begin thinking about the larger purpose that motivates her. Then, use the questions outlined above to put together a more comprehensive analysis of how this purpose influences the particular choices the writer makes.

Ellen Roche, "Military Recruiters on Campus Is a Bad Idea"

In this blog post, Ellen Roche, a college sophomore, offers her thoughts on the current debate over whether military recruiters should be allowed on campus.

The idea of having military recruiters on campus, I have to admit, doesn't sound like the kind of thing colleges or universities should encourage. College is supposed to be about learning, expanding your mind, growing as a person. Imagine how distracting it would be to have these recruiters around here bothering hard-working students. College should be about making your life better and learning new things. The military, however, is all about   5
learning how to destroy life. No matter how much the recruiters dress it up and hide behind sales tactics, the military is about learning how to kill. What's more, most of the armed forces are made up of people who come from poor families and lower class back- grounds with little education. The military prefers people who do not ask questions and will do what they are told. That is why military recruiters frequent community college   10
campuses. They aren't going to get many affluent blue bloods to join, so they cynically aim for children of the working class instead. Should the decision be made to allow military recruiters on campus, there would be a surge of anti-war activity. Students need to stop this unnecessary and dangerous move.

■ Thinking Rhetorically About Purpose: A Step-by-Step Guide

Now, let's now see how the guidelines above can be used as the basis for putting to- gether a more formal, step-by-step, rhetorical analysis:

Step One: *Planning for Purpose: What is the Writer's Basic Goal?*

   ○ Clearly, the writer's main goal is to argue against military recruiters on college campuses. In making this case, though, the writer seems to have a number of other goals in mind as well. Among them:

   › To present a critique of military violence and what she views as the true purpose behind the military altogether—namely, to "destroy" and "kill."

   › To question the rationale behind military recruitment itself, which the writer defines as an effort to manipulate and exploit "working class kids."

   › To define college life and military life as fundamentally incompatible.

   › To mobilize college students to oppose military recruitment.

Step Two: *Acting Upon Purpose: How Does This Goal Influence Other Rhetorical Choices the Writer Makes?*

   ○ The effort to argue against military recruitment leads the writer to describe college life and military life in opposite terms. Because she wants her readers to look upon military recruitment as an inappropriate, even immoral intrusion, she describes college in language that highlights fundamental differences. For example:

> College is supposed to be about learning, expanding your mind, growing as a person.

> College should be about making your life better and learning new things.

o At the same time, the writer chooses language that describes the military in the exact opposite terms:

> The military . . . is all about learning how to destroy life.

> The military is about learning how to kill.

o Because another of the writer's goals is to question the military's motives, she also uses language that makes recruitment seem like a threat to college students. She speaks of "hard-working" students who don't need the efforts of recruiters "distracting" them. She accuses the military of "cynically" targeting "children of the working class."

o And finally, because she also wants her audience to understand the importance of getting involved, the writer makes the decision to conclude her post with an explicit call to action:

> Students need to stop this dangerous and unnecessary move.

Step Three: *Rethinking Purpose: How Do You Evaluate This Goal? How Effectively Does the Writer Achieve It?*

o I think the writer does an effective job of communicating her basic point that military recruitment should not be allowed. The language she uses makes clear to her readers where she stands on this issue. If the writer's goal is to make sure that her opposition to this practice comes across vividly, the essay definitely succeeds.

o In relation to the writer's other goals, however, I'm less sure the essay is entirely effective. While she clearly wants readers to judge the military harshly, I'm not sure her decision to make negative blanket statements helps accomplish this. Statements like "the military . . . is all about learning how to destroy life" are such black-and-white generalizations that they make the claim itself feel less believable.

o This applies to the way the writer describes campus life as well. Once again, her tendency to speak in sweeping generalizations undercuts the broader attempt to present college life as the opposite of military life. Why can't there be a place for the military on college campuses? Why can't conversations between students and recruiters become part of the "learning" and "growing" process the writer associates with higher education?

Step Four: *Refining Purpose: What Aspects of This Writing Would You Change? How Would They Affect the Goal?*

○ If I were the writer here, I would have tried to present a more balanced assessment of this debate. It is possible to present the other side of an argument, I believe, while still making a strong case for your own point of view. In fact, I think this strategy would help the writer here accomplish her goal more effectively. It would help her readers see that her own position is more fully thought out.

Step Five: *Putting It Into Writing: How Do You Summarize Your Findings in Writing?*

○ The strength of this essay is in how clearly and forcefully the writer conveys her own opinions. Readers can have little doubt about where this writer stands on the question of military recruitment on college campuses, or on what response college students themselves should have. At times, however, the language the writer uses to make her case runs the risk of simplifying the question at hand. From this perspective, it seems as if the clarity and forcefulness of her writing might actually be working against her own goals.

Informal Writing Selections

This section invites you to undertake this kind of work yourself. Bringing together a sampling of the informal writing you might easily come across in your own daily life, it provides you with a chance to put into practice the rhetorical analysis modeled above.

Let's start by working our way through a sample of this rhetorical analysis. While reading the selection below, pay close attention to the comments and the questions. They are designed to serve as a model for the analysis you will conduct with the other selections that follow.

Courtney Wittmann, "Best Warriors Highlight Army Strong Values"

This essay by Courtney Wittmann is part of a larger promotional campaign undertaken by the US Army to educate the general public about the contributions and sacrifices of US soldiers.

Two weeks after the Army's Annual Best Warrior Competition the winners are acclimating to their new roles as spokesmen for the Army, the competitors have settled back into their daily Soldier routines and I am still amazed by the dedication and strength of 24 individuals I witnessed throughout the week-long competition.

The language here reflects the writer's goal to present a positive portrait of army life.   5

As a civilian employee of the Army, I am surrounded by our Nation's bravest on a daily basis, but working Best

Warrior gave me a greater understanding and appreciation
10   for those I serve. I was able to witness, first hand, what it
takes to face adversity head on and prevail, what it takes to
perpetuate through pitfalls and what it takes to soldier on
in times of trouble. I was able to witness Army Strong.
Throughout the week, warriors woke while the sun was still
15   sleeping only to face hostage situations, medical evacua-
tions and provide casualty assistance. As the night faded to
day, Soldiers' mental and physical abilities continued to be
pushed and tested by written examinations, land naviga-
tion, rifle qualifications and combatives. The sound of gun-
20   fire and explosions persisted late into the night and left
participants with minimal sleep, night after night.

Emphasizing the sacrifices the soldiers endure. This strategy seems designed to create sympathy and support for the work these soldiers undertake.

Despite the haze of sleep deprivation and physical exhaustion, warriors upheld the words of the Soldiers Creed:
I am disciplined, physically and mentally tough, trained
25   and proficient in my warrior tasks and drills. Their excitement and professionalism never faltered throughout the
week's worth of tests. As I approached participants for interviews, comments or requests I was always greeted with
enthusiasm and friendliness, even as the pressures of the
30   competition remained. The week-long competition offered
me a glimpse into the day-to-day life of a Soldier. In the
short timeframe of a week, the experience allowed me to
absorb true, gritty Army culture and better my ability to
share the Soldier story.

Is the writer going too far here? Is it really necessary to stress the soldiers' "enthusiasm" and "friendliness" along with their hard work and sacrifice?

35   The extreme perseverance, dedication and professionalism exhibited by the 24 competitors at Best Warrior, and
Soldiers everywhere, is what makes my job so enjoyable. The
dedication and vigor instilled in the individuals that make
up our Army are unparalleled by most and the Best Warrior
40   Competition reiterated that working with and for individuals encompassing such qualities is a privilege to say the least.

The conclusion sheds light on the writer's overall goal. She doesn't only want us to support the work these soldiers undertake, she also wants us to further this support by offering our own stories, too.

Now that you've read about my experience, do you have a
story about working with Soldiers? Do you know a Soldier
who is Army Strong? Tell me about it!

Source: Army Live, October 20, 2010
http://armylive.dodlive.mil/index.php/2009/10/best-warriors-highlight-army-strong-values/

Step One: *Planning for Purpose: What is the Writer's Basic Goal?*

o The writer's basic goal is to create an extremely positive impression of soldiers in the US Army and to make clear to readers how necessary and

important the work they perform truly is. We can see evidence of this goal in the language the writer uses, beginning with the title and continuing throughout the piece:

› "Best Warriors" and "Strong Values"

› "excitement and professionalism"

› "enthusiasm and friendliness"

› "perseverance, dedication and professionalism"

○ More specifically, the writer wants her readers not only to be aware of the army's contributions but to be appreciative and grateful as well. We see evidence of this goal when the writer expresses amazement at the soldiers' "dedication and strength" or when she speaks of the "privilege" of working with such individuals. In moments like these, it is clear that the writer wants readers to share her own feelings of admiration and indebtedness.

Step Two: *Acting Upon Purpose: How Does This Goal Influence Other Rhetorical Choices the Writer Makes?*

○ The goal of instilling admiration and gratitude within readers explains why the writer provides so many examples of soldiers' dedication and sacrifice. For example:

> Throughout the week, warriors woke while the sun was still sleeping only to face hostage situations, medical evacuations and provide casualty assistance.

> Soldiers' mental and physical abilities continued to be pushed and tested by written examinations, land navigation, rifle qualifications and combatives.

○ The same goal of celebrating Army life is also evident in the key term the writer uses to describe US soldiers: "warriors." This is not an objective or neutral descriptor. It is clearly designed to conjure images of heroism, valor, and sacrifice.

○ The writer's desire to emphasize the discipline and sacrifice of these soldiers in particular comes across in other language the essay employs—for example, her description of the Soldier's Creed:

> I am disciplined, physically and mentally tough, trained and proficient in my warrior tasks and drills.

Step Three: *Rethinking Purpose: How Do You Evaluate This Goal? How Effectively Does the Writer Achieve It?*

○ It is not difficult to identify the goals behind this essay because the writer uses language that conveys her attitude and feelings so clearly. As a result, there is little doubt that readers are meant to admire and appreciate the work of the US Army soldiers.

o In some respects, though, the language is so enthusiastic and admiring that it risks undermining this goal. While the list of military tasks and characteristics is impressive, it is so universally positive that readers may be tempted to question how realistic the writer is being.

o The writer presents an intimate account of soldiers' lives, which in many ways is an effective tactic for furthering the larger goal of celebrating army life. As a first-hand witness, she can personally testify to how challenging the work of soldiering is. On the other hand, this proximity also suggests that the writer may be a little too close to this issue to offer a truly objective assessment, a bias that could undermine her overall goal.

Step Four: *Refining Purpose: What Aspects of This Writing Would You Change? How Would They Affect the Goal?*

o Because some of the language the writer uses seems over the top, I might recommend that she include more objective descriptions of the soldiers' duties and tasks and fewer words and phrases that do nothing but praise. In the long run, including more examples and objective descriptions could make the sacrifices of these soldiers come across as even more compelling.

o I would also consider altering the way the essay ends. Concluding with an explicit appeal to readers to share their own "Soldier" story might strike some readers as a too blatant attempt to influence their opinions. What if readers don't have a "Soldier" story? Or what if their "Soldier" story isn't as celebratory as the one presented here? Should the writer assume that all other "Soldier" stories would present the same kind of portrait?

Step Five: *Putting It Into Writing: How Do You Summarize Your Findings in Writing?*

o While the writer achieves the main goal of celebrating the strength and sacrifices of US soldiers, the essay undermines the effectiveness of this message by too often overstating or overselling these accomplishments. By relying more on complimentary language than concrete example, the writer runs the risk of raising doubts about her objectivity.

Now, it's your turn. Read through each of the selections below. Then, use the step-by-step outline above to conduct your own rhetorical analysis of purpose.

Matt Kibbe, "Take America Back"

Founded by former House Majority Leader Dick Armey, FreedomWorks is a website dedicated to advancing conservative political causes, encapsulated in its tagline: "Lower Taxes, Less Government, More Freedom."

To all freedom-loving citizens:

The very principles that define the uniquely American experiment—constitutionally-constrained government, individual liberty and free enterprise—are threatened with extinction by the arrogant and ambitious agenda of Barack Obama, Nancy Pelosi, Harry Reid, and others on the liberal left. Today, like no other time in our lives, the stakes are higher and the outcomes more decisive for the future of our children and our grandchildren.

The good news is that we can **Take America Back**. Over the past year, you've taken part in an unprecedented surge of grassroots activism in the limited government movement. Maybe you turned out for the Tea Party protests that swept across the nation last spring and summer, witnessed firsthand the outpouring of emotion at August town hall meetings, made the trip to FreedomWorks' own 9/12 Taxpayer March on Washington (with up to 800,000 other freedom-loving activists in attendance), or cast a ballot in the remarkable election upsets in Virginia, New Jersey, and Massachusetts. No matter how you've been a part of it, it's clear that more citizens than ever before are exercising their civic duties and demonstrating against policies that threaten their pocketbooks as well as their fundamental freedoms.

The Tea Party's common-sense agenda of fiscal conservatism now represents the very middle of the American political spectrum. We believe that the government should not spend money it does not have, and should not take over our health care system or run auto companies. If we get organized today, we can become a game-changing political bloc not unlike the 9 million new voters that showed up to overturn Democratic control of Congress in 1994.

Now is the time to build upon this unprecedented grassroots uprising for freedom and **Take America Back** from the advocates of big government in both political parties, from the rent-seeking big corporations eager to use the power of government to enrich themselves at the expense of consumers and taxpayers, and from the web of left-wing special interests who feed at the public trough and consider it their right to do so.

This active grassroots conservatism is exactly the kind of political movement FreedomWorks has been working to build since their founding in 1984. We did not create the Tea Party movement, nor have we tried to control it, but we are working around the clock to support it, help it grow and increase its impact. We are working to make this remarkable patriotic uprising a force for massive and permanent change this November. And with the help of patriots like you, that is *exactly what we are going to do.*

Source: FreedomWorks. http://www.freedomworks.org/take-america-back-campaign-war-room

Visual Rhetoric: Andy Reynolds, "Voto Aqui"

This visual presents its own portrait of political participation in modern America. What does this image seem to saying about this issue? How does its portrait compare with the vision of political participation advanced in the FreedomWorks piece?

FIGURE 5.4

Alicia Criado, "After Waiting 13 Years, My Family Reunited"

Alicia Criado is the Economic Policy Field Coordinator for La Raza. The largest Hispanic civil rights organization in the United States, the National Council of La Raza has worked for over 20 years to achieve greater recognition of and advocacy for Hispanic Americans.

When I initially heard the current immigration reform bill introduced on April 17 proposed to remove or limit certain family-based immigration petitions all I could think about was my personal family story. Without these petitions, many of my family members currently living and helping to strengthen the United States' economy would not be here.

My family is similar to many Latinos families in that we are close-knit and this includes my extended family. My mom was the first in her family to immigrate to the U.S. and through the family immigration system my mom sponsored her mother and eventually her sibling living in Peru.

I cannot help but cringe when I hear people talk about immigrants who are undocumented and say that they should have come the "legal way" or formally applying for green cards. It shows that they don't know how few options exist for

5

10

people to enter and that even in the channels that exist, people must endure extraordinary long waiting periods. I make it a point to share with them that I have family members who immigrated the "legal way" and waited 13 years to do so. 15 Most people's reaction is usually one of shock and astonishment that it can take over a decade for a family to be reunified.

Since my family immigrated to the United States in 2006, three have become naturalized citizens and they have all secured employment and are investing in their community by purchasing homes and starting businesses. Like many immi- 20 grant families, my mom's siblings and mother live in close proximity of each other and provide emotional and financial support for each other. They also all help support my grandmother who will turn 86 next month.

Since 2006, my mom has also gone through many life changes such as divorcing my father and being laid off from her job at the peak of the Great Recession. Through 25 these life changes, her siblings and mother have helped make her transition in life easier. My mom attributes her ability to bounce back from these difficult times and slowly reestablish herself in large part to have her siblings and mother here.

Plain and simple, if family-based immigration petitions were restricted, or in the case of siblings, eliminated, my mother would not have the family support she 30 relies on today. Additionally, their community in Southern California would not benefit from the positive economic impact my family has contributed.

Although my loved ones had to wait 13 years before they could reunite with my mother, I'm thankful they had the opportunity to immigrate to this country and thrive. This unfortunately is not the case for many people who never receive visas after waiting 35 in visa backlogs or those who are unjustly separated from their relatives. My family's story not only sheds light on problems with our broken immigration system but also serves as a reminder of how policy affects real people's lives and can help strengthen our economy. I can personally attest to the importance of preserving family-based immigration petitions. And I know that my family's story is one of many that demonstrate 40 we have benefited by having the ability to reunify with our loved ones.

Source: © 2013 by the National Council of La Raza, May 16, 2013
http://blog.nclr.org/2013/05/16/after-waiting-13-years-my-family-reunified/

Jamie Kelley, "The Steroid Problem, and How to Fix It"

Jamie Kelley is a contributor to SIKids.com, a website produced in conjunction with Sports Illustrated *magazine that explores sports issues of particular interest to young people. This article appeared at the height of the debate over steroid use in professional sports.*

Sports and steroids seem to be going hand in hand these days. Just this past August two Major League Baseball players who were leading their teams to the playoffs tested positive for steroids and were suspended. A seven time Tour de France winner was stripped of all Tour de France titles and banned from cycling for life for allegedly using illegal performance-enhancing drugs (PEDs). Some have suggested that PEDs should become legal because so many athletes in every kind of athletic competition are users.

There are different types of performance-enhancing drugs that athletes can use to make themselves better. Anabolic steroids help you develop a lean body and muscle growth quickly. Stimulants are used to electrify the athlete's brain and body by increasing the level of concentration, stamina, and aggressiveness. A third type of steroids are painkillers, which help the athlete make it through the long and grueling season. When athletes use performance-enhancing drugs they are also prone to a high injury risk. Many players who use steroids end up on the disabled list because the increase in muscle mass and speed is greater than the strength of the body's ligaments, tendons, etc.

Former New York Yankee pitcher David Wells said that "25–40% of baseball players are juiced." If that's true that means as many as 480 of the possible 1,200 baseball players that play in a single season are using PEDs. The numbers don't lie, there has been a steady power rise since the 1980s. Hall of Famers Cal Ripken, Jr., and Mike Schmidt, who played from 1981–2001 and 1972–1989, respectively, averaged 20–30 home runs a year, which is lower than the average today. In 1981, Schmidt led the league with a "mere" 31 home runs. In the 1980s there would also only be a handful of players who were hitting 25–35 plus home runs, today that number has become the norm for top Major League Baseball hitters. Home run leaders in the 1980s averaged 41.19 home runs a season, in the 1990s 51.8 home runs a season, and since 2000 have averaged 49 home runs a season. The modern game has moved away from the small ball type of play that was perfected throughout the years. Today pretty much every team has a player who averages 25–35 home runs a season. Yes, there have been advancements in how a player is trained and there are certainly players who have their own pure talent, but it seems that in recent years if a player is having a really productive season the subject of steroid use is immediately brought to the table.

PEDs don't just affect Major League Baseball, they affect every sport, one of which is professional cycling. Three-time Spanish Tour de France winner Alberto Contador was found guilty of using banned performance-enhancing drugs during the 2010 Tour de France. Contador was banned for two years from professional cycling and even though he was able to return this past August, his career is shattered because of his choice to use PEDs.

Lance Armstrong has won the Tour de France seven times. He has also been banned from cycling for life for allegedly using illegal banned substances while in the Tour de France. In June of this year the U.S. Anti-Doping Agency (USADA) charged Armstrong with having used illicit performance-enhancing drugs throughout his racing career. Armstrong brought a lawsuit against the USADA to federal court claiming that the USADA did not have jurisdiction and that his right to due process was being violated. On August 20th, 2012, a U.S. District Judge ruled in favor of the USADA, but the judge did question the USADA timing and motivation of their investigation into Armstrong and their obvious "single minded determination to force Armstrong to arbitrate." On August 23rd, 2012, Lance Armstrong released a statement in which he continued to claim his innocence but also that he would not be challenging the USADA's charges any longer. "There comes a point in every man's life when he has to say, 'Enough is enough.' For me, that time is now." Armstrong wrote in a statement: "Today I turn the page. I will no longer address this issue, regardless of the circumstances." *The New York Times* reported that, "according to the WADA Code," Armstrong's failure to contest such serious charges of anti-doping rules violations means that he forfeits all awards and prizes earned after August 1, 1998, including his Tour titles, and is banned from any sport that uses the World Anti-Doping Code.

Armstrong is one of the most famous athletes to have allegedly used PEDs, and while many people believe that he did use banned substances, many people believe that he did not use steroids. Until the USADA decides to release any concrete evidence against Armstrong, I along with many believe that he is innocent.

The differences in opinion in the Armstrong case lead right into the debate about whether or not performance-enhancing drugs should be allowed into professional sports. If PEDs were legal, all athletes and players would not be under certain disadvantages, they could all be even. Nobody would be suspended for cheating and there would be no speculation about if the home-run leaders were users or not. The opposite side of that debate is that, does the sport community, from fans to natural athletes to coaches etc., really want to be a part of something where you can legally cheat? This is a very pressing issue that needs to be dealt with. People are certainly fed up with the use of PEDs in sports today and they just want the game to go on without all of this surmising if a player is juicing or not, whether that means legalizing PEDs or not.

Back in the day of Ted Williams, Jesse Owens, Jim Thorpe, and Jackie Robinson steroids were a non-issue. These players had risen to their high standards by pure hard work. It was the golden age of athletics. Today we have veered off course of the golden age. While there are still great, natural athletes I don't believe that they are the majority but in fact possibly the minority. If PEDs are legalized into sports, we would be disappointing all of the games predecessors who fought and played hard to get athletics where they are today.

If steroids are legalized the players who do choose to use them are putting themselves at a major health risk. Lyle Alzado, a former NFL defensive end, died at the age of 43 due to brain cancer which was caused because of his consistent use of steroids. Alzado was one of the first professional athletes ever to use steroids. "I started taking anabolic steroids in 1969 and never stopped. It was addicting, mentally addicting. Now I'm sick, and I'm scared." Alzado said. "My last wish? That no one else ever dies this way." What Alzado was saying is that, yes steroids may be helping you in the short term but they're killing you in the long term.

Why do these athletes use performance-enhancing drugs? In reality it's because they want a big payday. If you're talented at what you do and are able to lead a team to the championship, you get to sign a new contract so that you can help the team the next season. But when you sign this contract there are more zeroes at the end of it than there were before. In the end it's greed and addiction. Don't get me wrong there are definitely players who earn that big contract, players like Mike Trout, Stephen Strasburg, and Cristiano Ronaldo. They all worked hard and earned that respect from their clubs. Same goes for Olympic athletes, they want endorsements, but the only way they can get endorsements is if they win. Some Olympic athletes think that the only way that they can win is if they use performance-enhancing drugs, because crossing that finish line a second earlier could be worth millions of dollars. I'm certainly not accusing all athletes of using steroids, far from it. In fact in recent years there has been a surge of younger players arriving onto the scene because they have worked as hard as they could. Players just like Trout and Bryce Harper, and Olympic athletes like Ryan Lochte, Missy Franklin, and Shelly-Ann Fraser-Pryce. They have all gotten to where they are today by pushing their limits. These athletes are certainly not the only ones who have reached their goal by training hard, they're but some of many. But there still are those players and athletes who want the money and think that using PEDs will secure those extra zeroes.

I am definitely still a believer that we can bring back the golden age of athletics. But the only way we can do that is to get rid of the use of performance-enhancing drugs in athletic competition. The way to do that is for commissioners, presidents, and athletes to come together and draw out a plan that offers severe penalties and possible immediate expulsion for an athlete if they test positive for PEDs. For instance, at this time the MLB has a three-strike rule for violators of their drug policy. Test positive once, the player gets a 50-game suspension. Test positive a second time and the player is suspended for 100 games. If they test positive a third time they are banned from baseball for life. While this may seem like an adequate policy it certainly isn't working. In my opinion, Major League Baseball needs to incorporate a two-strike rule. One positive test and the player in question is suspended for one year, test positive a second time and the player is banned for life.

All athletics, not just Major League Baseball, all over the world need to incorporate immensely stern drug policies, from the Barclays Premier League to the International Olympic Committee to the National Football League. All of these leagues, and all those in between, need to make the imperative decision to stop the use of performance-enhancing drugs. If each league is able to come together in their respective divisions and are able to resolve the problem of steroid use, the return of the golden age of athletics in this day and age is not far off.

Source: SIKids.com, September 19, 2012
http://www.sikids.com/kid-reporter-blogs/2012/09/19/the-steroid-problem-and-how-to-fix-it

Bryan Johnson, "Make State-Church Separation Absolute"

Bryan Johnson is a first-year graduate student at Colorado State University in Fort Collins and is pursuing an MFA in creative writing. He has an English *degree from Purdue University and has worked as a copywriter while writing fiction. He was awarded a $500 scholarship from the Freedom From Religion Foundation for this essay.*

In a speech to the Greater Houston Ministerial Association in 1960, presidential candidate John F. Kennedy said "I believe in an America where the separation of church and state is absolute . . . where no Catholic prelate would tell the president how to act, and no Protestant minister would tell his parishioners for whom to vote; where no church or church school is granted any public funds or political preference." 5

Kennedy emphasized that there were "far more critical issues" that faced the nation than his Catholicism, and the same thing holds true today. In an age where unemployment and poverty are rampant, overseas wars kill our citizens and raise our deficit, and the world's richest country also has its largest prison population, religion has become a driving force in American politics. 10

God's name is used to justify policies in arenas as diverse as health care, civil rights for women and minorities, and even education. Yet invoking the bible does nothing to address the issues behind our country's problems; it only serves to muddy the waters with arbitrary loyalties, xenophobia, and unwillingness to compromise. The separation of church and state is essential for creating effective, rational policies and ensuring freedom and equality for all. 15

Government is most effective when it uses empirically proven, logic-based methods for solving real-world problems. These methods can be debated using facts learned through scientific research, from carefully recorded observations and from successful tactics used in other countries. But supernatural justifications for policy 20 require no such vetting process; once God comes to the table, the issue becomes a matter of faith, not fact. Supernatural solutions do not solve real-world problems.

In August 2011, Texas Gov. Rick Perry convened a daylong event in Houston called The Response, a call for Americans to "to pray and fast like Jesus did" to combat Texas' crippling drought and economic problems. It did nothing, of course, 25 to ease economic and drought woes. His April day of prayer for rain was similarly ineffective.

The funds and time used to promote these events could have been used to research realistic methods of combating drought and deficits, but instead it was used to create a conservative soapbox that did nothing to solve the problems 30 faced by Texans.

Religion is an entirely subjective way to create policy, since doctrine and beliefs differ between religions. Even Christian denominations disagree on the exact nature of the god they worship.

In American history, this has manifested itself in countless ways. For example, 35 slave owners and abolitionists both used the bible to defend their position in the 19th century. In modern times, the LGBTQ movement's fiercest critics often use God as their primary reason for fighting against marriage equality, yet there are plenty of progressive Christians who support marriage equality and use the bible to justify their claims. 40

Which God?

You cannot debate the idea of God in a courtroom or statehouse. You cannot objectively weigh the advantages and disadvantages of a policy that has been dictated by a higher power. When we use unverifiable, subjective reasoning to make decisions, we create unjustifiable, ineffective policy.

45   With God involved in policy-making, the question becomes "which God?" In the U.S., Christians make up the vast majority of the population, but our country is also a melting pot of Buddhists, Hindus, Muslims, atheists, agnostics and everyone in between.

Indeed, America was founded in part on the freedom to worship or not worship
50   any way you please, and it's this diversity that makes America what it is. Part of freedom *from* religion is protecting freedom *of* religion.

When the majority religion makes its way into government, it does so not by reconciling itself to all other faiths and nonfaiths, but by the power of demograph-
55   ics. This leads to unequal representation, which creates a government that cannot or will not hear the needs of all its citizens.

Religion-based rule is tribalism at its purest and enforces divisions that are based on arbitrary cultural labels. Recently, Louisiana passed a law allowing public funds to be used on vouchers to send children to a school of the parent's choosing. But lawmakers didn't realize those funds could also be used for non-Christian
60   schools: "Republican state Rep. Kenneth Havard objected to the [Islamic School of Greater New Orleans'] request for 38 government-paid student vouchers, saying he opposed any bill that 'will fund Islamic teaching.'"

Inevitably, the rights of minorities are trampled by the majority, especially when beliefs in an exclusive deity are used to justify that power.

65   Fifty-two years after Kennedy's historic speech in Houston, separation of church and state brought "vomit" to the mouth of presidential candidate Rick Santorum: "I don't believe in an America where the separation of church and state is absolute. The idea that the church can have no influence or no involvement in the operation of the state is absolutely antithetical to the objectives and vision of our country."

70   Santorum couldn't be further from the truth. This is a country founded on freedom of religion, not domination by religion. We need equal rights for all, not just for the majority. We need a country free from the tribalism and petty divisions that politicized religion breeds.

If we are to ever separate ourselves from our country's economic, social and ideo-
75   logical woes, we need a country where separation of church and state is absolute.

Source: Freethought Today, *December 2012*
*https://ffrf.org/publications/freethought-today/item/16993-make-state-church-
separation-absolute*

▮ Thinking Rhetorically About Purpose: Expanded Outline

Now that you've gotten some practice with this kind of work, use the expanded outline below to conduct a more extensive rhetorical analysis of one of the informal selections above.

Step One: *Planning for Purpose: What is the Writer's Basic Goal?*

º Based on your reading of this text, what do you think the writer is trying to accomplish here? What larger goals does the author have in mind?

º What effect on the target audience does writer want to have?

Step Two: *Acting on Purpose: How Does This Goal Influence the Writer's Choices?*

º How does the writer's goal influence the way this text is organized?

º How does the writer's goal influence the specific elements this text includes?

Step Three: *Rethinking Purpose: How Do You Evaluate This Goal?*

º How valid do you think the writer's goal is?

º How effectively does the writer accomplish it?

Step Four: *Refining Purpose: What Aspects of This Writing Would You Change?*

º Do you agree or sympathize with the goal the writer is trying to achieve?

º If you were the writer, would you revise this goal in any way?

Step Five: *Putting It Into Writing*

º How do you summarize your findings and reaction in writing?

Formal Writing Selections

As writers, every choice we make stems from some objective we hope to accomplish. But this is also true in relation to countless other choices we make in our everyday lives. Whether in our role as student or worker, family member or friend, citizen or consumer, the day-to-day choices we make are shaped by some larger goal we believe is worth accomplishing. Understanding what these goals are and putting these goals into practice, however, are often easier said than done. How do we figure out which goals are truly worth pursuing? And how do we put together a plan for turning these goals into a reality?

Each of the following selections offers its own answer to these questions. Examining some of the most representative domains in contemporary life—from politics to the media to technology—they take a hard look at the factors and forces that shape the choices we are called upon to make in our daily lives. At the same time, these selections also provide another opportunity to analyze the question of purpose in rhetorical terms. Like the informal selections presented above, the readings gathered here are accompanied by questions designed to help you to identify the goals behind the choices each of these writers makes.

José Cruz, "College Affordability: Damned if You Go, Damned if You Don't?"

In the United States, we like to think of a college education as an opportunity equally available to everybody. For many, however, the enormous costs of such an education can conspire to keep this opportunity more of a dream than a reality. Indeed, with the spiraling cost of tuition, writes José Cruz, Vice President for Higher Education Policy and Practice at The Education Trust, many aspiring college students now find themselves confronting a paradox: While essential to their long-term professional and economic success, a college degree may nonetheless have become too expensive to afford.

"We can and must do a better job of translating our democratic ideals into policies and practices at all levels that sustain, rather than erode, opportunity."

I have traveled the tortuous road that separates the haves from the have-nots, so I'm intimately familiar with the structural barriers that stall upward mobility in America. It's not news to me that 20 percent of U.S. households earn half of all income, while the poorest 20 percent earn almost none. And though it pains me, I
5 can wrap my head around data that place inequality in the United States at higher levels than in other developed countries.

But I can't fully grasp how U.S. income inequality can be on par with that of Tunisia, Sri Lanka and Morocco, or how our intergenerational mobility roughly matches that of Nepal and Pakistan.
10 Higher education has long been heralded as an engine of opportunity in America. Now, more than ever, economic demands are making a post-secondary degree the surest way into the middle class. Indeed, we'll likely hear about it in Tuesday's State of the Union address, since the Obama administration has taken a number of steps to try to make college more affordable. But skyrocketing tui-
15 tion rates, plus policies that shift more and more financial aid away from those who need it most, are rendering the decision to go to college a damned if you go, damned if you don't proposition for too many hard-working students like Erica and Katrina.

Erica is a 19-year-old student at Fordham University, has a partial scholarship
20 and is paying the rest of her tuition through student loans. She estimates that she will owe $75,000 in student loans when she graduates.

And even at public institutions, students are encumbering similarly life-altering debt. Katrina attends the University of Illinois–Chicago, and will graduate this spring approximately $50,000 in the hole. Indeed, millions of students nation-
25 wide are in the same boat, staying awake at night, worrying about their financial futures.

The reality is that college is becoming increasingly unaffordable. Indeed, college tuition and fees are growing almost twice as fast as health care costs, and about four and a half times as fast as inflation. In addition, a soft inequality bias in federal, state and institutional policies is shaping the reality students face.   30

Over the past two decades, states have increased funding for grants unrelated to student financial need at almost five times the rate of need-based grants. In the 1990s, public four-year institutions invested twice as much grant aid on their low-income students as they did on more affluent ones. Today, spending on both groups is about equal. Private colleges, meanwhile, now spend nearly twice as   35
much on the wealthiest students as on the neediest.

But this isn't just an institutional problem. Just last year, more than $23 billion in federal financial aid dollars were diverted to education tax credits—some of which benefit families making more than $100,000 per year—leaving the Federal Pell Grant Program and the nearly 10 million low-income and working-class students   40
who rely on it vulnerable to cuts.

These policies spawn dreadful results. Today, low-income students must finance an amount equivalent to 72 percent of their family's annual income to attend a public university for one year, even after accounting for grant aid. So is it any surprise that by age 24, you're 10 times more likely to have a bachelor's degree if your   45
parents are wealthy than if they're poor? Or that for the first time in our nation's history, student loan debt tops credit card debt?

Colleges and universities need to control costs. But federal and state policymakers also should be targeting our scarce resources to make college more affordable for those students who have the least but can contribute the most to resurrecting   50
a strong middle class. Affordability, after all, depends not only on cost, but on students' ability to pay—without foreclosing on their future because of unfathomable student loan debt.

Policymakers can do much to reverse America's rising tide of inequality while managing their budgets. Here are three steps to get them started: 55

First, instead of fighting over how to reduce Pell Grant spending, federal policymakers should look elsewhere for cost savings. They could, for example, eliminate tax benefits for building private nonprofit educational facilities and lower the income caps for higher education tax credits and deductions.

Second, state policymakers should reverse the dangerous shift toward burden-   60
ing low-income students with the lion's share of college costs. Take California, which slashed $650 million from the California State University's budget this year, spiking tuition by nearly 23 percent. Combined with Governor Jerry Brown's recent proposal to slash the state Cal Grant program, this will be devastating to the state's economic recovery, amounting to a one-two punch against hard-working,   65
low- and middle-income students trying to afford college.

Third, institutional policymakers must end the financial aid arms race and commit to meeting the financial needs of low-income students—before offering scholarships and grants aimed at attracting elite students.

We can and must do a better job of translating our democratic ideals into poli-   70
cies and practices at all levels that sustain, rather than erode, opportunity. We can

make it not only possible, but probable that the growing numbers of low-income students can rise to the middle class, paving the way for less inequality and more social mobility in America.

Source: The Huffington Post, *January 20, 2012*
http://www.huffingtonpost.com/jose-cruz/affording-college-tuition_b_1216111.html

Discussion/Writing Prompts

1. For Cruz, higher education is a world in which our freedom of choice is becoming more and more constrained. Why do you think he paints such a negative portrait? What larger goal do you think he is trying to achieve by doing so? [Rhetorical Analysis of Purpose]

2. How would you characterize your own experiences negotiating the costs of a college education? Based on these experiences, would you say that Cruz's assessment is accurate? Can you think of an example in which you found your own opportunities or choices limited by financial factors? [Personal Reflection]

3. Cruz sees the current state of higher education as example of "the structural barriers that stall upward mobility in America." What does he mean by this? How, in your view, is the cost of a college education related to "upward mobility"? [Close Reading]

4. Much of Cruz's critique rests upon the statistics he cites about "tuition and fees," average "family income," and the availability of government financial aid. How are these data used to posit a cause-and-effect relationship between higher education costs and higher education opportunity? Do you think the use of this rhetorical mode is effective? Why, or why not? [Analyzing Rhetorical Modes]

5. According to Cruz, the best way to combat the rising cost of higher education is to champion policies that dramatically shift the burden of college costs away from "low-income students." Do you agree? Is this kind of solution fair? Is it feasible? [Argument]

6. Like Cruz, Sherry Turkle ("The Flight From Conversation") is interested in exploring the forces and factors that create divisions in modern society. How do you think Turkle would respond to Cruz's critique? Given her own argument in favor of greater community and connection in our day-to-day communications, how do you think she would evaluate Cruz's call for greater fairness and opportunity in higher education? [Compare and Contrast]

7. Cruz's dire assessment is far from the only view of college life. In the eyes of other observers, there is ample reason to feel optimistic about the future of higher education. Find a text (e.g., newspaper editorial, political speech, or college website) that presents just such a view, and examine the particular claims it makes. According to this author, what are the specific benefits or opportunities our current education scene offers? How do these claims compare to the claims Cruz makes? Which viewpoint do you find more convincing? Why? [Research]

Sherry Turkle, "The Flight From Conversation"

Few would disagree that the rise of the Internet has made life a good deal more convenient. Information once virtually inaccessible to us is now, quite literally, available at our fingertips. But this newfound convenience may come at a price, warns Sherry Turkle, a psychologist and professor at MIT and, most recently, the author of Alone Together: Why We Expect More From Technology and Less From Each Other. *Even as we enjoy enormous gains in communication, information, and the like, Turkle argues, it is possible that we are also suffering certain kinds of loss: in our ability to focus and think deeply, and in our willingness to maintain long-lasting connections.*

"Human relationships are rich; they're messy and demanding. We have learned the habit of cleaning them up with technology."

We live in a technological universe in which we are always communicating. And yet we have sacrificed conversation for mere connection.

At home, families sit together, texting and reading e-mail. At work executives text during board meetings. We text (and shop and go on Facebook) during classes and when we're on dates. My students tell me about an important new skill: 5 it involves maintaining eye contact with someone while you text someone else; it's hard, but it can be done.

Over the past 15 years, I've studied technologies of mobile connection and talked to hundreds of people of all ages and circumstances about their plugged-in lives. I've learned that the little devices most of us carry around are so powerful 10 that they change not only what we do, but also who we are.

We've become accustomed to a new way of being "alone together." Technology-enabled, we are able to be with one another, and also elsewhere, connected to wherever we want to be. We want to customize our lives. We want to move in and out of where we are because the thing we value most is control over where we 15 focus our attention. We have gotten used to the idea of being in a tribe of one, loyal to our own party.

Our colleagues want to go to that board meeting but pay attention only to what interests them. To some this seems like a good idea, but we can end up hiding from one another, even as we are constantly connected to one another. 20

A businessman laments that he no longer has colleagues at work. He doesn't stop by to talk; he doesn't call. He says that he doesn't want to interrupt them. He says they're "too busy on their e-mail." But then he pauses and corrects himself. "I'm not telling the truth. I'm the one who doesn't want to be interrupted. I think I should. But I'd rather just do things on my BlackBerry." 25

A 16-year-old boy who relies on texting for almost everything says almost wistfully, "Someday, someday, but certainly not now, I'd like to learn how to have a conversation."

In today's workplace, young people who have grown up fearing conversation show up on the job wearing earphones. Walking through a college library or the campus of a high-tech start-up, one sees the same thing: we are together, but each of us is in our own bubble, furiously connected to keyboards and tiny touch screens. A senior partner at a Boston law firm describes a scene in his office. Young associates lay out their suite of technologies: laptops, iPods and multiple phones. And then they put their earphones on. "Big ones. Like pilots. They turn their desks into cockpits." With the young lawyers in their cockpits, the office is quiet, a quiet that does not ask to be broken.

In the silence of connection, people are comforted by being in touch with a lot of people—carefully kept at bay. We can't get enough of one another if we can use technology to keep one another at distances we can control: not too close, not too far, just right. I think of it as a Goldilocks effect.

Texting and e-mail and posting let us present the self we want to be. This means we can edit. And if we wish to, we can delete. Or retouch: the voice, the flesh, the face, the body. Not too much, not too little—just right.

Human relationships are rich; they're messy and demanding. We have learned the habit of cleaning them up with technology. And the move from conversation to connection is part of this. But it's a process in which we shortchange ourselves. Worse, it seems that over time we stop caring, we forget that there is a difference.

We are tempted to think that our little "sips" of online connection add up to a big gulp of real conversation. But they don't. E-mail, Twitter, Facebook, all of these have their places—in politics, commerce, romance and friendship. But no matter how valuable, they do not substitute for conversation.

Connecting in sips may work for gathering discrete bits of information or for saying, "I am thinking about you." Or even for saying, "I love you." But connecting in sips doesn't work as well when it comes to understanding and knowing one another. In conversation we tend to one another. (The word itself is kinetic; it's derived from words that mean to move, together.) We can attend to tone and nuance. In conversation, we are called upon to see things from another's point of view.

Face-to-face conversation unfolds slowly. It teaches patience. When we communicate on our digital devices, we learn different habits. As we ramp up the volume and velocity of online connections, we start to expect faster answers. To get these, we ask one another simpler questions; we dumb down our communications, even on the most important matters. It is as though we have all put ourselves on cable news. Shakespeare might have said, "We are consum'd with that which we were nourish'd by."

And we use conversation with others to learn to converse with ourselves. So our flight from conversation can mean diminished chances to learn skills of self-reflection. These days, social media continually asks us what's "on our mind," but we have little motivation to say something truly self-reflective. Self-reflection in conversation requires trust. It's hard to do anything with 3,000 Facebook friends except connect.

As we get used to being shortchanged on conversation and to getting by with less, we seem almost willing to dispense with people altogether. Serious people muse about the future of computer programs as psychiatrists. A high school sophomore confides to me that he wishes he could talk to an artificial intelligence program instead of his dad about dating; he says the A.I. would have so much more in its database. Indeed, many people tell me they hope that as Siri, the digital assistant on Apple's iPhone, becomes more advanced, "she" will be more and more like a best friend—one who will listen when others won't.

During the years I have spent researching people and their relationships with technology, I have often heard the sentiment "No one is listening to me." I believe this feeling helps explain why it is so appealing to have a Facebook page or a Twitter feed—each provides so many automatic listeners. And it helps explain why— against all reason—so many of us are willing to talk to machines that seem to care about us. Researchers around the world are busy inventing sociable robots, designed to be companions to the elderly, to children, to all of us.

One of the most haunting experiences during my research came when I brought one of these robots, designed in the shape of a baby seal, to an elder-care facility, and an older woman began to talk to it about the loss of her child. The robot seemed to be looking into her eyes. It seemed to be following the conversation. The woman was comforted.

And so many people found this amazing. Like the sophomore who wants advice about dating from artificial intelligence and those who look forward to computer psychiatry, this enthusiasm speaks to how much we have confused conversation with connection and collectively seem to have embraced a new kind of delusion that accepts the simulation of compassion as sufficient unto the day. And why would we want to talk about love and loss with a machine that has no experience of the arc of human life? Have we so lost confidence that we will be there for one another?

We expect more from technology and less from one another and seem increasingly drawn to technologies that provide the illusion of companionship without the demands of relationship. Always-on/always-on-you devices provide three powerful fantasies: that we will always be heard; that we can put our attention wherever we want it to be; and that we never have to be alone. Indeed our new devices have turned being alone into a problem that can be solved.

When people are alone, even for a few moments, they fidget and reach for a device. Here connection works like a symptom, not a cure, and our constant, reflexive impulse to connect shapes a new way of being.

Think of it as "I share, therefore I am." We use technology to define ourselves by sharing our thoughts and feelings as we're having them. We used to think, "I have a feeling; I want to make a call." Now our impulse is, "I want to have a feeling; I need to send a text."

So, in order to feel more, and to feel more like ourselves, we connect. But in our rush to connect, we flee from solitude, our ability to be separate and gather

115   ourselves. Lacking the capacity for solitude, we turn to other people but don't
        experience them as they are. It is as though we use them, need them as spare parts
        to support our increasingly fragile selves.

        We think constant connection will make us feel less lonely. The opposite is true.
        If we are unable to be alone, we are far more likely to be lonely. If we don't teach
120   our children to be alone, they will know only how to be lonely.

        I am a partisan for conversation. To make room for it, I see some first, deliberate
        steps. At home, we can create sacred spaces: the kitchen, the dining room. We can
        make our cars "device-free zones." We can demonstrate the value of conversation
        to our children. And we can do the same thing at work. There we are so busy com-
125   municating that we often don't have time to talk to one another about what really
        matters. Employees asked for casual Fridays; perhaps managers should introduce
        conversational Thursdays. Most of all, we need to remember—in between texts
        and e-mails and Facebook posts—to listen to one another, even to the boring bits,
        because it is often in unedited moments, moments in which we hesitate and stut-
130   ter and go silent, that we reveal ourselves to one another.

        I spend the summers at a cottage on Cape Cod, and for decades I walked the
        same dunes that Thoreau once walked. Not too long ago, people walked with their
        heads up, looking at the water, the sky, the sand and at one another, talking. Now
        they often walk with their heads down, typing. Even when they are with friends,
135   partners, children, everyone is on their own devices.

        So I say, look up, look at one another, and let's start the conversation.

        Source: The New York Times, *April 21, 2012, © 2012 The New York Times.*
        http://www.nytimes.com/2012/04/22/opinion/sunday/the-flight-from-
        conversation.html?pagewanted=all&_r=0

▊ Discussion/Writing Prompts

1. One of Turkle's central goals is to warn readers about the dangers of Web-based
   communication. How effectively do you think her essay accomplishes this purpose?
   What aspects of this piece (e.g., tone, word-choice, or organization) are most
   effective? What aspects are least effective? [Rhetorical Analysis of Purpose]

2. What do you make of Turkle's central claim? Do your own experiences online
   confirm her suspicion that Web-based technologies are eroding our willingness and
   ability to connect? Can you think of an experience that either supports or refutes this
   proposition? [Personal Reflection]

3. Take a closer look at the title of this essay. Why do you think Turkle characterizes
   the challenges of online communication as a "flight" from conversation? What
   images or associations does this term conjure in your mind? And in your view, does
   this title effectively capture the larger argument she is making? [Close Reading]

4. Turkle organizes much of her essay around a series of anecdotes and/or examples about
   communicating online. Explore in greater detail the ways she uses this rhetorical

mode. What larger point is she using these examples to make? How effectively do these examples help her accomplish this goal? [Analyzing Rhetorical Modes]

5. As much as a critique of the Internet, Turkle's essay is also a call for change. In a two- or three-page essay, propose a set of changes to the Web that, in your view, would help to remedy the problems Turkle outlines here. What would these changes look like? What specific solution would they help bring about? [Argument]

6. Douglas Rushkoff ("Why I'm Quitting Facebook") shares with Turkle a deep skepticism about the supposed benefits of our new digital culture. How do their viewpoints compare? What are the key similarities and differences? And which critique do you find more effective? [Compare and Contrast]

7. Turkle's essay is part of a much larger body of work dedicated to studying the effects the Web is having on the ways we interact and communicate. Conduct some research of your own into this question. Choose an example of this research (e.g., journal article, book, or published study), and describe the particular ways it examines and discusses this issue. How do these findings compare to the conclusions Turkle draws? [Research]

Douglas Rushkoff, "Why I'm Quitting Facebook"

It is an article of faith among boosters of digital culture that the rise of social media represents a revolutionary leap forward in individual freedom. But when we venture online, are we fully in control of our choices? Or do the digital tools we use sometimes do the choosing for us? This is the provocative question noted media theorist Douglas Rushkoff ponders, a question that leads him to make a revolutionary decision of his own—to quit Facebook.

> *"Facebook does not exist to help us make friends, but to turn our network of connections, brand preferences and activities over time—our 'social graphs'—into money for others."*

I used to be able to justify using Facebook as a cost of doing business. As a writer and sometime activist who needs to promote my books and articles and occasionally rally people to one cause or another, I found Facebook fast and convenient. Though I never really used it to socialize, I figured it was OK to let other people do that, and I benefited from their behavior. 5

I can no longer justify this arrangement.

Today, I am surrendering my Facebook account, because my participation on the site is simply too inconsistent with the values I espouse in my work. In my up- coming book *Present Shock*, I chronicle some of what happens when we can no longer manage our many online presences. I have always argued for engaging with 10 technology as conscious human beings and dispensing with technologies that take that agency away.

Facebook is just such a technology. It does things on our behalf when we're not even there. It actively misrepresents us to our friends, and worse misrepresents those who have befriended us to still others. To enable this dysfunctional situation—I call it "digiphrenia"—would be at the very least hypocritical. But to participate on Facebook as an author, in a way specifically intended to draw out the "likes" and resulting vulnerability of others, is untenable.

Facebook has never been merely a social platform. Rather, it exploits our social interactions the way a Tupperware party does.

Facebook does not exist to help us make friends, but to turn our network of connections, brand preferences and activities over time—our "social graphs"—into money for others.

We Facebook users have been building a treasure lode of big data that government and corporate researchers have been mining to predict and influence what we buy and for whom we vote. We have been handing over to them vast quantities of information about ourselves and our friends, loved ones and acquaintances. With this information, Facebook and the "big data" research firms purchasing their data predict still more things about us—from our future product purchases or sexual orientation to our likelihood for civil disobedience or even terrorism.

The true end users of Facebook are the marketers who want to reach and influence us. They are Facebook's paying customers; we are the product. And we are its workers. The countless hours that we—and the young, particularly—spend on our profiles are the unpaid labor on which Facebook justifies its stock valuation.

The efforts of a few thousand employees at Facebook's Menlo Park campus pale in comparison to those of the hundreds of millions of users meticulously tweaking their pages. Corporations used to have to do research to assemble our consumer profiles; now we do it for them.

The information collected about you by Facebook through my Facebook page isn't even shared with me. Thanks to my page, Facebook knows the demographics of my readership, their e-mails, what else they like, who else they know and, perhaps most significant, who they trust. And Facebook is taking pains not to share any of this, going so far as to limit the ability of third-party applications to utilize any of this data.

Given that this was the foundation for Facebook's business plan from the start, perhaps more recent developments in the company's ever-evolving user agreement shouldn't have been so disheartening.

Still, we bridle at the notion that any of our updates might be converted into "sponsored stories" by whatever business or brand we may have mentioned. That innocent mention of a cup of coffee at Starbucks, in the Facebook universe, quickly becomes an attributed endorsement of their brand. Remember, the only way to connect with something or someone is to "like" them. This means if you want to find out what a politician or company you don't like is up to, you still have to endorse them publicly.

More recently, users—particularly those with larger sets of friends, followers and likes—learned that their updates were no longer reaching all of the people who had signed up to get them. Now, we are supposed to pay to "promote" our posts to our friends and, if we pay even more, to their friends.

Yes, Facebook is entitled to be paid for promoting us and our interests—but this wasn't the deal going in, particularly not for companies who paid Facebook for extra followers in the first place. Neither should users who "friend" my page automatically become the passive conduits for any of my messages to all their friends just because I paid for it. 60

That brings me to Facebook's most recent shift, and the one that pushed me over the edge. 65

Through a new variation of the Sponsored Stories feature called Related Posts, users who "like" something can be unwittingly associated with pretty much anything an advertiser pays for. Like e-mail spam with a spoofed identity, the Related Post shows up in a newsfeed right under the user's name and picture. If you like me, you can be shown implicitly recommending me or something I like—something you've never heard of—to others without your consent. 70

For now, as long as I don't like anything myself, I have some measure of control over what those who follow me receive in my name or, worse, are made to appear to be endorsing, themselves. But I feel that control slipping away, and cannot remain part of a system where liking me or my work can be used against you. 75

The promotional leverage that Facebook affords me is not worth the price. Besides, how can I ask you to like me, when I myself must refuse to like you or anything else?

I have always appreciated that agreeing to become publicly linked to me and my work online involves trust. It is a trust I value, but—as it is dependent on the good graces of Facebook—it is a trust I can live up to only by unfriending this particularly anti-social social network. 80

Maybe in doing so I'll help people remember that Facebook is not the Internet. It's just one website, and it comes with a price.

Source: CNN.com, February 25, 2013. © 2013 Cable News Network, Inc.
http://www.cnn.com/2013/02/25/opinion/rushkoff-why-im-quitting-facebook/

Discussion/Writing Prompts

1. In Rushkoff's view, sites like Facebook are dangerous because they redirect our personal choices to suit their own purposes. How much, if at all, would you say this same idea captures the goal Rushkoff himself has for his audience? To what extent does Rushkoff want to shape or direct the particular conclusions his readers choose? [Rhetorical Analysis of Purpose]

2. How accurate a portrait of Facebook does Rushkoff draw? How much of yourself do you see in his descriptions of the typical Facebook user? Can you think of an example from your own experience that either supports or challenges this portrait? [Personal Reflection]

3. "The true end users of Facebook," writes Rushkoff, "are the marketers who want to reach and influence us. They are Facebook's paying customers; we are the product. And we are its workers." What do you make of this claim? Is it fair to speak of individual Facebook users as "workers," laboring on behalf of advertisers? [Close Reading]

4. Rushkoff uses his own personal experiences online as a framework for the critique of Facebook he presents. In your view, is employing this rhetorical mode an effective strategy? What aspects of Rushkoff's critique are strengthened by the fact he presents them in narrative form? What aspects are weakened? [Analysis of Rhetorical Modes]

5. Rushkoff makes the decision to renounce Facebook because, in his view, this social media site treats the connections and friendships its users forge as mere commercial opportunities: "Facebook does not exist to help us make friends, but to turn our network of connections, brand preferences and activities over time—our 'social graphs'—into money for others." Write a two- or three-page essay in which you evaluate this particular claim. Do you agree with this assertion? Is the ultimate aim of Facebook to convert our social connections into money? If so, what do you think Facebook users themselves should do about this? [Argument]

6. Like Rushkoff, Sherry Turkle ("The Flight From Conversation") is interested in exploring the kinds of connections made possible by the rise of social media. How do these two writers' discussion of this issue compare? Do you see any similarities between Rushkoff's critique of Facebook and Turkle's examination of social disconnection? If so, what? [Compare and Contrast]

7. In many ways, Rushkoff's essay can be read as a response to the work of marketers and advertisers in general, whose job is to manipulate consumer desire for different products. Conduct some first-hand research into the ways advertising or marketing professionals describe their own work. How does this discussion compare to the critique Rushkoff offers? [Research]

Shankar Vedantam, "Partisanship Is the New Racism"

The emergence of our 24/7 media environment has brought with it both opportunities and perils. On the one hand, the explosion of media outlets has dramatically increased our ability to discuss and debate urgent social and political issues. On the other hand, these same outlets have also given rise to a potent and problematic new partisanship, in which political adversaries now attack, misrepresent, and malign each other with growing impunity. Shankar Vedantam, a science correspondent for National Public Radio and the author of The Hidden Brain: How Our Unconscious Minds Elect Presidents, Control Markets, Wage Wars, and Save Our Lives, *casts a sobering glance over this new environment and offers some thoughts about the place of—and causes behind—"partisanship" in modern American life.*

"Partisanship is the new racism. We love to criticize it, and we love to claim we've transcended it. We recognize it in our enemies but not in ourselves."

Republicans and Democrats in Congress are going to sit together—all chummy and united—during President Obama's State of the Union speech on Tuesday. I'm betting that this new post-partisan era will be a lot like the post-racial America that Obama supposedly ushered in.

Partisanship is the new racism. We love to criticize it, and we love to claim we've 5 transcended it. We recognize it in our enemies but not in ourselves. We use it to discriminate against others. And increasingly, we find sophisticated ways to mask it in a veneer of open-mindedness.

New psychological research and insights from political science suggest parallels between partisanship and racism. Both seem to arise from aspects of social iden- 10 tity that are immutable or slow to change. Both are publicly decried and privately practiced. Both are increasingly employed in ways that allow practitioners to deny that they are doing what they are doing.

Let's take these assertions one by one. Most of us don't think of partisanship as a matter of social identity. We think that party loyalties stem from our views about 15 government, abortion, guns, and foreign policy. But if you look at those issues, there is no logical reason why people who are against abortion rights should also support gun rights, as many conservatives do. There is no logical reason why those who support unions shouldn't also support a militaristic foreign policy—yet liberals tend to do one but not the other. The issues that bind liberals together and the ones that tie 20 conservatives together are all over the place. Most people see the incoherence in their opponents' views: Liberals, for example, mock conservatives for opposing abortion on the grounds that it takes human life while simultaneously supporting the death penalty. Conservatives shake their heads at liberals who pour onto the streets for antiwar protests, but only when the commander in chief is a Republican. 25

In recent years, a number of political scientists have argued that our party loyalties drive our views about issues, not the other way around. But if our views don't make us Democrats or Republicans, what does? Consider this thought experiment: I have two neighbors, Jack and Jill. Jill is an African-American woman and a yoga instructor. Jack is a white man and an evangelical Christian. I've told you nothing 30 about Jack and Jill's views about abortion, government, guns, taxes, or foreign policy. Yet most of us would have no trouble guessing that Jill is a Democrat and Jack is a Republican. How do we know this? Because social identity—race, gender, religious affiliation, geographical location—play an outsize (and largely hidden) role in determining our partisan affiliations. 35

When partisanship is seen as a form of social identity—I'm a Democrat because people like me are Democrats, or I'm a Republican because people like me are

Republicans—we can understand why so many blue-collar Kansans are Republicans and why so many Silicon Valley billionaires are Democrats, even though each group's rational interests might be better served by the other party. Partisanship as social identity helps explain why, if you're a black man in America, it's really, really difficult to be a Republican. Same goes if you are a white, male, evangelical Christian in rural Texas who supports Barack Obama. Social identities are not deterministic—there will always be some black Republicans and some born-again Christians who are liberals—but most of us stick with our social tribes. Any liberal who supported George W. Bush's adventure in Iraq would have been ostracized by his friends. A conservative who feels Barack Obama is a cool president will be made to feel like a traitor at church.

Here's the second way in which partisanship has become the new racism: We use it to discriminate against those who do not belong to our group.

In a recent experiment, researchers assigned Democrats and Republicans to play the role of a college admissions director and asked them to evaluate the applications of two students based on their SAT scores, GPA scores, and recommendation letters. Some applicants were described as enthusiastic members of the Young Democrats or Young Republicans and were said to have been campaign volunteers for Democratic or Republican presidential candidates.

When evaluators were not told about the applicants' partisan affiliations, 79 percent selected the candidate with the strongest scores. When the evaluators were told about the applicants' partisan affiliations—and the partisan affiliation of the candidate with the strongest score conflicted with the partisan loyalty of the evaluator—only 44 percent of evaluators chose the candidate with the strongest score.

The bias was evident among both Democratic and Republican evaluators. The study was published in the *Journal of Applied Social Psychology* and authored by Geoffrey D. Munro, Terell P. Lasane, and Scott P. Leary. Partisanship is also like racism in a third way: Studies have shown that racism is so socially proscribed that people exhibit it nowadays only when they can plausibly deny—to themselves and to others—that they are biased. One meta-analysis of studies, for example, found that "discrimination against blacks was more likely to occur when potential helpers had more opportunities to rationalize decisions not to help" by invoking "justifiable explanations having nothing to do with race."

Munro, Lasane, and Leary found the same pattern of behavior in partisanship. The partisan college evaluators were willing to acknowledge that applicants they chose who shared their political loyalties had lower test scores—an objective fact—but they selected the candidates anyway by inflating the importance of the recommendation letters that came with applications. Accepting candidates merely on the basis of low test scores would have shown the evaluators were biased. Accepting candidates on the basis of recommendation letters—and arguing the letters were more important than scores—allowed the evaluators to plausibly deny that they were biased.

If partisanship and racism are both tied to social identity, then a post-partisan   80
America is about as likely as a post-racial America. Our views on issues may change,
but our identities remain stable over decades. Democrats and Republicans sitting
together in Congress will no sooner put an end to partisanship than gay men, black
women, and Alabama hunters will give up their tribes.

Source: Slate, January 24, 2011. © 2011 The Slate Group.
http://www.slate.com/articles/health_and_science/the_hidden_brain/2011/01/
partisanship_is_the_new_racism.html

▉ Discussion/Writing Prompts

1. In making his argument, Vedantam connects "partisanship" to what is perhaps the
   most controversial issue in modern American life: "racism." Why do you make of
   this decision? What larger goal do you think Vedantam is trying to accomplish by
   making this comparison? [Rhetorical Analysis of Purpose]

2. In Vedantam's view, partisanship is so entrenched because it is so deeply tied to our
   "social identity." Do you agree? Do you have certain political convictions so deep
   that they define your very identity? Is there an example of one that confirms
   Vedantam's theory? If so, how? [Personal Reflection]

3. "If partisanship and racism are both tied to social identity," writes Vedantam, "then
   a post-partisan America is about as likely as a post-racial America." How would you
   define the terms "post-partisan" and "post-racial"? Do you agree with Vedantam that
   they share a certain meaning in common? [Close Reading]

4. In many ways, Vedantam's argument rests on his attempt to redefine what the term
   "partisanship" conventionally means. Where in the essay do you see evidence of
   Vedantam employing this rhetorical mode? And how effective do you find it to be?
   [Analysis of Rhetorical Modes]

5. According to Vedantam, part of what makes combatting partisan bias so difficult is
   that most people deny having any such bias themselves. Write an essay in which you
   propose and argue for a solution to this problem. What approach to political debate
   and conflict do you think would help people better acknowledge and counter their
   own biases? [Argument]

6. Like partisanship, envy is a concept that comes under a great deal of criticism.
   How does Vedantam's discussion of partisanship compare to F. Diane Barth's
   examination of envy ("Why Women Fear Envy")? To what extent do both writers
   attempt to challenge the ways these terms are typically understood? And how
   effective do you find each effort to be? [Compare and Contrast]

7. To test the validity of Vedantam's argument, research a current political issue
   and how it is debated. In what ways does this debate lend itself to "partisan"
   disagreement? And what biases do you detect? [Research]

Visual Rhetoric: Stuart Isett, "Occupy Seattle Protesters Join Police Brutality March"

What vision of public protest does this image present? Does it remind you in any way of Vedantam's discussion of partisanship?

FIGURE 5.12

Source: Mario Tama/Getty Images News/Getty Images

F. Diane Barth, "Why Women Fear Envy and Why We Don't Need To"

Over the centuries, to put it mildly, envy has gotten a lot of bad press. Derided as a vice, stigmatized as a sin, envy has come to be regarded as a quintessential sign of moral failure. But is there, asks F. Diane Barth, a psychotherapist and author who lives in New York City, another side to this question? Are there circumstances under which envy, especially for women, can be viewed as an empowering, even positive form of motivation?

"[W]e feel badly about the envy itself. Feeling these feelings makes us feel like we're bad."

One day many years ago a client who I will call Virginia* accused me of hurting her feelings by calling her competitive. This was ironic, since Virginia had spent long hours in therapy discussing her competitive feelings about her siblings, her co-workers, her friends, and even her boyfriend. But I understood what she meant. First, as psychoanalyst and author Adrienne Harris notes, despite years of social change women tend to feel our own envious and aggressive competitiveness "as a damning character flaw." And second, competitiveness breeds envy; and most women are terrified

5

*Names and identifying information changed to protect privacy.

of that feeling, whether it's our own directed at someone else, or someone else's directed at us.

Why is this? And what, if anything, can we do about it?

First of all, let's talk about what envy is. Lots of people interchange the words "envy" and "jealousy," so when I define how I'm using the word, you may decide that what I really mean is "jealousy." Although I put a lot of stock in choosing words carefully, in this case I actually don't think it matters which word we use—most of us dread the feelings I'm talking about, whatever we want to call them.

Dictionary.com defines envy as a feeling of discontent or covetousness with regard to another's advantages, success, possessions, etc. So when we envy someone for something they have, we want it for ourselves, and we feel angry or unhappy that we don't have it. That's easy enough, right? The problem is that these feelings do a double whammy to our self-esteem. In the first place, we feel like we are somehow inferior to the holder of whatever it is we covet—long legs, thick wavy hair, a great job, a terrific partner/spouse, a beautiful home, brilliant children, success, happiness, etc. In the second place, we feel badly about the envy itself. Feeling these feelings makes us feel like we're bad.

The British psychoanalyst Melanie Klein says that part of the reason we feel badly about feeling envious is that along with the desire to have what someone else has, we also feel like destroying them, or at least we want to damage both their good feelings and whatever it is that they possess that we believe is making them feel good. This is usually, although not always, not a conscious desire; but it is a powerful unconscious emotion that does nothing to help us feel better about ourselves.

For women, as Harris points out, there is the added feeling that we are being unfeminine, unlovable and *unattractive* (funny how often those ideas go together) by having these angry, antagonistic and potentially hurtful feelings towards someone else. Another psychoanalytic writer, Ruth Moulton, writes that we feel that we will lose the approval of others if we are too obvious about our desire to win, and, even today in our "lean in" times, it seems that envy is often viewed as a signal of "over the top" competitiveness. In order not to feel it we put ourselves down; or we hide our accomplishments; or we actually set ourselves up to lose. But of course these ploys don't work. They just make us feel worse about ourselves.

So where does this leave us?

It seems to me that, to paraphrase the old idea about imitation and flattery, envy is actually the highest form of flattery. Who has ever envied anything that she didn't admire? We want what someone else has because we think it makes them special in some way, and we think that if we had it, we would feel special too.

I think one problem with envy is that we keep it buried, away from the light of day, because we think it's so bad; but burying it is actually what makes it fester. When we can talk about it, it often opens up into a much milder feeling.

This happens in part because it often turns out that the same person we envy also envies us—sometimes for the very same thing we admire in them. When we express our envy in terms of admiration, we often get admiration in response. And when we don't, we often get genuine surprise and pleasure from the other person, which is sometimes just as good!

That's what happened with Virginia and me. One day after we had started talking about her envious feelings, I said, "Does it ever occur to you that I might envy something you have?" She was horrified at first, but after we talked some more, she was curious. "What could I possibly have that you would envy?" she demanded.

I told her that there were several things that I admired and envied in her, but one important one was the way she went after her goals. "You are so single-minded about them," I said. "You don't let yourself get distracted. You work hard, long into the night sometimes, until you accomplish what you set out to do. I envy that ability. I seem to have an automatic internal time limit, after which I have to stop."

She looked at me in stunned silence. "You envy that? And you don't hate me for it?"

I laughed. "Sure," I said, "Sometimes I hate you a little. But it's only because I wish I had that ability myself."

We spoke for many sessions about the idea that envy is always destructive. I had to agree with Virginia when she said, "I guess it's destructive when it can't be talked about. Once it's out in the open, we get a chance to share our envy—and our admiration of each other. Your envying me makes it much easier for me to let go of my wish to destroy you. Because now I know that I've got something too."

Envy, kept deep inside, feeds on itself because it doesn't make room for mutual admiration. Spoken about, it opens up room for acknowledgement of the fact that when we envy someone, it's often mutual. Far more often than anyone realizes, both people have something the other wants; and that idea goes a long way towards easing the pain of any envious feelings about what we don't have.

Source: Psychology Today, July 17, 2013. © 2013 Sussex Publishers, LLC.
http://www.psychologytoday.com/blog/the-couch/201307/why-women-fear-envy-and-why-we-dont-need

▉ Discussion/Writing Prompts

1. Barth makes the provocative argument here that "envy" may actually be beneficial to both our social relationships and our self-esteem. What would you say motivates Barth to make such an argument? What larger goal does she have in mind? [Rhetorical Analysis of Purpose]

2. Can you think of a moment when you were envious of somebody else? If so, who was it, and what aspect of this person's life did you envy? Looking back on it today, does this experience confirm Barth's thesis that envy can serve as a positive form of motivation? How or how not? [Personal Reflection]

3. In making her argument, Barth draws a distinction between constructive and destructive envy. How does Barth define these categories differently? How do her definitions compare with your own? Do you share her view that certain types of envy can be viewed as constructive? Why, or why not? [Close Reading]

4. "I think," writes Barth, "one problem with envy is that we keep it buried, away from the light of day, because we think it's so bad; but burying it is actually what makes it fester. When we can talk about it, it often opens up into a much milder feeling." In a short essay, evaluate the cause-and-effect mode she employs here. Is Barth correct? Does "burying" envy actually reinforce or exacerbate it? How?, [Analysis of Rhetorical Modes]

5. "Envy, kept deep inside," writes Barth, "feeds on itself because it doesn't make room for mutual admiration. Spoken about, it opens up room for acknowledgement of the fact that when we envy someone, it's often mutual. Far more often than anyone realizes, both people have something the other wants; and that idea goes a long way towards easing the pain of any envious feelings about what we don't have." In a three- to five-page essay, respond to Barth's argument here. Do you accept the claim that envy undermines our capacity for "mutual admiration"? Do you share her conviction that "acknowledging" envy holds the key to resolving this problem? Why, or why not? [Argument]

6. How do you think Sherry Turkle ("The Flight From Conversation") would respond to this essay? Does her argument about digital culture and disconnection seem in any way related to Barth's discussion of envy? In your view, are disconnection and envy related concepts? If so, how? [Compare and Contrast]

7. In support of her argument here, Barth makes reference to the work of other noted psychotherapists. Conduct some research of your own along these same lines. What does current psychoanalytic research suggest about the most effective ways to treat envy? Does this research support or challenge the argument Barth makes here? [Research]

Academic Writing Selections

The rhetorical analysis above doesn't only apply to writing found in the real world. It also offers a useful framework for examining the kinds of writing that are taught within the college classroom. While such academic work has traditionally been treated as both different and distant from the realm of popular writing, it can be analyzed just as effectively in rhetorical terms. Like their real world counterparts, the authors of these academic selections base their choices about how and what to write on considerations of purpose, audience, argument, voice, and credibility.

The two selections below illustrate this point vividly, demonstrating the extent to which academic writing is also shaped by rhetorical concepts. More specifically, these examples highlight the role that considerations of purpose play in shaping a writer's choices. Read each selection carefully. Then, answer the questions that follow.

Tillie Olsen, "I Stand Here Ironing"

What stories do we choose to tell about ourselves? And what do these stories say about how we view ourselves and the world around us? This short story by

Tillie Olsen, who is best known for her collection **Tell Me A Riddle,** *presents readers with a portrait of memory and family that addresses these questions.*

I stand here ironing, and what you asked me moves tormented back and forth with the iron.

"I wish you would manage the time to come in and talk with me about your daughter. I'm sure you can help me understand her. She's a youngster who needs help and whom I'm
5   deeply interested in helping."

"Who needs help." . . . Even if I came, what good would it do? You think because I am her mother I have a key, or that in some way you could use me as a key? She has lived for nineteen years. There is all that life that has happened outside of me, beyond me.

And when is there time to remember, to sift, to weigh, to estimate, to total? I will start
10   and there will be an interruption and I will have to gather it all together again. Or I will become engulfed with all I did or did not do, with what should have been and what cannot be helped.

She was a beautiful baby. The first and only one of our five that was beautiful at birth. You do not guess how new and uneasy her tenancy in her now-loveliness. You did not know her
15   all those years she was thought homely, or see her poring over her baby pictures, making me tell her over and over how beautiful she had been—and would be, I would tell her—and was now, to the seeing eye. But the seeing eyes were few or nonexistent. Including mine.

I nursed her. They feel that's important nowadays. I nursed all the children, but with her, with all the fierce rigidity of first motherhood, I did like the books then said. Though
20   her cries battered me to trembling and my breasts ached with swollenness, I waited till the clock decreed.

Why do I put that first? I do not even know if it matters, or if it explains anything.

She was a beautiful baby. She blew shining bubbles of sound. She loved motion, loved light, loved color and music and textures. She would lie on the floor in her blue overalls
25   patting the surface so hard in ecstasy her hands and feet would blur. She was a miracle to me, but when she was eight months old I had to leave her daytimes with the woman downstairs to whom she was no miracle at all, for I worked or looked for work and for Emily's father, who "could no longer endure" (he wrote in his good-bye note) "sharing want with us."

I was nineteen. It was the pre-relief, pre-WPA[1] world of the depression. I would start
30   running as soon as I got off the streetcar, running up the stairs, the place smelling sour, and awake or asleep to startle awake, when she saw me she would break into a clogged weeping that could not be comforted, a weeping I can hear yet.

After a while I found a job hashing at night so I could be with her days, and it was better. But it came to where I had to bring her to his family and leave her.

35   It took a long time to raise the money for her fare back. Then she got chicken pox and I had to wait longer. When she finally came, I hardly knew her, walking quick and nervous like her father, looking like her father, thin, and dressed in a shoddy red that yellowed her skin and glared at the pockmarks. All the baby loveliness gone.

[1]Works Progress Administration. This government program provided work to many unemployed people during the Depression.

She was two. Old enough for nursery school they said, and I did not know then what I know now—the fatigue of the long day, and the lacerations of group life in the kinds of nurseries that are only parking places for children.

Except that it would have made no difference if I had known. It was the only place there was. It was the only way we could be together, the only way I could hold a job.

And even without knowing, I knew. I knew the teacher that was evil because all these years it has curdled into my memory, the little boy hunched in the corner, her rasp, "why aren't you outside, because Alvin hits you? that's no reason, go out, scaredy." I knew Emily hated it even if she did not clutch and implore "don't go Mommy" like the other children, mornings.

She always had a reason why we should stay home. Momma, you look sick. Momma, I feel sick. Momma, the teachers aren't here today, they're sick. Momma, we can't go, there was a fire there last night. Momma, it's a holiday today, no school, they told me.

But never a direct protest, never rebellion. I think of our others in their three-, four-year-oldness—the explosions, tempers, the denunciations, the demands—and I feel suddenly ill. I put the iron down. What in me demanded that goodness in her? And what was the cost, the cost to her of such goodness?

The old man living in the back once said in his gentle way: "You should smile at Emily more when you look at her." What *was* in my face when I looked at her? I loved her. There were all the acts of love.

It was only with the others I remembered what he said, and it was the face of joy, and not of care or tightness or worry I turned to them—too late for Emily. She does not smile easily, let alone almost always as her brothers and sisters do. Her face is closed and sombre, but when she wants, how fluid. You must have seen it in her pantomimes, you spoke of her rare gift for comedy on the stage that rouses laughter out of the audience so dear they applaud and applaud and do not want to let her go.

Where does it come from, that comedy? There was none of it in her when she came back to me that second time, after I had to send her away again. She had a new daddy now to learn to love, and I think perhaps it was a better time.

Except when we left her alone nights, telling ourselves she was old enough.

"Can't you go some other time, Mommy, like tomorrow?" she would ask. "Will it be just a little while you'll be gone? Do you promise?"

The time we came back, the front door open, the clock on the floor in the hall. She rigid awake. "It wasn't just a little while. I didn't cry. Three times I called you, just three times, and then I ran downstairs to open the door so you could come faster. The clock talked loud. I threw it away, it scared me what it talked."

She said the clock talked loud again that night I went to the hospital to have Susan. She was delirious with the fever that comes before red measles, but she was fully conscious all the week I was gone and the week after we were home when she could not come near the new baby or me.

She did not get well. She stayed skeleton thin, not wanting to eat, and night after night she had nightmares. She would call for me, and I would rouse from exhaustion to sleepily call back: "You're all right, darling, go to sleep, it's just a dream," and if she still called, in a sterner voice, "now to go sleep, Emily, there's nothing to hurt you." Twice, only twice, when I had to get up for Susan anyhow, I went in to sit with her.

85 Now when it is too late (as if she would let me hold and comfort her like I do the others) I get up and go to her at once at her moan or restless stirring. "Are you awake, Emily? Can I get you something?" And the answer is always the same: "No, I'm all right, go back to sleep, Mother."

They persuaded me at the clinic to send her away to a convalescent home in the country where "she can have the kind of food and care you can't manage for her, and you'll be free 90 to concentrate on the new baby." They still send children to that place. I see pictures on the society page of sleek young women planning affairs to raise money for it, or dancing at the affairs, or decorating Easter eggs or filling Christmas stockings for the children.

They never have a picture of the children so I do not know if the girls still wear those gigantic red bows and the ravaged looks on the every other Sunday when parents can come 95 to visit "unless otherwise notified"—as we were notified the first six weeks.

Oh it is a handsome place, green lawns and tall trees and fluted flower beds. High up on the balconies of each cottage the children stand, the girls in their red bows and white dresses, the boys in white suits and giant red ties. The parents stand below shrieking up to be heard and the children shriek down to be heard, and between them the invisible wall 100 "Not To Be Contaminated by Parental Germs or Physical Affection."

There was a tiny girl who always stood hand in hand with Emily. Her parents never came. One visit she was gone. "They moved her to Rose Cottage" Emily shouted in explanation. "They don't like you to love anybody here."

She wrote once a week, the labored writing of a seven-year-old. "I am fine. How is the 105 baby. If I write my letter nicely I will have a star. Love." There never was a star. We wrote every other day, letters she could never hold or keep but only hear read—once. "We simply do not have room for children to keep any personal possessions," they patiently explained when we pieced one Sunday's shrieking together to plead how much it would mean to Emily, who loved so to keep things, to be allowed to keep her letters and cards.

110 Each visit she looked frailer. "She isn't eating," they told us.

(They had runny eggs for breakfast or mush with lumps, Emily said later, I'd hold it in my mouth and not swallow. Nothing ever tasted good, just when they had chicken.)

It took us eight months to get her released home, and only the fact that she gained back so little of her seven lost pounds convinced the social worker.

115 I used to try to hold and love her after she came back, but her body would stay stiff, and after a while she'd push away. She ate little. Food sickened her, and I think much of life too. Oh she had physical lightness and brightness, twinkling by on skates, bouncing like a ball up and down up and down over the jump rope, skimming over the hill; but these were momentary.

120 She fretted about her appearance, thin and dark and foreign-looking at a time when every little girl was supposed to look or thought she should look a chubby blonde replica of Shirley Temple. The doorbell sometimes rang for her, but no one seemed to come and play in the house or be a best friend. Maybe because we moved so much.

There was a boy she loved painfully through two school semesters. Months later she told me how she had taken pennies from my purse to buy him candy. "Licorice was his favorite and I brought him some every day, but he still liked Jennifer better'n me. Why, Mommy?" The kind of question for which there is no answer.

School was a worry to her. She was not glib or quick in a world where glibness and quickness were easily confused with ability to learn. To her overworked and exasperated teachers she was an overconscientious "slow learner" who kept trying to catch up and was absent entirely too often.

I let her be absent, though sometimes the illness was imaginary. How different from my now-strictness about attendance with the others. I wasn't working. We had a new baby, I was home anyhow. Sometimes, after Susan grew old enough, I would keep her home from school, too, to have them all together.

Mostly Emily had asthma, and her breathing, harsh and labored, would fill the house with a curiously tranquil sound. I would bring the two old dresser mirrors and her boxes of collections to her bed. She would select beads and single earrings, bottle tops and shells, dried flowers and pebbles, old postcards and scraps, all sorts of oddments; then she and Susan would play Kingdom, setting up landscapes and furniture, peopling them with action.

Those were the only times of peaceful companionship between her and Susan. I have edged away from it, that poisonous feeling between them, that terrible balancing of hurts and needs I had to do between the two, and did so badly, those earlier years.

Oh there are conflicts between the others too, each one human, needing, demanding, hurting, taking—but only between Emily and Susan, no, Emily toward Susan that corroding resentment. It seems so obvious on the surface, yet it is not obvious. Susan, the second child, Susan, golden- and curly-haired and chubby, quick and articulate and assured, everything in appearance and manner Emily was not; Susan, not able to resist Emily's precious things, losing or sometimes clumsily breaking them; Susan telling jokes and riddles to company for applause while Emily sat silent (to say to me later: that was *my* riddle, Mother, I told it to Susan); Susan, who for all the five years' difference in age was just a year behind Emily in developing physically.

I am glad for that slow physical development that widened the difference between her and her contemporaries, though she suffered over it. She was too vulnerable for that terrible world of youthful competition, of preening and parading, of constant measuring of yourself against every other, of envy, "If I had that copper hair," "If I had that skin. . . ." She tormented herself enough about not looking like the others, there was enough of the unsureness, the having to be conscious of words before you speak, the constant caring—what are they thinking of me? without having it all magnified by the merciless physical drives.

Ronnie is calling. He is wet and I change him. It is rare there is such a cry now. That time of motherhood is almost behind me when the ear is not one's own but must always be racked and listening for the child cry, the child call. We sit for a while and I hold him, looking out over the city spread in charcoal with its soft aisles of light. *"Shoogily,"* he breathes and curls closer. I carry him back to bed, asleep. *Shoogily.* A funny word, a family word, inherited from Emily, invented by her to say: *comfort.*

In this and other ways she leaves her seal, I say aloud. And startle at my saying it. What do I mean? What did I start to gather together, to try and make coherent? I was at the terrible, growing years. War years. I do not remember them well. I was working, there were four smaller ones now, there was not time for her. She had to help be a mother, and house-
170   keeper, and shopper. She had to set her seal. Mornings of crisis and near hysteria trying to get lunches packed, hair combed, coats and shoes found, everyone to school or Child Care on time, the baby ready for transportation. And always the paper scribbled on by a smaller one, the book looked at by Susan then mislaid, the homework not done. Running out to that huge school where she was one, she was lost, she was a drop; suffering over the unpre-
175   paredness, stammering and unsure in her classes.

There was so little time left at night after the kids were bedded down. She would struggle over books, always eating (it was in those years she developed her enormous appetite that is legendary in our family) and I would be ironing, or preparing food for the next day, or writing V-mail to Bill, or tending the baby. Sometimes, to make me laugh, or out of her
180   despair, she would imitate happenings or types at school.

I think I said once: "Why don't you do something like this in the school amateur show?" One morning she phoned me at work, hardly understandable through the weeping: "Mother, I did it. I won, I won; they gave me first prize; they clapped and clapped and wouldn't let me go."
185   Now suddenly she was Somebody, and as imprisoned in her difference as she had been in anonymity.

She began to be asked to perform at other high schools, even in colleges, then at city and statewide affairs. The first one we went to, I only recognized her that first moment when thin, shy, she almost drowned herself into the curtains. Then: Was this Emily? The control,
190   the command, the convulsing and deadly clowning, the spell, then the roaring, stamping audience, unwilling to let this rare and precious laughter out of their lives.

Afterwards: You ought to do something about her with a gift like that—but without money or knowing how, what does one do? We have left it all to her, and the gift has as often eddied inside, clogged and clotted, as been used and growing.
195   She is coming. She runs up the stairs two at a time with her light graceful step, and I know she is happy tonight. Whatever it was that occasioned your call did not happen today.

"Aren't you ever going to finish the ironing, Mother? Whistler painted his mother in a rocker. I'd have to paint mine standing over an ironing board." This is one of her commu-
200   nicative nights and she tells me everything and nothing as she fixes herself a plate of food out of the icebox.

She is so lovely. Why did you want me to come in at all? Why were you concerned? She will find her way.

She starts up the stairs to bed. "Don't get me up with the rest in the morning." "But I
205   thought you were having midterms." "Oh, those," she comes back in, kisses me, and says quite lightly, "in a couple of years when we'll all be atom-dead they won't matter a bit."

She has said it before. She *believes* it. But because I have been dredging the past, and all that compounds a human being is so heavy and meaningful in me, I cannot endure it tonight.

I will never total it all. I will never come in to say: She was a child seldom smiled at. Her   210
father left me before she was a year old. I had to work her first six years when there was
work, or I sent her home and to his relatives. There were years she had care she hated. She
was dark and thin and foreign-looking in a world where the prestige went to blondeness
and curly hair and dimples, she was slow where glibness was prized. She was a child of
anxious, not proud, love. We were poor and could not afford for her the soil of easy growth.   215
I was a young mother, I was a distracted mother. There were other children pushing up,
demanding. Her younger sister seemed all that she was not. There were years she did not
want me to touch her. She kept too much in herself, her life was such she had to keep too
much in herself. My wisdom came too late. She has much to her and probably little will
come of it. She is a child of her age, of depression, of war, of fear.   220

Let her be. So all that is in her will not bloom—but in how many does it? There is still
enough left to live by. Only help her to know—help make it so there is cause for her to
know—that she is more than this dress on the ironing board, helpless before the iron.
1961

Source: Tillie Olsen. Tell Me a Riddle, Requa I, and Other Works. *University of Nebraska Press. 1989.*

▪ Discussion/Writing Prompts

1. This narrative is organized as an extended flashback. What do you think motivates
   Olsen to organize her story this way? What larger goal is she trying to achieve by
   telling this story through a collection of memories? [Rhetorical Analysis of Purpose]

2. Is there a story from your past that you have found yourself reflecting upon or
   retelling frequently? If so, what is this story about? And what makes it so memorable
   and important? [Personal Reflection]

3. Reflecting upon her daughter, the narrator declares:

   > I think of our others in their three-, four-year-oldness—the explosions, the tem-
   > pers, the denunciations, the demands—and I feel suddenly ill. I put the iron
   > down. What in me demanded that goodness in her? And what was the cost, the
   > cost to her of such goodness?

   What kind of distinction is the narrator drawing here between her daughter and her
   other children? What realization about her daughter causes her to interrupt her
   ironing? What does she mean by the phrase "the cost of goodness"? [Close Reading]

4. This selection is an example of narration. How effective do you find this rhetorical mode
   to be? Do you think the decision to present this mother/daughter portrait in story form
   helps Olsen accomplish her main goals? How, or how not? [Analysis of Rhetorical Modes]

5. Olsen concludes her story by having her narrator speak the following words:

   > Let her be. So all that is in her will not bloom—but in how many does it? There
   > is still enough left to live by. Only help her to know—help make it so there is

cause for her to know—that she is more than this dress on the ironing board, helpless before the iron.

In a two- or three-page essay, identify and analyze the main points Olsen is trying to get across in this passage. What is the narrator saying here about her daughter's capacity to "bloom"? What's the difference between "blooming" and "knowing"? And how does the narrator use this distinction to say something about her relationship with her daughter? [Argument]

6. How do you think F. Diane Barth ("Why Women Fear Envy and Why We Don't Need To") would respond to this story? Given her own argument about female emotion, do you think she would be drawn to Olsen's portrait of a complicated mother/daughter relationship? Why, or why not? [Compare and Contrast]

7. Does Olsen's portrait here reflect or challenge prevailing models of parent/child relationships? To answer this question, research the ways our popular culture invites us to define the ideal family. What examples of the ideal family does our pop culture present to us? How do these examples define the ideal roles that parents and children are supposed to play? And what are the key differences between this ideal and the mother/daughter relationship presented in Olsen's story? [Research]

Stephen King, "Why We Crave Horror Movies"

What explains the enduring popularity of horror movies? Why are so many of us drawn to their depiction of menace, mayhem, and murder? Seeking to answer precisely this question, Stephen King, the author of dozens of best-selling horror and thriller novels, delves into the social and psychological needs such terrifying pop culture fare may actually satisfy.

Stephen King's name is synonymous with horror stories. A 1970 graduate of the University of Maine, King worked as a janitor in a knitting mill, a laundry worker, and a high school English teacher before he struck it big with his writing. Many consider King to be the most successful writer of modern horror fiction today. To date, he has written dozens

5   of novels, collections of short stories and novellas, and screenplays, among other works. His books have sold well over 250 million copies worldwide, and many of his novels have been made into popular motion pictures, including *Stand by Me, Misery, The Green Mile,* and *Dreamcatcher.* His books, starting with *Carrie* in 1974, include *Salem's Lot* (1975), *The Shining* (1977), *The Dead Zone* (1979), *Christine* (1983), *Pet Sematary* (1983), *The Dark Half*

10   (1989), *The Girl Who Loved Tom Gordon* (1999), *From a Buick 8* (2002), and *Everything's Eventual: Five Dark Tales* (2002), his first collection of short stories in nine years. Other works of his include *Danse Macabre* (1980), a nonfiction look at horror in the media, and *On Writing: A Memoir of the Craft* (2000). Each year King and his wife, novelist Tabitha King, donate at least 10 percent of their pretaxable income to charitable organizations, many of them

local. The widespread popularity of horror books and films attests to the fact that many   15
people share King's fascination with the macabre. In the following selection, originally
published in *Playboy* in 1982, a variation on "The Horror Movie as Junk Food" chapter
in *Danse Macabre,* King analyzes the reasons we flock to good horror movies.

I think that we're all mentally ill; those of us outside the asylums only hide it a little
better—and maybe not all that much better, after all. We've all known people who talk to   20
themselves, people who sometimes squinch their faces into horrible grimaces when they
believe no one is watching, people who have some hysterical fear—of snakes, the dark, the
tight place, the long drop . . . and, of course, those final worms and grubs that are waiting
so patiently underground.

When we pay our four or five bucks and seat ourselves at tenth-row center in a theater   25
showing a horror movie, we are daring the nightmare.

Why? Some of the reasons are simple and obvious. To show that we can, that we are not
afraid, that we can ride this roller coaster. Which is not to say that a really good horror
movie may not surprise a scream out of us at some point, the way we may scream when a
roller coaster twists through a complete 360 or plows through a lake at the bottom of the   30
drop. And horror movies, like roller coasters, have always been the special province of the
young; by the time one turns 40 or 50, one's appetite for double twists or 360-degree loops
may be considerably depleted.

We also go to re-establish our feelings of essential normality; the horror movie is
innately conservative, even reactionary. Freda Jackson as the horrible melting woman   35
in *Die, Monster, Die!* confirms for us that no matter how far we may be removed from
the beauty of a Robert Redford or a Diana Ross, we are still light-years from true
ugliness.

And we go to have fun.

Ah, but this is where the ground starts to slope away, isn't it? Because this is a very pe-   40
culiar sort of fun, indeed. The fun comes from seeing others menaced—sometimes killed.
One critic has suggested that if pro football has become the voyeur's version of combat,
then the horror film has become the modern version of the public lynching.

It is true that the mythic, "fairy-tale" horror film intends to take away the shades of
gray. . . . It urges us to put away our more civilized and adult penchant for analysis and to   45
become children again, seeing things in pure blacks and whites. It may be that horror
movies provide psychic relief on this level because this invitation to lapse into simplicity,
irrationality and even outright madness is extended so rarely. We are told we may allow
our emotions a free rein . . . or no rein at all.

If we are all insane, then sanity becomes a matter of degree. If your insanity leads you to   50
carve up women like Jack the Ripper or the Cleveland Torso Murderer,[1] we clap you away in

---

[1]*Jack the Ripper, Cleveland Torso Murderer:* serial murderers who were active in the 1880s
and the 1930s, respectively. [Eds.]

the funny farm (but neither of those two amateur-night surgeons was ever caught, heh-heh-heh); if, on the other hand, your insanity leads you only to talk to yourself when you're under stress or to pick your nose on your morning bus, then you are left alone to go about your business . . . though it is doubtful that you will ever be invited to the best parties.

The potential lyncher is in almost all of us (excluding saints, past and present; but then, most saints have been crazy in their own ways), and every now and then, he has to be let loose to scream and roll around in the grass. Our emotions and our fears form their own body, and we recognize that it demands its own exercise to maintain proper muscle tone. Certain of these emotional muscles are accepted—even exalted—in civilized society; they are, of course, the emotions that tend to maintain the status quo of civilization itself. Love, friendship, loyalty, kindness—these are all the emotions that we applaud, emotions that have been immortalized in the couplets of Hallmark cards and in the verses (I don't dare call it poetry) of Leonard Nimoy.[2]

When we exhibit these emotions, society showers us with positive reinforcement; we learn this even before we get out of diapers. When, as children, we hug our rotten little puke of a sister and give her a kiss, all the aunts and uncles smile and twit and cry, "Isn't he the sweetest little thing?" Such coveted treats as chocolate-covered graham crackers often follow. But if we deliberately slam the rotten little puke of a sister's fingers in the door, sanctions follow—angry remonstrance from parents, aunts, and uncles; instead of a chocolate-covered graham cracker, a spanking.

But anticivilization emotions don't go away, and they demand periodic exercise. We have such "sick" jokes as, "What's the difference between a truckload of bowling balls and a truckload of dead babies? (You can't unload a truckload of bowling balls with a pitch-fork . . . . a joke, by the way, that I heard originally from a ten-year-old). Such a joke may surprise a laugh or a grin out of us even as we recoil, a possibility that confirms the thesis: if we share a brotherhood of man, then we also share an insanity of man. None of which is intended as a defense of either the sick joke or insanity but merely as an explanation of why the best horror films, like the best fairy tales, manage to be reactionary, anarchistic, and revolutionary all at the same time.

The mythic horror movie, like the sick joke, has a dirty job to do. It deliberately appeals to all that is worst in us. It is morbidity unchained, our most base instincts let free, our nastiest fantasies realized . . . and it all happens, fittingly enough, in the dark. For those reasons, good liberals often shy away from horror films. For myself, I like to see the most aggressive of them—*Dawn of the Dead*, for instance—as lifting a trap door in the civilized forebrain and throwing a basket of raw meat to the hungry alligators swimming around in that subterranean river beneath.

Why bother? Because it keeps them from getting out, man. It keeps them down there and me up here. It was Lennon and McCartney who said that all you need is love, and I would agree with that.

As long as you keep the gators fed.

[2]*Leonard Nimoy* (b. 1931): television and film actor. [Eds.]

Source: King, Stephen. "Why We Crave Horror Movies" *originally published in Playboy, 1982.*

▨ Discussion/Writing Prompts

1. As the title of this essay suggests, King is clearly playing around with our conventional assumptions and expectations about horror movies. Why do you think he wants to do this? In your view, what effect does King aim to have on the way his readers think and feel about this type of cultural product? [Rhetorical Analysis of Purpose]

2. What are your own personal experiences with horror movies? Are you drawn to this particular genre? If so, what is it about these types of film that appeals to you? If not, what is it about such movies that you find unappealing? Based on your own experience, would you consider yourself to be part of King's intended or target audience here? Why, or why not? [Personal Reflection]

3. Here is how King opens his essay: "I think that we're all mentally ill; those of us outside the asylum only hide it a little better . . ." Why do you think King chooses to begin this way? In what ways do these opening lines prepare his readers for the argument about horror movies that follows? [Close Reading]

4. In many ways, King's discussion here unfolds as an argument about causes and effects. What is it, he asks, that generates our interest in horror movies? Do you find this causal explanation logical or persuasive? How, or how not? [Analysis of Rhetorical Modes]

5. "The mythic horror movie," writes King, "like the sick joke, has a dirty job to do. It deliberately appeals to all that is worst in us. It is morbidity unchained, our most base instincts let free, our nastiest fantasies realized . . . and it all happens, fittingly enough, in the dark." Write an essay in which you analyze and evaluate the hypothesis King is presenting here. Do you agree that horror movies are designed to deliberately activate our "base instincts" and "nasty fantasies"? And if so, do you share King's belief that this is what makes such movies so valuable? Why, or why not? [Argument]

6. Like King, Sherry Turkle ("The Flight From Conversation") makes an argument about the ways pop culture can influence our personal behavior. How do you think these two discussions compare? Despite the fact that they address such different topics, would you say that these writers share a common perspective on the power of popular culture? If so, how? [Compare and Contrast]

7. To test the validity of King's argument, spend some time watching horror movies. As you watch, keep a list of your feelings and reactions. Then, write a quick assessment of what this first-hand research tells you. Do your own reactions provide data in support of King's hypothesis? [Research]

▨ Tying It All Together

1. A number of the selections above focus on the risks posed by our new communications environment. Choose two such selections. Then, in a two or

three-page essay, describe and evaluate the specific dangers or risks each selection identifies. What do they share in common? What are their key differences? And what different responses or solutions does each propose?

2. Sherry Turkle ("The Flight From Conversation") and Douglas Rushkoff ("Why I'm Quitting Facebook") both turn their attention to the ways that modern media (e.g., advertising, social networking, or Web 2.0 technology) can influence individual behavior. Write a two- or three-page essay in which you argue against this particular view. In what ways can we think of modern media as having a more positive or empowering effect on our behavior? And in what ways does such a view help us challenge or revise the arguments these writers are advancing?

3. F. Diane Barth ("Why Women Fear Envy") and Shankar Vedantam ("Partisanship Is the New Racism") both connect their discussion to current social or political issues. Choose your own current issue. First, research the ways this issue gets depicted and debated within our media. What does the discussion of this issue look like? What are the key questions or problems around which this issue revolves? What are the key points about which people disagree? Next, analyze this issue in terms of purpose. What are the goals of those who are participating in this debate? What does each side hope to accomplish? How do these goals or objectives compare with your own? Why is this an issue you care about? And what effect would you like this debate to have?

Using the Steps of Rhetorical Analysis to Write Your Own Academic Essay

The same instruction this chapter presents for analyzing other people's writing can also serve as a guide for undertaking writing of your own. In particular, a number of the steps outlined above provide a useful framework for the kind of writing you are often called upon to do in the classroom. In the same way that these steps teach you to apply the rhetorical concept of purpose to what you read, they can also be used to help you better see the role this concept plays in your own essay writing. Take a look at the outline below. Organizing the writing process along the same rhetorical lines modeled above, it provides you with a map for how to use the concept of purpose to organize and create your own academic essay:

- *Step 1: Planning for Purpose*: What is your basic goal? What points or ideas do you want to get across? What information do you want to convey?
- *Step 2: Acting Upon Purpose*: How do these goals affect the way you organize your essay? How do they influence the points you raise or the language you use?
- *Step 3: Refining Purpose*: What additional changes can you make to your essay that help you better accomplish your goal? What material can you add, alter, or delete?

To see how these steps can be put into practice, let's take a look at a specific example. As you read over the essay below, pay attention to how considerations about purpose guide the writer's calculations and choices. To assist you in this work, take note of the comments and questions that accompany the essay in the margins. Then, turn your attention to the sample analysis that follows. In what ways does this discussion provide a model for using the three steps outlined above to write an academic essay of your own?

Student Essay: Iris Lopez, "Unintended Consequences: The Dangers of Social Media"

In this essay, Iris Lopez, a college student, makes a cause-and-effect argument about one of the key issues raised by the formal writing selections above: the role of social media in our daily lives.

Over the last decade, the rise of social media has changed almost every facet of our lives: from how we work to how we talk to how we socialize. Indisputably, many of these changes have been for the better. We can now connect to people in far-flung places that, in previous times, we would have had no connection to or even awareness of. We have access to amounts of different information these days that previous generations would have never imagined. For all these advantages, however, the rise of social media has also brought with it several unintended consequences. It has the potential to lead people to turn away from forms of organization and connection they previously might have participated in. It might also foster a culture of envy in which people are taught to compete against each other for greater and greater attention. And most dangerously, it runs the risk of encouraging us to accept a diminished, even false, idea of friendship itself, one that substitutes shallow connection for real connection.

5

Author's purpose: to question the benefits of social media.   10

15

Author's Thesis   20

The first potential effect of the rise of social media is *First Effect* a reduction in local community participation. As people come to rely more and more on tools like Twitter or Facebook to stay in touch, the possibility grows that the interest people have in local or face-to-face contact will decline. As more and more people turn to the Web to connect with people in far-away places, it seems logical to assume that those local organizations that formerly served as the cornerstone of neighborhood or community life (social clubs, churches) may now struggle to convince people to stay involved. We should worry about this change for a couple of

25

Author pursuing her goal by focusing first on the effect on community.

30

reasons. First, it could lead to people simply not knowing anything about the interests or concerns of their
35   neighbors. Without the face-to-face contact, people
in the same community might easily become strangers
to each other. The second reason this is worrisome is
that such a loss of face-to-face contact would make it
harder and harder for people to work together to
40   solve the problems of their community. If you don't
think of your neighbors as part of your community, the
community itself will suffer.

The rise of social media also has the potential to   *Second Effect*
foster greater degrees of envy and competition
45   among people. From Facebook "likes" to Re-Tweets,
much of the emphasis within social media is placed on
gaining attention from others. For many, the goal of
social media is not to convey important information or
share thoughts and feelings, but rather simply to be
50   known and noticed by those around them. This kind of
situation could (and indeed often does) lead people
to treat social media as a weapon for trying to outdo
or defeat others. Instead of using social media to   *Author focusing next on issue*
communicate real thoughts and feelings, people   *of competition.*
55   may increasingly be using them to polish their own
image. This is a dangerous trend because, like the
threat to community noted earlier, it could lead people
to become more and more self-concerned, less and
less interested in learning about the genuine needs
60   and concerns of those around them.

Lastly and most importantly, the rise of social
media might result in people embracing a diminished
notion of friendship. In a world where "friending" has
become a verb, something we can do with no more   *Third Effect*
65   effort than the click of a button, it is not too far-
fetched to wonder whether we are learning in our
online lives to treat friendship as something that re-
quires little or no commitment. Traditional, face-to-   *Author focusing on the issue of*
face models of friendship develop over time. They   *friendship*
70   involve an effort to truly get to know another person.
And most crucially, they require that we in turn allow
ourselves to be truly known by somebody else. None
of these requirements need to be met in online
friendship.

The rise of social media is one of the great revolutions of our time. This development has profoundly improved countless aspects of our lives. At the same time, however, this development has also subtly altered the ways we think about and interact with each other. Along with the convenience of connection has come the risk of isolation, where the same tools we use to reach out to each other simultaneously create boundaries that keep us all the more apart.

Conclusion 75

80

Author summarizing her key points.

Now, let's see how the rhetorical steps presented above help us understand the choices the writer makes to create this essay:

Step One: *Planning for Purpose: What is the Writer's Basic Goal?*

º As the title makes clear, the writer's main goal is to highlight the dangers of social media. Along with this general goal, though, are some more specific objectives as well. Among them:

› To make the case for the harmful effect our reliance on social media may be having on local communities.

› To question the motivation behind our growing desire to connect with other people online.

› To underscore the ways in which social media encourage a kind of narcissism among users.

› To encourage readers to reconsider more traditional models of friendship.

Step Two: *Acting Upon Purpose: How Does This Goal Influence Other Rhetorical Choices the Writer Makes?*

º The effort to highlight the dangers of social media leads the writer to draw firm lines between "face-to-face" life and online life. Because she wants her readers to look upon the online interactions as inherently less substantial and authentic than their face-to-face counterparts, she describes online life in language that highlights its inauthenticity. For example:

[T]he rise of social media might result in people embracing a diminished notion of friendship.

Instead of using social media to communicate real thoughts and feelings, people may increasingly be using them to polish their own image.

º At the same time, the writer chooses language that describes "face-to-face" interaction in opposite terms:

> [L]ocal organizations . . . served as the cornerstone of neighborhood or community life . . .

> Traditional, face-to-face models of friendship develop over time. They involve an effort to truly get to know another person.

Step Three: *Refining Purpose: How Do You Evaluate This Goal? How Effectively Does the Writer Achieve It?*

º The writer effectively makes clear her basic critique of social media. She organizes her three individual points clearly and logically, highlighting the common ideas or themes that link them together.

º At the same time, the writer undermines her main objective because her discussion fails to account for the objections others might offer in response. Her discussion doesn't acknowledge, for example, the possibility that social media are often used as a tool for creating new types of community. Instead, the writer treats social media as if their only purpose is to satisfy people's individual desires.

Group Work: Thinking Rhetorically About the Formal Selections

Thus far, this chapter has given you ample opportunity to analyze purpose individually. This activity invites you to undertake this same kind of work from a group perspective. Your group should select one of the formal selections above. Prepare for your group work by re-reading the selection. Then, with your group, use the outline presented at the beginning of the chapter, *Thinking Rhetorically About Purpose,* to analyze the role that purpose plays in this piece. Here is a quick recap of these steps:

• What larger goals seem to be motivating this writer?
• How fully does the author achieve these goals?
• Are these goals valid ones to pursue?
• What is my objective in reading this text?

Once you have completed this work, exchange your findings with another group. First, have your group re-read the selection these new findings examine. Then, discuss as a group how helpful you find this analysis. Do you agree with the conclusions about purpose this analysis draws? Do you evaluate the role of purpose in different or similar ways? Finally, summarize your key findings in a paragraph. Be prepared to share this written assessment with the rest of the class.

Different Purpose, Different Point: Understanding the Connection Between Informal and Formal Writing

Throughout this chapter, we have shifted back and forth between a focus on informal and formal writing. The array of selections under examination has ranged from short social network posts to in-depth professional essays. How do these types of writing compare? What are the key differences in language and tone, form and content, organization and context? And what happens to our understanding of purpose when we take these differences into account?

The activity presented here provides an opportunity to address these questions. First, choose an issue raised by one of the formal selections in this chapter (e.g., the cost of college education, the role of envy in public life, or the effect of Web technologies on personal behavior). Next, choose an informal venue (e.g., blog, Facebook post, tweet, or email), and write about this issue using the conventions of this particular form. Then, choose a formal venue (e.g., journal essay, magazine article, or academic analysis), and write about the same issue using the conventions particular to this form. When you're done, spend a few moments itemizing the specific ways these two writing samples are similar and different. In what ways did your choice of venue affect your overall goal? And how did this goal affect the larger point you were trying to make?

Connecting Purpose to Rhetorical Modes

As you learned in Chapter 4, across writing that may differ greatly in terms of genre or subject matter, it is still possible to note certain patterns emerge and repeat themselves. Called rhetorical modes, these patterns often play a significant role in helping a writer achieve a particular goal. It can be helpful, in fact, to think of these modes as a kind of rhetorical toolbox, helping accomplish the particular objectives a writer has in mind.

To better understand the connection between writerly purpose and rhetorical modes, try the following activity: Choose one of the examples of real world writing from the informal selections in this chapter. First, analyze this selection according to the five rhetorical categories (purpose, audience, argument, voice, credibility). Then, identify the specific rhetorical mode this selection uses to advance or achieve each of these rhetorical goals. How, for instance, does a strategy of narration or definition help reinforce the writer's overall argument? How well does a cause-and-effect strategy help bolster a writer's credibility? To help you complete this work, here is a quick recap of the major rhetorical modes:

- Narration
- Description
- Cause and effect
- Compare and contrast
- Definition

Speaking for Yourself

Choose an issue that is currently being debated. First, write a one-page description of where you stand on this issue. What are your own opinions? On which side of the debate do you fall? Next, choose a type of real world writing with which you are familiar (e.g., blog, social network post, tweet, email, or academic essay), and write out your views on this issue within the conventions of this form. When you're done, write another one-page essay in which you assess this real world example in terms of your goals or purpose. What effect on your audience were you hoping to have? What larger point were you trying to get across?

6 Audience

Imagine the following scenario: It's the beginning of the semester, and you find yourself in conversation with your roommate about what each of you did over summer vacation. Wanting to make the last three months sound as exciting as possible, you work hard to impress your listener with a tale of nonstop, fun-filled carousing. You lard your story with anecdotes about late-night parties and trips to the beach, while leaving out any mention of the two weeks you spend battling the flu or your part-time job mowing lawns.

Now, let's amend this picture slightly. Instead of your roommate, imagine yourself in the same conversation at the dinner table with a grandparent or across the table from a supervisor interviewing you for a job. Under these altered circumstances, chances are your story about "what I did on summer vacation" would look and sound a whole lot different. With a grandparent as your audience, you might think twice before launching into a lengthy description of the all-night parties you attended or boastful claims about how little sleep you got. Addressing yourself to a future employer, you might decide that adding a few details about that summer lawn-mowing job isn't such a bad idea after all. Depending on your audience, you'd make very different calculations about which topics to cover and which to omit, which details to highlight and which to downplay, and even what tone to strike or what language to use.

The foregoing hypothetical makes an important point: What we say, and how we say, it depends a lot upon *to whom* we are saying it—depends, that is, on audience. As writers, we all have some vision of the ideal reader we are trying to reach: the person whom we feel is best suited to the message we are trying to present. Whether sending an email, blogging about a current political issue, analyzing a work of literature, writing a scientific report, or posting a message on Facebook, our choices as writers are always based in part on our vision of the audience we are addressing. Depending on what this audience looks like, we will make very different decisions about what, and how, to write.

Audience and the Goals of Writing

To illustrate, consider the job letter. Most of us are familiar with what this kind of writing involves. A job letter, put succinctly, is where we make the case for why we should be hired. It is where we outline our key qualifications, highlight our skills and strengths, and connect these things to the specific requirements of the position we are seeking. As the author, the choices we make about how to organize and present this material—what background information to provide and what to omit, which skills to foreground and which to downplay—will change depending on the type of reader we imagine ourselves to be addressing. If we imagine a reader who wants to know only the relevant facts about our past work experiences, chances are we will write a job letter that reads more like an objective or neutral list of names and dates. If we imagine a reader who places a greater premium on interpersonal skills, we are likely to write a very different job letter, one that conveys much more personal information about ourselves and, perhaps, is written in a more informal, friendlier tone.

Of course, the corollary of this lesson is also true. Just as we make assumptions about the readers we are addressing, so too do writers make certain assumption *us*. An ad touting the benefits of a new antidepressant medication, for example, is likely to address itself to you as a reader actively searching for ways to become happier. A presidential speech announcing a new policy in Afghanistan will probably attempt to play upon your feelings of patriotism or concerns over national security. A tabloid expose' of a reality television star will speak to you as somebody truly interested in the lives of celebrities. In making its case *to* you, each of these examples is also making its case *about* you: who you are, what you care about, and what you want to be told.

In the real world today, it is especially important to understand the role that audience plays. As the rise of digital culture has brought us into closer and closer contact with each other, the relationship between writers and readers has likewise grown increasingly interactive. Whether it be a social media post or an iMessage, an email or a Wikipedia entry, authors engage in a constant back and forth with their audiences, attending to their responses, questions, and feedback. While exciting, this kind of interactivity also raises some important questions. Does the back-and-forth relationship between authors and audience change the ways we read or write? And if so, are these changes for the better?

How to Analyze Audience in Real World Writing

To answer these questions, we need an approach that helps us analyze audience in rhetorical terms. The framework below divides this analysis into a series of discrete steps, each of which helps you identify, analyze, and evaluate the role that audience plays in writing. To be sure, what follows is just an outline, and we will take a much closer and detailed look at this process in the pages ahead. For now, though, as you look over these steps, think about the ways you can use them to begin analyzing audience rhetorically.

Thinking Rhetorically About Audience

- **Step One: Identifying the Audience:** Who is the writer trying to reach? How would you define the intended or target audience?
- **Step Two: Addressing the Audience:** What does the writer say to this audience? And how does the writer go about saying it?
- **Step Three: Influencing the Audience:** What does the writer want this writing to do *for* the audience? To inform? To educate? To entertain? To persuade?

What does the writer want this writing to do *to* the audience? What reactions does the writer aim to elicit?

- **Step Four: Reflecting on the Audience:** How does this choice of audience influence the writer's own decisions and goals? How would these decisions and goals change if the writer targeted a different type of audience?
- **Step Five: What Kind of Audience Am I?:** How closely do I, as a reader, fit the definition of the target audience? Are my own responses in line with the responses the writer seems to be aiming for?
- **Step Six: Putting It Into Writing:** How do I summarize my own findings in writing?

To see how these guidelines can be put into practice, let's turn to a specific example. As you look over the selection below, notice how the sample analysis that follows uses the questions outlined above to explore the way this text defines and addresses its audience.

Connie Uhlrich, "Let Me Choose My Own Classes!"

This blog post by Connie Uhlrich, a high school senior, offers an example of the type of writing we might encounter ourselves.

It's been a while since my last posting, so I thought I'd catch everybody up on what's new. Like you, I've been doing a lot of thinking about the upcoming semester, now only one week (yikes!) away. As I sit in my favorite café enjoying my usual morning coffee my thoughts are turning to the new semester. Like everybody else, I'm trying hard to get excited for the start of the new school year. Not going so well. But can you blame me? Maybe   5
there are those who feel differently, but I for one am NOT psyched about having to take both calculus and physics at the same time. I mean, honestly, would anyone? It's not that I'm trying to avoid hard classes, I just don't get the whole idea of required course work. What's so wrong with letting students choose the classes they want to take? We are in high school, after all. Are teachers really worried we'd all end up taking things like underwater   10
basket weaving? I seriously doubt that would happen. I think kids would still choose challenging classes, but just the stuff they're really interested in. Not a great chance of this happening. Oh well. Maybe my caffeine buzz will kick in and improve my mood. Gotta go!

▌Thinking Rhetorically About Audience: A Step-by-Step Guide

Now, let's see how we can use the steps outlined above to analyze this example in a detailed and comprehensive way:

Step One: *Identifying the Audience: How Would You Define the Target Reader?*

   º The writer assumes a reader already acquainted with the basic details of her life, as indicated by the statement:

      I thought I'd catch everybody up on what's new.

Because she is only going to talk about "what's new," she assumes that the reader already knows what came before. If she were writing to an audience that was not familiar with her life, she would need to take an opportunity to provide additional background.

o She is writing to a reader of similar age and background. The phrases "Like you" and "Like everybody else" seem particularly important, as they explicitly define the reader as someone with the same basic attitude toward school.

o The writer assumes that the reader is already skeptical about mandatory classes and required coursework. The rhetorical questions posed seem to assume that the reader already agrees:

> I for one am NOT psyched about having to take both calculus and physics at the same time. I mean, honestly, would anyone?

This assumption works for an audience that feels the same way as the writer. If the piece were written for a different audience, including one who actually liked science and math, the writer could not use a rhetorical question like this and expect the same response from the readers.

o By making unsupported claims, the writer assumes a reader receptive to accepting claims at face value. Consider, for example, the statement:

> I think kids would still choose challenging classes, but just the stuff they're really interested in.

Because she doesn't provide evidence of this, the writer is assuming that her audience will agree with her. If this were a formal proposal to the school administration, the writer would need to use evidence to convince this audience that students would still elect to take legitimate courses. Because her *audience* would be different, her *approach* to that audience would need to change as well.

Step Two: *Addressing the Audience: How Does This Writer Speak to the Audience?*

o The writer speaks here using an intimate, familiar tone, one that reinforces the idea that she is addressing a readership of people she already knows. Her use of such terms as "stuff" and the concluding phrase "gotta go" make clear that her tone is intended to remain conversational.

o The writer's use of informal language relates as well to her use of humor. Her familiar tone is matched throughout this essay by one that is also often ironic, even sarcastic, as in her joking remark about "kids" opting to study "underwater basket weaving." This rhetorical strategy is far more likely to be effective in relation to an audience the writer already knows well. If she were to attempt this kind of humor or sarcasm with an unfamiliar audience, there is a far greater chance the writer would find her tone or larger point misunderstood.

○ The final strategy the writer employs is to pose rhetorical questions. For example:

> What's so wrong with letting students choose the classes they want?

It's clear that the writer wants her readers to answer this question in the same way she does—namely, that there's nothing wrong with letting students choose. And again, this is a strategy that works far more effectively with an audience the writer already knows than with one who is encountering her writing for the first time. An unfamiliar reader would be far less likely to give the writer the benefit of the doubt and automatically agree with the point of view she is expressing.

Step Three: *Influencing the Audience: What Are the Writer's Larger Goals?*

○ At the most basic level, the writer clearly wants to focus her readers' attention on the problem of required classes. She seems intent on getting her audience to question whether compulsory coursework actually enhances student learning.

○ Beneath this argument runs a second, unspoken message—namely, that students are mature and responsible enough to be trusted with the freedom to choose their own classes. This can be seen in such statements as:

> I think kids would still choose challenging courses, but just the stuff they're really interested in.

The implication here is that the courses students would find "interesting" would also be subjects worth studying in their own right.

Step Four: *Reflecting on the Audience: What Type of Reader Would Best Respond to These Goals?*

○ For these goals to be achieved, the writer needs an audience whose own experiences and background in school resonate with the problem she identifies: an audience of school-age "kids" who have the same concerns about required coursework as she does.

○ This essay would work perhaps most effectively for an audience of fellow students with a similar aversion to taking math and science classes. In many ways, in fact, it seems as if the writer is assuming that her readers already share this aversion, as when she poses the rhetorical question about wanting to take "calculus and physics" at the same time:

> I mean, honestly, would anybody?

∘ This argument would work less effectively for an audience in search of harder evidence or concrete proof. Because the writer uses her own experiences as a reference point, her readers are left having to accept that her feelings on this matter reflect the feelings of others as well.

Step Five: *What Kind of Audience Am I?*

∘ In many ways, I am drawn in by the writer's informal tone and use of humor. I like the way this familiar tone invites me to identify with the points she makes. Having given this same question some thought myself, I may well be one of the target readers the writer has in mind.

∘ The rhetorical question she poses about mandatory classes and student choice reflect concerns I have long had, too, and I find myself in general sympathy with the basic points she raises.

∘ That said, I am also the type of reader who responds best to arguments that include concrete support. In this sense, I find my sympathy for the writer's points undermined a bit by my desire for a fuller explanation of why this kind of change is really necessary. What difference would greater student "choice" make? In what specific ways would this enhance student learning or student experience in the classroom?

∘ In the end, I wish the writer didn't assume I already agreed with her position. I would have found it more persuasive to hear a comparison of her own views with the views of those who disagree, and thereby demonstrate how her view has greater merit.

Step Six: *Putting It Into Writing*

∘ This post raises an issue that is highly relevant to students in high school. Should classes be mandatory, or is it better to allow students to choose for themselves? The author does a good job of making her own viewpoint clear, stating her own preference for student choice repeatedly throughout. This strategy works well, in my opinion, for a reader who already agrees with the author's own point. There are many students who feel limited by teachers and administrators setting the agenda and that it would be far better for students to pursue their own interests. But there are also lots of students who feel differently, who don't believe their education would be enhanced if required coursework were done away with. And the author does very little to convince this type of audience to change their minds. Rather than go into greater depth about why student choice is better, the writer instead assumes that readers will automatically agree with her just because she expresses this view. This approach won't work well for an audience with a different attitude toward school. This type of reader needs to be told a) what is wrong with letting teachers make decisions about classes and b) what specifically would be better if students were given this choice. For this reason, I find this discussion less than fully effective.

Informal Writing Selections

Now that you've seen what this analysis looks like, try putting it into practice yourself. This section brings together a representative sample of informal writing, the kind of writing you might easily come across in your own day-to-day life. Using the format above as your guide, analyze each of these selections along the same rhetorical lines. In each case, how does the writer define, address, and attempt to influence the intended audience? What kinds of assumptions does each writer make about who these target readers are? About what they need and what they are looking for?

To help you begin answering these questions, let's start by working our way through a sample of what this rhetorical analysis might look like. As you read the selection below, pay close attention to both the questions that appear in the margins and the more extended responses to the step-by-step questions that follow. How does this material help you gain a better understanding of the role that audience plays here?

PositivelyPresent.com, "Get Happier!"

PositivelyPresent.com is a website that promotes self-help advice and advertises its self-help services to potential clients.

You want to be happier, don't you? We all do! I'm a firm believer that happiness comes from within. It's a choice that you have to make every moment of your life. That being said, it doesn't hurt to have some external help. I love to read and learn about happiness and find ways to bring more happiness into my life and not too long ago, I discovered the website happier.com. What is happier.com? Well, for anyone interested in proactively working on their personal happiness, it's everything you could ever need and more! Read this summary of the site:

> happier.com is a new website launching today designed to help people not just be happier but "do happier." This innovative website provides online

What sort of connection with the audience is the writer trying to establish here?

Writer offering to serve as a model for readers to follow. How effective is this rhetorical tactic? How might a reader respond?

5

Writer transitioning from "personal happiness" to the benefits of the website.

10

15   tools and exercises for users to make an immediate
      positive impact on their lives. The website allows
      users to participate for free by taking 4 validated tests
      with instant feedback on strengths, optimism, happi-
      ness, and positivity. More than 100 exclusive videos
20   from the world's leading happiness researchers and   *Shift to discussion about*
      practitioners are also included in this section of the   *financial cost designed to make*
      site. Premium users can subscribe for just $5 a month   *the program more appealing to*
      for access to more than a dozen research-backed   *potential customers. What kind*
      tools customized to increase happiness, resilience,   *of reader would find this*
25   optimism, engagement, and meaning.   *rhetorical move most effective?*

        This site is *legit*. Why? Because happier.com was   *Another rhetorical strategy*
      created by Doug Hensch and Andrew Rosenthal to in-   *designed to enhance the*
      spire happiness in others, and the foundation of the   *website's appeal.*
      site is positive psychology. To develop the site, Hensch   *The writer makes a special*
30   and Rosenthal had the privilege of working with   *point here of highlighting the*
      Dr. Martin Seligman—also known as the "father of   *professional credentials of the*
      positive psychology." When I first started reading up   *program's founders. How*
      on positive psychology (and I'm still learning more   *might the inclusion of this*
      about it every day), I quickly found out that Seligman   *information enhance a reader's*
35   was the go-to guy and the fact that he's assisted with   *confidence in this program?*
      this site is a pretty sure sign that you'll find just what *Writer returning to the rhetorical*
      you need to help create a happier you.   *strategy of the beginning: posing*
        Now, I know what you're probably thinking: "Can't I   *rhetorical questions which are*
      do all of this stuff on my own? Can't I just do research   *then answered. This strategy*
40   and create documents and read books?" Sure, of   *would likely be most effective*
      course you can . . . but will you? If you're like me, it   *with readers who may still feel*
      helps to have a place to organize everything and, if   *undecided about this kind of*
      your happiness is something that's really important to   *self-help program.*
      you (I know it is to me!), this is well worth the few   *Writer working, again, to*
45   bucks you have to shell out to keep it all together. And   *establish that sense of*
      you get access to all of this great stuff that you won't   *connection and identification*
      find anywhere else. How do I know all about it even   *with the readers.*
      though it's just officially launched? I had the wonder-   *Writer appealing to an*
      ful privilege of trying it out for awhile before it was   *audience's sense of feeling*
50   officially released and I can't say enough good things about *special. What kind of reader*
      it. Access to experts, tools, videos, and a whole commu-   *would respond positively?*
      nity of people who, like you, are interested in learning   *Writer concluding here with*
      more about happiness. What could be better than that?   *final question. How does the*
                                                                  writer hope readers will
                                                                  answer it?

Source: Dani DiPirro, from "Get Happier (.com)!" PositivelyPresent.com, September 23,
2009. http://www.positivelypresent.com/2009/09/gethappierdotcom.html

Step One: *Identifying the Audience: How Would You Define the Target Reader?*

○ The ideal or intended reader is:

> › Someone who shares a desire to become "happier" and who believes in the potential for self-help programs to achieve this goal.

> › Someone who is not happy enough as is and is looking for outside assistance to become happier.

> › Someone who believes in the potential of self-help programs to improve one's life search of guidance and life advice and is comfortable with the world of self-help.

> › Someone without a formal background or expertise in psychology but with a healthy respect for scientific credentials.

○ This reader would be drawn to a text like this because:

> › The text guarantees that its program will lead to greater happiness.

> › The text outlines a simple, clear, step-by-step formula to follow.

> › The text references well-known experts to bolster its claims.

○ The reader *least* likely to respond well to this text is:

> › Someone who already feels happy or contented with life.

> › Someone who is skeptical of self-help programs.

> › Someone who is wary of being asked for money online.

Step Two: *Addressing the Audience: How Does This Writer Speak to the Audience?*

○ The key ideas or messages are:

> › That personal happiness is attainable for everyone.

> › That everyone is capable of becoming happier than they currently are.

> › That attaining personal happiness requires the assistance of credentialed experts.

○ The writer adopts a tone:

> › That creates a confidential, intimate connection with the reader.

> › That reassures the reader the cost of this program is reasonable.

> › That invokes the authority of scientific expertise.

Step Three: *Influencing the Audience: What Are the Writer's Larger Goals?*

- ○ The writer's goals are:

  - › To get readers to buy the self-help program being sold.

  - › To cultivate within readers a belief in the advice and guidance of credentialed experts.

  - › To serve as a role model for readers to follow.

- ○ The writer's central argument or main point is:

  - › That personal happiness is just around the corner.

  - › That personal happiness is attainable if one is willing to work on it as a project.

  - › That the path to personal happiness requires a modest investment of time and money.

- ○ The writer tries to achieve this by:

  - › Serving as a role model.

  - › Posing a series of rhetorical questions, which are then answered.

  - › Defining the psychologist referenced as the "father of positive psychology" and the "go-to guy."

Step Four: *Reflecting on the Audience: What Type of Reader Would Best Respond to These Goals?*

- ○ The most effective strategies the writer employs include:

  - › The intimate, confiding tone designed to establish a bond of trust between writer and audience.

  - › The rhetorical questions, which the writer both asks and answers and which thereby enhance the impression of the writer's knowledge and competence.

  - › The specific information and details about the psychological experts.

- ○ The audience most likely to respond to these strategies is:

  - › A reader actively searching for ways to become more "happy."

  - › A reader predisposed to believe that happiness can be found through the advice of "experts."

Step Five: *What Kind of Audience Am I?*

   ° I am an ideal reader for this text because:

      › I share the writer's belief that it's always possible for people to become happier.

      › I have thought about ways to improve my own personal happiness.

   ° I am *not* an ideal reader for this text because:

      › I am sometimes skeptical of information I encounter online.

      › I believe in the importance of "personal happiness" but wonder whether a program can help me achieve this goal.

      › I have taken psychology classes in college and would like to know more about the work of the experts cited here.

Step Six: *How Do I Put All of This Into Writing?*

   ° Here's how I would summarize my evaluation of this text:

> The overall goal is to encourage readers to accept and adopt the happiness guidelines outlined by the writer. Directed toward an audience already predisposed toward the benefits of self-help, the writer offers to serve as a role model for how one can "achieve happiness." The use of an intimate, familiar tone along with descriptions of the founders' expertise combine to create the impression that this writer is genuinely interested in enhancing the happiness of the audience.

Now, it's your turn. For each of the selections below, use these same six steps outlined above to undertake your own analysis of audience.

Girlshealth.gov, "Why Fitness Matters"

Girlshealth.gov is a government website dedicated to providing young women information and advice about maintaining a healthy lifestyle.

Exercise is an important part of a lifetime of good health! Exercising is also fun and is something you can do with friends. Regular exercise provides both mental and physical health benefits.

What is Physical Fitness?
A condition or state of being that helps you look, feel and do your best. It is the ability to do tasks full of energy, and still be able to do other things with your time, such as schoolwork and activities with family and friends. It is a basis for good health and well-being. Fitness involves performance of the heart and lungs, and the muscles of the body. Fitness can also influence how alert you are and how you feel emotionally.

     5

Mental health benefits of exercise

One of the great things about exercise is that it can improve your mental health. Regular exercise can help you feel less stressed, can improve your self-esteem, and can help you to feel ready to learn in school. Kids who exercise may also have reduced symptoms of anxiety and depression.

Exercise can also improve your overall mood. Did you have an argument with a friend? Or did you do poorly on a test? A workout at the gym or a brisk 30-minute walk will make your brain produce chemicals that will make you happier and more relaxed than before you started working out.

What if you're having trouble sleeping? Again, it's exercise to the rescue! Regular exercise can help you fall asleep faster and help you sleep deeper. A good night's sleep can improve your concentration and productivity in school the next day.

Physical health benefits of exercise

Another great thing about exercise is that it can keep your body healthy. Kids who exercise often have a healthier body weight than kids who don't exercise. Exercise makes your bones solid, improves your heart and lungs, and makes your muscles strong.

Exercise can also affect specific diseases that affect adolescents and teens. New research shows that teens who exercise regularly (about 60 minutes of brisk exercise each day) burn more calories and use blood sugar more efficiently than teens who don't exercise. This could protect you from developing type 2 diabetes. Why should this concern you? Well, in recent years, a lot of health problems that doctors saw only in adults are now seen in young people. For example, 15 years ago type 2 diabetes was rare among adolescents, but now it accounts for almost 50 percent of new cases of diabetes in young people. In fact, type 2 diabetes used to be called 'adult-onset diabetes,' but the name was changed because so many young people were developing the disease.

Here is something else to consider: children and adolescents who are overweight are more likely to become adults who are overweight. If you start good habits (like daily exercise) when you are young, you will be likely to continue them when you're older.

New research shows that exercise during the teen years (beginning at age 12) can help protect girls from breast cancer when they are older. Also, regular physical activity can help prevent colon cancer later in your life.

Get moving!

The more time you spend in front of the television or playing video games, the less time you have to be active. Not being active is called sedentary (say: sed-un-tair-ee). Leading a sedentary lifestyle can cause weight gain and even obesity (dangerously high weight), which can lead to type 2 diabetes, high cholesterol levels, and high blood pressure. These three health issues can hurt your heart and make it easier for you to get certain diseases. Make physical activity a regular part of your life. It can help you protect your health! Obesity can also hurt your self-esteem, too.

Source: http://www.girlshealth.gov/fitness/whygetfit

Visual Rhetoric: Justin Bilicki, "We Are Destroying the Earth"

This political cartoon by Justin Bilicki was published in 2012.

FIGURE 6.4

Source: Union of Concerned Scientists/Justin Bilicki
http://www.dailydawdle.com/search/label/political%20cartoon

Peter Hakim and Cameron Combs, "Why the US Should Legalize Marijuana"

While public attitudes regarding marijuana use have undergone significant change over the last several years, federal policy regarding such use has yet to reflect this. Addressing this gap, the essay below, first posted to the Miami Herald *website in 2014, makes the case for legalization.*

Tiny Uruguay made waves a month ago by becoming the first nation anywhere to fully legalize the sale and use of recreational marijuana. Colorado and Washington, however, had already beaten them to the punch, and a handful of other states are expected soon to follow suit.

In addition, 18 states and the District of Columbia permit marijuana for medical   5
purposes. A proposal to legalize medical marijuana could appear on Florida's ballot in November.

What this all means is that the United States is without a national policy toward marijuana. Although legally banned throughout the country by federal law, cannabis use is, in practice, governed by an incoherent patchwork of state regulations, and   10
further muddled by staggering disparities in enforcement and punishment.

Legalizing cannabis, a step most Americans now favor, is the only way out of this jumble, particularly after President Obama made clear that he would not enforce a federal ban on marijuana use in those states where it was now lawful. "We have other fish to fry," he said. In another interview, he said marijuana is no more harmful than alcohol.

Legalization should also contribute to easier relations with Mexico and other neighbors to the south on issues of public security.

To be sure, legal marijuana comes with costs and risks. The American Medical Association considers cannabis a "dangerous drug," while the American Psychiatric Association asserts that its use impedes neurological development in adolescents and can cause the "onset of psychiatric disorders."

Some studies suggest it interferes with learning and motivation. It should be anticipated that legalization will lead to greater use, at all ages, as marijuana becomes more accessible and less expensive, and the cultural and social stigmas surrounding its consumption literally go up in smoke. Abuse and addiction—including among juveniles—will rise as well.

But keeping marijuana illegal also carries a high price tag. Particularly devastating are the human costs of arresting and jailing thousands upon thousands of young Americans each year. Roughly one-third of all U.S. citizens are arrested by age 23. Racial and ethnic minorities are most vulnerable. African-American marijuana users are over three times more likely to be arrested and imprisoned than whites, even though the two groups consume the drug at virtually the same levels.

With cannabis accounting for roughly half of total drug arrests, legalization would sharply reduce this egregious disparity. It would also save money by reducing the U.S. prison population. A half a million people were incarcerated for drug offenses in 2011, a ten-fold jump since 1980—at an average annual cost per prisoner of more than $20,000 in a minimum-security federal facility.

Cannabis legalization would also help to lift an unneeded burden from U.S. foreign policy in Latin America, where Washington's drug war has long strained diplomatic relations.

Most governments in the hemisphere have concluded that U.S. anti-drug policies are just not working and, in many places, are actually contributing to mounting levels of crime, violence and corruption. Colombia has been a notable exception. With U.S. support of nearly $10 billion, the country has become far more secure in the past dozen years.

Yet Juan Manuel Santos, Colombia's president and arguably Washington's closest ally in the region, is now a leading advocate of alternative drug strategies. In an exhaustive report last year, prompted by President Santos, the Organization of American States analyzed a range of alternative policy approaches, including cannabis legalization.

Few Latin American countries are actively contemplating legalization *a la uruguaya*. But many have stopped arrests for use and possession of marijuana, and virtually all are keeping a close watch on developments in Uruguay. Nowhere is

there much enthusiasm for cooperating with the United States in its continuing ef-   55
forts to eradicate drug crops and interrupt drug flows.

A decision by the U.S. government to legalize marijuana would be a bold step
toward breaking today's bureaucratic and political inertia and opening the way for
a genuine hemisphere-wide search for alternative strategies.

Cannabis legalization will not be a cure-all. It will not solve other critical drug   60
abuse problems or change the security question dramatically—and as noted, it
comes with substantial risks. It would not be an attractive option if there were other
ways to address the twin tragedies of mass imprisonment of young Americans and
Washington's ineffective and widely unpopular anti-drug programs overseas. But
nothing else is visible on the horizon.   65

Source: Miami Herald, *January 26, 2014*
http://www.miamiherald.com/2014/01/26/3891371/why-the-us-should-legalize-
marijuana.html

CNN.com, "Kate and William Bring Home Royal Baby Boy"

CNN.com is the online arm of the Cable News Network.

They looked like "a normal couple" as they left the hospital, one bystander said.

Of course, most normal couples don't have a crowd of reporters, photographers and
random well-wishers waiting for them to show off their new baby.

Prince William and Catherine, the Duchess of Cambridge, emerged from St. Mary's
Hospital in London on Tuesday evening to give the public its first view of the new heir   5
to the British throne, joking that the still-unnamed boy had more hair than his father.
Catherine and William took turns holding the child, wrapped in a cream-colored blanket,
as they waved to well-wishers outside.

The couple is "still working on a name," William said, "so we'll have that as soon as we
can." But he added, "He's got her looks, thankfully."   10

The prince has already changed his first diaper, the couple told reporters.

"It's very emotional. It's such a special time," Catherine said.

The couple left the hospital Tuesday evening, with William carrying the boy out in a car
seat and installing him in the back of a black SUV. Then he got behind the wheel for the trip
to their residence at Kensington Palace.   15

On their way out, they walked out down the same steps where Diana, Princess of Wales,
and Prince Charles gave the world its first look at Prince William 31 years ago.

"It was so exciting. It was fantastic," said Eliza Wells, one of those gathered outside the
hospital. "The crowd erupted, because everyone's been waiting so long for it."

William and Catherine "both seemed very relaxed, even with the press there and the   20
crowd," Wells said. "They just seemed like a normal couple."

Shortly before the departure, Charles stopped by for a brief visit with his first grand-
child, accompanied by his wife, Camilla, the Duchess of Cornwall. He told reporters it was
"marvelous."

25 And Catherine's parents, Carole and Michael Middleton, visited earlier, with Carole Middleton telling reporters the royal baby is "absolutely beautiful."

She said both mother and baby are doing "really well" and that she and her husband were "so thrilled" at being grandparents.

Bells, Gun Salutes

30 The 8-pound, 6-ounce boy was born Monday afternoon. He's third in line, behind Charles and William, for the British throne now held by his great-grandmother, Queen Elizabeth II.

Tuesday, London echoed with the sound of cannonades and music to mark the birth.

Guardsmen at Buckingham Palace, the queen's residence, played the Cliff Richard song "Congratulations" at the Changing of the Guard. The military ceremony, much beloved by 35 tourists, involves a new guard exchanging duty with the old guard in the palace forecourt.

The King's Troop Royal Horse Artillery in Green Park fired 41 shots in tribute to the boy, while the Honorable Artillery Company at the Tower of London fired 62 rounds.

At the same time the bells of Westminster Abbey, where William and Catherine were married in April 2011, began to peal, in keeping with royal tradition, and were set to con-40 tinue for more than three hours.

The news of the boy's birth, announced about four hours after the event Monday, prompted cheers and celebration among the crowds of well-wishers outside Buckingham Palace. At least one group of well-wishers brought flowers, champagne and a card for the Duke and Duchess of Cambridge.

45 Social media networks were also abuzz with the news, which made headlines around the world.

"We Could Not Be Happier"

The new parents spent some time with their baby before calling family members—starting with the queen—to announce the birth, a Kensington Palace source told CNN royal corre-50 spondent Max Foster.

"We could not be happier," said Prince William, according to the Kensington Palace source.

Prince William remained at Catherine's side throughout the labor, and the baby was born naturally. An official bulletin was placed on a gilded easel outside Buckingham Palace.

55 The celebrations for the arrival of the new prince—whose title will be His Royal Highness Prince (the baby's name) of Cambridge—were hard to miss in the capital.

The fountains at Trafalgar Square were dyed blue; the BT Tower, a London landmark, flashed the words "It's a boy"; and the London Eye was illuminated in patriotic red, white and blue.

60 Farther afield, Canada—where the British monarch is head of state—turned its side of the Niagara Falls blue to mark the birth, and the CN Tower in Toronto was lit up the same color.

Betting on a Name

It was a long wait for the media camped outside St. Mary's Hospital, but when the news of 65 the birth finally came, the excitement of the moment was huge.

The Sun newspaper, Britain's best-selling tabloid daily, changed its masthead Tuesday to "The Son" to mark the occasion, above a picture of the official birth announcement, while the Daily Express and Telegraph emblazoned "It's a boy" across their front pages.

Recognizing that excitement over the prince's arrival is not universal, the Guardian newspaper's website lets users switch to a royal baby-free version of the home page. The front page of UK satirical magazine Private Eye simply says: "Woman has baby." 70

Many bets are being placed as the wait continues for the baby's name to be announced. British bookmakers Ladbrokes have James as favorite, followed by Henry and George, Philip, Alexander and Richard.

William's name was announced a few days after birth; his brother Harry's on departure from hospital. 75

Some British parents have delayed naming their newborns in recent days in hopes of either copying or avoiding the royal name, he said.

Royal Joy

The official British Monarchy Twitter feed said: "The Queen and Prince Philip are delighted at the news of the birth of The Duke and Duchess of Cambridge's baby." 80

Charles Spencer, brother of the late Diana, Princess of Wales, welcomed the birth of the baby. "We're all so pleased: it's wonderful news," he said in a statement.

"My father always told us how Diana was born on just such a blisteringly hot day, at Sandringham, in July 1961. It's another very happy summer's day, half a century on." 85

British Prime Minister David Cameron said, "It is an important moment in the life of our nation, but I suppose above all, it's a wonderful moment for a warm and loving couple who got a brand new baby boy."

Tributes Around the World

The British monarch is also head of state in 15 Commonwealth countries, including Australia, Canada, New Zealand, Belize and Jamaica. 90

Canadian Prime Minister Stephen Harper offered his country's congratulations on the birth of a future king.

"The arrival of the newest member of the Royal Family, a future Sovereign of Canada, is a highly anticipated moment for Canadians given the special and warm relationship that we share with our Royal Family," he said in a statement. 95

Barack and Michelle Obama also gave their best wishes.

"The child enters the world at a time of promise and opportunity for our two nations," the U.S. president and first lady said in a statement. "Given the special relationship between us, the American people are pleased to join with the people of the United Kingdom as they celebrate the birth of the young prince." 100

Russia's President Vladimir Putin and Japan's Prime Minister Shinzo Abe also sent their congratulations.

On Twitter, topics related to the royal baby jumped to the top of the trending list in the United Kingdom on Monday morning. Worldwide, hashtags such as #RoyalBabyBoy and #Will&Kate were trending later Monday. 105

In a nod to modern times, Clarence House called for people to send news and images of any other new arrivals using the hashtag #WelcometotheWorld.

Source: CNN.com, July 23, 2013. © 2013 Cable News Network, Inc.
http://www.cnn.com/2013/07/23/world/europe/uk-royal-baby/index.html

---

Thinking Rhetorically About Audience: Expanded Outline

Now that you've gotten some practice with this kind of analysis, use the expanded outline below to work your way through one of the selections included above. What target audience does this text address? How does this choice of audience relate to the other rhetorical choices the writer makes?

Step One: *Identifying the Audience: How Does This Text Define Its Target Reader?*

o Based on your reading of this text, what type of person would you say is the ideal audience? What type of reader do you think would be most drawn to the information, messages and/or arguments it presents? Sketch as detailed a description of this hypothetical reader as you can. What is this reader looking for from this text? What are the reader's key interests or needs?

o Based on the above profile, explain *why* you think such a reader would be drawn to this particular text. Which features or aspects, in your view, would this reader find most appealing?

o Who would you say is the type of reader *least* likely to be drawn to this text? What aspects or features would this reader find least appealing? Why?

Step Two: *Addressing the Audience: How Does This Text Speak to Its Audience?*

o What specific topics, issues or questions does this text raise? What are the key ideas or messages being conveyed?

o How would you characterize the overall tone? What words or phrases stand out as especially important?

Step Three: *Influencing the Audience: What Are the Writer's Larger Goals?*

o Overall, what goal would you say this text has for its intended audience? What reaction does it try to elicit?

o What larger point is the writer trying to get across? What argument is the writer trying to make?

o What features of this text seem designed to help achieve this goal? Which aspects of this text do you think its target audience would find most appealing? Why?

Step Four: *Reflecting on the Audience: What Type of Reader Would Best Respond to These Goals?*

º Which elements of the text have the greatest effect on the target audience?

º Which elements have the least effect?

Step Five: *What Kind of Audience Am I?*

º Compare the goals this writer seems to have for the audience against your experience reading this text. Based on your own impressions and reactions, would you characterize yourself as an ideal reader of this text? Why, or why not?

Step Six: *How Do I Put All of This Into Writing?*

º How do you summarize the key findings in your analysis?

º How do you explain and justify your overall assessment of audience?

Formal Writing Selections

Audience is not only a key rhetorical element within the writing process, it is also a compelling social issue in its own right. Indeed, to focus upon audience is to begin taking stock of one of the most representative experiences in modern life: being cast into the role of watcher or spectator. From reality television shows to political campaigns, YouTube videos to Twitter feeds, our world is full of opportunities to act as an audience.

Because the experience of watching (and being watched) has come to feel so familiar, however, we don't always stop to consider what is significant about it. When we do, it becomes clear that this experience touches upon some of the most important questions of our day: how we define friendship, what boundaries we place around personal privacy, and how to find common ground within our political dialogue.

The essays below provide you with an opportunity to reflect upon some of the larger questions (social, intellectual, and ethical) that focusing on the role of audience raises. At the same time, these selections also provide an opportunity to continue the work of analyzing audience in rhetorical terms. Like the informal selections gathered above, the collection of formal readings here includes questions that ask you to think about how audience is being defined and addressed and how these choices in turn help shape the language, goals, and organization of the writing at hand.

Michael Solis, "Social Media: Obstacle to Friendship/Love"

The explosive popularity of social networking sites like Facebook raises important questions about the changing ways we approach the question of friendship. Have these new communication technologies fundamentally altered the way we think about, talk to. and define our "friends?" Answering

this question with a resounding "No," Michael Solis offers a critique of social
media and the new social norms to which these technologies have given rise.

"I know I've been defriended on Facebook for going too long without
replying to messages or for not writing 'happy bday' on walls."

When I was little, I remember my mom getting a message on her answering machine
from one of our neighbors, Mrs. Hartman (whom my brothers and I lovingly called
Mrs. Fartman). It turned out that Mrs. Fartman wasn't happy with my mother, who
hadn't responded to her last two messages.

5   "Fine—I get it, Leah!" Mrs. Fartman said, her voice a Roseanne-like shriek. "If
you don't want to talk to me anymore, then so be it!"

    Click. End of friendship.

    When I asked my mom (who was in the process of raising three devil children,
myself included) if she cared about losing one of her friends, she offered a tired

10 sigh and said, "Not really. I'm busy and didn't have time to call her back. If she can't
understand that, then what am I supposed to do? Maybe that's just something she
has to work out herself."

    Twenty years later, a lot has changed. Facebook is putting everyone's face online
multiple times over, distracting us from the pleasures of books. Tiny tweets zap

15 back and forth across the world at a rate that's impossible for anyone to keep up
with, unless you're Anne Marie-Slaughter. We have separate online profiles for
work and dating that we use when we're at work and sometimes even while on a
date, if it's that bad. Household answering machines are pretty much obsolete
when mobile phones put us in constant contact with one other on a 24/7 basis.

20   And to top it all off, there are a whole lot more Mrs. Fartmans out there than
there ever were before.

    I'm reminded of Mrs. Fartman each time someone tells me, "You didn't answer
my call," or "You didn't respond to my Facebook message," or "You didn't retweet
my tweet," or "You said you were gonna be on Skype," or "Didn't you read my

25 blog?" There's too much going on at once, and I can't keep it all focused. And
that's not like me—I used to be very focused. Extremely focused. So focused that
I had a teacher in elementary school who used to call me Mr. Focused. But now my
diligence has nothing to show for itself in this new digital age where communication is constant and feelings are so easily wounded.

30   I've tried to be honest with others about my online communication style, but
people in the virtual sphere don't respond well to the truth. You either have to stop
talking to them all together as if they don't exist, or you have to make something
up that's absolutely ridiculous just to satisfy them. Take, for instance, a recent
Facebook conversation I had with an acquaintance.

35   Facebook friend: "Where have you been? I tried calling you, but you didn't
answer."

    Me: "Sorry. I wasn't in the mood."

    Facebook friend: "Why not?"

Me: "I needed me time."

Facebook friend: "☺"   40

End of conversation. End of (Facebook) friendship.

What I should have said was something like, "I can't, I'm choking on a piece of rotten cheese" or "No-can-do, my parakeet has just had a heart attack and died," (the latter being a double lie, since I never had a parakeet to begin with). Instead, I took the "higher road" of honesty, but where did that get me?   45

Friendships aren't the only relationships affected negatively by social media. I recently went on a date with a partner of several months who started quizzing me—not about history or politics, but about his blog. The conversation ended with me admitting that I had never in fact read his blog. Said revelation caused his face to redden and his jaw to collapse—the same expression he might have gotten   50 had I punched him in the nose or flicked his grandmother's ear. Needless to say, the relationship came to a swift end.

Then there's the whole liking phenomenon. When people like something of mine on Facebook, I find it nice. Or I used to find it nice, until I discovered that there was an unspoken rule that if someone likes something of yours, you're sup-   55 posed to like something back of theirs, even if you don't like anything of theirs at all. It's like someone coming to your home and telling you that you have nice cur- tains. They can't just expect you to go to their home right away and tell them that they have nice curtains too, especially not when their curtains are ugly. Ugly cur- tains do not merit compliments, people!   60

I know people have stopped following me on Twitter because I haven't followed them back. People on LinkedIn have severed the virtual chains that once bound us because I haven't endorsed the professional qualifications they already say they have. And I know I've been defriended on Facebook for going too long without replying to messages or for not writing "happy bday" on walls. I get it. Really I do.   65

But I don't. Really. #notintheleastbit.

In the NGO [nongovernmental organization] world, we're taught to communi- cate with online donors as if we're having a real life conversation. If they say some- thing to you, you have to respond in kind. In a normal conversation, you can't just stand there, silent, when someone is speaking directly to you. If you do that,   70 people might think you've gone bonkers. Apparently, that holds true in the virtual sphere as well.

But I'm here to insist that it doesn't! Virtual conversations don't operate the same way as actual conversations. Sometimes they're faster, and sometimes they're slower. In one-on-one conversations, our attention is supposed to be undi-   75 vided, while online our choices are infinite. You might say hello to me, but instead of saying hello back I could be writing a dissertation, buying an ant farm, planting a garden made of virtual strawberries, teaching myself pilates, observing my hair's evolution over a decade of photos, or watching a video of a cat dancing to the Macarena. The fact that I don't say hello doesn't mean I don't want to. It just means   80 I'm distracted. "Busy," my mom might say, without the time to write back.

Sigh. I doubt that any of the Mrs. Fartmans out there will ever understand my grievances, but if they can't, what am I supposed to do? Maybe that's just something they have to work out themselves.

Source: The Huffington Post, August 26, 2013

http://www.huffingtonpost.com/michael-solis/social-media-obstacle-to-_b_3815356.html

Discussion/Writing Prompts

1. Solis makes a number of assumptions about the audience he is addressing, foremost among them that his readers are personally familiar with how social networking sites like Twitter and Facebook work. In your view, is this a valid assumption to make? Do you think the subsequent argument he makes about social media works best for an audience already acquainted with online technologies? If so, how? And how might this argument need to be amended if it were addressed to an audience with little or no experience online? [Rhetorical Analysis of Audience]

2. Surveying our media landscape, Solis writes:

   Facebook is putting everyone's face online multiple times over, distracting us from the pleasures of books. Tiny tweets zap back and forth across the world at a rate that's impossible for anyone to keep up with . . .

   How do you respond to this portrait? Do you agree that social media have created routines that lead us to become more and more "distracted"? Can you think of an example from your own experience that either confirms or challenges this characterization? [Personal Reflection]

3. Solis begins his essay by recalling a story about his mother receiving a message on her answering machine. Why do you think he opens by telling the story of an obsolete technology? What impression of new technologies like Twitter and Facebook does this kind of opening encourage readers to form? Given the larger argument Solis is making, do you think this is an effective way to establish audience expectations? Why, or why not? [Close Reading]

4. Solis uses the story of "Mrs. Fartman" to organize much of his overall argument here. How do you evaluate this rhetorical strategy? What does he gain by presenting his larger point about social media, friendship, and the like through this kind of narrative? Can you think of an alternative mode that might be more effective? [Analyzing Rhetorical Modes]

5. In many ways, Solis' thesis comes down to a basic observation: "Virtual conversations don't operate the same way as actual conversations." Do you agree? Are there fundamental differences between "virtual" and "actual" conversations? In a one-page essay, create an argument in which you either critique or defend the effect of "virtualization" on our personal interactions. In your view, is it valid to critique sites like Twitter and Facebook for the ways they differ from face-to-face contact? Why, or why not? [Argument]

6. Social media offer us extremely useful tools for staying in almost perpetual contact with each other. How do you think Christopher Calabrese and Matthew Harwood ("Destroying the Right to Be Left Alone") would respond to this possibility? Given their own argument about the dangers of surveillance, do you think these authors would share Solis' misgivings? Why, or why not? [Compare and Contrast]

7. Choose an example of a social media tool you think undermines or diminishes the quality of our personal interactions. First, describe this tool. Next, analyze the specific audience this tool is typically designed to reach. And finally, compare the effect this tool has on this audience to the conclusions Solis draws in his essay. Does your example support Solis' thesis? How, or how not? [Research]

Christopher Calabrese and Matthew Harwood, "Destroying the Right to Be Left Alone"

From security cameras to iPhone pictures, we have grown quite accustomed to the experience of being watched. In this day and age, many of us simply take it as a given that our day-to-day activities will be captured and put on display for one audience or another. But is this situation really normal? What are the consequences of living in a world where what we do and what we say automatically become public? What effect does such perpetual audienceship have on our right to privacy? Taking up precisely these questions, Christopher Calabrese and Matthew Harwood take a closer look at our emerging surveillance culture, exploring what happens when we find ourselves unable "to be left alone." Christopher Calabrese is a legislative counsel for privacy-related issues for the ACLU in Washington, DC. Matthew Harwood works for the ACLU in Washington, DC, as a media strategist.

> "Increasingly, the relationship between Americans and their government has come to resemble a one-way mirror dividing an interrogation room."

For at least the last six years, government agents have been exploiting an AT&T database filled with the records of billions of American phone calls from as far back as 1987. The rationale behind this dragnet intrusion, codenamed Hemisphere, is to find suspicious links between people with "burner" phones (prepaid mobile phones easy to buy, use, and quickly dispose of), which are popular with drug dealers. The 5 secret information gleaned from this relationship with the telecommunications giant has been used to convict Americans of various crimes, all without the defendants or the courts having any idea how the feds stumbled upon them in the first place. The program is so secret, so powerful, and so alarming that agents "are instructed to never refer to Hemisphere in any official document," according to a recently re- 10 leased government PowerPoint slide.

You're probably assuming that we're talking about another blanket National Security Agency (NSA) surveillance program focused on the communications of

innocent Americans, as revealed by the whistleblower Edward Snowden. We could
15 be, but we're not. We're talking about a program of the Drug Enforcement
Administration (DEA), a domestic law enforcement agency.

While in these last months the NSA has cast a long, dark shadow over American
privacy, don't for a second imagine that it's the only government agency system-
atically and often secretly intruding on our lives. In fact, a remarkable traffic jam of
20 local, state, and federal government authorities turn out to be exploiting technology to wriggle into the most intimate crevices of our lives, take notes, use them for
their own purposes, or simply file them away for years on end.

"Technology in this world is moving faster than government or law can keep up,"
the CIA's Chief Technology Officer Gus Hunt told a tech conference in March. "It's
25 moving faster I would argue than you can keep up: You should be asking the question of what are your rights and who owns your data."

Hunt's right. The American public and the legal system have been left in the dust
when it comes to infringements and intrusions on privacy. In one way, however, he
was undoubtedly being coy. After all, the government is an active, eager, and early
30 adopter of intrusive technologies that make citizens' lives transparent on demand.

Increasingly, the relationship between Americans and their government has
come to resemble a one-way mirror dividing an interrogation room. Its operatives
and agents can see us whenever they want, while we can never quite be sure if
there's someone on the other side of the glass watching and recording what we
35 say or what we do—and many within local, state, and federal government want to
ensure that no one ever flicks on the light on their side of the glass.

So here's a beginner's guide to some of what's happening on the other side of
that mirror.

You Won't Need a Warrant for That

Have no doubt: the Fourth Amendment is fast becoming an artifact of a paper-
40 based world.

The core idea behind that amendment, which prohibits the government from
"unreasonable searches and seizures," is that its representatives only get to invade
people's private space—their "persons, houses, papers, and effects"—after it
convinces a judge that they're up to no good. The technological advances of the last
45 few decades have, however, seriously undermined this core constitutional protection against overzealous government agents, because more and more people don't
store their private information in their homes or offices, but on company servers.

Consider email.

In a series of rulings from the 1970s, the Supreme Court created "the third-party
50 doctrine." Simply stated, information shared with third parties like banks and doctors no longer enjoys protection under the Fourth Amendment. After all, the court
reasoned, if you shared that information with someone else, you must not have
meant to keep it private, right? But online almost everything is shared with third
parties, particularly your private email.

Back in 1986, Congress recognized that this was going to be a problem. In re- 55
sponse, it passed the Electronic Communications Privacy Act (ECPA). That law was
forward-looking for its day, protecting the privacy of electronic communications
transmitted by computer. Unfortunately, it hasn't aged well.

Nearly three decades ago, Congress couldn't decide if email was more like a
letter or a phone call (that is, permanent or transitory), so it split the baby and 60
decreed that communications which remain on a third party's server—think
Google—for longer than 180 days are considered abandoned and lose any
expectation of privacy. After six months are up, all the police have to do is issue
an administrative subpoena—a legal request a judge never sees—demanding
the emails it wants from the service provider, because under ECPA they're 65
considered junk.

This made some sense back when people downloaded important emails to their
home or office computers and deleted the rest since storage was expensive. If, at
the time, the police had wanted to look at someone's email, a judge would have
had to give them the okay to search the computer where the emails were stored. 70

Email doesn't work like that anymore. People's emails containing their most personal information now reside on company computers forever or, in geek speak, "in
the cloud." As a result, the ECPA has become a dangerous anachronism. For
instance, Google's email service, Gmail, is nearly a decade old. Under that law,
without a judge's stamp of approval or the user ever knowing, the government can 75
now demand from Google access to years of a Gmail user's correspondence, containing political rants, love letters, embarrassing personal details, sensitive financial and health records, and more.

And that shouldn't be acceptable now that email has become an intimate repos-
itory of information detailing who we are, what we believe, who we associate with, 80
who we make love to, where we work, and where we pray. That's why common-
sense legislative reforms to the ECPA, such as treating email like a piece of mail,
are so necessary. Then the police would be held to the same standard electroni-
cally as in the paper-based world: prove to a judge that a suspect's email probably
contains evidence of a crime or hands off. 85

Law enforcement, of course, remains opposed to any such changes for a reason
as understandable as it is undemocratic: it makes investigators' jobs easier. There's
no good reason why a letter sitting in a desk and an email stored on Google's
servers don't deserve the same privacy protections, and law enforcement knows
it, which is why fear-mongering is regularly called upon to stall such an easy fix to 90
antiquated privacy laws.

As Department of Justice Associate Deputy Attorney General James Baker put
it in April 2011, "Congress should also recognize that raising the standard for
obtaining information under ECPA may substantially slow criminal and national
security investigations." In other words, ECPA reform would do exactly what the 95
Fourth Amendment intended: prevent police from unnecessarily intruding into
our lives.

Nowhere to Hide

"You are aware of the fact that somebody can know where you are at all times, because you carry a mobile device, even if that mobile device is turned off," the CIA's Hunt explained to the audience at that tech conference. "You know this, I hope? Yes? Well, you should."

You have to hand it to Hunt; his talk wasn't your typical stale government presentation. At times, he sounded like Big Brother with a grin.

And it's true: the smartphone in your pocket is a tracking device that also happens to allow you to make calls, read email, and tweet. Several times every minute, your mobile phone lets your cell-phone provider know where you are, producing a detail-rich history of where you have been for months, if not years, on end. GPS-enabled applications do the same. Unfortunately, there's no way to tell for sure how long the companies hang onto such location data because they won't disclose that information.

We do know, however, that law enforcement regularly feasts on these meaty databases, easily obtaining a person's location history and other subscriber information. All that's needed to allow the police to know someone's whereabouts over an extended period is an officer's word to a judge that the records sought would aid an ongoing investigation. Judges overwhelmingly comply with such police requests, forcing companies to turn over their customers' location data. The reason behind this is a familiar one: law enforcement argues that the public has no reasonable expectation of privacy because location data is freely shared with service or app providers. Customers, the argument goes, have already waived their privacy rights by voluntarily choosing to use their mobile phone or app.

Police also use cell-phone signals and GPS-enabled devices to track people in real time. Not surprisingly, there is relatively little clarity about when police do this, thanks in part to purposeful obfuscation by the government. Since 2007, the Department of Justice has recommended that its U.S. attorneys get a warrant for real-time location tracking using GPS and cell signals transmitted by suspects' phones. But such "recommendations" aren't considered binding, so many U.S. Attorneys simply ignore them.

The Supreme Court has begun to weigh in but the issue is far from settled. In *United States v. Jones*, the justices ruled that, when officers attach a GPS tracking device to a car to monitor a suspect's movements, the police are indeed conducting a "search" under the Fourth Amendment. The court, however, stopped there, deciding not to rule on whether the use of tracking devices was unreasonable without a judge's say so.

In response to that incomplete ruling, the Justice Department drew up two post-*Jones* memos establishing guidelines for its agents and prosecutors regarding location-tracking technology. When the American Civil Liberties Union (ACLU) filed a Freedom of Information Act request for those guidelines, the Justice Department handed over all 111 pages, every one of them redacted—an informational blackout.

The message couldn't be any clearer: the FBI doesn't believe Americans deserve   140
to know when they can and cannot legally be tracked. Supreme Court Justice
Sonia Sotomayor drove home what's at stake in her concurring decision in the
Jones case. "Awareness that the Government may be watching chills associational
and expressive freedoms," she wrote. "And the Government's unrestrained power
to assemble data that reveal private aspects of identity is susceptible to abuse . . .   145
[and] may 'alter the relationship between citizen and government in a way that is
inimical to democratic society.'"

The ability of police to secretly track people with little or no oversight is a power
once only associated with odious police states overseas. Law enforcement agencies in the United States, however, do this regularly and enthusiastically, and they   150
do their best as well to ensure that no barriers will be thrown in their way in the
near future.

Sting(ray) Operations

During one of his last appearances before Congress as FBI director, Robert Mueller
confirmed what many insiders already assumed. Asked by Senator Chuck Grassley
whether the FBI operates drones domestically and for what purpose, Mueller re-   155
sponded, "Yes, and for surveillance." This was a stunning revelation, particularly
since most Americans associate drone use with robotic killing in distant lands.

And, Grassley followed up, had the FBI developed drone guidelines to ensure
that American privacy was protected? The Bureau, Mueller replied, was in the beginning phase of developing them. Senator Dianne Feinstein, hardly a privacy   160
hawk, seemed startled by the answer: "I think the greatest threat to the privacy of
Americans is the drone, and the use of the drone, and the very few regulations that
are on it today," she said.

The senator shouldn't have been shocked. The government's adoption of
new intrusive technologies without bothering to publicly explore their privacy   165
implications—or any safeguards that it might be advisable to put in place first—
isn't an aberration. It's standard practice. As a result, Americans are put in the
position of secretly subsidizing their own surveillance with their tax dollars.

In July, for example, the ACLU published a report on the proliferating use of
automatic license-plate readers by police departments and state agencies across   170
the country. Mounted on patrol cars, bridges, and overpasses, the cameras for
these readers capture the images of every license plate in view and run them
against databases for license plates associated with stolen cars or cars used in a
crime. Theoretically, when there's a hit, police are alerted and someone bad goes
to jail. The problems arise, however, when there's no hit. Most police departments   175
decide to hang onto those license-plate images anyway, creating yet another set
of vast databases of innocent people's location history that's easy to abuse.

Since technology almost always outpaces the law, regulations on license plate
readers are often lax or nonexistent. Rarely do police departments implement
data-retention time limits so that the license plates of perfectly innocent people   180

are purged from their systems. Nor do they set up rules to ensure that only autho-
rized officers can query the database when there's evidence that a particular license plate might be attached to a crime. Often there aren't even rules to prevent
the images from being widely shared with other government agencies or even
185   private companies. These are, in other words, systems which give law enforcement
another secret way to track people without judicial oversight and are ripe for privacy abuse.

As is often the case with security technology—for instance, full-body scanners
at airports—there's little evidence that license plate readers are worthwhile
190   enough as crime fighting tools to compensate for their cost in privacy terms. Take
Maryland. In the first five months of 2012, for every million license plates read in
that state, there were just 2,000 "hits." Of those 2,000, only 47 were potentially
associated with serious crimes. The vast majority were for minor regulatory violations, such as a suspended or revoked vehicle registration.

195   And then there's the Stingray, a device first used in our distant wars and so intrusive that the FBI has tried to keep it secret—even from the courts. A Stingray mimics
a cell-phone tower, tricking all wireless devices in an area to connect to it instead of
the real thing. Police can use it to track suspects in real time, even indoors, as well
as nab the content of their communications. The Stingray is also indiscriminate. By
200   fooling all wireless devices in an area into connecting to it, the government engages in what is obviously an unreasonable search and seizure of the wireless information of every person whose device gets caught up in the "sting."

And when the federal government isn't secretly using dragnet surveillance technologies, it's pushing them down to state and local governments through Depart-
205   ment of Homeland Security (DHS) grants. The ACLU of Northern California has, for
example, reported that DHS grant funds have been used by state and local police
to subsidize or purchase automated license-plate readers, whose images then flow
into federal databases. Similarly, the city of San Diego has used such funds to buy
a facial recognition system and DHS grants have been used to install local video
210   surveillance systems statewide.

In July, Oakland accepted $2 million in federal funds to establish an around-the-
clock "Domain Awareness Center," which will someday integrate existing surveillance cameras and thermal imaging devices at the Port of Oakland with the
Oakland Police Department's surveillance cameras and license plate readers, as
215   well as cameras owned by city public schools, the California Highway Patrol, and
other outfits and institutions. Once completed, the system will leverage more than
1,000 camera feeds across the city.

Sometimes I Feel Like Somebody's Watching Me

What makes high-tech surveillance so pernicious is its silent, magical quality. Historically, when government agents invaded people's privacy they had to resort to the
220   blunt instruments of force and violence, either torturing the body in the belief it could
unlock the mind's secrets or kicking down doors to rifle through a target's personal

effects and communications. The revolution in communications technology has made such intrusions look increasingly sloppy and obsolete. Why break a skull or kick down a door when you can read someone's search terms or web-surfing history?

In the eighteenth century, philosopher Jeremy Bentham conceived of a unique   225
idea for a prison. He called it a "panopticon." It was to be a place where inmates would be constantly exposed to view without ever being able to see their wardens: a total surveillance prison. Today, creating an electronic version of Bentham's panopticon is an increasingly trivial technological task. Given the seductive possibilities now embedded in our world, only strong legal protections would prevent   230
the government from feeling increasingly free to intrude on our lives.

If anything, though, our legal protections are weakening and privacy is being deval-
ued, which means that Americans with a well-developed sense of self-preservation increasingly assume the possibility of surveillance and watch what they do online and elsewhere. Those who continue to value privacy in a big way may do things that   235
seem a little off: put Post-it notes over their computer cameras, watch what they tweet or post on Facebook, or write their emails as if some omnipresent eye is read-
ing over their shoulders. Increasingly, what once would have been considered para-
noid seems prescient—self-defense and commonsense all rolled into one.

It's hard to know just what the cumulative effect will be of a growing feeling that   240
nothing is truly private anymore. Certainly, a transparent life has the potential to rob an individual of the sense of security necessary for experimentation with new ideas and new identities without fear that you are being monitored for deviations from the norm. The inevitable result for many will be self-censorship with all its corrosive effects on the rights of free speech, expression, and association.   245

The Unknown Unknowns

Note that we've only begun a tour through the ways in which American privacy is currently under assault by our own government. Other examples abound. There is E-Verify's proposed giant "right-to-work" list of everyone eligible to work in the United States. There are law enforcement agencies that actively monitor social media sites like Facebook and Twitter. There are the Department of Homeland   250
Security's research and development efforts to create cameras armed with almost omniscient facial recognition technology, not to speak of passports issued with radio frequency identification technology. There are networked surveillance camera feeds that flow into government systems. There is NSA surveillance data that's finding its way into domestic drug investigations, which is then hidden by the DEA from   255
defense lawyers, prosecutors, and the courts to ensure the surveillance data stream continues unchallenged.

And here's the thing: this is only what we know about. As former Defense Secre-
tary Donald Rumsfeld once put it, "there are also unknown unknowns—there are things we do not know we don't know." It would be the height of naïveté to believe   260
that government organizations across this country—from the federal to the munic-
ipal level—aren't engaged in other secret and shocking privacy intrusions that

have yet to be revealed to us. If the last few months have taught us anything, it should be that we are in a world of unknown unknowns.

265   Today, government agencies act as if they deserve the benefit of the doubt as they secretly do things ripped from the pages of science-fiction novels. Once upon a time, that's not how things were to run in a land where people prized their right to be let alone and government of the people, by the people, and for the people was supposed to operate in the open. The government understands this perfectly

270   well: Why else would its law enforcement agents and officers regularly go to re- markable lengths, sometimes at remarkable cost, to conceal their actions from the rest of us and the legal system that is supposed to oversee their acts? Which is why whistleblowers like Edward Snowden are so important: they mount the last line of defense when the powers-that-be get too accustomed to operating in the dark.

275   Without our very own Snowdens working in the county sheriff's departments or big city police departments or behemoth federal bureaucracies, especially with the world of newspapers capsizing, the unknowns are ever more likely to stay un- known, while what little privacy we have left vanishes.

Source: The Huffington Post, September 22, 2013
http://www.huffingtonpost.com/christopher-calabrese/destroying-the-right-to-b_b_
3973526.html

▥ Discussion/Writing Prompts

1. Calabrese and Harwood assume that their readers share their belief that government efforts to watch over us have been carried too far. Do you share this belief? How do your own thoughts about surveillance influence the way you respond to these authors' main point? How do you think an audience with fewer concerns over surveillance might react to this piece? [Rhetorical Analysis of Audience]

2. According to Calabrese and Harwood, it is highly dangerous not to be concerned about the extent of government surveillance. What do you think? Can you think of an experience from your own life when you were reassured by the fact you were under surveillance? What were the circumstances, and what did this experience feel like? [Personal Reflection]

3. "What makes high-tech surveillance so pernicious," write Calabrese and Harwood, "is its silent, magical quality." What do you think the authors mean by this? In what way are the types of surveillance they describe "silent" and "magical"? Why would these particular qualities make such surveillance "pernicious"? [Close Reading]

4. The authors include a good deal of description to support their claims about government surveillance and its threat to privacy. They describe how different surveillance technologies work, and they describe the history behind different government surveillance practices and policies. What do you think is the goal behind this strategy? What are the authors trying to accomplish by including so much description here? Do you find it effective? Why, or why not? [Analyzing Rhetorical Modes]

5. The argument here depends in large measure on the author's claim that privacy (what they call "being left alone") is a fundamental "right." In a one-page essay, make your own argument about how we should view the "right to be left alone." Do you agree that "being left alone" is a "right"? If so, how far should this right extend? If not, what do you think is a more valid way to define such privacy? [Argument]

6. Take a closer look at "Kate and William Bring Home Royal Baby Boy" by Laura Smith-Spark and Matt Smith. Do you see any parallels between the ways CNN.com covers the lives of celebrities and the authors' discussion of surveillance here? In your view, does it make sense to think of websites like these as evidence that we're learning to accept greater and greater invasion of our privacy? [Compare and Contrast]

7. Research the ways in which the issue of government surveillance is currently debated. Choose a source (e.g., journal or website) that takes a clear stand on this debate. Does it argue for or against government surveillance? What reasons does it offer to support this position? What evidence does it cite? Are you convinced? Why, or why not? [Research]

Allison Brennan, "Microtargeting: How Campaigns Know You Better Than You Know Yourself

---

Among the many audience roles we are called upon to play, none is perhaps more vital than that of voter. With voter participation hovering somewhere around 50%, however, this is not a role we all regularly assume. Many believe this situation might change, though, as campaigns become better and better skilled at directing their messages to particular subsets of the general electorate. But does such political microtargeting actually lead to a more motivated and better informed voting public? Allison Brennan offers some preliminary answers, taking a closer look at the tactics and technologies that have remade the modern political campaign.

"[W]hen a political spot pops up while surfing the Web, there's a good chance it's aimed right at you."

Political ads on the airwaves have been so pervasive this year that voters in battleground states probably see them in their sleep. But when a political spot pops up while surfing the Web, there's a good chance it's aimed right at you.

The practice is called microtargeting and like a lot of marketing techniques on the Internet aimed at identifying consumer tastes and behaviors, it is an information-age approach that is helping change how political groups identify and interact with voters. 5

Moreover, microtargeting may give pollsters, campaigns and interest groups a sharper idea of how candidates and issues may fare at the ballot box, raising concerns about personal privacy in a medium where government regulation is minimal.

In fact, "there is none," said Chris Calabrese, legislative counsel for the American Civil 10 Liberties Union.

"Anonymity has been crucial to our political process. It's the reason for the secret ballot, it's the reason the Federalist Papers were anonymous," he said.

Surfing the Web leaves a trail of browser history that allows marketing companies to glean insight into personal interests.

Do you read *The New York Times* or watch Fox News? Do you have children? Do you shop in high-end stores or hunt for bargains on eBay? Do you support the Sierra Club or Club for Growth?

Political strategy firms like Democratic DSPolitical and Republican CampaignGrid are gathering or buying up that data. They then match it to the publicly available voter rolls that were digitized as a part of a new federal law aimed at efforts to help improve voting procedures after the ballot controversies of the 2000 election.

What these firms receive is detailed information about how often a potential voter has cast a ballot in addition to data on what they read, where they shop and other consumer behavior tracked for decades off line.

Jim Walsh of DSPolitical said the company has so far aggregated more than 600 million cookies—or tags on Internet user IP addresses that track movements online—and has worked to match them against lists of some 250 million voters in the United States.

This all is aimed at helping them determine how someone might vote and then reaching them wherever they go online.

It is so efficient and such a natural extension of direct mail that Walsh called the way microtargeting is being used today "inevitable."

In response to privacy advocates, CampaignGrid President Jordan Lieberman and Walsh said they aren't doing anything that hasn't been done before.

"The data has been commercially available data for years—we're not targeting you by who you voted for; we're targeting you if you tend to vote or participate in the democratic process," Lieberman said.

And he said these strategies infringe less on privacy because they don't use names or physical mailing addresses like direct mail.

"The reality is that we are more focused on privacy and we have more privacy protections than direct mail . . . has used for decades," Lieberman said.

This they said is because lists generated from browser histories are stripped of any personal information before they are used to target potential voters. Both companies said they use a third party vendor to remove that data and match the files.

Lieberman wouldn't identify CampaignGrid's vendor, calling it "part of the special sauce."

DSPolitical and CampaignGrid aren't the only ones in the game.

Google, Facebook and other data powerhouses are also in on the action, albeit in a different way.

For instance, Google said it doesn't collect or allow its advertisers to use personally identifiable information, including political information, to reach potential customers or voters. But it does allow marketers, political or otherwise, to target its users based on specific demographic information.

The company launched its Google Political Toolkit and campaign tools via YouTube, offering candidates the chance to "promote your videos using Google AdWords for video to reach exactly the audience you want—by age, gender, location or other criteria." 55

Facebook is also using its vast amount of personal information during the election.

Currently there are more than 110,000 political Facebook pages in the United States and more than 11,000 U.S.-based pages for politicians, according to a Facebook spokesman.

While Facebook doesn't hand over personally identifiable information, it does allow advertisers to seek out subsections of the population based on their preferences on Facebook. 60

ProPublica also reported on how other search engine giants are selling their users' browser history to campaigns.

What companies, who follow a model of self regulation, and campaigns are doing isn't popular with the public.

When asked if they wanted "political advertising tailored to your interests," 86% of 65 Americans surveyed said they did not, according to a study from the University of Pennsylvania's Annenberg School of Communication released last July.

Sixty-four percent said their support for a candidate would decrease if they found out a candidate was microtargeting them differently than their neighbor. The study also found that 20% more respondents reacted more strongly to political targeting than they did to 70 being targeted as a consumer.

"There's a lot to say in favor of campaigns targeting voters in this way, (but) there is a lot to be concerned about," said Eitan Hersh, a political science professor at Yale University who studies the impact of microtargeting on campaigns and the political process.

"People like being targeted in many ways," said Hersh. "Many people like that Amazon 75 knows what kind of books they like. If a campaign knows that you're of this religion and this race and went to college, you're likely to have a different set of values . . . the campaign is likely to reach out to you on those attributes."

But there is always a danger that the campaign will misfire or that the ads will seem like "pandering," Hersh said. 80

"The downside, of course, is that we might not like being stereotyped," he explained.

Still, microtargeting makes an uphill process easier for the campaigns, especially at the presidential level.

"How do you start by trying to convince 200 million people that they should vote for you?" asked Hersh. 85

"The task is hard. Data helps and permits campaigns to talk to people about issues they care about," he continued.

And the data does help.

Besides ads that show up before a YouTube video or banner ads on the websites users visit, they dictate scripts that door-to-door canvassers read. They also improve efficiency 90 of campaign voter turnout efforts and reduce costs since ads online are significantly less expensive than television spots.

In the age of DVR, microtargeting can also guarantee that voters actually see campaign ads.

"We can serve a pre-roll video ad," Walsh said, referring to ads viewers see before videos
95   online, "which is great stuff, it forces you to watch it before you get to your content. The big
problem for advertisers these days is that everyone is fast forwarding through their
videos."

A sign of how often these ads are used by political campaigns—"online video inventory
has been sold out," Lieberman said, in many of the key battleground states looking into the
100   final days of the campaign.

Privacy and civil liberties activists don't propose shutting down online advertising. Instead, they favor an opt-in versus the opt-out option currently available to consumers and
voters—a "Do Not Track" mechanism.

Calabrese says the trick is not getting browsers to add the mechanism, but getting other
105   Web companies to agree to it. Yahoo recently said it would not honor the "Do Not Track"
button Microsoft is installing in Microsoft Explorer 10.

"The pushback has been that there is a business model out there that wants to track you
all the time," Calabrese said. "They can wring more and more advertising dollars out of you."

But don't look for this practice to end. Lieberman says it's just the beginning.
110   Looking toward the next election cycle, CampaignGrid signed a deal with AT&T combining AT&T's mobile network with its online voter data files.

The next frontier is to reach voters with ads on their "IP-addressable" television sets,
serving the same targeted ads that people see online, during the commercial breaks on
their favorite shows. And Lieberman says they are adding data crunching power to what he
115   calls "rich data sets."

As Duke political science professor Sunshine Hillygus said, "There's no turning back on
microtargeting."

Source: CNN.com, November 5, 2012. © 2012 Cable News Network, Inc.
http://www.cnn.com/2012/11/05/politics/voters-microtargeting/

Discussion/Writing Prompts

1. This essay addresses an audience presumed to view the issue of voter participation as
   an important civic question. What specific features of the essay reflect this
   assumption? Where in this essay do you see the most visible proof that the author
   views the audience in this way? [Rhetorical Analysis of Audience]

2. How would you characterize the role you play as voter? Do you vote regularly? What
   determines this decision? Has the advent of online campaigning affected or altered
   this role? [Personal Reflection]

3. What do you make of the term "microtargeting"? What vision of political
   campaigning does it suggest? How does it differ from the more conventional
   definition of political campaigning? [Close Reading]

4. Brennan clearly intends for the practice of microtargeting to stand for a broader set
   of changes transforming the nature of political campaigning. How well do you think

this strategy of exemplification works? In your view, does microtargeting capture some of the larger ways the modern political campaign is changing? [Analyzing Rhetorical Modes]

5. "[M]icrotargeting," Brennan writes, "may give pollsters, campaigns and interest groups a sharper idea of how candidates and issues may fare at the ballot box, raising concerns about personal privacy in a medium where government regulation is minimal." In a two-page essay, make an argument about the particular type of "regulation" you think should govern the practice of microtargeting. In your view, what limits should be placed around the kind of information about voters that campaigns are allowed to gather? What restrictions should be imposed on how such information is used? Why? [Argument]

6. In presenting the discussion of microtargeting, Brennan quotes Christopher Calabrese. In ways does Calabrese and Harwood's examination of privacy and surveillance ("Destroying the Right to Be Left Alone") support or reinforce the larger points about microtargeting Brennan is trying to make? [Compare and Contrast]

7. Choose a campaign website. Then, write a description of the ideal or target audience this site seems designed to reach. What information particular to this audience do you think this site is "microtargeting"? Do you find this effort to be effective? Why, or why not? [Research]

Daniel Solove, "Why Privacy Matters, Even When You Have 'Nothing to Hide'"

When you confide your misgivings about someone to a single friend, the consequences are likely to be limited. But what happens when the audience for your complaint numbers in the millions? This, says Daniel J. Solove, John Marshall Harlan Research Professor of Law at the George Washington University Law School, is the situation that we, as users and consumers of the Internet, now face. What happens to our reputation, he asks, when every last tidbit of information about us—whether accurate or bogus—can be uploaded and disseminated online?

"One can usually think of something that even the most open person would want to hide."

When the government gathers or analyzes personal information, many people say they're not worried. "I've got nothing to hide," they declare. "Only if you're doing something wrong should you worry, and then you don't deserve to keep it private."

The nothing-to-hide argument pervades discussions about privacy. The data-security expert Bruce Schneier calls it the "most common retort against privacy advocates." The legal scholar Geoffrey Stone refers to it as an "all-too-common refrain." In its most compelling form, it is an argument that the privacy interest is generally minimal, thus making the contest with security concerns a foreordained victory for security.

10   The nothing-to-hide argument is everywhere. In Britain, for example, the government has installed millions of public-surveillance cameras in cities and towns, which are watched by officials via closed-circuit television. In a campaign slogan for the program, the government declares: "If you've got nothing to hide, you've got nothing to fear." Variations of nothing-to-hide arguments frequently appear in

15   blogs, letters to the editor, television news interviews, and other forums. One blogger in the United States, in reference to profiling people for national-security purposes, declares: "I don't mind people wanting to find out things about me, I've got nothing to hide! Which is why I support [the government's] efforts to find terrorists by monitoring our phone calls!"

20   The argument is not of recent vintage. One of the characters in Henry James's 1888 novel, *The Reverberator*, muses: "If these people had done bad things they ought to be ashamed of themselves and he couldn't pity them, and if they hadn't done them there was no need of making such a rumpus about other people knowing."

    I encountered the nothing-to-hide argument so frequently in news interviews,

25   discussions, and the like that I decided to probe the issue. I asked the readers of my blog, *Concurring Opinions*, whether there are good responses to the nothing-to-hide argument. I received a torrent of comments:

- My response is "So, do you have curtains?" or "Can I see your credit-card bills for the last year?"
30 - So my response to the "If you have nothing to hide . . ." argument is simply, "I don't need to justify my position. You need to justify yours. Come back with a warrant."
- I don't have anything to hide. But I don't have anything I feel like showing you, either.
35 - If you have nothing to hide, then you don't have a life.
- Show me yours and I'll show you mine.
- It's not about having anything to hide, it's about things not being anyone else's business.
- Bottom line, Joe Stalin would [have] loved it. Why should anyone have to say more?

40   On the surface, it seems easy to dismiss the nothing-to-hide argument. Everybody probably has something to hide from somebody. As Aleksandr Solzhenitsyn declared, "Everyone is guilty of something or has something to conceal. All one has to do is look hard enough to find what it is." Likewise, in Friedrich Dürrenmatt's novella "Traps," which involves a seemingly innocent man put on trial by a group of

45   retired lawyers in a mock-trial game, the man inquires what his crime shall be. "An altogether minor matter," replies the prosecutor. "A crime can always be found."

    One can usually think of something that even the most open person would want to hide. As a commenter to my blog post noted, "If you have nothing to hide, then that quite literally means you are willing to let me photograph you naked?

And I get full rights to that photograph—so I can show it to your neighbors?" The Canadian privacy expert David Flaherty expresses a similar idea when he argues: "There is no sentient human being in the Western world who has little or no regard for his or her personal privacy; those who would attempt such claims cannot withstand even a few minutes' questioning about intimate aspects of their lives without capitulating to the intrusiveness of certain subject matters."

But such responses attack the nothing-to-hide argument only in its most extreme form, which isn't particularly strong. In a less extreme form, the nothing-to-hide argument refers not to all personal information but only to the type of data the government is likely to collect. Retorts to the nothing-to-hide argument about exposing people's naked bodies or their deepest secrets are relevant only if the government is likely to gather this kind of information. In many instances, hardly anyone will see the information, and it won't be disclosed to the public. Thus, some might argue, the privacy interest is minimal, and the security interest in preventing terrorism is much more important. In this less extreme form, the nothing-to-hide argument is a formidable one. However, it stems from certain faulty assumptions about privacy and its value.

To evaluate the nothing-to-hide argument, we should begin by looking at how its adherents understand privacy. Nearly every law or policy involving privacy depends upon a particular understanding of what privacy is. The way problems are conceived has a tremendous impact on the legal and policy solutions used to solve them. As the philosopher John Dewey observed, "A problem well put is half-solved."

Most attempts to understand privacy do so by attempting to locate its essence—its core characteristics or the common denominator that links together the various things we classify under the rubric of "privacy." Privacy, however, is too complex a concept to be reduced to a singular essence. It is a plurality of different things that do not share any one element but nevertheless bear a resemblance to one another. For example, privacy can be invaded by the disclosure of your deepest secrets. It might also be invaded if you're watched by a peeping Tom, even if no secrets are ever revealed. With the disclosure of secrets, the harm is that your concealed information is spread to others. With the peeping Tom, the harm is that you're being watched. You'd probably find that creepy regardless of whether the peeper finds out anything sensitive or discloses any information to others. There are many other forms of invasion of privacy, such as blackmail and the improper use of your personal data. Your privacy can also be invaded if the government compiles an extensive dossier about you.

Privacy, in other words, involves so many things that it is impossible to reduce them all to one simple idea. And we need not do so.

In many cases, privacy issues never get balanced against conflicting interests, because courts, legislators, and others fail to recognize that privacy is implicated. People don't acknowledge certain problems, because those problems don't fit into a particular one-size-fits-all conception of privacy. Regardless of whether we call something a "privacy" problem, it still remains a problem, and problems

shouldn't be ignored. We should pay attention to all of the different problems that
spark our desire to protect privacy.

95   To describe the problems created by the collection and use of personal data,
many commentators use a metaphor based on George Orwell's *Nineteen Eighty-
Four*. Orwell depicted a harrowing totalitarian society ruled by a government
called Big Brother that watches its citizens obsessively and demands strict discipline. The Orwell metaphor, which focuses on the harms of surveillance (such as
100 inhibition and social control), might be apt to describe government monitoring of
citizens. But much of the data gathered in computer databases, such as one's race,
birth date, gender, address, or marital status, isn't particularly sensitive. Many
people don't care about concealing the hotels they stay at, the cars they own, or
the kind of beverages they drink. Frequently, though not always, people wouldn't
105 be inhibited or embarrassed if others knew this information.

    Another metaphor better captures the problems: Franz Kafka's *The Trial*. Kafka's
novel centers around a man who is arrested but not informed why. He desperately
tries to find out what triggered his arrest and what's in store for him. He finds out
that a mysterious court system has a dossier on him and is investigating him, but
110 he's unable to learn much more. *The Trial* depicts a bureaucracy with inscrutable
purposes that uses people's information to make important decisions about them,
yet denies the people the ability to participate in how their information is used.

    The problems portrayed by the Kafkaesque metaphor are of a different sort
than the problems caused by surveillance. They often do not result in inhibition.
115 Instead they are problems of information processing—the storage, use, or analysis
of data—rather than of information collection. They affect the power relationships
between people and the institutions of the modern state. They not only frustrate
the individual by creating a sense of helplessness and powerlessness, but also
affect social structure by altering the kind of relationships people have with the
120 institutions that make important decisions about their lives.

    Legal and policy solutions focus too much on the problems under the Orwell-
ian metaphor—those of surveillance—and aren't adequately addressing the
Kafkaesque problems—those of information processing. The difficulty is that commentators are trying to conceive of the problems caused by databases in terms of
125 surveillance when, in fact, those problems are different.

    Commentators often attempt to refute the nothing-to-hide argument by point-
ing to things people want to hide. But the problem with the nothing-to-hide argument is the underlying assumption that privacy is about hiding bad things. By
accepting this assumption, we concede far too much ground and invite an unpro-
130 ductive discussion about information that people would very likely want to hide.
As the computer-security specialist Schneier aptly notes, the nothing-to-hide argument stems from a faulty "premise that privacy is about hiding a wrong." Surveillance, for example, can inhibit such lawful activities as free speech, free
association, and other First Amendment rights essential for democracy.

The deeper problem with the nothing-to-hide argument is that it myopically 135 views privacy as a form of secrecy. In contrast, understanding privacy as a plurality of related issues demonstrates that the disclosure of bad things is just one among many difficulties caused by government security measures. To return to my discussion of literary metaphors, the problems are not just Orwellian but Kafkaesque. Government information-gathering programs are problematic even if no informa- 140 tion that people want to hide is uncovered. In *The Trial*, the problem is not inhibited behavior but rather a suffocating powerlessness and vulnerability created by the court system's use of personal data and its denial to the protagonist of any knowledge of or participation in the process. The harms are bureaucratic ones—indifference, error, abuse, frustration, and lack of transparency and 145 accountability.

One such harm, for example, which I call aggregation, emerges from the fusion of small bits of seemingly innocuous data. When combined, the information becomes much more telling. By joining pieces of information we might not take pains to guard, the government can glean information about us that we might indeed 150 wish to conceal. For example, suppose you bought a book about cancer. This purchase isn't very revealing on its own, for it indicates just an interest in the disease. Suppose you bought a wig. The purchase of a wig, by itself, could be for a number of reasons. But combine those two pieces of information, and now the inference can be made that you have cancer and are undergoing chemotherapy. That might 155 be a fact you wouldn't mind sharing, but you'd certainly want to have the choice.

Another potential problem with the government's harvest of personal data is one I call exclusion. Exclusion occurs when people are prevented from having knowledge about how information about them is being used, and when they are barred from accessing and correcting errors in that data. Many government 160 national-security measures involve maintaining a huge database of information that individuals cannot access. Indeed, because they involve national security, the very existence of these programs is often kept secret. This kind of information processing, which blocks subjects' knowledge and involvement, is a kind of due-process problem. It is a structural problem, involving the way people are 165 treated by government institutions and creating a power imbalance between people and the government. To what extent should government officials have such a significant power over citizens? This issue isn't about what information people want to hide but about the power and the structure of government.

A related problem involves secondary use. Secondary use is the exploitation of 170 data obtained for one purpose for an unrelated purpose without the subject's consent. How long will personal data be stored? How will the information be used? What could it be used for in the future? The potential uses of any piece of personal information are vast. Without limits on or accountability for how that information is used, it is hard for people to assess the dangers of the data's being in the 175 government's control.

Yet another problem with government gathering and use of personal data is distortion. Although personal information can reveal quite a lot about people's personalities and activities, it often fails to reflect the whole person. It can paint a distorted picture, especially since records are reductive—they often capture information in a standardized format with many details omitted.

For example, suppose government officials learn that a person has bought a number of books on how to manufacture methamphetamine. That information makes them suspect that he's building a meth lab. What is missing from the records is the full story: The person is writing a novel about a character who makes meth. When he bought the books, he didn't consider how suspicious the purchase might appear to government officials, and his records didn't reveal the reason for the purchases. Should he have to worry about government scrutiny of all his purchases and actions? Should he have to be concerned that he'll wind up on a suspicious-persons list? Even if he isn't doing anything wrong, he may want to keep his records away from government officials who might make faulty inferences from them. He might not want to have to worry about how everything he does will be perceived by officials nervously monitoring for criminal activity. He might not want to have a computer flag him as suspicious because he has an unusual pattern of behavior.

The nothing-to-hide argument focuses on just one or two particular kinds of privacy problems—the disclosure of personal information or surveillance—while ignoring the others. It assumes a particular view about what privacy entails, to the exclusion of other perspectives.

It is important to distinguish here between two ways of justifying a national-security program that demands access to personal information. The first way is not to recognize a problem. This is how the nothing-to-hide argument works—it denies even the existence of a problem. The second is to acknowledge the problems but contend that the benefits of the program outweigh the privacy sacrifice. The first justification influences the second, because the low value given to privacy is based upon a narrow view of the problem. And the key misunderstanding is that the nothing-to-hide argument views privacy in this troublingly particular, partial way.

Investigating the nothing-to-hide argument a little more deeply, we find that it looks for a singular and visceral kind of injury. Ironically, this underlying conception of injury is sometimes shared by those advocating for greater privacy protections. For example, the University of South Carolina law professor Ann Bartow argues that in order to have a real resonance, privacy problems must "negatively impact the lives of living, breathing human beings beyond simply provoking feelings of unease." She says that privacy needs more "dead bodies," and that privacy's "lack of blood and death, or at least of broken bones and buckets of money, distances privacy harms from other [types of harm]."

Bartow's objection is actually consistent with the nothing-to-hide argument. Those advancing the nothing-to-hide argument have in mind a particular kind of appalling privacy harm, one in which privacy is violated only when something

deeply embarrassing or discrediting is revealed. Like Bartow, proponents of the
nothing-to-hide argument demand a dead-bodies type of harm.   220

Bartow is certainly right that people respond much more strongly to blood and
death than to more-abstract concerns. But if this is the standard to recognize a
problem, then few privacy problems will be recognized. Privacy is not a horror
movie, most privacy problems don't result in dead bodies, and demanding evidence of palpable harms will be difficult in many cases.   225

Privacy is often threatened not by a single egregious act but by the slow accre-
tion of a series of relatively minor acts. In this respect, privacy problems resemble
certain environmental harms, which occur over time through a series of small acts
by different actors. Although society is more likely to respond to a major oil spill,
gradual pollution by a multitude of actors often creates worse problems.   230

Privacy is rarely lost in one fell swoop. It is usually eroded over time, little bits
dissolving almost imperceptibly until we finally begin to notice how much is gone.
When the government starts monitoring the phone numbers people call, many may
shrug their shoulders and say, "Ah, it's just numbers, that's all." Then the government might start monitoring some phone calls. "It's just a few phone calls, nothing 235
more." The government might install more video cameras in public places. "So
what? Some more cameras watching in a few more places. No big deal." The increase in cameras might lead to a more elaborate network of video surveillance.
Satellite surveillance might be added to help track people's movements. The government might start analyzing people's bank records. "It's just my deposits and   240
some of the bills I pay—no problem." The government may then start combing
through credit-card records, then expand to Internet service providers' records,
health records, employment records, and more. Each step may seem incremental,
but after a while, the government will be watching and knowing everything about us.

"My life's an open book," people might say. "I've got nothing to hide." But now 245
the government has large dossiers of everyone's activities, interests, reading
habits, finances, and health. What if the government leaks the information to the
public? What if the government mistakenly determines that based on your pattern
of activities, you're likely to engage in a criminal act? What if it denies you the right
to fly? What if the government thinks your financial transactions look odd—even if 250
you've done nothing wrong—and freezes your accounts? What if the government
doesn't protect your information with adequate security, and an identity thief obtains it and uses it to defraud you? Even if you have nothing to hide, the government can cause you a lot of harm.

"But the government doesn't want to hurt me," some might argue. In many   255
cases, that's true, but the government can also harm people inadvertently, due to
errors or carelessness.

When the nothing-to-hide argument is unpacked, and its underlying assumptions examined and challenged, we can see how it shifts the debate to its terms,
then draws power from its unfair advantage. The nothing-to-hide argument speaks 260

to some problems but not to others. It represents a singular and narrow way of conceiving of privacy, and it wins by excluding consideration of the other problems often raised with government security measures. When engaged directly, the nothing-to-hide argument can ensnare, for it forces the debate to focus on its narrow understanding of privacy. But when confronted with the plurality of privacy problems implicated by government data collection and use beyond surveillance and disclosure, the nothing-to-hide argument, in the end, has nothing to say.

Source: The Chronicle of Higher Education, May 5, 2011
http://chronicle.com/article/Why-Privacy-Matters-Even-if/127461/

265

◼ Discussion/Writing Prompts

1. Solove's argument is clearly directed toward an audience concerned about threats to their privacy. What kind of reader, in your view, would be most susceptible to this type of argument? What type of reader would be least susceptible? And which type do you more closely resemble? [Rhetorical Analysis of Audience]

2. Solove's examination of privacy and surveillance raises a fundamental question about who owns our personal information. Can you think of a moment in your life where you had to confront this question? What personal information did this involve? And what was the specific threat to your ownership over it? [Personal Reflection]

3. "[T]he problem with the nothing-to-hide argument," Solove writes, "is the underlying assumption that privacy is about hiding bad things. By accepting this assumption, we concede far too much ground and invite an unproductive discussion about information that people would very likely want to hide." Write a short response in which you analyze this claim. What specific objection is Solove raising about the "nothing-to-hide argument"? And do you agree that endorsing this view involves accepting a false assumption that "privacy is about hiding bad things"? [Close Reading]

4. Much of Solove's argument here revolves around his attempt to redefine the notion of "privacy" itself. What particular rhetorical strategies does he use to achieve this goal? Given what Solove wants to teach his readers about privacy, do you think this rhetorical mode is effective? How, or how not? [Analyzing Rhetorical Modes]

5. Near the end of this essay, Solove poses a number of rhetorical questions:

   What if the government leaks [your personal] information to the public? What if the government mistakenly determines that based on your pattern of activities, you're likely to engage in a criminal act? What if it denies you the right to fly? What if the government thinks your financial transactions look odd—even if you've done nothing wrong—and freezes your accounts? What if the government doesn't protect your information with adequate security, and an identity thief obtains it and uses it to defraud you?

In a two-page essay, analyze and assess the way these questions help Solove convey his larger argument. Based on what he has to say about privacy elsewhere in the essay, how do you think Solove would answer these questions? Based on these answers, what would you say is the larger point about privacy he is trying to make? And do you find yourself convinced? [Argument]

6. Allison Brennan ("Microtargeting: How Campaigns Know More About You Than You Know About Yourself") examines a particular example of personal data gathering. Do you think her essay serves as proof of Solove's thesis? Are there any aspects of her discussion that challenge the conclusions about privacy Solove draws? [Compare and Contrast]

7. Choose an organization or website dedicated to gathering personal information about its users. First, describe what this entity looks like. What is its focus or purpose? Next, describe the profile of the audience it addresses. What kind of information defines this typical user? If you found yourself targeted, what information would you want to make sure was kept private? [Research]

Visual Rhetoric: Tim Robberts, "Young Woman Peering Inside Laptop Screen"

Like Solove's essay above, this image makes a point about the eroding boundaries around personal privacy. What would you say the message here is? And how does it compare to what Solove has to say on the same subject?

FIGURE 6.11

Source: Tim Robberts/Digital Vision/Getty Images

Jim Taylor, "Popular Culture: Reality TV is NOT Reality"

Our airwaves are filled with examples of reality television: shows that purport to present viewers with an unmediated slice of "real life." But how real are these portraits? And what are the implications for viewers of accepting them at face value? Posing precisely these questions, Jim Taylor, an adjunct professor of psychology at the University of San Francisco, looks beneath the surface of reality television, at the choices and calculations the makers of such cultural fare use to create their portraits. Rather than an actual glimpse of "real life," he argues, these shows instead offer audiences fictionalized stories designed to promote a carefully chosen and highly selective set of ideas.

"Only in George Orwell's 1984 reality can people be watched every moment of the day like on Big Brother."

What attracts millions of Americans each week to this cultural phenomenon known as "reality TV?" Where did the purveyors of shows such as *Survivor, Jersey Shore,* and *Wife Swap,* get the idea (I know, from Europe!), and why do so many of us buy into the idea that reality TV resembles reality in any way, shape, or form?
5   Only in George Orwell's *1984* reality can people be watched every moment of the day like on *Big Brother.* Only in William Gerald Golding's *Lord of the Flies* reality can people "eliminate" one another on a desert island like on *Survivor.* Only in Ira Levin's *The Stepford Wives* reality are all of the women attractive, shapely, and predominantly white like on the *Real Housewives* franchise. Only in Andy Warhol's
10   "fifteen minutes" reality do people whose only claim is that they won a reality TV show make them worthy of the fame and fortune of talk show appearances, book contracts, and speaking tours. Yet this is the "reality" of reality TV to which we are exposed and it is the reality that some of us may come to believe can be our reality.

15   Reality TV promotes the worst values and qualities in people—and disguises them all as entertainment. Reality TV has made the Seven Deadly Sins—pride, avarice, envy, wrath, lust, gluttony, and sloth—attributes to be admired. Throw in selfishness, deceit, spite, and vengeance—all qualities seen routinely on reality TV—and you have the personification of the worst kind of person on Earth. Reality
20   TV makes heroic decidedly unheroic values, characters, and behavior.

Why would popular culture want to communicate such destructive values, you may ask. The answer is, because popular culture has no values; it's amoral. It doesn't care about us and it has no sense of social responsibility. Popular culture is concerned with only one thing, money, and it will do everything and sacrifice any-
25   thing to achieve that end, including hurting the society it is meant to serve.

Some argue that reality TV is just giving us what we want. But I don't recall any demonstrations or picket lines outside of the television studios clamoring for reality TV shows. Admittedly, if viewers didn't want these shows they would "vote them off the island" by not watching them, thus ensuring cancellation. But doing
30   so would be like driving by a horrendous car wreck and having the strength not to look at the carnage.

The messages that popular culture sends us about success and failure—as communicated through the unreality of "reality" TV—are particularly destructive. Success, as defined by our culture and conveyed through reality TV—wealth and fame, most notably—is so revered, yet, in the reality in which most of us live, so   35 utterly unattainable. We get the message from reality TV that we must become successful at any cost, even if success can be achieved only by dishonesty and subterfuge. The unfortunate results of these messages can be found throughout our culture. We see increased cheating in schools, the use of performance-enhancing drugs in sports, and criminal behavior in our youth and, among our   40 adult population, lying on resumes, frivolous law suits, and corporate greed. Anything to become a success! Reality TV obviously doesn't cause such behavior, rather that it is just another symptom of the decline of values that used to limit this behavior. And reality TV is now an omnipresent conduit through which these truly atrocious messages are communicated to America. And if you think these mes-   45 sage are fundamentally benign, think again. The more people are exposed to any message, even terrible ones, the more likely they will be accepted as the norm.

There is no worse fate in our culture than to be labeled a failure, yet, so narrowly defined by our culture (not being wealthy, famous, powerful, or beautiful), it is almost a certainty for most of us. Failure alone though is not punishment enough   50 for the "losers" in reality TV. They must also be demeaned, dehumanized, and publicly humiliated. These losers must suffer the indignity of banishment from reality TV shows by hosts, such as the cold, yet venerated, Donald Trump—"You're fired!"—and judges such as the mean-spirited Simon Cowell on *American Idol* (I realize that these shows differ from other unscripted shows, but no greater author-   55 ity than realitytvworld.com lumps them all together). Despite this despicable behavior, we are encouraged to feel excitement and glee in seeing others suffer. As we cringe outwardly at the barbs that are thrown at the well-meaning contestants, we inwardly giggle in guilty pleasure at seeing the failing contestants in pain. Most of the joy of reality TV is not in seeing contestants succeed, but rather in seeing   60 them not only fail, but fail in the most humiliating ways. We celebrate every luscious moment of this depravity!

Why do so many of people not only watch reality TV (I understand that everyone has a right to be entertained as they choose), but become so consumed by it that there are Web sites, blogs, magazine and newspaper articles, and constant talk   65 around the water cooler? One answer is vicarious stimulation. Reality TV is exciting when life is often mundane. It is interesting when life can be dull. Reality TV is dangerous when life can be all too secure. It is emotionally powerful—excitement, joy, embarrassment, shame—when life can be emotionally void. And many of us want it that way because we are loath to take risks and feel so deeply in our own lives.   70

Reality TV has become the public executions of our times. We sit on the edge of our seats waiting eagerly for the guillotine to fall, yet don't want the end to come too quickly. We want to savor the lingering death of humiliation and rejection. And when

the "execution" finally occurs, we feel conflicted in enjoying others' "deaths," yet relief
75   in our continued existences, guilty for the exhilaration we feel, yet giddy in knowing
that we are "survivors" of our own reality show called Life. In these times of economic
and global uncertainty, thanks to the contestants' symbolic deaths on reality TV, we
can return to our lives feeling somehow better, safer . . . that we are going to be okay.

Or maybe I'm just overthinking the reality TV thing and the shows are just fun to
80   watch. Just sayin'.

Source: Psychology Today, January 31, 2011. © 2011 Sussex Publishers, LLC.
http://www.psychologytoday.com/blog/the-power-prime/201101/popular-culture-reality-
tv-is-not-reality

Discussion/Writing Prompts

1. How do you think an avid watcher of reality television would respond to Taylor's critique?
   What specific objections might such an audience offer? [Rhetorical Analysis of Audience]

2. How closely do you conform to the profile of the typical reality television viewer
   Taylor presents here? Do you see any aspects of yourself in his description of the
   reality television audience? If so, what? [Personal Reflection]

3. "Reality TV," Taylor writes, "has become the public executions of our times." What
   does he mean by this? In your view, is it valid to compare reality television to a
   "public execution"? Why, or why not? [Close Reading]

4. Underneath Taylor's discussion of reality television is an unspoken cause-and-effect
   argument about what the popularity of such shows is doing to the people who watch
   them. Write a one-page essay in which you identify and analyze the cause-and-effect
   relationship between reality television shows and reality television viewers that Taylor
   is presenting here. According to Taylor, how do reality shows affect the way their
   audiences view the world around them? And why, in his view, should we worry about
   this? [Analyzing Rhetorical Modes]

5. Taylor writes: "Reality TV is exciting when life is often mundane. It is interesting
   when life can be dull. Reality TV is dangerous when life can be all too secure." What
   larger point is Taylor trying to make here? What argument is he advancing here
   about the effect reality television has on its target audience? [Argument]

6. Like Taylor, Michael Solis ("Social Media: Obstacle to Friendship/Love") worries
   about the ways our modern media culture can foster habits that harm the general
   public. In your view, does Taylor's critique of reality television fit the definition of an
   "obstacle" presented by Solis? How, or how not? [Compare and Contrast]

7. One of the key objections Taylor levels against reality television has to do with the
   way it caters to the baser instincts of its audience. Choose an example of a reality
   show that you think deliberately appeals to its viewers' baser emotions (e.g., envy,
   fear, or anger). Then, analyze the particular rhetorical strategies this show uses to
   address and manipulate its audience in this way. [Research]

Academic Writing Selections

The rhetorical analysis modeled above doesn't only apply to the types of informal and formal writing found in the real world. It can also serve as an equally useful framework for examining what is often termed classic writing: essays by well-known authors that have stood the test of time and come to be regarded as models of sound academic writing. Like their real world counterparts, such classic writing lends itself just as well to rhetorical analysis.

The two selections below illustrate this point vividly, demonstrating the extent to which even classic texts are shaped by rhetorical concepts. More specifically, these examples highlight the role that considerations about audience play in shaping a writer's choices. Read each selection carefully. Then, answer the questions that follow.

George Orwell, "Shooting an Elephant"

Have you ever felt pressured to act in a way that violates your personal sense of right and wrong? When confronted by such pressures, how do you summon the strength to do what is right? George Orwell considers these philosophical questions by placing them in the specific historical context of 20th-century British colonialism.

In Moulmein, in lower Burma, I was hated by large numbers of people—the only time in my life that I have been important enough for this to happen to me. I was subdivisional police officer of the town, and in an aimless, petty kind of way anti-European feeling was very bitter. No one had the guts to raise a riot, but if a European woman went through the bazaars alone somebody would probably spit betel juice 5
over her dress. As a police officer I was an obvious target and was baited whenever it seemed safe to do so. When a nimble Burman tripped me up on the football field and the referee (another Burman) looked the other way, the crowd yelled with hideous laughter. This happened more than once. In the end the sneering yellow faces of young men that met me everywhere, the insults hooted after me when I was at a safe 10
distance, got badly on my nerves. The young Buddhist priests were the worst of all. There were several thousands of them in the town and none of them seemed to have anything to do except stand on street corners and jeer at Europeans.

All this was perplexing and upsetting. For at that time I had already made up my mind that imperialism was an evil thing and the sooner I chucked up my job and got 15
out of it the better. Theoretically—and secretly, of course—I was all for the Burmese and all against their oppressors, the British. As for the job I was doing, I hated it more bitterly than I can perhaps make clear. In a job like that you see the dirty work of Empire at close quarters. The wretched prisoners huddling in the stinking cages of the lock-ups, the grey, cowed faces of the long-term convicts, the 20
scarred buttocks of the men who had been Bogged with bamboos—all these oppressed me with an intolerable sense of guilt. But I could get nothing into perspective. I was young and ill-educated and I had had to think out my problems in the

utter silence that is imposed on every Englishman in the East. I did not even know that the British Empire is dying, still less did I know that it is a great deal better than the younger empires that are going to supplant it. All I knew was that I was stuck between my hatred of the empire I served and my rage against the evil-spirited little beasts who tried to make my job impossible. With one part of my mind I thought of the British Raj as an unbreakable tyranny, as something clamped down, in saecula saeculorum, upon the will of prostrate peoples; with another part I thought that the greatest joy in the world would be to drive a bayonet into a Buddhist priest's guts. Feelings like these are the normal by-products of imperialism; ask any Anglo-Indian official, if you can catch him off duty.

One day something happened which in a roundabout way was enlightening. It was a tiny incident in itself, but it gave me a better glimpse than I had had before of the real nature of imperialism—the real motives for which despotic governments act. Early one morning the sub-inspector at a police station the other end of the town rang me up on the phone and said that an elephant was ravaging the bazaar. Would I please come and do something about it? I did not know what I could do, but I wanted to see what was happening and I got on to a pony and started out. I took my rifle, an old 44 Winchester and much too small to kill an elephant, but I thought the noise might be useful in terrorem. Various Burmans stopped me on the way and told me about the elephant's doings. It was not, of course, a wild elephant, but a tame one which had gone "must." It had been chained up, as tame elephants always are when their attack of "must" is due, but on the previous night it had broken its chain and escaped. Its mahout, the only person who could manage it when it was in that state, had set out in pursuit, but had taken the wrong direction and was now twelve hours' journey away, and in the morning the elephant had suddenly reappeared in the town. The Burmese population had no weapons and were quite helpless against it. It had already destroyed somebody's bamboo hut, killed a cow and raided some fruit-stalls and devoured the stock; also it had met the municipal rubbish van and, when the driver jumped out and took to his heels, had turned the van over and inflicted violences upon it.

The Burmese sub-inspector and some Indian constables were waiting for me in the quarter where the elephant had been seen. It was a very poor quarter, a labyrinth of squalid bamboo huts, thatched with palmleaf, winding all over a steep hillside. I remember that it was a cloudy, stuffy morning at the beginning of the rains. We began questioning the people as to where the elephant had gone and, as usual, failed to get any definite information. That is invariably the case in the East; a story always sounds clear enough at a distance, but the nearer you get to the scene of events the vaguer it becomes. Some of the people said that the elephant had gone in one direction, some said that he had gone in another, some professed not even to have heard of any elephant. I had almost made up my mind that the whole story was a pack of lies, when we heard yells a little distance away. There was a loud, scandalized cry of "Go away, child! Go away this instant!" and an old woman with a switch in her hand came round the corner of a hut, violently shooing away a crowd of naked children. Some more women followed, clicking their tongues and exclaiming; evidently there was something that the children ought not to have seen. I rounded the hut and saw a man's dead body sprawling in the mud. He was an Indian, a black Dravidian coolie, almost naked, and he could not have been dead many minutes. The people said that the elephant had come suddenly upon him round the corner of the hut, caught him with its trunk, put its foot on his back and ground him into the earth. This was the rainy season and the ground was soft, and his face had scored a trench a foot deep and a couple of yards long. He was lying on his belly with arms crucified and head sharply twisted to one side. His face was coated with mud, the eyes wide open, the teeth bared and grinning with an expression of unendurable agony. (Never tell me, by the way, that the dead look peaceful. Most of the corpses I have seen looked devilish.) The friction of the great beast's foot had stripped the skin from his back as neatly as one skins a rabbit. As soon as I saw the dead man I sent an orderly to a friend's house nearby to borrow an elephant rifle. I had already sent back the pony, not wanting it to go mad with fright and throw me if it smelt the elephant.

The orderly came back in a few minutes with a rifle and five cartridges, and meanwhile some Burmans had arrived and told us that the elephant was in the paddy fields below, only a few hundred yards away. As I started forward practically the whole population of the quarter flocked out of the houses and followed me. They had seen the rifle and were all shouting excitedly that I was going to shoot the elephant. They had not shown much interest in the elephant when he was merely ravaging their homes, but it was different now that he was going to be shot. It was a bit of fun to them, as it would be to an English crowd; besides they wanted the meat. It made me vaguely uneasy. I had no intention of shooting the elephant—I had merely sent for the rifle to defend myself if necessary—and it is always unnerving to have a crowd following you. I marched down the hill, looking and feeling a fool, with the rifle over my shoulder and an ever-growing army of people jostling at my heels. At the bottom, when you got away from the huts, there was a metalled road and beyond that a miry waste of paddy fields a thousand yards across, not yet ploughed but soggy from the first rains and dotted with coarse grass. The elephant was standing eight yards from the road, his left side towards us. He took not the slightest notice of the crowd's approach. He was tearing up bunches of grass, beating them against his knees to clean them and stuffing them into his mouth.

I had halted on the road. As soon as I saw the elephant I knew with perfect certainty that I ought not to shoot him. It is a serious matter to shoot a working elephant—it is comparable to destroying a huge and costly piece of machinery—and obviously one ought not to do it if it can possibly be avoided. And at that distance, peacefully eating, the elephant looked no more dangerous than a cow. I thought then and I think now that his attack of "must" was already passing off; in which case he would merely wander harmlessly about until the mahout came back and caught him. Moreover, I did not in the least want to shoot him. I decided that I would watch him for a little while to make sure that he did not turn savage again, and then go home.

110   But at that moment I glanced round at the crowd that had followed me. It was an immense crowd, two thousand at the least and growing every minute. It blocked the road for a long distance on either side. I looked at the sea of yellow faces above the garish clothes—faces all happy and excited over this bit of fun, all certain that the elephant was going to be shot. They were watching me as they would

115   watch a conjurer about to perform a trick. They did not like me, but with the magical rifle in my hands I was momentarily worth watching. And suddenly I realized that I should have to shoot the elephant after all. The people expected it of me and I had got to do it; I could feel their two thousand wills pressing me forward, irresistibly. And it was at this moment, as I stood there with the rifle in my hands, that

120   I first grasped the hollowness, the futility of the white man's dominion in the East. Here was I, the white man with his gun, standing in front of the unarmed native crowd—seemingly the leading actor of the piece; but in reality I was only an absurd puppet pushed to and fro by the will of those yellow faces behind. I perceived in this moment that when the white man turns tyrant it is his own freedom that he

125   destroys. He becomes a sort of hollow, posing dummy, the conventionalized figure of a sahib. For it is the condition of his rule that he shall spend his life in trying to impress the "natives," and so in every crisis he has got to do what the "natives" expect of him. He wears a mask, and his face grows to fit it. I had got to shoot the elephant. I had committed myself to doing it when I sent for the rifle. A sahib has

130   got to act like a sahib; he has got to appear resolute, to know his own mind and do definite things. To come all that way, rifle in hand, with two thousand people marching at my heels, and then to trail feebly away, having done nothing—no, that was impossible. The crowd would laugh at me. And my whole life, every white man's life in the East, was one long struggle not to be laughed at.

135   But I did not want to shoot the elephant. I watched him beating his bunch of grass against his knees, with that preoccupied grandmotherly air that elephants have. It seemed to me that it would be murder to shoot him. At that age I was not squeamish about killing animals, but I had never shot an elephant and never wanted to. (Somehow it always seems worse to kill a large animal.) Besides, there

140   was the beast's owner to be considered. Alive, the elephant was worth at least a hundred pounds; dead, he would only be worth the value of his tusks, five pounds, possibly. But I had got to act quickly. I turned to some experienced-looking Burmans who had been there when we arrived, and asked them how the elephant had been behaving. They all said the same thing: he took no notice of you if you left him

145   alone, but he might charge if you went too close to him.

    It was perfectly clear to me what I ought to do. I ought to walk up to within, say, twenty-five yards of the elephant and test his behavior. If he charged, I could shoot; if he took no notice of me, it would be safe to leave him until the mahout came back. But also I knew that I was going to do no such thing. I was a poor shot

150   with a rifle and the ground was soft mud into which one would sink at every step. If the elephant charged and I missed him, I should have about as much chance as a toad under a steam-roller. But even then I was not thinking particularly of my own

skin, only of the watchful yellow faces behind. For at that moment, with the crowd watching me, I was not afraid in the ordinary sense, as I would have been if I had been alone. A white man mustn't be frightened in front of "natives"; and so, in general, he isn't frightened. The sole thought in my mind was that if anything went wrong those two thousand Burmans would see me pursued, caught, trampled on and reduced to a grinning corpse like that Indian up the hill. And if that happened it was quite probable that some of them would laugh. That would never do.

There was only one alternative. I shoved the cartridges into the magazine and lay down on the road to get a better aim. The crowd grew very still, and a deep, low, happy sigh, as of people who see the theatre curtain go up at last, breathed from innumerable throats. They were going to have their bit of fun after all. The rifle was a beautiful German thing with cross-hair sights. I did not then know that in shooting an elephant one would shoot to cut an imaginary bar running from ear-hole to ear-hole. I ought, therefore, as the elephant was sideways on, to have aimed straight at his ear-hole, actually I aimed several inches in front of this, thinking the brain would be further forward.

When I pulled the trigger I did not hear the bang or feel the kick—one never does when a shot goes home—but I heard the devilish roar of glee that went up from the crowd. In that instant, in too short a time, one would have thought, even for the bullet to get there, a mysterious, terrible change had come over the elephant. He neither stirred nor fell, but every line of his body had altered. He looked suddenly stricken, shrunken, immensely old, as though the frightful impact of the bullet had paralysed him without knocking him down. At last, after what seemed a long time—it might have been five seconds, I dare say—he sagged flabbily to his knees. His mouth slobbered. An enormous senility seemed to have settled upon him. One could have imagined him thousands of years old. I fired again into the same spot. At the second shot he did not collapse but climbed with desperate slowness to his feet and stood weakly upright, with legs sagging and head drooping. I fired a third time. That was the shot that did for him. You could see the agony of it jolt his whole body and knock the last remnant of strength from his legs. But in falling he seemed for a moment to rise, for as his hind legs collapsed beneath him he seemed to tower upward like a huge rock toppling, his trunk reaching skyward like a tree. He trumpeted, for the first and only time. And then down he came, his belly towards me, with a crash that seemed to shake the ground even where I lay.

I got up. The Burmans were already racing past me across the mud. It was obvious that the elephant would never rise again, but he was not dead. He was breathing very rhythmically with long rattling gasps, his great mound of a side painfully rising and falling. His mouth was wide open—I could see far down into caverns of pale pink throat. I waited a long time for him to die, but his breathing did not weaken. Finally I fired my two remaining shots into the spot where I thought his heart must be. The thick blood welled out of him like red velvet, but still he did not die. His body did not even jerk when the shots hit him, the tortured breathing continued without a pause. He was dying, very slowly and in great agony, but in some world remote from me where not even a bullet could damage him further. I felt that I had got to put an end to that dreadful noise. It seemed dreadful to see the great beast Lying there, powerless to move and yet powerless to die, and not even to be able to finish him. I sent back for my small rifle and poured shot after shot into his heart and down his throat. They seemed to make no impression. The tortured gasps continued as steadily as the ticking of a clock.

In the end I could not stand it any longer and went away. I heard later that it took him half an hour to die. Burmans were bringing dash and baskets even before I left, and I was told they had stripped his body almost to the bones by the afternoon.

Afterwards, of course, there were endless discussions about the shooting of the elephant. The owner was furious, but he was only an Indian and could do nothing. Besides, legally I had done the right thing, for a mad elephant has to be killed, like a mad dog, if its owner fails to control it. Among the Europeans opinion was divided. The older men said I was right, the younger men said it was a damn shame to shoot an elephant for killing a coolie, because an elephant was worth more than any damn Coringhee coolie. And afterwards I was very glad that the coolie had been killed; it put me legally in the right and it gave me a sufficient pretext for shooting the elephant. I often wondered whether any of the others grasped that I had done it solely to avoid looking a fool.

Source: George Orwell. from A Collection of Essays by George Orwell. *Houghton Mifflin Harcourt Publishing Company.*

Discussion/Writing Prompts

1. Orwell's story is directed toward an audience presumed to have some familiarity with the British colonial system. What attitude toward colonialism does Orwell seem to want his readers to adopt? What kind of reaction does his story seem intended to elicit? [Rhetorical Analysis of Audience]

2. As the title suggests, this narrative revolves around Orwell's struggle to resolve his feelings about having to "shoot an elephant." How relatable do you find this struggle to be? Do you have any personal experience with hunting or killing animals? In your mind, what ethical questions does this practice raise? [Personal Reflection]

3. Here is how the narrator in the story describes the moments after he shoots the elephant:

   [The elephant] was breathing very rhythmically with long rattling gasps, his great mound of a side painfully rising and falling. His mouth was wide open—I could see far down into caverns of pale pink throat. I waited a long time for him to die, but his breathing did not weaken. Finally I fired my two remaining shots into the spot where I thought his heart must be. The thick blood welled out of him like red velvet, but still he did not die.

   Analyze the language Orwell uses here. What kind of reaction do descriptive terms like "pale pink throat" or "long rattling gasps" seem designed to evoke? How does the language here shape your response to this scene? [Close Reading]

4. Do you think the commentary about colonialism in Orwell's story is more effective because it is presented through the mode of narration? What specific aspects of the narrative do you find most effective in communicating the key points that Orwell is trying to get across? [Analyzing Rhetorical Modes]

5. Here is how Orwell describes the moments before he fires his rifle at the elephant: "[A]s I stood there with the rifle in my hands . . . I first grasped the hollowness, the futility of the white man's dominion in the East. Here was I, the white man with his gun, standing in front of the unarmed native crowd—seemingly the leading actor of the piece; but in reality I was only an absurd puppet pushed to and fro by the will of those yellow faces behind. I perceived in this moment that when the white man turns tyrant it is his own freedom that he destroys." In a two-page essay, analyze and assess the argument Orwell is making here. What point is he trying to get across by describing himself as a "leading actor" and "absurd puppet?" And how is this view connected to what he subsequently says about the destruction of his own "freedom"? [Argument]

6. From a very different perspective, Daniel Solove ("Why Privacy Matters, Even When You Have 'Nothing to Hide'") considers the consequences of living in a world that feels like we are constantly being watched. How does Solove's commentary about this issue compare to Orwell's? Do you find any common ground between Solove's call for greater "privacy" and Orwell's reaction to finding himself on display? What are the key similarities and differences? [Compare and Contrast]

7. Research the history of British colonialism in Asia. What did this colonial system look like? How did it operate? Then, write an essay using this historical information to re-examine Orwell's story. Based on your research, do you find this story to be an accurate portrayal, or persuasive critique, of British colonialism? Why, or why not? [Research]

Jhumpa Lahiri, "Rice"

What can we learn about ourselves, our family, and our history from what we eat? To what extent can the practices and rituals around meal preparation become a way of preserving ties between parents and children? Using her own family as a case study, Jhumpa Lahiri, the author of numerous short stories and two novels, The Namesake *(2003) and* Lowland *(2013), answers these questions by recounting her father's methodical, and memorable, ways in the kitchen.*

My father, seventy-eight, is a methodical man. For thirty-nine years, he has had the same job, cataloguing books for a university library. He drinks two glasses of water first thing in the morning, walks for an hour every day, and devotes almost as much time, before bed, to flossing his teeth. "Winging it" is not a term that comes to mind in describing my father. When he's driving to new places, he does not enjoy getting lost.

In the kitchen, too, he walks a deliberate line, counting out the raisins that go into his oatmeal (fifteen) and never boiling even a drop more water than required for tea. It is my father who knows how many cups of rice are necessary to feed four, or forty, or a hundred and forty people. He has a reputation for *andaj*—the Bengali word for "estimate"—accurately gauging quantities that tend to baffle other cooks. An oracle of rice, if you will.

But there is another rice that my father is more famous for. This is not the white rice, boiled like pasta and then drained in a colander, that most Bengalis eat for dinner. This other rice is pulao, a baked, buttery, sophisticated indulgence, Persian in origin, served at festive occasions. I have often watched him make it. It involves sautéing grains of basmati in butter, along with cinnamon sticks, cloves, bay leaves, and cardamom pods. In go halved cashews and raisins (unlike the oatmeal raisins, these must be golden, not black). Ginger, pulverized into a paste, is incorporated, along with salt and sugar, nutmeg and mace, saffron threads if they're available, ground turmeric if not. A certain amount of water is added, and the rice simmers until most of the water evaporates. Then it is spread out in a baking tray. (My father prefers disposable aluminum ones, which he recycled long before recycling laws were passed.) More water is flicked on top with his fingers, in the ritual and cryptic manner of Catholic priests. Then the tray, covered with foil, goes into the oven, until the rice is cooked through and not a single grain sticks to another.

Despite having a superficial knowledge of the ingredients and the technique, I have no idea how to make my father's pulao, nor would I ever dare attempt it. The recipe is his own, and has never been recorded. There has never been an unsuccessful batch, yet no batch is ever identical to any other. It is a dish that has become an extension of himself, that he has perfected, and to which he has earned the copyright. A dish that will die with him when he dies.

In 1968, when I was seven months old, my father made pulao for the first time. We lived in London, in Finsbury Park, where my parents shared the kitchen, up a steep set of stairs in the attic of the house, with another Bengali couple. The occasion was my *annaprasan*, a rite of passage in which Bengali children are given solid food for the first time; it is known colloquially as a *bhath*, which happens to be the Bengali word for "cooked rice." In the oven of a stove no more than twenty inches wide, my father baked pulao for about thirty-five people. Since then, he has made pulao for the *annaprasans* of his friends' children, for birthday parties and anniversaries, for bridal and baby showers, for wedding receptions, and for my sister's Ph.D. party. For a few decades, after we moved to the United States, his pulao fed crowds of up to four hundred people, at events organized by Prabasi, a Bengali cultural institution in New England, and he found himself at institutional venues—schools and churches and community centers—working with industrial ovens and stoves. This has never unnerved him. He could probably rig up a system to make pulao out of a hot-dog cart, were someone to ask.

There are times when certain ingredients are missing, when he must use almonds instead of cashews, when the raisins in a friend's cupboard are the wrong color. He makes it anyway, with exacting standards but a sanguine hand. 50

When my son and daughter were infants, and we celebrated their *annaprasans*, we hired a caterer, but my father made the pulao, preparing it at home in Rhode Island and transporting it in the trunk of his car to Brooklyn. The occasion, both times, was held at the Society for Ethical Culture, in Park Slope. In 2002, for my son's first taste of rice, my father warmed the trays on the premises, in the giant 55 oven in the basement. But by 2005, when it was my daughter's turn, the representative on duty would not permit my father to use the oven, telling him that he was not a licensed cook. My father transferred the pulao from his aluminum trays into glass baking dishes, and microwaved, batch by batch, rice that fed almost a hundred people. When I asked my father to describe that experience, he expressed no 60 frustration. "It was fine," he said. "It was a big microwave."

Source: The New Yorker, November 23, 2009
http://www.newyorker.com/magazine/2009/11/23/rice-2

Discussion/Writing Prompts

1. Lahiri's description of her father is aimed toward an audience unacquainted with the traditions of Bengali cooking. How do you think this account would be different were it targeted toward an audience already familiar with these traditions? What aspects of this description do you think Lahiri might choose to change? [Rhetorical Analysis of Audience]

2. Are there any food-related rituals or traditions in your own family? Can you think of a particular dish that, in your view, captures or reflects something important about your family? Do you find any parallels between your own example and the description of pulao that Lahiri offers? [Personal Reflection]

3. Lahiri begins her essay by offering the following description:

   My father, seventy-eight, is a methodical man. For thirty-nine years, he has had the same job, cataloguing books for a university library. He drinks two glasses of water first thing in the morning, walks for an hour every day, and devotes almost as much time, before bed, to flossing his teeth.

   What impression of Lahiri's father does this description establish? What particular words or phrases stand out? And why do you think Lahiri chooses to start her essay by offering this particular description? [Close Reading]

4. Much of this essay is devoted to describing not only Lahiri's father but also the specific process by which her father goes about preparing pulao. How effective do you find these descriptive modes to be? What do these descriptions teach us about

Lahiri's family and their experiences living in the United States? [Analyzing Rhetorical Modes]

5. Lahiri concludes her essay with one final description of her father preparing pulao:

> My father transferred the pulao from his aluminum trays into glass baking dishes, and microwaved, batch by batch, rice that fed almost a hundred people. When I asked my father to describe that experience, he expressed no frustration. "It was fine," he said. "It was a big microwave."

What is significant about the fact that this description places so much emphasis on the "microwave" her father uses? What larger point is Lahiri using this particular detail to make? [Argument]

6. Based on his essay, what kind of reality television show do you think Jim Taylor ("Popular Culture: Reality TV is NOT Reality") would create for Lahiri's family? What aspects of family life would he decide to showcase? Which aspects of family life would he decide not to showcase? Why? [Compare and Contrast]

7. Choose a particular food, and research its social and cultural history. Where did this food originate? What groups or communities have the strongest traditions associated with it? Then, write a short essay relating your research to Lahiri's essay. What does her description of "pulao" tell us about her own cultural traditions? [Research]

Tying It All Together

1. Many of the readings assembled above raise the same basic question. For all the new forms of communication our latest technologies make possible, do they truly enable greater connection? Do they foster more helpful, honest, or productive exchanges between writers and audiences? Choose two selections that, in your view, provide answers to these questions. Then, write a two- or three-page essay in which you compare the respective answers each provides.

2. Christopher Calabrese and Michael Harwood ("Destroying the Right to Be Left Alone"), Allison Brennan ("Microtargeting"), and Daniel Solove ("Why Privacy Matters") all invite readers to think about where the line between what is public and what is private should be drawn. Write a two-page essay in which you describe and evaluate the ways each of these writers addresses the issue of privacy. According to each writer, is there any aspect of our lives that can or should still be considered off-limits to public scrutiny or display? According to your own view, where should the boundary between the public and the private be drawn? What guidelines, limits, or restrictions should be placed on what others are allowed to see about us? Why?

3. A key feature of writing in the digital age involves readers' ability to talk back to the writing they encounter. But this newfound power also raises important questions. Is it always a good idea for writers to have such direct and immediate access to audience

feedback? To what extent does the availability of such feedback adversely affect what an author chooses to write? Answer these questions by conducting some research of your own online. Choose an online text that, in your view, showcases a specific connection between authors and audience. Then, in a two- or three-page essay, conduct a rhetorical analysis of the role that the audience plays here. Who is the target audience? What assumptions does the text make concerning what this audience cares about or wants to know? What effect upon its audience does the text want to have? And what specific aspects of the text would you point to as evidence of this?

Using the Steps of Rhetorical Analysis to Write Your Own Academic Essay

The same instruction this chapter presents for analyzing other people's writing can serve as a guide to the writing you do yourself. Take a look at the outline below. Organizing the writing process along the same rhetorical lines modeled above, it provides you with a map for how to use the concept of audience to organize and create your own essay:

- *Step One: Identifying the Audience*: What kind of reader are you trying to reach? How would you define your intended or target audience?
- *Step Two: Addressing the Audience*: What rhetorical choices do you make to address your audience?
- *Step Three: Influencing the Audience*: What specific goals do you have for your audience? Do you want to educate? Entertain? Persuade? Inform?

To see how these steps can be put into practice, let's take a look at a specific example. As you read over the essay below, pay attention to how considerations about audience guide the writer's calculations and choices. To assist you in this work, take note of the comments and questions that accompany the essay in the margins. Then, turn your attention to the sample analysis that follows. In what ways does this discussion provide a model for using the steps outlined above to write an essay of your own?

Student Essay: Luke VanderMeer, "Censoring Free Speech: A Contradiction in Terms"

This essay by Luke VanderMeer, a college student, employs the definition mode to address a key question: Under what circumstances is it permissible to limit free speech?

Democracy is founded on the idea that all people, regardless of background or belief, have the right to express their views, whatever they may be. Since its founding, for example, the United States has championed freedom of speech as one of the basic pillars of a democratic society, a universal

Opening with a definition of "democracy"

5

right that government should be allowed to place very few constraints upon. For this reason, censorship has long been regarded in American society as being incompatible with democracy. Because it's primary objective is to restrict free
10 speech, censorship of public expression is not only counter to our nation's democratic ideals, it is fundamentally anti-American.

Presenting definition of "censorship"

First and foremost, censorship involves an intentional effort to stifle the ability of citizens to freely air and ex-
15 change their views. What this means is that censorship targets one of the basic features of democracy itself. In a society in which people are no longer free to express their views, there is a greater risk that decisions about how this society is to be governed will be made without any input
20 from the people themselves. The famous philosopher John Stuart Mill argues in his work, *On Liberty*, that protecting free speech is key to preventing governments from exercising tyranny over their citizens. If citizens live in fear that their ideas and views are going to be censored, it is far less
25 likely that they will express views that go against the wishes of those in power.

Developing definition of "censorship"

Citing outside authority to bolster main point

In order for a democratic society to actually function as a democracy, there need to be strong rules in place preventing the censoring of public speech. Citizens must have open
30 access to all ideas so that they may come to a deep understanding of critical issues. Such access is critical for the public to be able to properly form opinions and make decisions.

Using definition to advance an argument about limiting censorship

A related reason to oppose censorship is that doing so en-
35 sures that a society will continue to progress socially and politically. Throughout history, it is often the case that many ideas considered by the general public to be offensive or wrong turn out over time to represent ideas a society needs to embrace in order to continue advancing. A case in
40 from our own history is the Civil Rights Movement from the 1960's. When people first began demanding equal rights for African Americans, many white Americans (especially in the South) regarded this position as too radical. Imagine if those protesting in favor of these rights were
45 prohibited from expressing these views publicly. It is conceivable our society would not have achieved the enormous progress in civil rights that it did. It is frightening to

Offering reason in support of argument

Using historical example as evidence to support argument

imagine that such important ideas could be withheld from humanity, and another reason why censorship should never be tolerated.

50

Some in favor of censorship argue that this practice is useful because it allows a government to protect its citizens from harmful speech. Thus, they argue, censorship should be allowed in cases of speech that grossly offends, or even harms, others. But this view of censorship raises questions of its own. Where do we draw the line between speech that is too offensive and speech that is permissible? Who should be in charge of making this distinction? And what happens in situations where people disagree? For example, some argue that the public expression of views challenging the government should be deemed "treasonous," and thus banned. But who should be in charge of making this determination? One person's definition of "treasonous" speech might easily strike somebody else as a legitimate, even necessary, expression of political opposition. Because there is such a slippery slope, the best solution is always to err on the side of allowing more, rather than less, speech. Otherwise, you run the risk of suppressing ideas that should be aired.

Challenging an alternative definition of censorship

55

60

Using hypothetical example as further support for main point

65

Another point raised by advocates of censorship is that different standards should apply where children are concerned. While it is true that children are not as fully developed as adults, and are thus potentially more susceptible to the influence of dangerous speech, it does not automatically follow that banning certain forms of expression is the answer. A better solution for children is to present them with support and guidance about how to properly understand and evaluate the ideas to which they are exposed. Children are never going to learn how to think for themselves, how to decide what ideas they accept and what they reject, if they are never allowed to hear these ideas for themselves.

Challenging another alternative definition of censorship

70

75

80

Overall, advocates of censorship support this policy because they regard certain forms of expression as simply too dangerous to be tolerated. While understandable, the potential danger posed by such ideas is far outweighed by the importance of allowing free speech. It is true that some ideas can pose serious threats to public welfare. But in the long run, the public welfare is far better served by allowing people to take responsibility for everything they hear and

Recapping main points

85

90   say. Once censorship begins, it is difficult to stop it. Because
        the question of what to ban and what to allow is so subjec-
        tive, there is never any sound basis on which to define what
        censorship should be. Given this, I would argue that censor-
        ship should be opposed.

Now, let's see how the rhetorical steps presented above help us understand the choices the writer makes to create this essay:

Step One: *Identifying the Audience: What Kind of Reader Is the Author Trying to Reach?*

- o On one level, it appears that the writer is addressing a general audience, composed of people who do not necessarily have strong objections to the notion of censorship. In more specific terms, though, it appears that the writer imagines himself addressing a type of reader who might be susceptible to the argument that censorship is useful and therefore needs to hear the argument against it.

Step Two: *Addressing the Audience: What Choices Does the Writer Make to Reach this Audience?*

- o The writer makes his case against censorship primarily by providing the audience a set of guidelines for how to define this concept. From the outset, for example, he draws a connection between censorship, free speech, and democracy, noting that "censorship has long been regarded in American society as being incompatible with democracy." The writer pursues this same strategy throughout the essay, arguing at another point that the "censoring of public speech" is incompatible with the "functioning of democracy."

- o To sway his readers' viewpoint, the writer also points to historical examples designed to prove how dangerous and ill-advised censorship actually is. He cites, for instance, the American Civil Rights Movement, using this example to prod readers to think skeptically about the validity of censorship: "Imagine if those protesting in favor of these rights were prohibited from expressing these views publicly."

Step Three: *Influencing the Audience: What Specific Goals Does the Writer Have for This Audience?*

- o Clearly, the writer employs these strategies to both educate and persuade his audience. The author's discussion of censorship in the opening paragraph, for example, is designed to provide readers with some basic information about what censorship involves. But these definitions are also designed to shape readers' attitudes toward censorship, to encourage them to form skeptical attitudes toward this concept. This same strategy is at work in other parts of the essay as well. In the historical and hypothetical examples, for instance, the writer clearly wants not only to provide his readers with further information but also to use this information to help them reach negative conclusions about censorship.

Group Work: Thinking Rhetorically About the Formal Selections

Throughout this chapter, you have been given ample opportunity to analyze audience on your own. Now, let's undertake this same kind of work from a group perspective. Your group should select one of the formal selections above. Prepare for your group work by re-reading the selection your group has been assigned. Then, with your group, use the outline presented at the beginning of the chapter, *Thinking Rhetorically About Audience*, to analyze the role that audience plays in this piece. Here is a quick recap of these steps:

• How does this text define its audience?
• How does this text address its audience?
• How does this text attempt to influence its audience?
• What kind of audience am I?
• How do I put this into writing?

Once you have completed this work, exchange your findings with another group. First, have your group re-read the selection these new findings examine. Then, discuss as a group how helpful you find this analysis. Do you agree with the conclusions about audience this analysis draws? Do you evaluate the role of audience in different or similar ways? Finally, summarize your key findings in a paragraph. Be prepared to share this written assessment with the rest of the class.

Changing Contexts, Shifting Audiences: Understanding the Connection Between Informal and Formal Writing

Throughout this chapter, we have shifted back and forth between a focus on informal and formal writing. How do these types of writing compare? What are the key differences in language and tone, form and content, organization and context? And what happens to our understanding of audience when we take these differences into account?

The activity presented here provides us with an opportunity to address these questions. First, choose a topic or issue raised by one of the selections in this chapter (e.g., government surveillance, reality television, or the problems of modern political campaigns). Next, choose an informal venue (e.g., blog post, Facebook post, tweet, or email), and write about this issue using the conventions of this particular form. Then, choose a formal venue (e.g., journal essay, magazine article, or academic analysis), and write about the same issue using the conventions particular to this form. When you're done, spend a few moments itemizing the specific ways these two writing samples differ. In what ways did your choice of venue affect the audience you aimed to address? How did this choice of audience influence other rhetorical choices: tone or voice, language or word choice, purpose or goal?

Connecting Audience to Rhetorical Modes

As you learned in Chapter 4, writing that differs in terms of genre may still share certain rhetorical patterns or modes. To better understand how rhetorical considerations of audience relate to the question of rhetorical modes, try the following activity: Choose one of the examples of real world writing from the informal selections in this chapter. First, describe the intended or target audience you believe this writing seeks to address. Then, choose the rhetorical mode (narration, description, cause-and-effect, compare-and-contrast, or definition) you feel is most prominent in this writing, and analyze the particular ways it helps the writer reach and influence the target audience.

Speaking for Yourself

Now that you have gotten some practice analyzing audience in relation to other people's writing, see how much of this work you can put into practice yourself. Choose a genre or type of real world writing with which you are familiar (e.g., political blog, social network site, or online magazine), and create your own example. What topic do you want to explore? What issues or questions do you want to raise? What messages or claims do you want to convey? What information or images do you want to include? When you're done, sketch a portrait of the reader you would consider to be the ideal or target audience for your text. Why did you choose this particular type of reader?

7 Argument

Members of the Tea Party Caucus gather in Congress to denounce the "socialist" policies of President Obama. Kanye West publicly feuds with Jimmy Kimmel over disparaging remarks the host makes in his late-night monologue. Before a television audience of millions, a married couple engage in a shouting match on the reality television show *The Real Housewives of New Jersey*. While they span widely different contexts and raise very distinct issues, these three media moments do share one crucial thing in common: Each attests to the central place that *argument* occupies in modern life. Whether it's partisan commentators shouting past each other on a Sunday talk show or dysfunctional spouses trading accusations on *Dr. Phil*, a snarky exchange we may find ourselves having over email or a scathing movie review we happen across online, ours is a world in which arguing has emerged as one of our most familiar forms of address—the default discourse of everyday life.

And yet it's far from clear that we have been taught to think about argument in ways that do full justice to the term. To be sure, our airwaves are filled with examples of people arguing. But such examples also tend to define argumentation itself in very limited ways: as little more than a pitched battle between entrenched adversaries, in which the only goal is to dominate, defeat, or silence the opposition. So commonplace has this notion become, in fact, that it has even leeched into the language we use to talk about argument. We speak of arguments as things to be "won" or "lost," tallying a given speaker or writer's claims as so many "points" to be scored against an opponent.

What Point Am I Trying to Make?

The truth, however, is a bit more complicated. While argument does involve putting up our views against those of other people, this doesn't mean that argument is solely about conflict. In its fullest form, in fact, argument works as a powerful vehicle for *exchanging* views rather than stifling them: a way to spur to dialogue and create common ground.

This is particularly true when it comes to analyzing argument in writing. Whatever the setting or topic, virtually every type of writing is designed to make some larger point. And to analyze such points (or arguments) effectively, there are any number of rhetorical questions we might pose: What message is the writer trying to get across? What makes this message important? What reasoning or evidence does this writer offer to support this message? And most importantly, do I find any of this convincing?

How to Analyze Argument in Real World Writing

The outline below provides you with a framework for conducting this rhetorical analysis in a more systematic way. Take a look at these steps, and familiarize yourself with the kinds of analysis each asks you to undertake. As you do this, also think about how you might use these steps to begin analyzing argument yourself.

▪ Thinking Rhetorically About Argument

- **Step One: Identifying the Issue Within the Argument:** What larger point is the writer is trying to make? What makes this issue debatable?
- **Step Two: Defining the Purpose Behind the Argument:** What larger goal is the writer trying to accomplish by making this argument?
- **Step Three: Exploring the Assumptions Underlying the Argument:** What assumptions does the writer seem to be making about why this argument is important?
- **Step Four: Defending the Argument:** What kinds of support does the writer offer to bolster the argument?
- **Step Five: Revising the Argument:** What critiques or counterpoints to this argument might a reader make? What changes or revisions might make this argument more effective?
- **Step Six: Putting It Into Writing:** How do you summarize your findings in writing?

To put these guidelines into practice, let's turn to an example. As you look over the selection below, use the questions outlined above to begin thinking about the particular decisions the writer makes to construct, advance, and defend this argument.

Alex Echov, "The Credit Card Trap"

This editorial by Alex Echov, a college junior, takes a stand on the issue of credit card use among college students. As such, it models exactly the kind of argumentative writing you might easily come across in your own daily life.

Student credit card debt continues to rise at an incredible rate. On average, students leave college with over $4,000 in credit card debt. This is a travesty and has to stop. Certainly students themselves need to take a degree of responsibility here, but this doesn't get to the heart of the matter. What about the credit card compa-
5   nies? Should they be allowed to lure unsuspecting young people into credit card deals that often have sky-high interest rates? And what about college administrators? Is it right that these people exercise no oversight or control over credit card use by students? Everyone involved in this issue should start by being more honest about what's really going on. This will lead to solutions that help resolve this very
10   difficult question.

▨ Thinking Rhetorically About Argument: A Step-by-Step Guide

Now, let's see how these questions and observations can be used as the basis for putting together a more formal, step-by-step, rhetorical analysis:

Step One: *Identifying the Issue: What Topic Does the Writer Raise? What Makes It Arguable?*

- ° The writer is clearly interested in the issue of credit card debt and, more specifically, on the effect that such debt has upon the average college student.

- ° In many ways, it seems like the writer is talking back to the credit card companies themselves, who most likely go to great lengths to assure college students there is absolutely nothing wrong with signing up for credit cards or accumulating consumer debt.

- ° From this perspective, what makes this issue arguable is that it involves a disagreement over whether credit card companies are pursuing business practices that help or hurt college students.

Step Two: *Defining the Purpose: What Goal is the Writer Trying to Achieve?*

- ° This writer has a point of view that is deeply critical of the ways credit card companies market to college students. Part of the goal therefore is to make the reader more critical or skeptical about the motives of the credit card companies themselves. We can see this goal in the writer's use of such terms as "travesty," and "sky-high interest rates." This goal is also evident in the questions the writer poses. For example:

    > Should [credit card companies] be allowed to lure unsuspecting young people into credit card deals . . . ?

- ° Another goal the writer seems to have is to convince readers that college-age students are not yet ready to handle the responsibility of credit card debt. This message comes across in the writer's comments about how credit card companies "lure" college students or the characterization of these students as "unsuspecting." The clear implication here is that students are being manipulated or duped.

- ° A third goal has to do with the attitude toward college administrators that the writer wants the audience to adopt. By suggesting that administrators have a role to play in regulating the behavior of credit card companies on campus, the writer appears to be assigning responsibility for this problem more broadly.

Step Three: *Exploring the Assumptions: What Assumptions Does the Writer Make About This Issue?*

- ° In advancing this critique, the writer is clearly working from the assumption that the motives behind the credit card companies' behavior are suspect.

This is made clear in the writer's assertion, near the end, that people need to be more "honest about what's really going on." The implication here is that credit card companies are not being "honest" with their customers and that part of the problem with student debt overall stems from their willingness not to be truthful.

o Another assumption underlying this critique is that college students are not yet responsible enough to be entrusted with their own decisions. While the writer does call for students to be more responsible, the overriding message is that this will not be enough to solve this problem. What is needed instead, the writer implies, is for others (e.g., college administrators or the credit card companies) to take responsibility and police this situation.

Step Four: *Defending the Argument: How Does the Writer Justify This Stance?*

o The writer believes that college student consumer debt is a real problem that needs to be tackled. In support of this view, the writer offers statistical evidence, citing the average debt of a typical college student.

o In addition, the writer also chooses language designed to play upon fears about the size and scope of the problem. For example:

Student credit card debt continues to rise at an incredible rate.

This is a travesty and has to stop.

Step Five: *Revising the Argument: What Critiques or Counterpoints Might Be Made?*

o It could be argued that the writer is overlooking the benefits that credit cards might offer the average college student. While the issue of debt is a serious one, the writer doesn't acknowledge the possibility that some students could have legitimate reasons for using a credit card. How would the writer react to stories of students needing a credit card to buy books for class or to pay part of their tuition? What effect would these stories have on the writer's overall argument?

o Another potential critique has to do with the way the writer is handling the question of responsibility. In the discussion about credit card companies, the writer seems to downplay the possibility that college students themselves should exercise more responsibility for their actions. Even though the writer calls on students to do this, the rest of the essay clearly treats this problem as the fault of those other than the students themselves. How well would this argument stand up to a call for greater individual responsibility?

Step Six: *Putting It Into Writing: How Do I Summarize My Findings in Writing?*

º The writer has clearly identified a pressing social problem. It is undeniable that large amounts of consumer debt, at perilously high rates of interest, have saddled many college students with a problem that may take years to resolve. On the other hand, the writer seems too quick, in my view, to assign full responsibility for this to the credit card companies themselves. True, the terms of these credit card deals do not always serve the interest of the students, but these students are still, at the end of the day, free to choose, or not to choose, to sign up. What is missing from this discussion is an assessment of the problem that assigns responsibility more broadly.

Informal Writing Selections

Now, try putting this kind of analysis into practice yourself. Using the example above as your guide, look more closely at the larger point each of the following selections attempts to make. In each case, how does the writer attempt to get this point across? What language does the writer use, what support does the writer provide, to persuade readers to accept this point?

To address these questions, let's start by taking a look at some sample analysis. As you read the selection below, pay attention first to the comments and questions that appear in the margins. Then, turn your attention to the sample discussion that follows. And finally, use the step-by-step approach outlined above to analyze the collection of informal selections below.

Adam Copeland, "I Will Pray on National Day of Prayer but NOT Because Congress Told Me To"

This essay is excerpted from A Wee Blether, *a blog by Adam Copeland that explores issues of religion and spirituality in modern life.*

Today is National Day of Prayer. I know Congress passes strange celebrations and remembrances all the time of which nobody takes notice. National Day of Prayer (NDP) is different, however, even unique. Churches around the country are holding prayer breakfasts this morning. Services will take place tonight. The country is praying because Congress told us to . . . .

Interesting decision to use the word "strange." To what extent does this preview the larger argument to come?

5

In a recent "Sightings" article Martin Marty discussed the changing nature of government-related religion with the phrase "when Baptists were Baptists

10

they knew this . . ." He also connects the decline of organized religion in Europe to the established state church. I wonder if the current religious environment in the US is confusing our historical awareness. The Establishment Clause of the First Amendment makes clear "Congress shall make no law respecting an establishment of religion." The Free Exercise Clause says Congress can't prohibit the free exercise of religion.

The writer is offering a lot of different support for his argument here: a history of "organized religion" in Europe, the Constitution. Does this evidence support the larger argument?

Historians are certainly not clear and consistent with their take on the religious beliefs of the "founding fathers," and we've wrestled with interpreting the First Amendment for hundreds of years. But, even if we know what and how Franklin and John Hancock prayed, I think that misses the point. The Constitution is bigger than the sum of vision of the founding fathers—who owned slaves, never imagined women would preach, or we'd have a lesbian cabinet official etc.

The awesome religious freedom we have in the US is a huge part of what makes this country so vibrant, free, and hopeful. Our government, even though it is made up of us, doesn't tell us what to believe about God nor how to practice those beliefs.

Key part of the argument. Writer drawing a firm distinction between personal religious belief on the one hand and government sponsorship of religious belief on the other.

I will certainly pray today, but not at a NDP breakfast or service. Instead, I'll take the advice of a guy named Jesus, who I call "the Christ" and the savior of the world. He advised once, "And when you pray, do not be like the hypocrites, for they love to pray standing in the synagogues and on the street corners to be seen by men. I tell you the truth, they have received their reward in full. But when you pray, go into your room, close the door and pray to your Father, who is unseen. Then your Father, who sees what is done in secret, will reward you" (Matt. 5:5–6).

Interesting way to conclude. Does this biblical quotation help the writer's overall argument?

Source: A Wee Blether, May 6, 2010
http://www.adamjcopeland.com/2010/05/06/ndp/

Step One: *Identifying the Issue: What Topic Does the Writer Raise? What Makes It Arguable?*

o The fundamental question in this essay has less to do with whether it is proper or not for individuals to pray than with who should ultimately be in charge of making this decision. Clearly, this writer is someone who believes, personally, in the value of prayer. What he objects to is the notion that prayer should be encouraged or compelled by the government.

º This point about the importance of individual choice is expressed in the essay's title, which draws a line between choosing to pray and being "told" to pray.

Step Two: *Defining the Purpose: What Goal Is the Writer Trying to Achieve?*

º The writer's main goal is to get his readers to think more skeptically about what it means for the government to sponsor holidays like National Prayer Day. He refers to this holiday as a "strange celebration," for instance, and speaks of the hypocrisy of those who sponsor it.

º In doing so, the writer also clearly is challenging those who, in recent years, have called upon (mostly Christian) religion to be given a more prominent place in public life. Arguing against this view, he repeatedly emphasizes the personal aspects of prayer, linking this to the ideals of liberty and individual freedom.

Step Three: *Exploring the Assumptions: What Assumptions Does the Writer Make About This Issue?*

º One of the main assumptions behind this essay is that the debate over prayer and freedom of choice has a long and prominent history. The writer's references to the "founding fathers," implies that this debate dates back to the earliest days of the Republic.

º In critiquing National Prayer Day, the writer also betrays his assumption that holidays such as these amount to a requirement that all Americans pray. By using National Prayer Day a symbol of mandatory prayer, the writer implies that such commemorations have the power to force people to engage in prayer, even if they do not wish to.

Step Four: *Defending the Argument: How Does the Writer Justify This Stance?*

º Much of the writer's argument rests on the opposition he establishes between compulsory prayer on the one hand and individual liberty on the other. We can see this in the emphasis he places on "[t]he awesome religious freedom we have in the US" and in the ways he casts America itself as a "vibrant, free, and hopeful" country.

º As noted above, the writer justifies his stance in part by pointing to American history. Arguing against the claim that mandatory prayer can be validated by looking to the religious beliefs of the "founding fathers," he cites other historical precedents that subsequent generations of Americans have come to reject, such as owning slaves and denying women the franchise.

º The writer further justifies his view by citing Christian theology. Most notably, he quotes a biblical passage that defines prayer as an essentially private act ("close the door and pray to your Father").

Step Five: *Revising the Argument: What Critiques or Counterpoints Might Be Made?*

○ One could certainly argue that the writer is overestimating the power of holidays like National Day of Prayer to force people to pray. A potential counterpoint might treat such holidays as more of a generic endorsement of prayer rather than a command for individuals to engage in prayer themselves.

○ Another counterpoint relates to the historical evidence the writer cites. Why isn't it valid to consider the religious convictions of the "founding fathers"? If these are the figures responsible for creating our Constitution, shouldn't their own views on religious belief and prayer be part of our considerations today?

Step Six: *Putting It Into Writing: How Do I Summarize My Findings in Writing?*

○ While he tends to present the issue in stark, either/or terms, the writer makes a valid point about the need to preserve individual freedom and individual choice when it comes to something as personal as prayer. And just as importantly, he uses precedent from American history to justify his claim. The result is a discussion of events like National Prayer Day that demonstrates how truly "American" it is to treat prayer itself as a solely personal decision.

Now, it's your turn. For each of the selections below, use these same six steps outlined above to undertake your own analysis of argument.

Kristi Myllenbeck, "You're Vegan, We Get It"

The Spartan Daily *is the campus newspaper for San Jose State University.*

Want to hear a joke? "How do you know if a person is vegan? Don't worry, they'll tell you."

The joke is a little harsh, but it brings up a good point. Why can't someone simply adopt a lifestyle or way of consuming nourishment without feeling like they have to brag about it?

For those of you who may not know, the vegan lifestyle is defined by not consuming or
5   coming into contact with animal products, most notably dairy, eggs and meat.

Some vegans may decide to not consume honey or products that come from insects. In addition, vegans don't wear leather or use down comforters.

Does making these decisions constitute an attitude of complete smugness though? I'm not so sure.

10   I understand it takes a ton of dedication to commit to the vegan lifestyle, but you'd think that those who respect and love Mother Earth and all things living would be, in general, just a tad more agreeable.

Okay, I'm not saying all vegan people are awful by any means. I'm just saying some vegans I know constantly look down on anyone who doesn't adopt the same lifestyle.

15   I've met handfuls of vegan/vegetarian people on either side—both boastful and modest.

Some people who are vegan or vegetarian feel the need to belittle people who enjoy eating meat, while others simply go about their business without making a spectacle out of their dietary choices.

I understand going vegan has myriad health and environmental benefits, and that's awesome. But why can't you just be an animal activist and do well for the Earth without being a pretentious asshole? 20

You can so easily decline that piece of milk chocolate by saying, "No, thank you" instead of "EW, I can't eat THAT, I'm VEGAN." I can assure you, almost nobody cares that you're vegan.

I can hear all the vegan students reading this grumbling and groaning. Don't worry. As you know, there is another side to the story. 25

Meat-eaters can be just as vicious and rude, if not more. On top of that, those who do not eat meat are confronted with a variety of situations.

There's the situation where there is nothing to eat besides fries at the restaurant your friends choose. There's the jerk who interrogates you about why someone would ever give up bacon, God forbid. And of course, there's the quintessential friend's dad who straight-up 30 makes fun of you for not eating meat, with no valid argument to back up his taunting.

Nowadays, there are so many dietary fads that people brag about, I can hardly keep anything straight.

I think what is most important is that we take care of our bodies, regardless of what that may mean for each person. It comes down to common courtesy and being respectful of one 35 another.

You make the choices you do because it's best for you, whether it relates to religion, study habits, eating meat, whatever. Notice the "you." It doesn't say other people.

I'm all for education and opening others' eyes to new possibilities, especially if it can positively affect someone's health, but there is a right and wrong way to go about it. 40

I am a huge supporter of not forcing beliefs on others.

I think with a little more sensibility and respect on both sides, the food world and world in general could definitely be a better and more peaceful place.

Source: The Spartan Daily, *October 10, 2013*
http://spartandaily.com/109629/youre-vegan-get

Debate.org, "Where Else Would Our Children Learn Patriotism?"

This comment was posted on the website Debate.org in 2013 as part of an online discussion about whether the Pledge of Allegiance should be recited in school.

As a math teacher at a High School I take the time to explain each sentence to my students, so they can understand the meaning behind each statement Bellamy wrote as the pledge of allegiance. I realize the "under God" portion was not a part of the original version and am okay with people's religious beliefs keeping them from saying the pledge. However, I do feel it is still important for them to respect 5 the idea of supporting our country by at least rising and standing silently during the pledge. To me the pledge of allegiance is as American as apple pie and the national anthem at a baseball game. I do it to show my students how much I love my country, and to show respect to the sacrifices that countless numbers of men and women have given for me and my family to live in this wonderful country. Unfortunately, many of our citizens seem to take this sacrifice for granted and feel entitled to more benefits or subsidies and/or freedoms than our forefathers intended us to have.

Source: Debate.org, 2013
http://www.debate.org/opinions/should-the-pledge-of-allegiance-be-said-in-schools

Visual Rhetoric: Chris Knorr, "The Pledge of Allegiance and an American Flag"

This picture offers its own take on the issue of government-sponsored prayer. What sort of argument does this image make? How does it compare with the claims made by the anonymous post above?

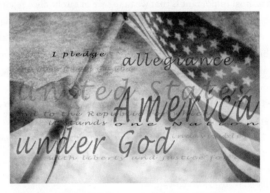

FIGURE 7.5

Source: Design Pics/Chris Knorr/Design Pics/Getty Images

Amanda Hall, "College Affordability and the Growing Cost of Education"

Rock the Vote is a nonpartisan, nonprofit organization dedicated to engaging young people in the political process.

The problem of college affordability is not a new preoccupation in America. In fact, scholars have been tracing this growing issue since the late 1990s. Today the major components of the problem remain the same, concerns about: the growing cost of education, student indebtedness and the financialization of higher education

The Growing Cost of Education:

It is impossible to deny that the cost of education has increased over the years. According to the US Department of Education's National Center for Education Statistics, the average cost of attending a 4-year, either public or private, institution doubled between 1990 and 2010. And according to the research, the cost also doubled for the same data set between 1980 and 1990. The difference between the 1990s and now, however, is context. Over the last decade our economy has suffered through a national terror attack, two wars, numerous natural disasters, labor outsourcing via globalization, a housing market collapse, a recession, and we finally became cognizant of corporate deregulation and the extent to which corporations were extracting economic rents from our economy. These events, especially the latter ones, have directly contributed to the ever-growing income divide in our nation, which compounds the college affordability question, including the lower and middle class' ability to pay.

Institutions claim that the cost of education is rising because state and federal governments have slashed spending on higher education and as a result, that cost has been transferred to students. While this is true in most places across America, there are other factors that subscribe to rising costs. Athletic programs, extravagant recreational facilities, and specialized food services have all contributed to growing costs. Moreover, basic economic theory tells us that colleges have an incentive to limit access to their universities by keeping costs high. When a product, like higher education, is costly, demand is higher than universities that are not as expensive. In this way, universities can use an economic factor, like cost, to increase their selectivity.

Additionally, non-classroom costs, like administrative overhead and payrolls, have ballooned, adding another line item to student's college bills. Professor salaries have not increased with administrative salaries and higher college costs, which makes us question a university's intent and, what appears to be, unbalanced fiscal allocations.

From a policy standpoint, Congress needs to take steps to ensure that colleges are held accountable for their soaring costs. The value-add of an expensive college should be palpable immediately after a student graduates from the institution in the form of transferable skills, job prospects, and career guidance. But, instead, universities are spending on ostentatious dining and athletic facilities for the student's in-residence use, a venture that has marginal impact on a student's return on investment post-graduation. Policymakers can financially incentivize universities to tie their costs to their post-graduates' success levels. This will 1) hold colleges accountable for their costs and 2) improve college effectiveness with emphasis on post-graduate opportunities.

45   The key to understanding the growing cost of education is internalizing that higher education is a business that provides a specific, and in most cases, covenanted product. Like all consumer products the government and the citizenry should hold educational enterprises accountable for the effectiveness of their product.

Source: Rock the Vote, August 29, 2013
http://www.blog.rockthevote.com/2013/08/issue-analysis-college-affordability-and-the-growing-cost-of-education.html

---

Visual Rhetoric: John Darkow, "Student Loan Debt"

This cartoon offers a satiric take on the issue of college affordability. What is the main point this cartoon is trying to advance? How does it compare to the argument about college affordability presented above?

Student Loan Debt   #100026

BY JOHN DARKOW, COLUMBIA DAILY TRIBUNE, MISSOURI - 10/28/2011 12:00:00 AM

FIGURE 7.7

Source: Columbia Daily Tribune, October 28, 2011. John Darkow/Copyright Cagle Cartoons.
http://www.politicalcartoons.com/cartoon/b83396d4-4fcc-440c-97c3-b260cff69c7d.html

---

Penny Lee, "The Problem With a $15 Minimum Wage"

USNews.com is the website for the newsmagazine US News and World Report.

At the height of the recession, the U.S. had an unemployment rate of 10 percent. Since the economic recovery began in January 2009, irrespective of one's views about the health aspects of fast food, these restaurants have added jobs more than twice as fast as the U.S. average, which has helped lower the unemployment rate to 7.8 percent.

Demonstrations by workers and union officials are now taking place across the country, claiming that it is not enough to provide a job, but that companies "owe" employees a higher salary that provides them a "livable wage"—currently being proposed at double the existing minimum wage, to offer employees a certain level of economic security and dignity.

As an example of how this impacts companies that have large numbers of minimum wage workers, it is estimated that a wage increase to $15 an hour would cost McDonald's $8 billion. The negative impact wouldn't be felt just with workers, by hiring less, but would also impact investors, suppliers and customers, who would pay increased prices.

Different jobs require different skill sets and are compensated based on the market value for the aptitude required and the service rendered. When defining what amounts to a fair wage, shouldn't the fair question be what corresponds to the market value of what the worker produces?

President Obama recently called for the raising of the minimum wage saying, "Nobody who works full-time should have to raise their children in poverty." But, in a free market system, should we allow for workers and employers to contract with one another based on an above-board, negotiated rate or attempt to dictate standards of living through minimum wage adjustments?

Recently, Walmart announced that it was prepared to invest in Washington, D.C., and open six new stores, projected to create 1,800 jobs, albeit many at a mandated minimum wage rate of $8.25. But, the D.C. City Council voted to force them to offer a higher minimum wage of $12.50. Without a veto by the mayor, Walmart has since announced that they will pull out of the D.C. market, rather than pass along the higher labor costs to its customers.

The council attempted to bully a large corporation by changing an existing minimum wage law and, in the end, denied 1,800 people a chance to work. The council members can indeed boast that they fought and stood on the side of workers, but the reality is that there are now 1,800 fewer jobs in D.C. Where I'm from, that's called winning the battle and losing the war.

While an extraordinary amount of focus of late seems to be on the hourly wage worker, what seems to be missing from the debate is the opportunity for upward mobility. 40 percent of the executives at McDonalds started out receiving an hourly wage. 50 percent of McDonalds franchise owners were at one time hourly wage employees. Similarly, Walmart gives out more than 160,000 promotions a year. These are all individuals who are able to gain a higher wage and better standard of living through experience and on the job training, gaining the kind of skill sets needed to live out the American dream.

To move America forward, the protest shouldn't be directed at those employers that provide jobs, but about how we put the policies in place that encourage more hiring, increase productivity and lower costs to do business. There need to be policies in place that allow for entrepreneurs to make their dreams a reality and extend opportunities to others.

50   A recent report noted, "Without entrepreneurs, there would have been no new net growth in the U.S. for the last 20 years." Policymakers need to continue to strike a balance on government regulation that puts the necessary safe guards on industry, while not choking the ability to innovate, grow and create more job opportunities, promotions, and advancement.

Source: USNews.com, September 9, 2013
http://www.usnews.com/opinion/blogs/penny-lee/2013/09/04/the-problem-with-
striking-workers-and-a-15-minimum-wage

■ Thinking Rhetorically About Argument: Expanded Outline

Now that you've gotten some practice with this kind of analysis, use the expanded outline below to work your way through one of the selections included above. How does this text construct and defend its argument? How does the treatment of argument relate to the other rhetorical choices the writer makes?

Step One: *Identifying the Issue: What is the Main Topic This Selection Addresses?*

o What specific topics does this selection explore? What issues does it raise?

o What makes this topic arguable? What are the different opinions, that people tend to have about this issue?

o Who, in your view, is most likely to care about this issue? How would you characterize the views of the different sides who engage in this debate?

Step Two: *Defining Purpose: What Goal is the Writer Trying to Accomplish?*

o What viewpoint on this issue does the author express? What central point about this issue does the writer want to make?

o How does the writer want readers to respond to this point?

Step Three: *Exploring Assumptions: What Assumptions Does the Writer Make About This Issue?*

o Why does the writer feel this issue is important?

o What does the writer assume readers already know about this issue?

o What does the writer assume readers do not already know about this issue?

Step Four: *Defending the Argument: How Does the Writer Justify This Stance?*

○ How does the text go about specifically advancing the writer's point of view? What strategies of persuasion (e.g., logical deduction, statistics/facts, or emotional appeal) does the writer use?

○ What forms of support does the writer offer? Is this support logical or convincing?

Step Five: *Revising the Argument: What Critiques or Counterpoints Might I Offer?*

○ Why do I care about this issue? Do I have the same viewpoint on this issue as the writer?

○ What flaws do I detect in the writer's argument?

○ What changes would I make to address these flaws?

Step Six: *Putting It Into Writing*

○ How do I summarize my findings in writing?

Formal Writing Selections

Our modern culture is rife with countless feuds, struggles, and conflicts. And while it may be easy to create a list of such arguments, much harder to address is the question of how we actually got here. What explains this uptick in public disagreeableness? What aspects of our contemporary culture are to blame? This, in a nutshell, is the question the selections below attempt to address. Offering a representative sampling of the dialogues, diatribes, and debates taking place today, these pieces shine a light on some of the most contentious issues that bedevil and divide us.

To fully understand these issues, this section approaches the essays from two related perspectives. First, it invites you to analyze each essay as its own form of argument. What rhetorical strategies, it asks, does each essay use to convey and support its main point? Second, it invites you to analyze each essay as its own reflection *upon* argument: an inquiry into how and why we argue in the ways that we do.

Myisha Cherry, "Twitter Trolls and the Refusal to Be Silenced"

When we find ourselves arguing with another person face to face, we can generally rest assured that our conflict won't rise beyond a certain threshold. But what happens to such restraint when our arguments go online? Under the Web's protective cloak of anonymity, many speak to others in ways that mislead, mock, and malign. Taking aim at one of the key examples of this trend, Myisha Cherry, an adjunct professor of philosophy at the City University of New York, shares her thoughts about the growing threat of "Twitter trolling."

"Twitter has been a space to share information but it has also been a space where civility can be thrown out the window, free speech is hailed and abused and where the silencing of individuals, particularly women and minorities, has become commonplace."

On August 4, 2013, some Twitter users boycotted the service in what was known as the #TwitterSilence Campaign. The boycott was in response to rape and bomb threats directed at feminist users. Such threats included, "a bomb has been placed outside your home," sent to historian Mary Beard. Caroline Criado-Perez, a cam-
5   paigner who was successful with getting Jane Austen on the British bank note, received tweets like "kill yourself before I do." They've also received rape threats, which because of their explicit nature, I refuse to repeat here.

Twitter has been a space to share information but it has also been a space where civility can be thrown out the window, free speech is hailed and abused and where
10   the silencing of individuals, particularly women and minorities, has become commonplace.

In 140 characters or less, trolls use Twitter like the Westboro Baptist Church uses funeral picket lines: to hail insults against others. Actor Jamie Fox was called a "stupid Ni**a" on Twitter for a wearing a Trayvon Martin Shirt at an award show.
15   Latino American Singer Mark Anthony was called a "sp*c" on Twitter after singing God Bless America at the 2013 MLB All-Star Game. A female Asheville, North Carolina, legislator recently was targeted by a fake GOP Tweeter account calling her "an argument for eugenics." In addition, everyday people who use Twitter to express their concerns about political oppression and social ills are also targets of
20   these threats and insults.

Twitter UK has responded by making the report abuse process easier by allowing users to report abuses through a one-click process. Twitter has been quoted as saying that they want people to feel safe and that they do not tolerate abuse. For some, this is an important step in the service fulfilling its ethical obligation.
25   But what is the moral and political obligation of those who receive these threats? Should they take them seriously and retreat, or should they remain defiant? These are the questions that came up in response to this past weekend's #TwitterSilence Campaign.

Some believed that the political and moral thing to do was to boycott the ser-
30   vice. Author Caitlin Moran wrote on her blog:

> I'm pro the mooted 24-hour walk-out on 4th of August, because not only is it a sym-
> bolic act of solidarity . . . but because it will also focus minds at Twitter to come up
> with their own solution to the abuses of their private company. You know—the

popularity of social networking sites waxes and wanes with ferocious rapidity. Twitter might currently be the hot thing—but it only takes a couple of bad months 35 for it to become the new Friends Reunited, the new MySpace, the new Bebo.

For Moran, the boycott would be an act of solidarity for those who have been abused on Twitter, a way to challenge Twitter to change its policies and for Twitter to see the value of its large percentage of users: women.

However, others saw it another way. British Journalist Damian Thompson called 40 it an "attention-seeking stunt" and went on to suggest, "What's happened instead is that the temporary disappearance of a certain breed of feminist and right-on blokes has reduced the volume of preachy, shouty messages on Twitter."

Historian Mary Beard, who has received death threats, joined the boycott. However, Caroline Criado-Perez felt a different moral and political obligation. Although 45 she respected others' decision to boycott, she refused to participate. Her reason was because she refused to be silenced.

The Counter-Revolution of Silencing

When we think of the actions of trolls, the main objective of their Internet harassment is not merely to annoy, but to silence users. Silencing is a technique used to shut people up from talking about and taking a stand against oppression. As blog- 50 ger Kinsey Hope argues, it can include trolling, offensive jokes, slurs, threats and dismissal of emotions. For Hope, the purpose is to disable and dismiss voices.

As a writer who uses social media, I too have been the victim of trolls. I know how with each read of insulting comments, I am tempted to be silent. However, I realize that is their aim and giving in will be doing exactly what the trolls want me 55 to do: remain silent. So, it's the act of continuing to speak, in spite of the insulting and threatening reactions, that makes my speech act more revolutionary.

Silencing is nothing new. People have tried to silence multiple voices throughout history. For example, Martin Luther King, Jr., received constant death threats in addition to threats of public exposure of his personal sexual acts if he did not kill himself. 60 The act of dismissing women's anger as hysteria has long been a form of silencing. Feminists have been silenced by being long regarded as "man-haters." The overall purpose of these techniques is to cause the individual to shut up. And with the Internet, silencing has gotten quick, direct, loud, ingenious, bolder and more anonymous.

Standing Up to Trolls

However, I believe boycotting in ways that keep our voices silent is counterproduc- 65 tive. I believe continuing to speak despite the hate one may receive via the Internet does several things.

Firstly, the refusal to retreat from Twitter for 24 hours, delete one's account all together or to stop speaking out about injustice online is saying that one refuses to be silenced by the insults of others. It's a powerful stance against intimidation. 70 It's to be defiant despite others' willingness to keep you quiet.

Secondly, refusing to be silenced is an acknowledgement that safety should be taken seriously, but it does not neglect the fact that one's truth *should* be told and injustice must be fought at all cost. As poet and activist Audre Lorde suggests,

75 "your silence will not protect you." The alternative of sitting in "safe corners mute as bottles" would still make us afraid. She notes, "We have been socialized to respect fear more than our own need for language and definition." Although social media threats can make us afraid and insults can make us offended, being silenced will not make things better. Oppression will still exist. Now more than ever is the

80 time to reclaim our need for language, particularly anti-oppressive language that can be shared across the world with the click of a button.

Thirdly, the refusal to be silenced also shows that one's words against oppression are more powerful than the words of trolls. If the online weapons of trolls are to be rendered powerless, we must allow our words to do the talking, the challeng-

85 ing, the revealing and the changing. We must do this instead of allowing insults and harassment to have the power to make our powerful voices mute. The horrific truths of oppression and injustice must be expressed. If not by us, then by who?

Each time I get online to share information and to join the fight against injustice, I remind myself of the old civil rights hymn that is as powerful now as it was in the

90 1960's:

Don't you let nobody turn you 'round/Turn you 'round/turn you 'round/Well don't you let nobody turn you 'round/You got to keep on walkin', keep on talkin'

Our words have power. It is up to us who we allow to have the last word. Trolls or Truth? For me, I choose the latter.

Source: The Huffington Post, *August 6, 2013*
http://www.huffingtonpost.com/myisha-cherry/trolls-and-the-refusal-to-be-silenced_b_3708466.html

Discussion/Writing Prompts

1. Cherry's thesis rests upon the assumption that online comments have the power to "silence" our own voices. Is it possible to analyze Cherry's essay along these same lines? In what ways does this essay seem to invite or encourage other voices to weigh in on this topic? Where in the essay do you see evidence of this? [Rhetorical Analysis of Argument]

2. According to Cherry, verbal abuse is a hallmark of online communication. Does this claim resonate with your own experience? Can you think of a moment online where you found yourself face to face (so to speak) with an abusive or threatening comment? If so, what was your response? [Personal Reflection]

3. Take a moment to consider the title of this essay. How accurate does the phrase "Twitter Trolls" seem to you? What image or association does it evoke? And what larger point about online conflict do you think Cherry is trying to make by using it? [Close Reading]

4. In making her argument about online harassment, Cherry uses stories from her own life as part of her support. How persuasive do you find this rhetorical strategy to be? What aspect of her larger argument does Cherry's decision to employ this narrative mode help her advance? [Analyzing Rhetorical Modes]

5. This essay offers several reasons why those opposed to online harassment should not remain silent: It's "a powerful stance against intimidation"; it's "an acknowledgement that safety should be taken seriously"; and it "shows that one's words against oppression are more powerful than the words of trolls." Choose one of the factors listed here. Then, write an essay in which you argue either for or against its validity in helping to combat "Twitter Trolls." [Argument]

6. How does Cherry's argument about "Twitter Trolls" compare to Lisa Bonos' discussion of in "The Art of the Digital Breakup"? What similarities do you see between these two forms of online conflict? Do you think Bonos would consider the stories cited in Cherry's piece to be useful in presenting her own thesis? Why, or why not? [Compare and Contrast]

7. There is an ample body of social and scientific research into the causes behind anger, rage, and conflict online. Conduct some research of your own into some of the ways these questions have been studied. What kinds of research are out there? What types of researchers take up these questions? And what are their findings? [Research]

Lisa Bonos, "The Art of the Digital Breakup"

We have long been accustomed to thinking about relationships— particularly the breakup of a relationship—as a highly personal matter. With the rise of social networking sites, however, this long-held assumption is being turned on its head. Nowadays, argues Lisa Bonos, it is becoming just as common for a divorce to be broadcast online as it is for it to be shared between close relatives or friends. What, she asks, are the effects of such a momentous and sudden change? And are we fully prepared to deal with all of its consequences?

"[F]rom what I've seen in my own dating life and what I've heard in conversations with other singles and relationship experts, technology has made our breakups even worse."

So I went through a bad breakup recently.

It wasn't tough because of the feelings I had for the guy. Rather it was because of the way things ended. After 10 days of silence from him, during which I calmly texted, called and e-mailed, he e-mailed me to say he was overwhelmed with work and couldn't handle a relationship. No call, no conversation. Two months of dating—we'd met each other's friends and were seeing each other every weekend— dissolved in one impersonal paragraph.

5

Of course, when was the last time you were rejected and thought: Ah, that felt good? Still, from what I've seen in my own dating life and what I've heard in conversations with other singles and relationship experts, technology has made our breakups even worse.

With so much of life happening on the Internet—and about 23 percent of couples now meeting online—it's inevitable that "I'm just not that into you" ends up in our inboxes, sandwiched between bills, notes from our bosses and e-cards from Mom. And it's not unheard of for Facebook users to get news about their romances when the other person changes his or her status from "in a relationship" to "single"—without talking about it first.

A digital rejection can be efficient and effective: The dumper can control the message; the dumpee can't interrupt or argue. No body language to misread, no tears to witness, no awkward hugs and no breakup sex. But we miss out on a lot when we outsource uncomfortable conversations to our e-mail accounts. In exchange for efficiency and emotional distance, we often give up a chance for real closure—and to show the other person that you care for them and respect the effort you put into the relationship. A face-to-face breakup vs. splitting up digitally is the difference between ending a romance with a namaste bow or using a karate chop.

So where should we put the dividing line between digital and real-time rejection? Online dating consultant Laurie Davis, founder of eFlirt Expert, tells her clients that after three dates, if they want to cut things off, they should call. Not surprisingly, a lot of them disagree. "In such a digital society," Davis says, "our fallback is that we have any difficult conversation by e-mail or text."

Or we avoid the conversation altogether, which can be even rougher than outright rejection. A 30-year-old D.C. lawyer who had been on a few dates with a woman who didn't respond to his texts said that, instead of silence, he would have preferred a simple message turning him down.

"I'd rather have people tell me straight up why something isn't working out," he said. Otherwise, "my mind will go to the most negative place."

Some digital breakups, though, can take you to a positive place. A 28-year-old D.C. nonprofit worker I recently spoke with received an "I'm just not feeling it" note that was so kind, she said, that she didn't mind that the rejection was digital. A man she'd been out with three times complimented her for being "an amazing combination of fun, attractive and smart" but said that he felt "there's something missing." He ended by apologizing for delivering the news by e-mail but said that he wanted to express how he was feeling—and he's better at doing that in writing. He also offered to discuss it more in person if she wanted.

She liked the note so much that she used it as an outline for the next digital breakup—one she initiated—and she's even passed it along to about five friends who've used it, too. They began referring to it as "the breakup e-mail template," she said.

Another 27-year-old D.C. dater has a digital breakup script that is short enough to send via text or Gchat: "Now just isn't a great time to be dating. I'm just going to focus on my non-romantic relationships." She developed the terse rejection note with a friend about two years ago, she says, when she was casually dating and was "trying to find a way to end things nicely . . . and digitally."

Of course, the problem is when a digital rejection is more callous than nice.

Ilana Gershon, an associate professor of communication and culture at Indiana University, says a breakup text or e-mail is often just the beginning of a conversation—the 21st-century version of "We need to talk"—that might lead to an in-person meeting. But that transition is rarely smooth. In her 2010 book, *The Breakup 2.0: Disconnecting Over New Media*, Gershon writes about a young man who initiated a breakup conversation with his girlfriend via text message. Because the couple had used texting only for joking around, the woman didn't know if he was serious. Once he confirmed (via text, of course) that he was, she had no interest in continuing the conversation.

No surprise, the consensus among the undergraduates Gershon has surveyed is that a digital breakup equals a bad breakup.

But there are two exceptions to keep in mind: Dating experts are careful to point out that if you're in an abusive relationship or are concerned for your safety, choose the method with the most distance, which might be e-mail. And Jodyne Speyer, author of *Dump 'Em: How to Break Up With Anyone From Your Best Friend to Your Hairdresser*, suggests that when the other person has an overpowering personality, e-mail might be a more effective way to deliver bad news.

Bad news is better than no news. For those who don't get so much as a rejection text, Audrey Melnik has a tool to help them find out what they might have said or done to turn someone off. Through her Web site, WotWentWrong.com, singles can send messages to dates who've disappeared, requesting feedback. A recipient can write his own response or choose from prepackaged answers, including: "Too much fighting; You are selfish; You don't make me feel attractive; You text instead of calling."

Taking the outsourcing of emotional conversations one step further, Bradley Laborman, founder of IDump4U.com, will make breakup phone calls on others' behalf for a $10 fee. He's made hundreds of calls in three years, he says, because he's tired of people dragging relationships out because they don't want to be the bad guy. He even posts the audio of selected breakup calls online.

Suddenly, my breakup e-mail isn't looking so harsh.

Regardless of how a breakup talk begins, there's a good chance the conversation will eventually make its way into Gchat or e-mail. Once the shock of rejection has settled, e-mail can be at its most productive in the breakup process. A dumpee who was caught off guard by an in-person breakup might want to follow up with things he didn't think to say in the moment. Or an ex might want to make clear that she still would like to keep in touch.

That's the kind of e-mail a 29-year-old neuroscience researcher in Washington received recently. He and his ex, who had been friends for seven years before dating for four, dissected their phone breakup over e-mail for about a week. While he said the correspondence gave him some added closure, the fact that he could

95   read and reread her words, and that she kept popping up in his inbox, made the
      breakup more difficult. "It was like getting re-broken-up with," he said.

          "We're so good at blurring our memories and forgetting details and fuzzying
      them out," he said of in-person or phone breakups. But with e-mail, you can pull
      up each person's words, and all those feelings come rushing back. And the notes
      are forever forwardable—another reason to avoid sending them in the first place.

100   As technology moves deeper into our lives, we have to work harder to maintain
      intimacy in our most delicate conversations. There aren't many dating rules that I
      believe in, but Davis, the online dating coach, has the right idea: If you want to
      break things off digitally, do it early—after one or two dates. Beyond that, talk
      over the phone or in person.

105   But no matter how many rules you make or how hard you try for a compassionate
      breakup, there's always a chance the other person will think it's cruel.

          After my first e-mail rejection six years ago—which included the gem "I don't
      feel that special tingle in my feet when we're together; the unexplainable feeling
      that knocks you over when you're in love"—I've tried hard not to reject anyone
110   through their inbox.

          A few years later, that conviction led me to make a date that had an unmen-
      tioned agenda: a breakup talk. When I matter-of-factly told him, a few bites into
      our tapas, that I just wanted to be friends, he was upset about the message—but
      more about its delivery.

115   "Why couldn't you have just done this in an e-mail?" he asked.

      Source: The Washington Post, *August 23, 2012. © 2012 The Washington Post.*
      http://www.washingtonpost.com/opinions/the-art-of-the-digital-breakup/2012/08/23/
      636f4cce-b4c5-11e1-9e4c-5a6a137d65e1_story.html

▮ Discussion/Writing Prompts

1. One of Bonos' assumptions here is that publicizing a private conflict like a breakup
   changes the way we experience that conflict. If you had to write an essay in support
   of this thesis, what sort of evidence would you cite? Can you think of an example of a
   publicized conflict that proves Bonos' point? [Rhetorical Analysis of Argument]

2. Have you ever mediated or resolved a conflict online? What did this conflict involve?
   How did you use a particular social media tool to resolve it? When you compare your
   own experiences with those depicted here, does the phenomenon of "digital breakup"
   seem typical or unusual? [Personal Reflection]

3. "A digital rejection," writes Bonos, "can be efficient and effective: The dumper can
   control the message; the dumpee can't interrupt or argue." What do you think is the
   greatest potential benefit to breaking up online? And how does it compare to Bonos'
   discussion here? [Close Reading]

4. Write an essay in which you use the rhetorical mode of process to create a step-by-step
   explanation of the rules one should follow to properly execute an online breakup.

How do your instructions compare to those discussed by Bonos? [Analyzing Rhetorical Modes]

5. Underneath Bonos' portraits of online breakups lies an even more fundamental question: Are our personal relationships enhanced or diminished when we transport them online? In an essay, offer your own answer to this question. In your view, has the rise of social media made it easier or more difficult to interact and understand each other? How? [Argument]

6. How do you think Geoffrey Nunberg ("Swearing: A Long and #%@&$ History") would respond to Bonos' essay? Do you think he would find in her discussion of online breakups support for his own thesis about the role of conflict in public life? How, or how not? [Compare and Contrast]

7. There is a growing body of scholarship examining the effect that online technologies are having on our personal and social lives. Educators and commentators of all stripes are offering their thoughts about what the rise of digital culture is doing to us as a society. Choose two or three examples of this scholarship, and write a two-page essay in which you both summarize and respond to their assessments. What do these experts claim the rise of digital technologies is doing to us? What specific consequences do they identify? And finally, do you agree with their assessments? [Research]

Geoffrey Nunberg, "Swearing: A Long and #%@&$ History"

It has become fashionable of late to bemoan the decline in civility in today's society. But is this really a recent development? Taking the longer view, Geoffrey Nunberg, a well-known linguist and adjunct professor in the School of Information at the University of California–Berkeley, offers a quick tutorial in the history of profanity in America. And what we learn is that rudeness and confrontation are anything but modern innovations.

"Well, profanity makes hypocrites of us all. But without hypocrisy, how could profanity even exist?"

Sometimes it's small government you need to keep your eye on. Take Middleborough, Mass., whose town meeting recently imposed a $20 fine for swearing in public. According to the police chief, the ordinance was aimed at the crowds of unruly teenagers who gathered downtown at night yelling profanities at people, not just someone who slams a finger in a car door. But whatever the exact idea was, nobody thought it was a good one. The ordinance had the rare distinction of being denounced by Fox News commentators, the editorial writers at *The Washington Post,* and the director of the Massachusetts ACLU. There are some people who want to keep government out of the marketplace and some people who want it kept out of the bedroom, but pretty much everybody is spooked at having it police what we say to the neighbor who starts his leaf blower at 7:15 on a Sunday morning.

But that's where the consensus ended, as the commentaries drifted off into culture-war faceoffs between moralists and modernists. To the moralists, the pervasiveness of swearing is a clear symptom of the collapse of civility and the coarsening of American culture. As they tell it, the dissolution began with the foul-mouthed demonstrators and hippies of the '60s and was amplified by Hollywood, rock music and hip-hop, turning us into a society that has lost all sense of shame or stigma.

This is an old tune. Social critics in the 1940s railed at the unchecked profanity of the returning GIs. In the '20s they were lambasting the vogue for four-letter words among the society slummers called mucker posers, the well-bred young people who felt the need "to emulate the manners and language of the longshoreman," as one critic put it. And so on down to the Victorians, whose sermons and statutes were full of references to public profanity. But then as the philosopher Montesquieu observed, people have been complaining about the decline of manners and morals since the time of Horace and Aristotle. They couldn't all have been right, he said, or men would be bears today.

The moralists are correct about one thing, though: This language has become more widespread and more audible than at any time since the early 19th century. I'd put the turning point in the '70s, when the styles and attitudes that emerged in the '60s were domesticated and divested of any subversive meaning—the moment when jeans, long hair and casual vulgarity became universal signs of democratic informality.

But a modernist could argue that the ubiquity of four-letter chatter actually makes it less of a concern. In a piece criticizing the Middleborough ordinance, the linguist John McWhorter said that it's time to bring our sense of "dirty" into line with our modern come-as-you-are American spirit. True, there are one or two genuinely taboo words. But the rest of this language has gotten so ordinary that's it's not profane, merely colorful. Just make sure kids learn not to use it at inappropriate times, the same way they have to learn not to burp in public.

That's the modernist point of view: Potty mouths are like potholes, just another of life's little inconveniences. They're there, they swear, get used to it. That uncompromising rationality may seem miles from the keening philippics of the moralists. Yet most of us slip easily between one position and the other. Just note the reactions when a political figure is caught dropping the F-bomb. To the opposition, it's gutter talk that shows his classlessness. To his own partisans, it's a "demonstration of earthy authenticity." And then when somebody from the other party uses the same word a week later, the two sides just exchange their copy.

But each view has its appeal. The moralists have a point. Vulgar language may be a fact of modern life, but it's more troubling than potholes. It's infuriating to hear someone behind you in the movie line swearing energetically, even if you don't happen to have a 6-year-old in tow. In one recent survey, three-quarters of the respondents said that parents should teach their kids that "cursing is always wrong." But not a lot of parents teach that lesson by example. The proportion of

Americans who claim they never curse runs anywhere from 5 to 15 percent, and 55
you figure some of them must be telling the truth. But while the rest of us may officially disapprove of swearing, we also engage in it enthusiastically—and even,
regrettably, at the family dinner table *devant les enfants.*

Well, profanity makes hypocrites of us all. But without hypocrisy, how could profanity even exist? To learn what it means to swear, a child has to both hear the 60
words said and be told that it's wrong to say them, ideally by the same people.
After all, the basic point of swearing is to demonstrate that your emotions have
gotten the better of you and trumped your inhibitions. That's why the words have
to be regarded as bad, not just inappropriate, so there's a real weight to using
them. Swear words don't describe your feelings; they manifest them. Throwing the 65
F-word at somebody isn't just a particularly colorful and emphatic way of saying,
"I'm awfully vexed with you right now," any more than "Ow!" is just an emphatic
way of saying, "Gee, that hurts."

In the end, neither the modernists nor the moralists can ever win the argument.
Each needs the other too much. The particular vocabulary items may change over 70
time, but swearing itself can never become so ordinary that we no longer consider
it naughty. You can't have profanity if there are no prudes left to be shocked by it.
Let's give credit to the good people of Middleborough, Mass., for helping to keep
the old traditions alive.

Source: NPR.org, July 11, 2012
http://www.npr.org/2012/07/24/156623763/swearing-a-long-and-history

Discussion/Writing Prompts

1. Nunberg's essay addresses the growing public concern over the rise of incivility in
   modern society. As you consider Nunberg's argument and the way he goes about
   making it, how well do you think his essay functions as a solution to this problem?
   Does Nunberg make his own argument in ways that differ from the historical
   examples of incivility he cites? And does this make his argument more effective?
   [Rhetorical Analysis of Argument]

2. While profanity has long been a hallmark of American public discourse, notes
   Nunberg, our era is unique in terms of the sheer amount of such speech we are exposed
   to: "This language has become more widespread and more audible than at any time
   since the early 19th century." Based on your own experience as a media consumer,
   would you say Nunberg's claim is true? Do you feel overwhelmed by the volume of
   profane speech circulating throughout our pop culture? And what are your chosen
   strategies for dealing with such material? [Personal Reflection]

3. Nunberg presents the debate over profanity in public life as a contest between
   "modernists" and "moralists." How do you understand these two terms? Do you find
   them to be useful or accurate descriptors of the opposing sides? How, or how not?
   [Close Reading]

4. For Nunberg, the growing prevalence of "four-letter words" in popular culture is symptomatic of a broader trend toward greater vulgarity. In your view, is this a fair conclusion to draw? Do you find Nunberg's use of the exemplification mode here to be convincing? How, or how not? [Analyzing Rhetorical Modes]

5. While it addresses the rise of profanity in American life, Nunberg's essay declines to include actual examples of profane or vulgar speech. Why do you think he opts for this rhetorical strategy? In your view, does omitting swear words from this essay reinforce or undermine the larger point Nunberg is making about the place of profanity in public life? [Argument]

6. How do you think Myisha Cherry's example of "Twitter Trolls" ("Twitter Trolls and the Refusal to Be Silenced") relates to Nunberg's historical overview of profanity? How neatly, in your view, does this online behavior fit into Nunberg's category of vulgar or abusive behavior? What are the key similarities and differences between the two? [Compare and Contrast]

7. Nunberg's argument rests upon the claim that public profanity has a long history in the United States. Conduct some first-hand research in which you test the validity of this claim. Choose a controversy or conflict from some earlier moment in American history. First, research the basic history of this conflict. What issues did it concern? What participants or parties did it involve, and how did their points of view differ? When you're done, write a one-page response in which you discuss whether or not this historical precedent reinforces Nunberg's own argument. [Research]

Bonnie Erbe, "As Religious Affiliation Declines, What's the Impact?"

The last several years have witnessed a growing trend among Americans to identify themselves as religiously unaffiliated. What, asks Bonnie Erbe, who hosts the PBS show To the Contrary *and writes a syndicated column for the Scripps Howard News Service, is the impact of such a dramatic social change? And is it possible that this decline in publicly professed religion is actually a change for the better?*

"Speaking as one of the non-affiliated, I must say it is liberating to know there are more of us and more non-Christians as well."

As America morphs from one nation under one Christian god to an amalgam nation under many gods, more scholars are asking whether the phrase "one nation under God" in our Pledge of Allegiance still applies.

Most recently, historian Molly Worthen posed the question in *The New York Times* and never really gave an answer. She referred to the increase of what she called "Chreasters—Americans who attend church only on Christmas and Easter," making their rare appearances in church this time of year. She also pointed to a

Pew Research Center poll released in October showing that Americans who have no religious affiliation account for 20 percent of the population, up from 16 percent in 2008.

Certainly, four decades of massive immigration have changed not only the complexion of America's skin, turning us browner, but also the panoply of our faiths. The ballooning population of Asian-Americans includes large numbers of Muslims, Hindus, Buddhists and all manner of non-Christian faiths with solid followings on U.S. soil.

As our non-affiliated population increases, so does our non-Christian population. That has huge implications for us as we move forward. Speaking as one of the non-affiliated, I must say it is liberating to know there are more of us and more non-Christians as well. Sometimes, pop and political culture give one the idea we are a decidedly, oppressively Christian nation that does not take it lightly when we deviate from church dogma.

One such episode was the 2012 political season's fixation on reproductive rights. This was prompted by three bizarre statements made by white male candidates about the intersection of church doctrine and pregnancy. Another was the Catholic overreaction to the Obama health care plan. "Obamacare" requires employers to cover contraception in their employees' health plans. The church hierarchy turned around and sued the administration, claiming its health care law violates the First Amendment guarantee of religious liberty.

The Obama administration offered a compromise, saying insurance companies would have to provide contraception for employees who wanted it—so Catholic employers could avoid directly providing birth control. But that wasn't good enough for the church, and the lawsuits persist.

If we didn't still see ourselves as one nation under one god, none of this would matter very much. But the fact that we do gives the Catholic Church the right to sue over something like this.

It requires a huge leap of faith (pun intended) to jump from the free-exercise clause to claiming that requiring insurance companies used by Catholic employers (schools, hospitals and the like) to provide birth control to employees who want it (many of whom are not Catholic) somehow violates the right to religious liberty. Yet Catholic prelates feel justified enough in their zeal to overturn this policy that they are willing to invest millions of dollars in lawsuits to try to have it overturned.

Clearly, they and other Christian church leaders still see us as one nation under one god. But as the Pew poll indicates, this is changing. Another Pew poll released two years ago on the "millennial" generation and its relationship with faith should be even more troubling to Christian leaders.

It showed the following, quoting from the Pew website: "Americans ages 18 to 29 are considerably less religious than older Americans. Fewer young adults belong to any particular faith than older people do today. They also are less likely to be affiliated than their parents' and grandparents' generations were when they were young."

One day, Christian leaders will wake up and recognize that their era is crumbling. If that means they will have decreasing power in the political realm, it will be a blessing for all of us—regardless of whether the "one nation under God" pledge still applies.

Source: Long Island Newsday, *December 26, 2012*
http://www.newsday.com/opinion/oped/as-religious-affiliation-declines-what-s-the-impact-bonnie-erbe-1.4377570

Discussion/Writing Prompts

1. "One day," writes Erbe, "Christian leaders will wake up and recognize that their era is crumbling. If that means they will have decreasing power in the political realm, it will be a blessing for all of us . . ." Based on your reading of this essay, where does Erbe provide support for this claim? And how persuasive do you find this support to be? [Rhetorical Analysis of Argument]

2. This essay invites readers to take seriously the idea that formal religious affiliation does its adherents more harm than good. Do you agree? Can you think of an example in your own life where a religious affiliation gave rise to a personal conflict? Can you think of an example in which the opposite is true? [Personal Reflection]

3. Erbe uses the term "non-affiliated" rather than "non-believer" to make her argument here. How do you understand each term? Is "non-affiliated" the best term to illustrate her point about the changing portrait of religious belief in America? Why, or why not? [Close Reading]

4. Part of Erbe's argument involves drawing a comparison between the realms of religion and politics. Write a short essay in which you evaluate the effectiveness of this rhetorical strategy. Does the use of a compare-and-contrast mode here enhance the power of Erbe's argument? How, or how not? [Analyzing Rhetorical Modes]

5. Erbe's worries about the political effects of religious affiliation raises an even more fundamental question about the relationship between religious terminology and religious identity. Does the language we use to describe our religious affiliation actually influence the way we define ourselves? [Argument]

6. How do you think E.J. Dionne ("Will We Keep Hating Government?") would react to the claims about religion Erbe makes here? Given how polarizing religious differences can be, do you think Dionne would see any connections to his own discussion of political conflict?

7. Erbe grounds part of her argument on recent Pew Research Center data that show "20 percent of the population" currently eschew any religious affiliation. Choose a study of this kind, and research its findings. What type of experiment does it conduct? How valid do you find its organization and methodology to be? Why? [Research]

E.J. Dionne, "Will We Keep Hating Government?"

We hear a lot of alarmist talk these days about the dangers posed by
"big government." The problem, however, is that this phrase can mean
very different things to different people. Ritually invoked as a political
boogeyman, "big government" has come to serve as a catchall phrase for
any number of disparate, unrelated concerns. All of which leads E.J. Dionne
to wonder whether we might be better off doing away with this epithet
altogether.

> *"Ever heard the one about the guy who hated government until a*
> *deregulated Wall Street crashed, an oil spill devastated the Gulf of Mexico, a*
> *coal mine collapsed, and some good police work stopped a terrorist attack?"*

Ever heard the one about the guy who hated government until a deregulated Wall
Street crashed, an oil spill devastated the Gulf of Mexico, a coal mine collapsed, and
some good police work stopped a terrorist attack?

Rarely has the news of the day run so counter to the *spin* on the news of the day.
It's hard to argue that the difficulties we confront were caused by an excessively   5
powerful "big" government. Rather, most of them arose from the government's
failure to do its job in the first place.

The central tasks of democratic government, after all, typically involve standing
up for the many against the few, the less powerful against the more powerful.
Government is supposed to make sure that corporations are properly supervised   10
when they turn public resources (the environment in the Gulf of Mexico, for example) into private gain. It is charged with protecting those with weaker bargaining
positions (coal miners, for example) against the harm that those in stronger bargaining positions might inflict.

Its duty is to keep the private economy running smoothly by preventing fraud,   15
shady dealing and forms of self-interested behavior that threaten the entire system.
And yes, it's supposed to keep us safe from physical harm, as it did in New York City.

Especially in the economic sphere, government in recent years failed to carry
out too many of these basic functions. That explains why this moment's anti-
government feeling reflects two entirely different strains of thinking.   20

Public attention has largely gone to the strain exemplified by the tea party
movement, opposition to government bailouts and an absolute hatred of
Congress. This is the old-fashioned, garden-variety conservatism that somewhere
between a fifth and a third of Americans have long subscribed to. These are the
citizens you see on television at the anti-Obama rallies, the members of Congress   25
who give speeches denouncing "overregulation," and the think tankers who insist
that the private sector always performs more efficiently and effectively than
"government bureaucrats."

Their views were definitively summarized many years ago by former House
Majority Leader Dick Armey, now a tea party friend, who declared: "The market is   30

rational and the government is dumb." Because they have always thought and voted the same way, partisans of this view do not account for shifts in opinion, let alone swing elections.

35 The more important and dynamic force behind the current disillusionment with government comes instead from those who actually believe it can and should be effective. They do not think that the market is automatically rational or that the government has to be dumb. They are not fed up with government because their ideology or philosophy tells them to be, but because they don't think government has been doing a proper job of promoting prosperity, equity and fair-dealing.

40 So far, the Obama administration has missed the opportunity to demonstrate to such voters how it is changing the way government works. How is its approach to writing and enforcing regulations different from what was done before? How is its management of the agencies different? How are its priorities different? What specific past failures is it addressing?

45 As Al Gore understood when he embarked on his "reinventing government" project for President Clinton, such an undertaking is more essential for liberals and progressives than for conservatives. Conservative ideas generally gain ground when government is discredited. But progressives who insist on government's constructive role can't succeed unless they persuade voters that public agencies 50 are up to the missions they undertake.

Starting with the newly urgent threat of domestic terrorism and the environmental disaster in the Gulf, the administration does not lack for obvious challenges to which it must respond effectively. Competence is the antidote to the electorate's sick feeling about public authority.

55 But President Obama must also press on with the defense of government he offered in his recent University of Michigan commencement address. And he has a new piece of evidence that will help him make his case that government in a free society is not a distant force, but rather something that all of us influence and shape.

60 We need to remind ourselves that a bomb could have devastated Times Square in the absence of the most basic form of cooperation between an observant merchant and a responsible police officer.

This is what happens when government is seen as being in partnership with democratic citizens. And there's nothing dumb about it.

Source: Truthdig.com, May 6, 2010. © 2010 The Washington Post.
http://www.truthdig.com/report/item/will_we_keep_hating_government_20100506

▓ Discussion/Writing Prompts

1. One of the implications of Dionne's discussion is that our current political discourse encourages us to treat political opponents as enemies. Do you agree that this is the case? And if so, do you find this to be a useful or a harmful tendency? [Rhetorical Analysis of Argument]

2. Can you think of a recent media example that exemplifies the disdainful attitude toward government that Dionne sets about to criticize here? What kind of example is it? A news story? Political speech? Blog post? Website? And how convincing do you find the argument it makes? [Personal Reflection]

3. Take a closer look at the essay's title. What do you make of Dionne's use of the term "we"? In your view, is it accurate to suggest that we all hate government? Do you see yourself within the "we" Dionne invokes here? And why do you think he chose this way of introducing his essay? [Close Reading]

4. "The central tasks of democratic government, after all," writes Dionne, "typically involve standing up for the many against the few, the less powerful against the more powerful." How do you respond to this definition? Is this how you would characterize the primary function of government? Or would you propose an alternative definition? If so, what? [Analyzing Rhetorical Modes]

5. Dionne makes a spirited argument in defense of the idea that government is not only relevant but, in fact, essential to a democratic society. Write an essay in which you respond to Dionne's central claim. Do you share his conviction about how important and useful government is? If so, why? If not, in what ways do you see government as unimportant? [Argument]

6. How does Bonnie Erbe's discussion of religious non-affiliation ("As Religious Affiliation Declines, What's the Impact?") compare to Dionne's defense of government? Do these two writers share a common vision of how society should work? Of what forces are responsible for fostering the common good? [Compare and Contrast]

7. Dionne's essay is part of a much larger debate regarding the proper role government should play in everyday life. Choose another public figure (e.g., writer, politician, or pundit) who is part of this debate, and research the particular arguments this person makes. What views on this question are being advanced? How do they compare with what Dionne has to say? [Research]

Academic Writing Selections

The rhetorical analysis modeled above doesn't only apply to the types of informal and formal writing found in the real world. It can also serve as an equally useful framework for examining the kinds of writing that are often taught within the college classroom and have come to be regarded as models of sound academic writing. Like their real world counterparts, the authors of these academic selections base their choices about how and what to write on considerations of purpose, audience, argument, voice, and credibility.

The two selections below demonstrate the extent to which academic writing is also shaped by rhetorical concepts. More specifically, these examples highlight the role that considerations about argument play in shaping a writer's choices. Read each selection carefully. Then, answer the questions that follow.

Thomas Jefferson, "The Declaration of Independence"

Few arguments are more central to American identity and American values than the Declaration of Independence. One of the founding documents of American society, the Declaration offers a clear, compelling manifesto about equality, freedom, and universal human rights.

When in the Course of human events, it becomes necessary for one people to dissolve the political bands which have connected them with another, and to assume among the powers of the earth, the separate and equal station to which the Laws of Nature and of Nature's God entitle them, a decent respect to the opinions of
5   mankind requires that they should declare the causes which impel them to the separation.

   We hold these truths to be self-evident, that all men are created equal, that they are endowed by their Creator with certain unalienable Rights, that among these are Life, Liberty and the pursuit of Happiness.—That to secure these rights, Gov-
10   ernments are instituted among Men, deriving their just powers from the consent of the governed,—That whenever any Form of Government becomes destructive of these ends, it is the Right of the People to alter or to abolish it, and to institute new Government, laying its foundation on such principles and organizing its powers in such form, as to them shall seem most likely to effect their Safety and
15   Happiness. Prudence, indeed, will dictate that Governments long established should not be changed for light and transient causes; and accordingly all experience hath shewn, that mankind are more disposed to suffer, while evils are sufferable, than to right themselves by abolishing the forms to which they are accustomed. But when a long train of abuses and usurpations, pursuing invariably the same
20   Object evinces a design to reduce them under absolute Despotism, it is their right, it is their duty, to throw off such Government, and to provide new Guards for their future security.—Such has been the patient sufferance of these Colonies; and such is now the necessity which constrains them to alter their former Systems of Government. The history of the present King of Great Britain is a history of repeated
25   injuries and usurpations, all having in direct object the establishment of an absolute Tyranny over these States. To prove this, let Facts be submitted to a candid world.

   He has refused his Assent to Laws, the most wholesome and necessary for the public good.
30   He has forbidden his Governors to pass Laws of immediate and pressing importance, unless suspended in their operation till his Assent should be obtained; and when so suspended, he has utterly neglected to attend to them.

He has refused to pass other Laws for the accommodation of large districts of people, unless those people would relinquish the right of Representation in the Legislature, a right inestimable to them and formidable to tyrants only. 35

He has called together legislative bodies at places unusual, uncomfortable, and distant from the depository of their public Records, for the sole purpose of fatiguing them into compliance with his measures.

He has dissolved Representative Houses repeatedly, for opposing with manly firmness his invasions on the rights of the people. 40

He has refused for a long time, after such dissolutions, to cause others to be elected; whereby the Legislative powers, incapable of Annihilation, have returned to the People at large for their exercise; the State remaining in the mean time exposed to all the dangers of invasion from without, and convulsions within.

He has endeavoured to prevent the population of these States; for that purpose 45 obstructing the Laws for Naturalization of Foreigners; refusing to pass others to encourage their migrations hither, and raising the conditions of new Appropriations of Lands.

He has obstructed the Administration of Justice, by refusing his Assent to Laws for establishing Judiciary powers. 50

He has made Judges dependent on his Will alone, for the tenure of their offices, and the amount and payment of their salaries.

He has erected a multitude of New Offices, and sent hither swarms of Officers to harrass our people, and eat out their substance.

He has kept among us, in times of peace, Standing Armies without the Consent 55 of our legislatures.

He has affected to render the Military independent of and superior to the Civil power.

He has combined with others to subject us to a jurisdiction foreign to our constitution, and unacknowledged by our laws; giving his Assent to their Acts of pre- 60 tended Legislation:

For Quartering large bodies of armed troops among us:

For protecting them, by a mock Trial, from punishment for any Murders which they should commit on the Inhabitants of these States:

For cutting off our Trade with all parts of the world: 65

For imposing Taxes on us without our Consent:

For depriving us in many cases, of the benefits of Trial by Jury:

For transporting us beyond Seas to be tried for pretended offences:

For abolishing the free System of English Laws in a neighbouring Province, establishing therein an Arbitrary government, and enlarging its Boundaries so as to 70 render it at once an example and fit instrument for introducing the same absolute rule into these Colonies:

For taking away our Charters, abolishing our most valuable Laws, and altering fundamentally the Forms of our Governments:

75   For suspending our own Legislatures, and declaring themselves invested with power to legislate for us in all cases whatsoever.

He has abdicated Government here, by declaring us out of his Protection and waging War against us.

He has plundered our seas, ravaged our Coasts, burnt our towns, and destroyed
80   the lives of our people.

He is at this time transporting large Armies of foreign Mercenaries to compleat the works of death, desolation and tyranny, already begun with circumstances of Cruelty & perfidy scarcely paralleled in the most barbarous ages, and totally unworthy the Head of a civilized nation.

85   He has constrained our fellow Citizens taken Captive on the high Seas to bear Arms against their Country, to become the executioners of their friends and Brethren, or to fall themselves by their Hands.

He has excited domestic insurrections amongst us, and has endeavoured to bring on the inhabitants of our frontiers, the merciless Indian Savages, whose known rule
90   of warfare, is an undistinguished destruction of all ages, sexes and conditions.

In every stage of these Oppressions We have Petitioned for Redress in the most humble terms: Our repeated Petitions have been answered only by repeated injury. A Prince whose character is thus marked by every act which may define a Tyrant, is unfit to be the ruler of a free people.

95   Nor have We been wanting in attentions to our Brittish brethren. We have warned them from time to time of attempts by their legislature to extend an unwarrantable jurisdiction over us. We have reminded them of the circumstances of our emigration and settlement here. We have appealed to their native justice and magnanimity, and we have conjured them by the ties of our common kindred to disavow these
100   usurpations, which would inevitably interrupt our connections and correspondence. They too have been deaf to the voice of justice and of consanguinity. We must, therefore, acquiesce in the necessity, which denounces our Separation, and hold them, as we hold the rest of mankind, Enemies in War, in Peace Friends.

We, therefore, the Representatives of the united States of America, in General
105   Congress, Assembled, appealing to the Supreme Judge of the world for the rectitude of our intentions, do, in the Name, and by Authority of the good People of these Colonies, solemnly publish and declare, That these United Colonies are, and of Right ought to be Free and Independent States; that they are Absolved from all Allegiance to the British Crown, and that all political connection between them
110   and the State of Great Britain, is and ought to be totally dissolved; and that as Free and Independent States, they have full Power to levy War, conclude Peace, contract Alliances, establish Commerce, and to do all other Acts and Things which Independent States may of right do. And for the support of this Declaration, with a firm reliance on the protection of divine Providence, we mutually pledge to each
115   other our Lives, our Fortunes and our sacred Honor.

Source: archives.gov

▨ Discussion/Writing Prompts

1. Among other things, the Declaration of Independence was intended to serve as a justification for the right of American colonists to form their own government. On this basis, how effective do you find this argument to be? Do Jefferson's claims about the right to "Life, Liberty and the pursuit of Happiness" provide a sufficient rationale for his subsequent claim about the right to self-government? Why, or why not? [Rhetorical Analysis of Argument]

2. Can you think of a recent debate in which the Declaration of Independence has been invoked to support one side's particular point of view? If so, what issue did this debate involve? In what way did the participants in this debate appeal to the Declaration? And how effective do you find this strategy to be? [Personal Reflection]

3. To countless generations, the following statement has come to stand as a summation of the Declaration's core argument:

   > We hold these truths to be self-evident, that all men are created equal, that they are endowed by their Creator with certain unalienable Rights, that among these are Life, Liberty and the pursuit of Happiness.

   Take a closer look at these lines. How effectively do you think they encapsulate the main argument Jefferson is making? What particular words or phrases stand out? [Close Reading]

4. In the body of the Declaration, Jefferson presents a list of grievances against "the present King of Great Britain." Choose one of them. Then, analyze how effectively this particular grievance serves as support for the larger argument Jefferson is making here. Does this grievance provide a logical or persuasive reasoning in favor of Jefferson's argument regarding the right to self-government? What are the strengths and/or deficiencies of this reasoning? [Analyzing Rhetorical Modes]

5. "[W]hen a long train of abuses and usurpations, pursuing invariably the same Object evinces a design to reduce [citizens] under absolute Despotism," Jefferson writes, "it is their right, it is their duty, to throw off such Government, and to provide new Guards for their future security." In this passage, Jefferson makes an argument in defense of the idea that popular self-government is not only a "right" but a "duty." Write an essay in which you respond to this claim. Do you agree with Jefferson's assertion that self-government is a "duty"? Why or why not? [Argument]

6. Compare Jefferson's argument in the Declaration to E.J. Dionne's discussion in "Will We Keep Hating Government?" Do these two writers share a common vision of what government is or should be? [Compare and Contrast]

7. Research some of Thomas Jefferson's other writings. What parallels do you see between these writings and the Declaration of Independence? What differences? [Research]

Elizabeth Cady Stanton, "Address to the Seneca Falls Convention"

Elizabeth Cady Stanton was a noted 19th-century abolitionist as well as a major pioneer in the women's rights movement of that era. She is widely credited as the driving force behind the 1848 Seneca Falls Convention, an antislavery meeting at which Stanton presented her famous address on the "rights of Woman."

We have met here today to discuss our rights and wrongs, civil and political, and not, as some have supposed, to go into the detail of social life alone. We do not propose to petition the legislature to make our husbands just, generous, and courteous, to seat every man at the head of a cradle, and to clothe every woman in male attire.

5   None of these points, however important they may be considered by leading men, will be touched in this convention. As to their costume, the gentlemen need feel no fear of our imitating that, for we think it in violation of every principle of taste, beauty, and dignity; notwithstanding all the contempt cast upon our loose, flowing garments, we still admire the graceful folds, and consider our costume far

10   more artistic than theirs. Many of the nobler sex seem to agree with us in this opinion, for the bishops, priests, judges, barristers, and lord mayors of the first nation on the globe, and the Pope of Rome, with his cardinals, too, all wear the loose flowing robes, thus tacitly acknowledging that the male attire is neither dignified nor imposing.

15   No, we shall not molest you in your philosophical experiments with stocks, pants, high-heeled boots, and Russian belts. Yours be the glory to discover, by personal experience, how long the kneepan can resist the terrible strapping down which you impose, in how short time the well-developed muscles of the throat can be reduced to mere threads by the constant pressure of the stock, how high the

20   heel of a boot must be to make a short man tall, and how tight the Russian belt may be drawn and yet have wind enough left to sustain life.

But we are assembled to protest against a form of government existing without the consent of the governed—to declare our right to be free as man is free, to be represented in the government which we are taxed to support, to have such dis-

25   graceful laws as give man the power to chastise and imprison his wife, to take the wages which she earns, the property which she inherits, and, in case of separation, the children of her love; laws which make her the mere dependent on his bounty. It is to protest against such unjust laws as these that we are assembled today, and to have them, if possible, forever erased from our statute books, deeming them a

30   shame and a disgrace to a Christian republic in the nineteenth century. We have met to uplift woman's fallen divinity upon an even pedestal with man's. And, strange as it may seem to many, we now demand our right to vote according to the declaration of the government under which we live.

This right no one pretends to deny. We need not prove ourselves equal to Daniel

35   Webster to enjoy this privilege, for the ignorant Irishman in the ditch has all the civil

rights he has. We need not prove our muscular power equal to this same Irishman to enjoy this privilege, for the most tiny, weak, ill-shaped stripling of twenty-one has all the civil rights of the Irishman. We have no objection to discuss the question of equality, for we feel that the weight of argument lies wholly with us, but we wish the question of equality kept distinct from the question of rights, for the proof of the one does not determine the truth of the other. All white men in this country have the same rights, however they may differ in mind, body, or estate.

The right is ours. The question now is: how shall we get possession of what rightfully belongs to us? We should not feel so sorely grieved if no man who had not attained the full stature of a Webster, Clay, Van Buren, or Gerrit Smith could claim the right of the elective franchise. But to have drunkards, idiots, horse-racing, rum-selling rowdies, ignorant foreigners, and silly boys fully recognized, while we ourselves are thrust out from all the rights that belong to citizens, it is too grossly insulting to the dignity of woman to be longer quietly submitted to.

The right is ours. Have it, we must. Use it, we will. The pens, the tongues, the fortunes, the indomitable wills of many women are already pledged to secure this right. The great truth that no just government can be formed without the consent of the governed we shall echo and re-echo in the ears of the unjust judge, until by continual coming we shall weary him

There seems now to be a kind of moral stagnation in our midst. Philanthropists have done their utmost to rouse the nation to a sense of its sins. War, slavery, drunkenness, licentiousness, gluttony, have been dragged naked before the people, and all their abominations and deformities fully brought to light, yet with idiotic laugh we hug those monsters to our breasts and rush on to destruction. Our churches are multiplying on all sides, our missionary societies, Sunday schools, and prayer meetings and innumerable charitable and reform organizations are all inoperation, but still the tide of vice is swelling, and threatens the destruction of everything, and the battlements of righteousness are weak against the raging elements of sin and death.

Verily, the world waits the coming of some new element, some purifying power, some spirit of mercy and love. The voice of woman has been silenced in the state, the church, and the home, but man cannot fulfill his destiny alone, he cannot redeem his race unaided. There are deep and tender chords of sympathy and love in the hearts of the downfallen and oppressed that woman can touch more skillfully than man.

The world has never yet seen a truly great and virtuous nation, because in the degradation of woman the very fountains of life are poisoned at their source. It is vain to look for silver and gold from mines of copper and lead.

It is the wise mother that has the wise son. So long as your women are slaves you may throw your colleges and churches to the winds. You can't have scholars and saints so long as your mothers are ground to powder between the upper and nether millstone of tyranny and lust. How seldom, now, is a father's pride gratified, his fond hopes realized, in the budding genius of his son!

80   The wife is degraded, made the mere creature of caprice, and the foolish son is heaviness to his heart. Truly are the sins of the fathers visited upon the children to the third and fourth generation. God, in His wisdom, has so linked the whole human family together that any violence done at one end of the chain is felt throughout its length, and here, too, is the law of restoration, as in woman all have fallen, so in her elevation shall the race be recreated.

85   "Voices" were the visitors and advisers of Joan of Arc. Do not "voices" come to us daily from the haunts of poverty, sorrow, degradation, and despair, already too long unheeded. Now is the time for the women of this country, if they would save our free institutions, to defend the right, to buckle on the armor that can best resist the keenest weapons of the enemy—contempt and ridicule. The same reli-

90   gious enthusiasm that nerved Joan of Arc to her work nerves us to ours. In every generation God calls some men and women for the utterance of truth, a heroic action, and our work today is the fulfilling of what has long since been foretold by the Prophet—Joel 2:28:

95   And it shall come to pass afterward, that I will pour out my spirit upon all flesh; and your sons and your daughters shall prophesy.

We do not expect our path will be strewn with the flowers of popular applause, but over the thorns of bigotry and prejudice will be our way, and on our banners will beat the dark storm clouds of opposition from those who have entrenched them-selves behind the stormy bulwarks of custom and authority, and who have fortified

100   their position by every means, holy and unholy. But we will steadfastly abide the result. Unmoved we will bear it aloft. Undauntedly we will unfurl it to the gale, for we know that the storm cannot rend from it a shred, that the electric flash will but more clearly show to us the glorious words inscribed upon it, "Equality of Rights."
Source: teachingamericanhistory.org

▋Discussion/Writing Prompts

1. Stanton opens her speech by reassuring the male listeners in her audience about all of things she will not do. For example:

   We do not propose to petition the legislature to make our husbands just, gener-ous, and courteous . . .

   [W]e shall not molest you in your philosophical experiments with stocks, pants, high-heeled boots, and Russian belts.

   How do you evaluate this rhetorical strategy? Do you think it is an effective way to introduce her larger argument about women's rights? Why, or why not? [Rhetorical Analysis of Argument]

2. In your view, is Stanton's argument still current? Can you think of an example or experience from your own life that demonstrates the continuing relevance of the issues Stanton raises? [Personal Reflection]

3. "[T]o have drunkards, idiots, horse-racing, rum-selling rowdies, ignorant foreigners, and silly boys fully recognized," Stanton writes, "while we ourselves are thrust out from all the rights that belong to citizens, it is too grossly insulting to the dignity of woman to be longer quietly submitted to." Take a moment to examine the specific language Stanton employs here. How do you react to her description of "drunkards, idiots, rum-selling rowdies, ignorant foreigners, and silly boys"? And what do you think is Stanton's goal in using such language? In your view, does such language strengthen or undermine the argument she is making for equal rights? [Close Reading]

4. In advancing her argument about "Equality of Rights," Stanton makes a bold prediction: "The right is ours. Have it, we must. Use it, we will." Based on the rest of the speech, how does Stanton envision this prediction coming true? What kind of description does she offer of the specific "uses" to which these rights for women will be put? [Analyzing Rhetorical Modes]

5. "The world has never yet seen a truly great and virtuous nation," Stanton writes, "because in the degradation of woman the very fountains of life are poisoned at their source." Write a short essay in which you identify and analyze the particular argument Stanton is making here. What kind of connection is she drawing between being a "great nation" and sanctioning the "degradation of woman"? What is she referring to in the phrase "fountain of life"? And how does the point she makes here relate to her broader argument about "Equality of Rights"? [Argument]

6. In arguing for the rights of women, Stanton makes the following statement:

   > [W]e are assembled to protest against a form of government existing without the consent of the governed—to declare our right to be free as man is free, to be represented in the government which we are taxed to support . . .

   To what extent does Stanton's statement here echo the language Thomas Jefferson uses in the Declaration of Independence? Can you think of any reason why Stanton might want to intentionally echo Jefferson? Do you think his claims about self-government and equality help to support the argument Stanton is advancing? How, or how not? [Compare and Contrast]

7. Research the history of the Seneca Falls Convention. What was the original purpose of this meeting? What key figures attended? What larger social impact did this event have? [Research]

Tying It All Together

1. Myisha Cherry ("Twitter Trolls and the Refusal to Be Silenced,") and Lisa Bonos ("The Art of the Digital Breakup") both focus on the role that online technologies have played in reshaping how and why we argue. In a two-page essay, assess their respective commentaries in comparison with each other. What does each essay have to say about the ways that online technologies and venues have changed argument? How does each essay invite us to think and feel about such changes? And which perspective, finally, do you find more compelling? Why?

2. Whatever the issue at hand, argument is always, on some level, about how we define *difference*. More than any other rhetorical activity, arguing sheds light on the ways we are taught to look at and think about those who—by virtue of their background or beliefs, their views or values—are not the same as us. Indeed, to look at argument is to realize how quickly another person's difference can start to seem not just, yes, different but downright threatening as well. Choose three selections from among those assembled above that, in your view, addresses this issue in some way. Then, write a three- to five-page essay in which you analyze how these selections can be understood as an inquiry into the relationship between argument and difference. What sort of commentary about or critique of this process does each selection offer? Do these essays go about analyzing this relationship in ways that are similar or different?

3. A number of writers in this chapter argue that the growing prevalence of argument in our culture has led to an equivalent loss of understanding, connection, and intimacy. Test the validity of this hypothesis yourself. First, choose an issue that is currently being debated publicly and research it. What sort of disagreement does this issue involve? What is the debate and what viewpoints does it put into conflict? Then, in a two- or three-page essay, analyze the ways that each side in this debate talks to, and talks about, each other. How do the various participants in this debate appear to think about those with whom they differ? In your view, are these assessments valid?

Using the Steps of Rhetorical Analysis to Write Your Own Academic Essay

The same instruction this chapter presents for analyzing other peoples' writing can also serve as a guide for undertaking your own. In particular, a number of the steps outlined above provide a useful framework for the kind of writing you are often called upon to do in the classroom. In the same way that these steps teach you to apply the rhetorical concept of argument to what you read, they can also be used to help you better see the role that argument plays in your own essay writing. Take a look at the outline below. Organizing the writing process along the same rhetorical lines modeled above, it provides you with a map for how to use the concept of argument to organize and create your own academic essay:

- **Step One: Identifying the Issue Within the Argument:** What is the larger point you are trying to make? What, in your view, makes this issue debatable?
- **Step Two: Defining the Goal Behind the Argument:** What larger goal are you trying to accomplish by making this argument? What do you want your audience to see, know, or understand that they don't already?
- **Step Three: Defending the Argument:** What kinds of support will best bolster the argument you are making?

To see how these steps can be put into practice, let's take a look at a specific example. As you read over the essay below, pay attention to the ways that considerations about argument guide the writer's calculations and choices. To assist you in this work, take note of the comments and questions that accompany the essay in the margins. Then, turn your attention to the sample analysis that follows. In what ways does this discussion provide a model for using these three steps to write an academic essay of your own?

Student Essay: Andrea MacBride, "Dolls: A Legacy of Stereotypes"

This essay by Andrea MacBride deals with one of the key issues raised in the academic writing selections above: social and cultural attitudes toward women.

The first Barbie Doll was created in the late 1950s at a time in American society when attitudes toward women were not nearly as progressive as today. Since then, the marketplace for dolls has expanded dramatically, as the arrival of countless Barbie-like imitators has provided new generations of young girls with a seemingly endless array of choices. And yet while such dolls have remained among the most popular toys in America for decades, they have also become the subject of intense debate and controversy. For many parents, educators, and child-welfare advocates, the continuing popularity of the doll industry represents a worrisome trend in American life. More specifically, these critics worry, this type of toy poses a threat to the positive image and self-esteem of young girls. In this essay, I make the case that these kinds of fears are well-founded, arguing that, despite all of the progress that has been made over the last several decades, the American doll industry continues to promote standards of female beauty and ideas about female power that are misguided and dangerous.

Establishing Context

5

10

Previewing Argument

15

Much of what makes the modern doll industry dangerous concerns the ways these toys promote unhealthy messages about bodies and body image to young girls. Despite the advances achieved by the women's rights movement over the last several decades, the makers of Barbie, for example, continue to present a doll that sets impossible physical standards. Many critics have noted, for instance, that the body proportions of the typical Barbie are entirely unrealistic, bearing no relationship to real life. Simply put: They are not measurements any real woman could actually achieve. Despite this fact, thousands of young girls every year spend hours playing with a doll that sets an impossible standard for their own bodies. The risk here is that young girls who

First Main Point

20

25

Supporting Example

30

buy such dolls might easily end up identifying with a body type they can never achieve in life, and feel as a result that
35   their actual body proportions are somehow inadequate.

Another key issue concerns the messages many dolls pro-
mote about female power. Despite the ways the American workplace has changed over the last century, despite the fact that women are now represented in every profession, many
40   contemporary toy companies continue to market dolls that define the role of women in sexist and stereotypical terms. Even today, it is not unusual to come across toys that teach girls to imagine themselves as "swimsuit models," "beauty queens," and "fairies." Not only do such dolls promote unreal-
45   istic standards of physical beauty, but perhaps even more dangerously, they suggest that, if you're female, your entire self-worth should be based on how you look. Entirely absent is any suggestion that females can or should be judged on the basis of other talents and attributes—such as intelligence or
50   professional accomplishment. The fact that we never see dolls that depict women in the role of scientist, teacher, or com-puter programmer says a lot about how far we still have to go.

Some defenders of the modern doll industry suggest that critics are simply making too big a deal out of a small con-
55   cern. Yes, they concede, many dolls continue to promote ste-reotypical images of and ideas about women, but these dolls are still just toys. Their purpose isn't to educate but to en-tertain, and from this perspective, critics who object to the dangerous messages they promote are missing the point.
60   Others, meanwhile, point out that not every modern doll promotes stereotypical ideas about women. There are, in fact, versions of the Barbie doll that present Barbie as a businesswoman, and even an astronaut. Despite this, how-ever, I would suggest that it is the defenders of the doll in-
65   dustry, and not the critics, who are really missing the point. Even if these exceptions to the rule exist, they are still ex-ceptions. The general rule still applies.

In the midst of this debate, a key question stands out. If the current situation isn't tolerable, what should be done? If
70   too many dolls on the market today promote too many mes-sages that are harmful to young girls, what changes in the doll industry should we work toward? In my opinion, the answer can be found not in banning certain types of dolls altogether, but by encouraging toy manufacturers to
75   modify and modernize the varieties of dolls they put on the

Second Main Point

Reasoning to Support Second Point

Addressing a Potential Counterargument

Conclusion: Proposing a Solution

market. Young girls (or boys for that matter) are never going to stop clamoring for new toys. The key therefore is not to stem the flow of available toys, but rather to encourage the development of toys that kids actually deserve.

Now, let's see how the rhetorical steps presented above help us understand the choices the writer makes to create this essay:

Step One: *Identifying the Issue Within the Argument: What Larger Point is the Writer Trying to Make?*

o The issue the writer is addressing here concerns the messages the modern doll industry promotes to young girls. More particularly, the writer makes the point that many of the most popular dolls promote messages about self-image and self-worth that are harmful to girls.

Step Two: *Defining the Purpose: What Goal is the Writer Trying to Achieve?*

o The writer clearly wants her audience to accept the premise that toys have the potential to affect the well-being of the children who use them. We can see this assumption at work from the beginning of the essay, when the writer warns her readers that "the American doll industry continues to promote standards of female beauty and ideas about female power that are misguided and dangerous."

o Another point the writer wants her readers to accept is that, despite the progress that has been made, sexist stereotypes are still commonplace in American culture. As she states, "The fact that we never see dolls that depict women in the role of scientist, teacher, or computer programmer says a lot about how far we still have to go."

Step Three: *Defending the Argument: How Does the Writer Justify This Stance?*

o Much of the writer's argument rests on her belief that an emphasis on physical appearance and "standards of female beauty" is inherently harmful to young women. In making her larger point about the modern doll industry, she focuses on the distinction between messages about intellectual or professional accomplishment and messages about physical appearance. The clear implication is that the former is a valid standard while the latter is not.

Group Work: Thinking Rhetorically About the Formal Selections

Throughout this chapter, you have been given ample opportunity to analyze argument on your own. This activity asks you to undertake this same kind of work from a group perspective. In your group, select one of the formal selections above. Prepare for your group work by re-reading the selection. Then, with your group, use the outline presented at the beginning of the chapter, *Thinking Rhetorically About Argument*, to analyze role that argument plays in this piece. Here is a quick recap of these steps:

- What is the main issue this selection addresses?
- What larger claim does this text make about this issue?
- What makes this claim convincing or persuasive?
- What kind of argument would I make?
- How do I put all of this into writing?

Once you have completed this work, exchange your findings with another group. First, have your group re-read the selection these new findings examine. Then, discuss as a group how helpful you find this analysis. Do you agree with the conclusions about argument this analysis draws? Do you evaluate the role of argument in different or similar ways? Finally, summarize your key findings in a paragraph. Be prepared to share this written assessment with the rest of the class.

Arguing in Context: Understanding the Connection Between Informal and Formal Writing

Throughout this chapter, we have shifted back and forth between a focus on informal and formal writing. How do these types of writing compare? What are the key differences in language and tone, form and content, organization and context? And what happens to our understanding of argument when we take these differences into account?

The activity presented here provides us with an opportunity to address exactly these sorts of questions. First, choose a topic or issue that has been raised by one of the formal selections in this chapter (e.g., cyberbullying, profanity in public life, or online dating). Next, choose an informal venue (e.g., blog, Facebook post, tweet, or email), and write about this issue using the conventions of this particular form. Then, choose a formal venue (e.g., journal essay, magazine article, or academic analysis), and write about the same issue using the conventions particular to this form. When you're done, spend a few moments itemizing the specific ways these two writing samples differ. In what ways did your choice of venue affect the argument you made?

Connecting Argument to Rhetorical Modes

As you learned in Chapter 4, writing that differs in terms of genre may still share certain rhetorical patterns or modes. To better understand how rhetorical considerations of argument relate to the question of rhetorical modes, try the following activity: Choose one of the examples of real world writing from the informal selections in this chapter. First, describe the larger point you think this writing attempts to get across. Then, choose the rhetorical mode (narration, description, cause and effect, compare and contrast, or definition) you feel is most prominent in this writing, and analyze the particular ways it helps the writer convey and support the argument.

Speaking for Yourself

Choose an issue that is important to you. It can apply to any given context or setting, concern any group or individual, and raise any topic. The only requirement is that it be a public issue—that is, one that different people take different sides on in some kind of public forum. First, define this issue in your own words. What is the key problem or question it addresses? Next, explain or reflect upon why you find this issue to be so important? What, in your view, makes this issue worth debating? Following this, describe the perspectives this debate puts into conflict. Once you've done all this, create an argument that shows how these differing points and positions can be reconciled.

8 Voice

Picture yourself walking into a library filled with people who are quietly reading. Would you shout out to a friend across the room, or would you instinctively lower your voice? Now, imagine that you're seated alongside hundreds of screaming fans at a weekend football game. Would you express your displeasure with the ref by whispering to the person next to you, or would stand up and yell like everybody else? Finally, consider what would happen if you found yourself unexpectedly jolted from a daydream during class by a question from your professor. Would you angrily dismiss the interruption and turn away, or would you make sure to respond in an attentive tone suitable to the moment?

We tend to think of our voice as something singular and fixed, a part of ourselves as natural as our height or the color of our eyes. But as the examples above suggest, this view doesn't capture the entire truth. When considered abstractly, it can easily seem that our voice is something inherent and unchanging, something that exists beyond the influence of setting or circumstance. In reality, however, our voice is extremely malleable. Depending upon where we are and with whom we are talking, we will make very different calculations about what language to use, what tone to adopt, and what style to employ.

Putting It Into Words

As writers, we confront this fact every day. Whether in a business letter or a lab report, a blog post or a letter to the editor, a Facebook post or a birthday card, we are consistently called upon in our writing to deal with the tricky question of which voice best fits the specific occasion. Think, for example, about all the different options at our disposal when we decide to communicate online. If we're tweeting friends about our daily routine, chances are we will employ a voice that veers toward the brief, chatty, and informal. If, on the other hand, we're blogging about the latest concert we've attended or an upcoming vacation, we might decide on a lengthier, more detailed presentation. And if, finally, we're composing an online essay in response to an assignment for school, we're more likely to adopt a more formal, serious style.

As writers, one of the most useful ways to make an informed decision about voice is to frame this choice in rhetorical terms. What style is best suited to the setting in which I am writing? What tone will best appeal to the audience I am targeting? What word choice or language will most help me accomplish my overall goal?

How to Analyze Voice in Real World Writing

The outline below provides a framework for addressing just these kinds of questions. Dividing the process into a series of discrete steps, it creates a model for how to identify, analyze, and evaluate voice in rhetorical terms. As you review these steps, think about the ways you can use them to begin analyzing voice rhetorically yourself.

▨ Thinking Rhetorically About Voice

- **Step One: Finding the Voice:** What overall impression does the writer convey? What basic style does the writer adopt?
- **Step Two: Assessing the Voice:** Does this style seem appropriate to the occasion? Is it designed to appeal to the writer's target audience? Does it help further the writer's larger goal?
- **Step Three: Expressing the Voice:** What specific elements in the text (e.g., words, phrases, sentences, and paragraphs) best help convey the writer's style?
- **Step Four: Refining the Voice:** What changes in language or organization would help convey the text's style even more effectively?
- **Step Five: Comparing the Voice:** How does the writer's style here compare to other styles that might have been employed?
- **Step Six: Putting It Into Writing:** How do I summarize my findings in writing?

To see how these guidelines can be put into practice, let's turn to a specific example. Read over the selection below. Then, look at the sample analysis that follows.

Jason Sulakis, "Personal Portrait"

This short essay by Jason Sulakis, a student in a freshman composition class, was written in response to his instructor's request for a short essay "describing how you see yourself." As such, it offers an example of exactly the sort of informal writing activity you might encounter in class or in a peer writing workshop.

How do I see myself? Well, the first thing is I am not afraid to say that I am a person who is willing to be completely honest with myself. I would never want to come across as cocky, but I truly believe that I have succeeded in becoming a leader and an example to many people around me. I am an athlete, for example, and the coaches preach to us daily about setting good examples of the program, ourselves, and our parents. Therefore, I make sure I am dressed appropriately; I make sure to talk at all times as if somebody important is listening; I don't talk trash or tear others down; I don't use foul language; I don't miss class. Now don't start thinking I believe that I am perfect—far from it. But I do feel I try a lot harder to set the right example to others. The most important thing about status is not how much of it you have, but what you do with it once you've got it. 5 10

Thinking Rhetorically About Voice: A Step-by-Step Guide

Now, let's now see how the steps modeled above can be used as a guide for analyzing this short writing in rhetorical terms:

Step One: *Finding the Voice: What Overall Impression Does the Writer Try to Convey?*

- o The writer clearly attempts to come across as confident and self-assured, as evidenced by such phrases as:

    "I am not afraid to say . . ."

    "I would never want to come across as cocky, but . . ."

- o The writer also tries to present himself as a positive role model, as in the sentence where he refers to himself as a "leader" and an "example."

- o It is also striking how often the writer begins sentences with the word "I." This strategy helps reinforce the sense of strength, conviction, and confidence he clearly wants to convey.

Step Two: *Assessing the Voice: Is This Style Appropriate to the Occasion?*

- o The confident tone the writer strikes seems appropriate to the assignment he has been given. This writer "sees" himself" as a person who doesn't have a lot of doubts about the way he is living his life. If he "saw himself" differently, if he wanted to come across as more uncertain or open-minded about his behavior, the writer would have struck a different tone at the beginning.

- o This tone also seems appropriate given the goal the writer wants to accomplish—namely, to encourage readers to follow his own example. Even though he acknowledges he is "far from [perfect]," the writer clearly believes that his actions and choices are the correct ones. This is most evident in the catalogue of behaviors he presents, which reads like a "to do" list we might be given by a parent or a teacher:

    "I make sure I am dressed appropriately . . ."

    "I don't talk trash or tear others down . . ."

    "I don't use foul language . . ."

    "I don't miss class."

Step Three: *Expressing the Voice: What Specific Elements Best Help Convey the Writer's Style?*

- o As noted above, the repeated use of "I" helps not only to establish a tone of self-confidence but also to reinforce the writer's view of himself as a person with something valuable to teach others. More specifically, though, the writer's use of "I" generally takes the form of "I don'ts": descriptions of things he does not do and, implicitly, doesn't want others to do either. This tactic makes the writer's overall tone here come across as more serious.

○ Related to this is the writer's use of words like "leader" and "example," which convey the unspoken message to readers that they should listen closely and emulate his actions.

○ The writer also makes the decision to emphasize his "honesty." This word choice seems to undermine the tone of confidence displayed elsewhere. Why bother to tell your readers that you're "willing to be completely honest" with yourself? Is the writer worried his readers won't believe this unless he says it?

Step Four: *Refining the Voice: What Changes Would Help Convey This Style More Effectively?*

○ If the writer's goal is to convince readers to view him as a role model, I'd suggest he change the way he phrases his advice. In addition to making statements about the choices he makes, it could be helpful to include a discussion of why he makes these choices. This would change the tone of the essay from one of unquestioned certainty to one of more open-ended dialogue.

○ Toward this same end, I think it might be more effective for the writer to shift from an overall tone of *declaring* his ideas to a tone of *explaining* his ideas. This would be particularly helpful, I think, at the end of the essay, where the writer begins to transition into what looks like a thesis or claim about "status." If he wants his readers to be persuaded by what he has to say about this issue, he will need to do more than simply state his view.

Step Five: *Comparing the Voice: How Does the Writer's Style Compare to the Other Styles That Might Have Been Employed?*

○ In one way or another, the advice the writer offers has to do with the importance of living up to the conventional or established rules: "dressing appropriately," "coming to class on time," and not using "foul language." I'm wondering if the writer could use a different style to make these same points. What would be different if this list of "do's and don'ts" were preceded by a sentence or two discussing the larger idea they all share in common?

○ The prompt asked the writer to reflect upon how he "sees" himself, which also seems like an opportunity to reflect upon the ways that others see him. I could imagine this writer using his own self-description as a comparison or contrast to the ways he is defined, rightly or wrongly, by those around him. This kind of essay could easily strike a more serious, analytical tone or a more ironic, humorous one.

Step Six: *Putting It Into Writing: How Do I Summarize My Findings in Writing?*

○ While the confident, assertive tone the writer employs succeeds in conveying an impression of certainty and self-assurance, there are moments where this style seems to work against the larger goal he is trying to achieve. The writer clearly wants to use his own choices as a model for his readers to follow. The problem here, however, is that readers may well find themselves less than fully convinced to do so because the writer's own confidence prevents him from more fully explaining or justifying his choices.

Informal Writing Selections

Now that you've seen what this kind of analysis looks like, try putting it into practice yourself. This section brings together a representative sample of informal writing, the kind of writing you might easily come across in your own day-to-day life. Using the step-by-step framework above as your guide, analyze each selection along the same rhetorical lines. In each case, how does the writer construct and present a particular type of voice? How does this voice influence the way this selection gets put together or the messages it contains? And what larger goal does the writer hope to achieve by writing in this particular tone or style?

Let's start by working our way through a sample of this rhetorical analysis. Pay close attention to the comments and the questions this sample analysis presents. It is designed to serve as a model for the kind of analysis you will conduct with the other selections included here.

Hailey Yook, "Positive Stereotypes Are Hurtful, Too"

Hailey Yook writes a column on "contemporary social issues" for The Daily Californian.

For the love of everything that's good and pure, can someone please explain to me what the phrase "You're so Asian" means? And while you're at it, let me know what criteria, scale and measurements one might use

5 for determining my degree of "Asian-ness." Maybe there's a panel of judges involved? I've heard the stereotypes one too many times to accept them as an integral part of my character and identity anymore.

The stereotype is an interesting concept, isn't it?
10 Particularly in its versatility. It can be comic and satirical and, at the same time, offensive and humiliating. My ethnicity mostly experiences positive stereotypes, such as the model-minority stereotype. But just like their negative counterparts, positive stereotypes strip

The writer's tone really draws me in. She uses a humorous approach to address a serious topic.

This is an effective rhetorical strategy, using an ironic voice here to preview her argument about the relationship between stereotypes and identity.

Impressive variety of word choices here. This strategy reflects how complicated the writer's feelings about these stereotypes are.

people of their individuality and alienate them for not meeting the standards that are imposed upon them.

Negative stereotypes are widely acknowledged as harmful, so they're often effectively rejected. But positive stereotypes, which are widely embraced and even considered flattering, can be equally detrimental. One particularly harmful positive stereotype of Asians is that they are all smart. A 2010 study about the model-minority stereotype showed that Asian Americans are most likely to be perceived as nerds. OK, so a lot of people think we're smart, and yes, it's good to be smart. Synonyms include intelligent, brilliant, bright . . . These terms couldn't offend anyone in their right mind. But there's a reason that out of all of the Asian stereotypes out there that could cause my identity to feel threatened, it's this one.

First off, it's important to recognize that this idea that every Asian person is smart is like any other stereotype—obviously false and easily ignorable. It's true that 42 percent of all Asian American adults have at least a college degree, which is the highest out of all major ethnic groups, but because of factors like stereotypes, sometimes it slips our minds that not every Asian person is the same. And due to the way that many people—of any racial background, including Asian—usually regard this "Asians-are-smart" stereotype as more acceptable than others, its implications change. According to this stereotype, intelligence is the result of having Asian genes. The stereotype that "Asians are smart" then becomes "Asians are smart only because they are Asian." Therefore, no matter how much effort, studying or practice an Asian person puts in, when he or she achieves academic excellence, it's likely that the common reaction will be along the lines of "Asians are so smart" or, you guessed it, "You're so Asian." It's difficult not to see that this person's achievement and intelligence are being attributed to one thing and one thing only—race.

Well, at least we're not being called stupid, right? I mean, we're being called smart for crying out loud. How could I complain about that? Despite how trite this may sound, it truly is a blessing and a curse. Many of us who are of Asian descent are, without even

This is a key point in the writer's overall argument: Even positive stereotypes can be harmful. 15

The writer is repeating her key argument here that positive stereotypes can be harmful. 20

25

Note how the writer moves back and forth between an informal, conversational tone and a more formal, serious presentation. 30

The inclusion of statistics here is an effective rhetorical strategy. The objective nature of the data complements the more subjective tone the writer adopts elsewhere. 35

40

45

50

The writer is returning here to a more informal, conversational tone. 55

having to prove ourselves first, already presumed to
be smart . . . which can be as nice as it sounds. But if
60   my race is taking all of the credit for my efforts and
accomplishments, what am I as an individual? Will my
capabilities and successes always be defined entirely
by my race? What if I feel that I don't meet these expectations, standards and pressures that my race im-
65   poses on me . . . Am I not truly Asian?

   I've never had that perfect 4.0, and I'm not the type
to strive for absolute perfection in every academic endeavor. So yes, I'm personally victim to the pressures
of this stereotype—to make sure I'm staying on top of
70   my studies because if I ever show signs of struggle, I'm
not being "Asian enough." I've witnessed during all of   *Another key rhetorical strategy:*
my years in the public school system how parents,   *The writer is using her own*
classmates and even teachers expect the Asian stu-   *personal experience as evidence*
dent to excel and even unknowingly guide them on   *to support her main point.*
75   paths of math and science without considering the in-
dividual student's interests and abilities. These pressures can cause some to crack. The model-minority
stereotype creates unnecessary stress, prevents students from acknowledging problems with stress and
80   seeking help and generates feelings of shame and re-
luctance in seeking academic assistance.

   Out of all of the stereotypes about my race, I find
this one to be the most limiting and oppressive. I feel
as though I, along with others, am boxed in by this
85   stereotype because even though it's easy to just ignore   *The writer is using emotionally*
assumptions that I'm as smart as I'm "supposed" to be,   *charged language here:*
it's hard to ignore that I'm regarded as smart only be-   *"oppressive" and "limiting."*
cause I am Asian. And it's even harder to ignore that
I'm not "Asian enough" if I struggle academically.
90   Stereotypes are inevitable, but something like intelli-   *The writer ends on a powerful*
gence can be so important to a person's life that attrib-   *note, using language that makes*
uting it merely to race and disguising it as a compliment *clear how objectionable she finds*
is more than a stereotype—it's an outright insult.   *these types of stereotypes to be.*

Source: The Daily Californian, *March 10, 2014*
http://www.dailycal.org/2014/03/10/positive-stereotypes-hurtful/

Step One: *Finding the Voice: What Overall Impression Does the Writer Want to Convey?*

   o The writer definitely wants to come across as someone who regards "Asian
   stereotypes" as a serious issue. We see evidence of this from the outset, where

she uses an urgent tone to introduce the topic: "For the love of everything that's good and pure, can someone please explain to me what the phrase 'You're so Asian' means?"

º More specifically, the writer wants to present herself as someone willing to think in more complex and critical ways about the assumptions that underlie this particular stereotype as well as the potential effect it has on those who are labeled by it. This impression comes through, for example, in such lines as:

> The stereotype is an interesting concept, isn't it?

> [P]ositive stereotypes strip people of their individuality and alienate them for not meeting the standards that are imposed upon them.

> It's difficult not to see that this person's achievement and intelligence are being attributed to one thing and one thing only—race.

Step Two: *Assessing the Voice: Is This Style Appropriate to the Occasion?*

º One of the writer's goals is to highlight how inaccurate the prevailing "Asian stereotype" actually is. One of her main rhetorical strategies for accomplishing this is to highlight the differences between the stereotype and the way she actually views herself. For example:

> I've heard the stereotypes one too many times to accept them as an integral part of my character and identity anymore.

> I've never had that perfect 4.0, and I'm not the type to strive for absolute perfection in every academic endeavor.

º As noted above, another goal is to challenge the influence these stereotypes exert. To further this goal, the writer repeatedly calls out what she views as the inherent absurdity of this stereotype, thereby inviting readers to question its power and validity. For example: "[I]t's important to recognize that this idea that every Asian person is smart is like any other stereotype—obviously false and easily ignorable."

Step Three: *Expressing the Voice: What Specific Elements Best Help Convey the Writer's Style?*

º Throughout the essay, the writer employs a humorous or ironic tone to convey her skepticism toward the stereotype of the "smart Asian." We can see this strategy at work in such sentences as:

> [L]et me know what criteria, scale and measurements one might use for determining my degree of "Asian-ness." Maybe there's a panel of judges involved?

> Well, at least we're not being called stupid, right? I mean, we're being called smart for crying out loud. How could I complain about that?

○ At other points in the essay, the writer complements this ironic approach with a more serious, critical tone that reflects the deep objections she harbors toward this stereotype. For example:

> Out of all of the stereotypes about my race, I find this one to be the most limiting and oppressive.

> [A]ttributing [intelligence] merely to race and disguising it as a compliment is more than a stereotype—it's an outright insult.

○ And finally, there are occasional moments where the writer strikes a tone that is neither ironic nor outraged but instead is more objective and factual. For example:

> It's true that 42 percent of all Asian American adults have at least a college degree, which is the highest out of all major ethnic groups, but because of factors like stereotypes, sometimes it slips our minds that not every Asian person is the same.

Step Four: *Refining the Voice: What Changes Would Help Convey This Style More Effectively?*

○ Overall, I find the mixture of tones the writer employs to be effective. The humorous tone not only grabs the reader's attention, it also encourages the reader to adopt a sympathetic attitude toward the issue. And by complementing this tone with one that is more pointed and critical, the writer is able to use that sympathetic connection with her reader to convey her more serious points about the dangers this stereotype poses.

○ If I have any questions about this strategy, they might concern the degree to which the writer seems to rely on an ironic or humorous tone. Does this reliance run the risk of undermining how seriously her readers will regard this issue? Is it possible to be too humorous in one's discussion of an important issue?

Step Five: *Comparing the Voice: How Does the Writer's Style Compare to the Other Styles That Might Have Been Employed?*

○ Rather than an informal, conversational style, the writer could have chosen to address this issue by adopting a more formal, analytical voice, one that examines the question of "Asian stereotypes" from a more distanced perspective. This approach would definitely have presented the issue in more structured, perhaps even academic, terms, but it might also have provided the writer with a better framework for advancing the serious critique she presents.

Step Six: *Putting It Into Writing: How Do I Summarize My Findings in Writing?*

○ The writer's overall goal is to encourage readers to think more closely and critically about the so-called "positive stereotypes" that are often applied to

Asian Americans. To accomplish this, the writer adopts a combination of ironic and serious tones, describing what she views as the inherent absurdity of these stereotypes while simultaneously advancing an important argument about the ways they can undermine one's identity. At times, however, it seems as if this goal is hindered a bit by the writer's overreliance on a humorous or ironic tone, a strategy that runs the risk of undermining the seriousness of the issue at hand.

Now, it's your turn. For each of the selections included below, use these same six steps outlined above to undertake your own analysis of voice.

The Onion, "Ah, To Be Young, Rich, White, Male, College-Educated, Straight, and in Love"

Ironically celebrating itself as "America's Finest News Source," The Onion has long enjoyed a reputation as one of the nation's most popular satirical publications.

I may be getting on in years, but I still consider myself a bit of a romantic. Why, just today, I was strolling through the park when I happened to spy a young, upper-class, straight male Caucasian sharing a kiss with his beloved, and I tell you, my heart nearly skipped a beat. The very sight of it filled me with a deep yearning and sense of elation that stirred this old man to his core. And I thought to myself, "Ah, to be   5
young, wealthy, white, male, college-educated, heterosexual, and in love!"

There's really nothing quite like it.

When you're in your twenties, a man, descended from Anglo-Saxon genes, born into immense luxury, able-bodied, surrounded by friends, family, and authority figures who support you, mentally alert, straight, possessing a degree from a re-   10
spected four-year institution, and head over heels in love, the world just seems like a magical place, doesn't it? The sun shines brighter, the breeze blows sweeter, and it feels like you're on top of the world! Anyone who's ever been captivated like that and has had all the advantages life has to offer handed to them on a silver platter because of their race, class, family history, and education level knows exactly what   15
I'm talking about.

I mean, just knowing that you've got that special someone—as well as the monumental opportunities afforded to you by being an affluent white male in his twenties who was born into a democratic society with limitless social mobility— can make you feel like the luckiest man alive. Yes, when you're in love and the   20
recipient of every possible benefit imaginable—be it lifelong financial stability or peerless social stature—it feels like it's just you, the object of your enchantment, and your unshakeable position within the top echelon of privilege. Nothing else matters.

Just think about how rare young love is! What a special thing it is to have found   25
someone who truly cares about you! And, similarly, how special it is to have never faced discrimination due to your race, gender, sexuality, religious preference, or

social class; to live in a safe, crime-free neighborhood; to have enjoyed a stable childhood in which you never felt afraid for yourself or your loved ones; to possess
30   a strong, healthy body and mind that allows you to surmount any obstacles that would impede less fortunate individuals; and to have parents whose financial prosperity ensures that you will always have a safety net in the unlikely event that even the merest trace of hardship or want should at any point intrude upon your life.

It makes you feel, well, pretty much invincible.

35   Ah, youth! Ah, love! Ah, living under a government that neither oppresses its people nor prevents them from pursuing their ambitions, having no children and no debt to prevent you from doing whatever you want at all times, being enrolled in health insurance, having free access to the numerous conveniences afforded by modern technology, living in a large metropolitan area with an array of job oppor-
40   tunities and unlimited diversions, and having been swept off your feet by the girl of your dreams! It truly is a gift.

So drink deep of love, you young, amorous, entitled, and racially favored men! Enjoy your romantic infatuation, just as you enjoy your separation from the troubles afflicting the billions of people who, simply by virtue of who they are, can
45   never aspire to the life you live, cloistered within an impermeable bubble of wealth and social mastery that no harm or worry can ever breach. It truly is as marvelous as the old poets say.

I just wish everyone could experience that feeling

Source: The Onion, October 23, 2013. © 2013, by Onion, Inc.
http://www.theonion.com/articles/ah-to-be-young-rich-white-male-
collegeeducated-str,34320/

Adrian Rodriguez, "Body Art Stereotypes Misrepresent Tattoo and Piercing Culture"

Golden Gate Xpress *is a newspaper for San Francisco State University.*

It wasn't until the artist lifted his handheld machine from my skin—as it buzzed like a dental drill—and wiped my ink and blood splattered arm clean that I realized I had just made a decision that would affect me for the rest of my life.

I was shaky and fatigued. I looked down at my forearm, swollen and red from the
5   irritation and I thought to myself the old cliché, "There is no turning back now."

I had just gotten tattooed.

Although it wasn't my first, this one in particular—a traditionally stylized portraiture of the Greek god, Poseidon—was definitely the most bold. The tattoo was an extension of a piece I had gotten a few years earlier, covering my forearm down to
10   the bend of my wrist. Even living in San Francisco, it's hard finding a job where I don't have to wear long sleeves to cover it up.

According to a study by Harris Interactive, currently one in five people in the U.S. has at least one tattoo. Although this 21 percent tattooed population is actively growing, 40 percent of people think this progression is a change for the worse, according to Pew Research Center.

It's interesting how perspectives are so different. In the study by Harris Interactive, people with tattoos generally seemed to have a positive outlook on each other and themselves, whereas people without tattoos were much more critical of their inked-up counterparts.

The study showed that "At least two in five (without tattoos) say that people with tattoos are less attractive (45 percent) or sexy (39 percent)," and "One quarter say that people with tattoos are less intelligent (27 percent), healthy (25 percent) or spiritual (25 percent)."

I can definitely understand how a person's physical attraction to another can be affected by body art—some tattoos, piercings and modifications are a bit extreme. However, the perception that those with tattoos are less intelligent, healthy or spiritual is completely ridiculous.

I knew what I was getting into each time I modified my body, whether it was a tattoo, stretching my ears or piercing my septum, but it doesn't give anyone the right to judge or harass a person with prejudices because someone is different.

There are times when people, usually in their late 30s or older, approach me and ask me, "What're you going to do when you're older? Didn't you think of that?" They make a face full of disgust thinking about old wrinkly tattoos.

My response? Well, I'm going to be an old guy with tattoos. It makes no difference if I have tattoos or not, we all get old.

At work I was waiting on a customer. I was polite, helpful and attentive as I usually am. She stared me straight in the eye, blatantly ignoring everything I said and told me, "You're going to grow out of that, you know?"

It caught me off guard. She made herself clear and pointed out that my "earlobes have holes big enough to fit bottlenecks through" and she said I was going to grow out of it. She said I made a mistake and I was going to regret it when I was older.

She didn't know me. She still doesn't know me. All she knew was I had holes in my ears and she looked at me like I was a stupid punk kid.

Every person is different, having had unique experiences in life. Yes, I think tattoos look bad ass and I feel like my piercings and tattoos give my look a bit of an edge; but next time you're standing in front of me I'd appreciate it if you had the respect and decency to hear what I have to say, rather than assuming that I'm going nowhere in life.

People just don't understand the tattoo culture. Honestly, I barely understand it. All I know is that I like tattoos. I like piercings. I don't regret any single modification I have done, whether it be a tattoo, stretched ears or a stretched septum. This is me and I am not afraid to show it. My piercings and tattoos have nothing to do with my heart and determination.

Source: Golden Gate XPress, May 11, 2013
http://www.goldengatexpress.org/2013/05/11/body-art-stereotypes/

Visual Rhetoric: Ed Fischer, "Pink Slime Burger"

This cartoon clearly aims to be a commentary on our contemporary eating habits. How do you understand the relationship between the visual image and the written text? How would you characterize the voice here?

FIGURE 8.5

Source: Ed Fischer/www.CartoonStock.com.
http://www.cartoonstock.com/cartoonview.asp?catref=efin2859

Denis Storey, "Why We Hate Congress"

In this post for BenefitsPro.com, a website that explores issues of importance to what it calls the "benefits community," blogger Denis Storey zeroes in on the public's growing antipathy toward Congress, giving voice to the anger and dismay so many Americans feel toward their elected leaders.

I know it's not just me—at least not this time. Most of us hate Congress—typically much more than we hate the president—unless you're a rodeo clown from my home state, of course. According to the latest poll from NBC News and *The Wall Street Journal*, a staggering 83 percent of Americans disapprove of the way Congress does (or doesn't do) its job. Who says we can't agree on anything?

But my favorite part of the poll? An all-time high six out of 10 voters said they "would vote to defeat and replace every single member of Congress" if such an item were actually on the ballot.

But why do we hate them so much? I have a few theories. The following list is by no means definitive, just a few things that spring to mind. Please add your own additions to my list in the comments section. 10

All That Recess

For starters, both chambers of Congress aren't in session at the same time much more than half the calendar year, which makes for a pretty light workload. Add to that the lack of people actually showing up to work—oh, and that European vacation in August—and it makes it pretty hard for the average hard-working American to relate. Which brings me to . . .

They're Loaded

According to some number crunching from the nonpartisan, nonprofit Center for Responsive Politics, the 113th Congress is the richest on record—largely because of the latest batch of freshman—with the median net worth sitting at $1,066,515. Or almost exactly $1 million more than the average voter.

Additionally, more than half are worth at least a cool mil each, according to the study. Hardly representative of the people, huh? Speaking of which . . .

Obamacare Exemption

Did I mention Congress and its staff—not to mention the union representing thousands of federal employees—are exempt from the Patient Protection and Affordable Care Act? So what's good enough for us isn't nearly good enough for them. 'Nuff said.

And we know about this because . . .

Because We See It All. In Real Time

We live in a world, where every vote, quote and foible is spread worldwide in seconds. Before 24-hour news cycles, social media and satellites, freshmen members of Congress enjoyed more slack—both professionally and personally—than they do today.

If you screw up your first day on the job—whether it's a questionable selfie on Twitter or an innocent misstatement to a hometown television reporter—its headline news.

But if you make every House vote or Senate subcommittee hearing, represent your constituents faithfully and stay off the Sunday morning talk shows, your reward (if you're lucky) is crickets.

And despite all of this . . .

We Keep Electing Them

Talk about the devil you know. The success rate of incumbents running for re-election is a numbing 90 percent. Which begs the question: Do we hate them because they're so successful?

Either way, I guess it's true that we get the government we deserve.

Source: BenefitsPro.com, August 12, 2013. © 2013 Summit Professional Networks.
http://www.benefitspro.com/2013/08/12/why-we-hate-congress?t=regulatory

Valerie Frankel, "Your Three Biggest Stressors, Solved"

SELF Magazine *ranks as one of the most widely read publications in the "self-help" genre of magazines. Targeted primarily toward a female readership, it offers instruction and guidelines on a range of topics— from weight loss to relationship issues.*

#1 Worry: Your Cash

"I'm afraid that I'm going to be broke forever. After my car payment, grad school tuition, rent and groceries, I barely have anything left over to put into savings."

—Rebecca, 25, North Carolina

5   **Take action:** First, know that this is temporary—your salary will likely go up. But the only way to reduce your money anxiety *now* is to be in control of your finances, says Manisha Thakor, founder and CEO of MoneyZen Wealth Management in Santa Fe. Step one is to make a budget. "About 50 percent of your paycheck should go to needs, like rent, and 30 percent to wants, like dinners out," Thakor says. The last 20 percent
10   is key: That's what you should put away. If you want to have money, you gotta start saving now. "Living paycheck to paycheck is scary," says Thakor. "Savings give you a cushion." So feel fab about whatever you can stash, even if it's only $20 a month.

#2 Worry: Your Job

"I have a good job—I just don't love the field I'm in. I fear that if I don't make a move
15   soon, I'll be unhappy at work forever, but I'm scared to give up my steady paycheck."

—Erin, 24, Chicago

Take action: It's normal when you're starting out to think you're stuck for life in the career you've chosen, but that's not true, Dr. Birndorf says. "You can always change jobs, but first, ask yourself: Do you really not like the industry you're in, or are you just
20   in a crappy low-level position?" If it's the former, make a six-month plan to score a happier gig—research careers, network. This buys you time to make a smart move but also relieves stress, because you're actively seeking what's next. If it's the latter, the answer may be to stick it out, because things will get better. And remember, work is only work: You can do what you love—volunteer, travel—on your own time.

#3 Worry: Your Guy

25

"I always fall for guys who don't want to get serious, guys I can tell won't be good to me. I'm panicked that if I can't break this pattern, I'll never have a healthy, lasting relationship."

—Katherine, 26, New York City

30   **Take action:** Let yourself off the hook a little bit—there's no deadline to find Mr. Right. Besides, dating the wrong guys has some benefits—experience, fun, great stories to share with your friends over beers. To break the pattern, though, you need to hash out what's driving it, says Rachel Sussman, a therapist in New York City.

Is it the thrill of being with a "bad boy"? Or maybe you're not ready to settle down yet, so you go for dudes you know aren't marriage material. Once you are ready and you understand what you don't want (guys who do x, y and z), it will be easier to find what you do want—and deserve: a smart, fun guy who treats you well.

Source: SELF Magazine, *April 19, 2013*
http://www.self.com/life/health/2013/04/three-biggest-stressors-solved/

35

▓ Thinking Rhetorically About Voice: Expanded Outline

Now that you've gotten some practice with this kind of work, use the expanded outline below to conduct a more extensive rhetorical analysis of one of the informal selections above:

Step One: *Finding the Voice: What Overall Impression Does the Writer Try to Convey?*

- ° How would you define the style the writer adopts? What sort of tone does the writer adopt? What types of language? What specific words or phrases stand out?

- ° What impression of the writer does this speaking style convey? Based on the tone, language, word choice, and so on, how would you characterize this writer?

- ° Can you think of an alternative voice this writer might have adopted? How, in your view, would this affect or alter the effectiveness of this piece?

Step Two: *Assessing the Voice: Is This Style Appropriate to the Occasion?*

- ° Who is the target audience? What style best appeals to such a readership?

- ° What is the writer's overall goal? How does this style help the writer accomplish this goal?

- ° What form does this writing take? Does the style reflect the style that is typical for this form?

Step Three: *Expressing the Voice: What Specific Elements Best Help Convey the Writer's Style?*

- ° What specific topics, issues, or questions does this text raise? What are the key ideas or messages being conveyed?

- ° What words, images, or phrases stand out as especially important? Why?

- ° What larger point, message, or argument is this voice designed to help convey?

- ° How would you characterize the overall structure or organization? What information or statements stand out to you as being especially important?

Step Four: *Refining the Voice: What Changes Would Help Convey This Style More Effectively?*

o What changes in language, structure, or tone would make the writer's style more appealing to the target audience?

o What changes in language, structure, or tone would help strengthen the writer's main points?

o What changes in language, structure, or tone would help the writer better accomplish the overall goal?

Step Five: *Comparing the Voice: How Does This Style Compare to Other Style That Might Be Employed?*

o How does the writer's voice compare to the voice others might use to address the same topic?

o What sort of style would you adopt if you were the author of this piece?

Step Six: *Putting It Into Writing*

o How do I summarize my findings in writing?

Formal Writing Selections

As writers, few things create as immediate and lasting an impression as the voice we choose to adopt. Depending on the words we choose, the tone we adopt, or the style we employ, readers will draw very different conclusions about who we are. But how do we know which voice to use? If there isn't any such thing as a single, authentic voice, what are the factors that determine the particular voice we choose?

Each of the selections below addresses this question from a different perspective. Taken together, they offer a portrait of the pressures and factors in our culture that influence the ways our voices are both shaped and heard. And in doing so, they also provide another opportunity to analyze different types of voice in rhetorical terms. Like the informal selections gathered above, the readings here include questions that invite you to think about how different writers construct their own voice and, in turn, how these choices help to shape the content, organization, and goal of the writing itself.

Brian Moen, "Myth of Objectivity"

We have longed harbored fantasies about the unbiased voice: the belief that the point of view devoid of all personal bias is by definition the most credible and legitimate. But is such objectivity even attainable, let alone desirable? Taking a closer look at media coverage of politics over the years, Brian Moen, writing in the campus newspaper for the University of California–Davis, answers: perhaps not. Seeking to challenge the myth of objectivity, he offers some surprising thoughts on the importance of bias in modern life.

"No one is forcing anyone to write anything. The world is comprised of institutions that craft the society to fit whatever upholds their power."

We live in a world full of death, suffering and extreme despotism. There are some hard problems to fix. Some other highly pervasive problems are not so hard. The endurance of hard problems doesn't need an explanation: We haven't solved them because they're hard.

But what is the explanation for the persistence of the easy problems? Well, I   5
think their very existence is proof of a thesis that I frequently supply and that I want to try to further explicate here. People cannot solve problems that should be easily fixed because some powerful institutions do not want those problems fixed. It would reduce their power.

Every institution acts in this way. This is what causes the manipulation of ideolo-   10
gies. The most powerful groups naturally filter information. By coercing information, our actions are controlled and the easy problems remain.

No one is forcing anyone to write anything. The world is comprised of institutions that craft the society to fit whatever upholds their power.

This has two important effects. One—those people who honestly and sincerely   15
hold the beliefs that uphold power will naturally be selected for. Megyn Kelly or Brian Williams, these people really believe the totally bogus stuff that they say. It's not that the media is full of liars who want to uphold power.

It is full of people who were selected for success because they happened to be properly submissive to the ideology that they were indoctrinated into. Success in   20
news media is the ability to seem critical and feel critical while being really, really not critical. Have you heard of any major muckraking journalists exposing big truths lately? I haven't.

Second—powerful institutions can exclude or minimize voices that would question the framework in which they address issues. This topic is dealt with thoroughly   25
by *Democracy Now!* host Amy Goodman. In her book *Breaking the Sound Barrier*, she argues that through sheer volume, corporate media (the media most crafted by elite institutions) drowns out real dissent.

If there are hundreds of web pages and news sites with heavy advertising bombarding people, then the one skeptical page that they come across will seem weird   30
and false. Furthermore, by repetition and reaffirmation, a sort of confirmation bias can be built into people's thinking.

That is, people are presented with fact X and fact Y by corporate media. Then later, they get fact Z. All three facts cohere nicely, and it all seems to fit. It all works; it must be true! Since X and Y seem true, then this gives Z credence. Since Z seems   35
true, it gives X and Y credence. It is a circular method of self-affirmation. It is an astoundingly effective form of manipulation. Now imagine this type of confirmation bias, not with three facts, but with thousands.

That is the framework of thought imposed upon us.

40   The underlying idea that enables this can be reduced. The myth of objectivity is as rampant as it is ludicrous. There is no objective standpoint. What is called "objective" is merely the very center of accepting the framework of the elites' discourse. That center is non-challenging. "Objective" simply means "non-critical."

People have assumed that fair assessment of facts means conforming to the
45   prevailing assessments. That is a failure. That is not what objectivity is supposed to mean. In fact, eminent biologist Stephen Jay Gould proposed this very idea in the sciences: "Objectivity must be operationally defined as fair treatment of data, not absence of preference."

The mere fact that news media would choose to report one thing and not an-
50   other is a statement of preference, a statement of value. Human speech is riddled with implicit value judgments. To think that any report of news could be devoid of preference or ideology is absurd. The myth of objectivity is the most blatant example of Newspeak ideology—anything that doesn't sound like corporate media is radical and non-objective.

55   Objectivity is good when it is real objectivity—the fair treatment of data. Ironically, if we treat the data fairly, we will easily come to the conclusion that major media is not really objective, not even close.

Major corporate conglomerates are not going to pay you to undermine world-
views that they benefit from. If you're a real journalist, then these groups will treat
60   you with hostility. If you are a fake journalist, an intellectual submissive, then you may be in for a highly successful career in journalism.

Source: The California Aggie, *March 14, 2013*
http://www.theaggie.org/2013/03/14/column-myth-of-objectivity/

▧ Discussion/Writing Prompts

1. Even with the issue of objectivity as its theme, it is far from certain that the essay adopts an objective tone itself. Take a closer look at this piece. What tone does Moen strike? What language does he employ? Based on this evidence, would you characterize his voice here as objective? And if not, how would you describe the attitude he displays? [Rhetorical Analysis of Voice]

2. "If there are hundreds of web pages and news sites with heavy advertising bombarding people," Moen writes, "then the one skeptical page that they come across will seem weird and false." To what extent do your own personal experiences confirm this insight? Can you think of a moment when a skeptical or unorthodox piece of writing struck you as "weird and false"? Reflecting upon this experience now, do you think your reaction was warranted? Why, or why not? [Personal Reflection]

3. In assessing bias in today's media, Moen declares: "Objectivity is good when it is real objectivity—the fair treatment of data." How do you respond to the definition of "objectivity" Moen offers? What, in your view, is the most effective way to ensure that the data presented to us are "fair"? [Close Reading]

4. Moen's argument hinges upon the way he redefines the concept of objectivity: "There is no objective standpoint. What is called 'objective' is merely the very center of accepting the framework of the elites' discourse." How effective do you find this rhetorical strategy to be? In your view, does Moen succeed in discrediting the more conventional or typical definition of objectivity? How, or how not? [Analyzing Rhetorical Modes]

5. Choose a current political topic that, in your view, might benefit from a more biased treatment in the media. What is this topic? What issues or questions does it involve? And how might a more biased discussion actually be for the better? [Argument]

6. How does Moen's discussion of "bias" compare with William J. Astore's discussion of "euphemism" ("The United States of Euphemism")? Do you see any contradiction in these respective arguments? Or, in your view, does Astore's critique of euphemistic language support Moen's argument about the need to rethink our definition of media objectivity? [Compare and Contrast]

7. How might we go about testing the hypothesis about "confirmation bias" that Moen advances here? When we take a closer look at the way our current popular media cover politics, what degree of objectivity do we discover? To answer these questions, conduct some first-person research. Choose two or three examples of publications (e.g., journals, newspaper articles, websites, or blogs) that discuss a specific, topical political issue. Next, analyze these texts for the different forms of "confirmation bias" you feel each displays. Then, write a two-page summary of your findings. [Research]

Carl Elliot, "The Perfect Voice"

What is the connection between our voice and our identity? While it may feel most natural to think of our voices as immutable markers of who we are, the truth, as Carl Elliot points out, is that our voices are susceptible to a striking array of change. From elocution training to regional accents, from vocal training to surgery, the factors that shape our voice raise complicated questions about which aspects of our voice constitute proof of the "real us."

"How exactly is a voice related to an identity? Many of us feel as if our voices are, in some vague and undefined way, our voices, an immutable part of who we are, but in fact our voices are changing all the time."

In 1985, the English physicist Stephen Hawking lost his voice. Hawking suffers from amyotrophic lateral sclerosis, or ALS, a degenerative neurological illness. Over the years Hawking's illness had left his voice increasingly slurred and difficult to understand, but it was not until an episode of pneumonia forced him to have a tracheostomy that Hawking lost his voice completely. After the tracheostomy, Hawking could not speak at all. He could communicate only by raising his eyebrows when someone pointed to the correct letter on a spelling card.

5

Several years later, a computer specialist from California sent him a computer
program called Equalizer. Equalizer allowed Hawking to select words from a series
of menus on a computer screen by pressing a switch, or by moving his head or
eyes. A voice synthesizer then transformed the words into speech. The computer
was a vast improvement on the spelling card system, and for the most part, Hawking was also pleased with the voice synthesizer. "The only trouble," he wrote in a
1993 essay, "is that it gives me an American accent." Yet Hawking then went on to
say that after many years of using the voice synthesizer, the American voice came
to feel like his own. He started to identify with that voice, and feel as if it were really
his. "I would not want to change even if I were offered a British-sounding voice,"
Hawking wrote. "I would feel I had become a different person."

The anthropologist Gregory Bateson used to ask his graduate students if a blind
man's cane is part of the man. Most students would say no, that the limits of a
person stop at his skin. But if Hawking is right, then the answer may be more complicated. For despite the fact that Hawking's "voice" was computer-synthesized,
despite the fact that it came from a set of audio speakers rather than from his
mouth, despite the fact that the synthesized voice sounded mechanical, robotic,
and worse still, American, Hawking eventually came to feel that it was *his* voice.
Hawking's identity, at least in his view, does not stop at the boundaries of his skin.

How exactly is a voice related to an identity? Many of us feel as if our voices are,
in some vague and undefined way, *our* voices, an immutable part of who we are,
but in fact our voices are changing all the time. The voice of a person at five years
of age will sound different from the voice of the same person at age forty-five, and
her voice will sound different again at age seventy-five. An Alabaman man living in
North Dakota will probably not speak with the same accent that he speaks with
back in Tuscaloosa. A black American may sound different when speaking to other
black Americans at home or at church than she does when speaking to white
Americans and the office. Our voices even sound noticeably different to us from
the inside, first-person standpoint than they sound to other people. For many of
us, it still comes as a mild shock to hear our own voices on tape.

Hawking's remarks about his voice synthesizer reflect two tensions in modern
identity that run through many debates over enhancement technologies. The first
is a tension between the natural and the artificial, or more broadly, between what
is *given* and what is *created*. The reason it initially sounds jarring to hear Hawking
say he identifies so closely with a computer-generated voice is precisely because it
has been generated by a computer, rather than by nature itself. Yet the fact that
Hawking does identify with the computer-generated voice reflects something about
the flexibility of modern identity. It is not uncommon these days for people to say
they feel more like themselves while taking Prozac or typing in an on-line chat
room, or that it was only after undergoing cosmetic surgery or taking anabolic
steroids that their bodies began to look the way they were meant to look. Statements like these sound odd (and merit a deeper look) precisely because they con-
found what we expect to hear. We may expect to hear that an artificial technology

makes a person feel *better* about herself, but we don't usually expect to hear that it makes her feel *like* herself.

Related to this tension between the given and the created is a second tension, between the self as it feels from the inside and the self as it is presented to others. Most modern Westerners have some sense that there is a gap between the self and self-presentation—between the self that sits alone in a room, thinking, and the self that hops up on the stage to crack jokes and take questions from the audience. We also tend to think that the true self is one that sits alone, a solitary self that endures over time, while the on-stage self is a mere persona, a type of useful role-playing that can be used or discarded as circumstances demand. But when Hawking the Englishman says he identifies with his American accent, and would feel like a different person with a British-sounding voice, he closes this gap between self and self-presentation. An accent is not part of the self that sits silently in a room. It is a part of the self that is presented to others. By identifying so closely with his accent, Hawking is identifying less with his solitary self than with his self-presentation. This makes the gap between the two somewhat questionable.

The voice is a good place to start thinking about identity, because many of us don't even think about our voices until we are made self-conscious about them. Those occasions of self-consciousness usually come when our identities are in flux or subject to challenge. If I am an adolescent boy, I will become self-conscious when my voice begins to deepen and crack. If I move to England, I will become self-conscious when the natives roll their eyes at my American accent. If I get sex-reassignment surgery and become a woman, I will become self-conscious when I still sound like a man. My voice is always distinctly *my* voice, but often I will not think of it as such until someone calls attention to my identity.

If you were listening to me speak these words, you would hear them spoken with a noticeable southern drawl. Some people might call it a twang, though I myself prefer the more flattering term "lilt," which was the term Lilli Ambro used when she heard me speak. Ambro runs an "accident-reduction clinic" in Greensboro, North Carolina, called The Perfect Voice. Clients of The Perfect Voice come to Ambro for help in learning how to diminish, change, or erase their Southern accents. A speech pathologist by training, with a background in professional singing, Ambro is a southerner herself—a North Carolinian, educated at one of the very cradles of southern womanhood, Salem College. In fact, she speaks with more than a trace of a southern accent herself.

I had gotten in touch with Lilli Ambro after coming across a shelf of cassette tapes in a Berkeley bookshop aimed at helping recent Asian immigrants to the United States overcome their foreign accents. I had just spent several days with a research group talking about whether enhancement technologies were a form of liberation or self-betrayal, whether Prozac and sex-reassignment surgery help people change themselves or help them discover who they really are. Seeing these cassettes displayed in the bookshop, after walking out of the research meeting,

the thought struck me that the purpose of an accent change is not really so different from many of the enhancement technologies we had been discussing. That
95   thought eventually led me to The Perfect Voice, one of a number of accent-reduction clinics springing up throughout the South.

Southerners have a complicated relationship with their accents, a complex mixture of pride and shame and fierce defensiveness. It's like a little brother who is a drunk or maybe a little crazy and therefore somewhat embarrassing—you are always
100   shaking your head when his name is mentioned—but you can't really disown him because, well, damn it, he *is* family. Most southerners, when they talk to Yankees, will defend a southern accent as the most beautiful and melodic of all American accents, but deep down we are not really convinced this is true. Many of us modify our speech, often unconsciously, when we are around outsiders, and talk more southern
105   in the company of one another. Some of us even learn to speak Yankee at work or when we are visiting up North. Many of us wish not so much to get rid of our southern accents as to get a *better* one, an accent that evokes a genteel, mythical old South rather than, say, *The Beverly Hillbillies*. Nobody explicitly teaches us this, but we somehow absorb the lesson that north of the Mason-Dixon line a southern accent
110   generally codes for stupidity and simplemindedness. You can watch only so many movies and television shows featuring big-bellied southern sheriffs, sweaty fundamentalist preachers, and shotgun-carrying rednecks before the message sinks in. We learn early on that in certain settings, like universities, a southern accent needs to be moderated, if not effaced, or else you will not be taken seriously.

115   When I was growing up in Clover, our small corner of South Carolina, it would occasionally happen that someone in town would accomplish something worthy of attention from the local television news station. The high school football team would make it to the upper state championships. A local preacher would accidently burn down a church. Once, I remember, state law enforcement authorities staged an un-
120   dercover sting operation and caught a local policeman stealing chocolate Easter eggs and frozen steaks from the grocery store. When these newsworthy events occurred, teams of television news reporters would make the trip down I-77 from Charlotte to investigate. Our moment of fame. In anticipation, we would all sit around the television and look at Clover through the lens of the television cameras.

125   It was always a little embarrassing. The reporter would ask someone from Clover a question on camera, the Cloverite would answer, and my parents would immediately groan and shake their heads. "Why do they always pick these kinds of people to be on TV?" my father would say. "They sound like such hicks." It was true. They did sound like hicks. They would draw out their words in a country twang. They would say
130   *insurance*, with the emphasis on the first syllable. *Greenville* became *Grainville*. *Here* became *hair* and *hair* became *hay-ur*. They sounded like one of those guys with overalls and a banjo on *Hee Haw*. Yet we never noticed this until we saw these people on television. Had we come across the very same people in the barbershop or the public library or in church, it would never have occurred to us that they had a different
135   accent. To be honest, their accents were probably no different from ours.

What interested me about this was the way the distinctiveness of our local accent was hidden from us until we pulled back and saw it—or rather listened to it—from the position of someone else. It was only by watching television, looking through the lens of the camera, that we were able to see what we ordinarily took for granted. What local accents compared to the other ones on TV, which are all non-southern (that is to say, Yankee) accents. The television news southerners talk like Yankees when they are on TV. It is an unspoken convention: if you are on TV you talk like a Yankee. Everyone does. If you don't, you sound like a hick.

Lilli Ambro told me that most of her clients at The Perfect Voice are people who have to do a lot of public speaking, like actors or certain kinds of businesspeople. One was, unsurprisingly, a television news reporter. Another was an aspiring actress whose acting coaches had advised her that to have a successful career she would need to be able to switch her southern accent on and off. All were southerners except one. The exception was a man from Pennsylvania running for public office who wanted to reduce his northern accent in order to improve his chances for election. (The knife cuts both ways. In the South, a northern accent codes for arrogance and bad manners.) Most (though not all) of her clients were white. It goes without saying that most of these clients felt they needed to change their accents in order to succeed at work, and felt strongly enough about it that they were willing to pay $45/hour to undergo a successful "dialect change."

What sort of accents were these people trying to change? In her book on cosmetic surgery, sociologist Kathy Davis notes how difficult it was for her, as an outside observer, to guess exactly what feature of themselves the potential clients wanted cosmetic surgery for—that many of the women who wanted nose jobs did not have obviously large or misshapen noses, or that many of those who wanted breast reductions did not have obviously large or asymmetrical breasts. The "defects" that bothered them so much seemed to be exaggerated in their own eyes. So I wondered aloud to Ambro whether there was a parallel in her work—whether it was ever difficult for an outsider to see exactly why these people wanted their accents changed. "No," she replied immediately; it was not hard to see why these people wanted to change. They all have very "strong" southern accents, she said. When I pressed her on what she meant by this, it became clear that most of her clients sounded like country folks or hillbillies. They were worried not so much about sounding southern as about sounding like hicks. Which made sense: this was the South, after all, where most people talk with southern accents. The worry in the South is not to get rid of your accent, like an expatriate southerner trying to pass in the North, but rather to transform it into a better one (which generally means something closer to what Ambro calls a "standard American" accent). Ambro told me that she does not generally get clients who want to rid themselves of a Tidewater Virginia accent, say, or an old Charleston accent, or any of the accents that sound especially well bred to southern ears. Yet she did admit that she occasionally tried to convince some of her clients that accents that sounded objectionable to their own ears were actually quite lovely.

I have to confess that when I called Lilli Ambro, I was skeptical about the notion
of accent-reduction clinics, notwithstanding Ms. Ambro's good intentions and her
charming manners. Expatriate southerners like me are likely to worry excessively
that distinctive features of the South are going to disappear; that in a vast consumerist sea, an age of generic TV news anchors speaking standardized American,
southern accents will go the way of the corner barber shop and the porch swing.
(Or, possibly even worse, that a southern accent will become a curiosity piece to be
marketed to Yankees, like small-batch bourbon and alligator farms). But what worried me most was the sense that by trying to change your accent, you are rejecting
something of who you are. Unlike a Chinese or Cuban immigrant who speaks
English with an accent, we southerners are raised to speak the way we do. It is our
mother tongue. It is the first thing that non-southerners notice about us when we
open our mouths. To try to speak like a northerner, quite honestly, strikes me as
phoniness—perhaps necessary phoniness on occasion, and a kind of phoniness to
which we are all prone, but phoniness nonetheless. This is also what rubs me the
wrong way about some enhancement technologies, especially those designed to
efface markers of identity. They look pretty close to fakery.

I once had a colleague at McGill University who spoke with a perfect upper-class
English accent. It was only when I asked him what part of England he was from that
I found out he was born and raised in Ontario. He had spent a couple of years at
Oxford as a student many decades previously. Apparently he had adopted an
English accent while he was there, and had hung onto it ever since. I can't remember ever having met a southerner who would affect an Oxford accent (where I
come from, Oxford is a town in Mississippi), or who would even feel inclined to try,
but many southerners do try to talk standardized American, or what they think is
standardized American, saying "you" instead of "y'all" and articulating their words
very carefully. In the United Kingdom, the BBC has made a nod toward acknowledging the legitimacy of regional accents by occasionally substituting Scots-,
Irish-, and Welsh-accented newsreaders for the traditional Englishman. But in the
United States, the newsreaders all speak as if they come from nowhere—which to
a southern ear, usually sounds like somewhere up North. (A Tennessean I once met
in Chicago told me that all Americans should hang on to their native accents or
else we would all sound like we come from Indi-goddamn-ana.)

The newspaper piece that led me to The Perfect Voice was written for the
Greensboro News and Record by a reporter with the southern-accented name of
Parker Lee Nash. She is a self-described "southern girl, raised by bootleggers and
Baptists," and her attitude toward The Perfect Voice could probably be best described as ironic and gently mocking. (She writes that to talk like a Yankee, you
have to "open your mouth big and wide and relax your tongue so it flops up and
down like a dog lapping water.") What interested me most about her article
was the lighthearted remark she concluded with. After spending a day in accent-
reduction classes, learning things like how to say "ham" in such a way that it does
not contain two syllables, she concluded, "All the accent reduction classes in
America can't take the Southern out of me. Thank the Lord."

Implicit in that offhand remark, it seemed to me, was both the worry about accent change ("Am I trying to change who I am?") and the reassurance that this worry is misplaced ("No, being a southerner is about more than having a southern accent"). And so I began to wonder whether clients at an accent-reduction clinic had any mixed feelings about their change—whether they felt that putting on an accent was artificial, or a betrayal of their heritage.

When I put this question to Lilli Ambro, she proceeded (as southerners are inclined to do) to tell me a story. She once had a client who was a preacher. Or more precisely, he was a sort of junior preacher, an assistant to a more senior pastor in a local church. She wasn't sure what denomination, but it wasn't Presbyterian or Episcopalian—more likely it was Baptist, or some poor relation. This preacher was from out in the country and he had an appropriately countrified accent. His senior minister had told him that he needed to work on the way he spoke, or else the congregation wouldn't take him seriously. Hence his visit to The Perfect Voice. Interestingly enough, he did not last longer than a lesson or two. The reason, he said, was because he felt the accent-reduction classes were changing his personality. (Almost as an afterthought, Ambro added, "He never did pay his bill.")

As odd as this preacher's reaction initially sounded to me, I think I can understand it. To paraphrase Kurt Vonnegut, if you pretend for long enough, you may become what you are pretending to be. Yet when I mentioned the story to a colleague from the North, a philosopher at an Ivy League university, he was puzzled by the thought that anyone could feel that his identity was bound in anything as trivial and incidental as an accent. Southerners, of course, usually understand the connection between accent and identity right away. So does anyone from the United Kingdom, where accent is a very public marker of social class, perhaps even the most important one. The British often confess to tremendous anxiety about accent, and what it reveals about social standing. And indeed, expatriates of all sorts in the United Kingdom are constantly made aware of their accents, and what the accent reveals about their geographical origins. I suspect that the thought that an accent is incidental to identity would occur mainly to people who have never had attention called to their own.

In *Democracy in America*, Tocqueville contrasts the behavior of Englishmen in foreign countries with that of Americans. If two Englishmen meet in a foreign country, he says, they will pay no attention to one another. "But two Americans are at once friends," he writes, "simply because they are Americans." Tocqueville attributes this difference to the complexities of the English class system. Englishmen don't quite know how to behave with other Englishmen; until they begin to speak and listen carefully to one another, neither can immediately discern the other person's social class. Social class therefore becomes a matter for uncomfortable investigation. But Americans have no such class system to negotiate, and hence no need for investigation. The Americans are more comfortable with each other, because both know immediately where they stand.

Tocqueville sees very clearly the anxiety that uncertainty about social class can generate. What he did not anticipate was the way that Americans would replace anxiety about class with anxiety about status. Status does not demand uncomfortable investigation in quite the way that class does, because it is so obviously a matter for public display. Status is a matter of self-presentation. Europeans often assume that status in America depends on how much money you make, but money is only part of a complex equation. (As the transplanted Englishman Andrew Sullivan puts it, status has less to do with how much money you make than who returns your phone calls.) Unlike class, status is crucially dependant on what other people think of you. More than that, in fact, in some ways it *is* what other people think.

Status in America can come from many things, of course: wealth, education, achievement, beauty, talent, celebrity, or the family name that you have inherited. At least part of the American anxiety about status comes from the pressure to put these markers of status right out in front, like a walking self-advertisement. You must dress for success, develop a dazzling personality, sell yourself, make a good first impression. For Sullivan, this helps explain why Americans are so obsessed with their bodies. Americans are constantly worrying: Too fat or too thin? Too tall or too short? Breasts too large or too small? Is having no hair on your head cool (the way it is for black men) or does it make you a candidate for Rogaine (as it does for white men)? In the British class system, the body is secondary—as Sullivan puts it, it is "an unchanging, clammy, misshapen blob that performs the task of convey-ing the accent from one geographical location to another." But "for status-conscious Americans," Sullivan concludes, "the body is a walking nervous disorder."

American status contrasts sharply with British class, which is something that a person is born to, and which, as a consequence, is largely a settled affair. English people can't do anything about who their parents are, where they were sent to school, or how they came to speak the way they do. If an Englishman tries to change his accent, he may well be accused of class betrayal, or, even worse, American-style social climbing. But in America, people are expected to try to change their status. We encourage people to make more money, get better jobs, and marry up the social ladder. The status system in America can be both empow-ering and terrifying: empowering, because you can actually improve your social position, but terrifying, in that you can fail, with no one to blame but yourself.

Yet American status is nothing if not local. What counts as a marker of status for university professors is nothing like what counts for corporate executives; and status on a Philadelphia basketball court is measured on a different yardstick than status at a New Orleans debutante ball. The fact that the yardstick of status can differ so dramatically from one place or community to another is part of what drives the tension some Americans feel about their accents. An accent may drive your status up at work, but down at home; up in Manhattan, but down in Natchez; up for your day job at the phone company, but down for your night job at the bar. Even the lowly southern accent will count as a mark of status if you happen to be a bluegrass fiddler or a stock-car driver.

Or, for that matter, an airline pilot. In *The Right Stuff*, Tom Wolfe writes about that particular southern drawl that anyone who has traveled on American commer-cial airlines has heard over the public address system. It is always the same, writes

Wolfe: an easy, down-home southern voice that seems to get even easier and move more down-home when something alarming is happening to the plane. As the airplane shakes and rattles and jolts up and down a thousand feet a clip so that your stomach leaps up into your throat, a folksy voice will come on the intercom just as relaxed as a voice can be: "Now, folks, uh . . . This is the captain . . . ummmm . . . We've got a little ol' red light up here on the control panel that's tryin' to tell us that the *landin'* gears're not . . . uh . . . *lockin'* into position when we lower 'em . . . Faint chuckle, long pause, as if to say, *I'm not even sure all this is really worth going into—still, it may amuse you* . . ." Later, after the plane has dumped its excess fuel into the ocean and the flight attendants are walking briskly and tight-lipped down the aisles asking you to remove all sharp objects from your pockets and put your head between your legs—to "assume the position," as the pilot puts it, with "another faint chuckle ('*We do this so often, and it's so much fun, we even have a funny little name for it*')," even as your heart pounds and your palms sweat and your mind races through all things that could go wrong, you still cannot quite bring yourself to believe that the trouble could really be all that crucial, otherwise how could the pilot, who surely would know better than anyone else if the plane is in real danger, keep on drawling and chuckling in that relaxed, aw-shucks southern voice.

That voice may sound vaguely southern, writes Wolfe, but in fact it is Appalachian in origin; specifically, it is West Virginian. That voice is the pilot's approximation of the accent of Chuck Yeager, the legendary test pilot who broke the sound barrier in 1948 at what is now Edwards Air Force Base. Yeager's legend among the brothers of the pilot fraternity has been so powerful—his thirteen kills as a fighter pilot at the age of twenty-two, his record-breaking test flight in 1948 (which he performed, effortlessly, with two broken ribs), his general shit-kicking, cool-as-ice demeanor—that every pilot who has gone through Edwards Air Force Base after Yeager has wound up talking like a West Virginian. Since the military is the training ground for so many pilots, the accent has spread even further, from test pilots to fighter pilots to commercial pilots. Today when passengers hear a voice coming out of the cockpit, chances are the voice will sound like some approximation of Yeager's West Virginian drawl. In the world of airline pilots, suggests Wolfe, talking like a West Virginian is a marker of status.

Status is not everything, of course. Accents often mark status, but they are also a mechanism by which people demonstrate their solidarity with others who share their identity. If you talk the right way, you show that you stand side-by-side with your fellow West Virginians, or Highland Scots, or African Americans. Educated speakers of a dialect often hang on to a trace of that dialect, even as they try to speak the standard version of the language. In this way, you can have your cake and eat it too: you get the status advantages of speaking standard English and the solidarity advantages of speaking with a slight southern drawl. You raise yourself in the eyes of those who see your accent as a marker of backwardness, but you also steel yourself against the complaint that you have betrayed your heritage.

355

360

In the vast museum of American consumerist oddities, accent-reduction clinics like The Perfect Voice probably merit little more than a small corner display. Yet there are at least two aspects to them that are worth thinking about more carefully, in light of the consumerist forces that drive the development of enhancement technologies. One is the way the language of illness is used to describe, however lightheartedly, the process of changing your accent. You do it at a clinic, and you are treated by a speech pathologist. In fact, you are not really changing your accent; you are "reducing" it, as if it had somehow ballooned out of control, like your weight or your blood sugar, and you need treatment in order to rein it back in.

365

370

375

The other thing to notice is just what is being sold at the accent-reduction clinic. Enhancement technologies are usually marketed and sold by taking advantage of a person's perception that she is deficient in some way. Accent reduction is no different. What is being sold at the accent-reduction clinic is old-fashioned, American-style self-improvement, and the yardstick on which the self-improvement is measured is social status and success at work. The accent-reduction clinic takes advantage of the perception (or perhaps the reality) that non-southerners see a southern accent as something to be hidden or overcome, and that even southerners themselves see certain kinds of southern accents as better than others. (The reason why it is better to talk like Scarlett and Rhett than those guys in the overalls in *Deliverance* is clear enough. But behind the more subtle gradations of accent is a peculiar sort of ancestor worship practiced by some white southerners that associate certain accents with a distinguished genealogy.) If The Perfect Voice is in any way representative, the people most inclined to change their accents are those whose success at work depends on the successful public presentation of themselves—actors, businesspeople, newsreaders, and the occasional minister.

380

385

In the relationship between public performance and the inner life that produces the mixed feelings that I suspect many southerners would have about an accent-reduction clinic. Southerners are quite familiar with public performance, of course; there is a good reason for all those self-dramatizing southern women in the plays of Tennessee Williams. But self-dramatization is one thing, and pretending to be a Yankee is another. Talking like a northerner would strike many southerners as a necessary evil at best, and at worst, a form of selling your birthright. It is a form of "passing," of hiding what is distinctive about your cultural identity. (The proper southern response to being made to feel ashamed of your accent, of course, is to exaggerate it.)

Source: Better Than Well:
American Medicine Meets the American Dream *(W.W. Norton and Co., 2004)*

▮ Discussion/Writing Prompts

1. As Elliot notes, our voice is far from singular or unchanging. Rather than something fixed, voice is often the product of what we choose to make it. How would you apply this insight to Elliot himself? How would you describe the particular voice Elliot

goes about constructing in this essay? And what larger goal is he trying to accomplish by creating this particular voice? [Rhetorical Analysis of Voice]

2. Part of Elliot's investigation into voice involves a more particular examination of accents. Make a list of words you think are particular to how/where you grew up (e.g., region, peer group, socioeconomics, family, or education). Then, create a second list of words that typically get used to define the people who talk this way. How do these two lists compare? Looking over them, does it seem fair or valid to pass judgment about people based on the accents they use? [Personal Reflection]

3. How do you evaluate the title of this essay? In your view, is it possible to designate any individual voice as the "perfect voice"? Based on the essay, would you say Elliot shares or disagrees with your view? What do you think he means by the phrase "perfect voice"? [Close Reading]

4. To advance his argument, Elliot relates a story about "accent reduction," one of the "enhancement technologies" designed to improve our lives by altering our physical self. What larger point does Elliot use this story to make? Do you think this point is best conveyed in narrative form? Can you think of another mode that might be used to make this point even more effectively? [Analyzing Rhetorical Modes]

5. One of the central questions raised by Elliot's interest in "accent reduction" has to do with where the line separating self-presentation from impersonation should be drawn. In a two- or three-page essay, make an argument about where you think the line between legitimate enhancement ends and fakery begins. At what point do our concerns for making an impression lead us to "put on an act" that does not reflect who we truly are? [Argument]

6. How do you think Brian Moen ("Myth of Objectivity") would react to Elliot's inquiry into accents and identity? Given Moen's own skepticism toward the idea of a singular or objective voice, what view would he have on the question of accents? Do you think he would subscribe to the idea that accents reveal the so-called true or authentic self? [Compare and Contrast]

7. Research the ways that "accent reduction" programs are marketed online. What types of companies advertise these services? Do they seem reputable? Whom do they seem to be targeting? Next, compile a list of the specific benefits these companies claim that "accent reduction" will bring. How do these claims compare to the assessment offered by Elliot? [Research]

Deanna Zandt, "Can't We All Just Get Along? Polarization of Politics, the Internet and You"

It has become a cliché to note how polarized much of our political discourse is these days. But have we really stopped to think about the effect this kind of language is having on our politics itself? Taking a critical look at the

current inability of our political leaders to "get along," Deanna Zandt offers
some tart observations about the way that digital technology is providing
further outlets for polarizing speech.

"I have certainly noticed a ramp-up in ideological spewing on social networks
that has even lifelong-activist me wondering, 'Can't we all just get along?'"

There's a lot of talk about the extreme polarization of public, and specifically, political discourse as we ramp up into the final, could-not-be-over-soon-enough months
of the US presidential race. I'm always skeptical when there are claims that we are
more polarized than ever, but I have certainly noticed a ramp-up in ideological spew-
5   ing on social networks that has even lifelong-activist me wondering, "Can't we all
just get along?"

As it turns out . . . no. Entrepreneur Tara Hunt reminded us on Facebook earlier
today of the sociological phenomenon called "confirmation bias." Applicable to
both online and offline conversations, it works like this: If I see evidence that sup-
10   ports what I already believe, I will support that evidence. If the evidence is neutral, I
will interpret it in a way that supports what I believe. And, if the evidence completely contradicts what I believe, I will discount the evidence, dig my heels in
deeper and keep believing what I want.

"The facts will not set you free" is the bottom line.

15   On social networks, people are complaining about how polarized the political
discussion has become, and are wondering if hypotheses like the ones I support
saying that sharing online inspires empathy are completely wrong. This is where
things get a little tricky.

First, political rhetoric in general has indeed become more polar between Dem-
20   ocrats and Republicans in recent years. It's not just the Internet playing a role; all
media have. However, you only have to look back to the 1800s or so to see just how
little has really changed about the mud-slinging nature of the dialog. The change
is in how many people see it, not the content. We have a false notion of a mythic
public square in which delicate, thoughtful, high-minded dialog took place. (I keep
25   imagining this place complete with white-gloved slapping.) I can't find evidence
that this was ever the common way for the work of politics to hash itself out. But
we hold that myth dear when we gasp and point fingers at political foes getting
their hands (and mouths) dirty in the process.

Second, the kind of sharing that I'm seeing pass through my social network
30   streams is not the kind of sharing that I'm thinking of when I talk about empathy
online. The sharing that I see, especially the kind found in humorous political
memes, is much more related to a broadcast-style of communication than one that
centers on developing or deepening relationships. We are the pamphleteers of the
digital age when we post raucous rants and deliberate screeds that espouse our
35   beliefs and values. These are the bits that relate to confirmation bias the most:
they reinforce our values, no matter what their actual content.

The kind of sharing that generates empathy, and that can actually inspire change, is when we share our stories with one another. When we seek out connection through our experiences, we are much more likely to be open to the potential that things might not be as we have seen them, or are more complicated than we've been led to believe. This can work in any format; I'm thinking about listening to the speeches in the New York State Senate when it passed marriage equality rights, and how many social conservatives said that they were swayed to vote in favor by the personal stories that had been shared with them. Online, we can point to phenomena like Caine's Arcade, where for a few minutes, we all remembered what it was like to be a lonely kid dreaming about something bigger. 40 45

Those shift points are not about being scolded, guilted or berated into thinking differently about how the world operates. The magic that happens when we share stories with one another comes from our human wiring to empathize with one another. To walk in each others' shoes and have our capacity for understanding broadened just a little bit. The unfortunate nature of political systems don't necessarily promote authentic, empathetic sharing, but we can recognize it and celebrate it when we see it. 50

Source: Forbes.com, August 22, 2012. © 2012 Forbes.
http://www.forbes.com/sites/deannazandt/2012/08/22/cant-we-all-just-get-along-polarization-of-politics-the-internet-and-you/

Discussion/Writing Prompts

1. For Zandt, what is most worrisome about online discourse is its lack of "empathy." How would you evaluate Zandt's own essay along these lines? Can you identify any statements or sections that you feel reflect a lack of empathy? Does her choice of language overall help advance the essay's argument? How, or how not? [Rhetorical Analysis of Voice]

2. This essay proceeds from the assumptions that polarizing language is, by definition, an inferior form of speech. Do you agree? Can you think of an example from your own experience where you found hostile or confrontational language to be useful, even preferable? If so, what was this experience like? [Personal Reflection]

3. Zandt characterizes polarizing discourse online as "raucous rants and deliberate screeds." What does this language suggest about the larger argument Zandt is trying to make? What alternative words would you use in your own assessment of such polarizing discourse? [Close Reading]

4. As part of her solution to the problem of polarization, Zandt calls for a form of "sharing" that involves exchanging stories instead of trading insults. How effective a solution do you find this to be? Do you share Zandt's belief that this rhetorical mode has the capacity to resolve political conflicts? How, or how not? [Analyzing Rhetorical Modes]

5. Beneath Zandt's discussion of online conflict is a belief that digital technology has a unique capacity to foster conflict. Write an essay in which you argue either for or against this view. Do you agree that our online tools encourage us to act and talk in more divisive, confrontational ways? Can you think of an example that either supports or challenges this thesis? [Argument]

6. In many ways, Zandt's discussion of the polarization echoes Moen's examination of "confirmation bias" ("The Myth of Objectivity"). Write an essay in which you compare these respective discussions. In your view, does polarization offer an example of the type of "confirmation bias" that Moen references in his piece? What are the key similarities and differences? [Compare and Contrast]

7. Choose a topic that, in your view, fits the definition of a polarizing issue. Then, research the ways this issue is presented in the wider media. To do this, you'll need to find at least three separate texts (e.g., newspapers, websites, magazines, or blogs) in which this topic is being discussed. Once you've assembled this material, write a one-page essay analyzing the degree to which this discussion encourages "polarization." [Research]

Patricia Williams, "Anti-Intellectualism Is Taking Over the US"

A basic tenet of progress holds that, as our society advances socially and technologically, so too does it improve intellectually. This, however, may not always be the case. Indeed, it's possible that, as we evolve, our interest in and commitment to serious ideas actually diminish. Exploring just this possibility, noted author and legal scholar Patricia Williams, who is also a professor of law at Columbia University, wonders whether "anti-intellectualism" has become the guiding standard for how Americans now talk to each other.

"There has been an unfortunate uptick in academic book bannings and firings, made worse by a nationwide disparagement of teachers, teachers' unions and scholarship itself."

Recently, I found out that my work is mentioned in a book that has been banned, in effect, from the schools in Tucson, Arizona. The anti-ethnic studies law passed by the state prohibits teachings that "promote the overthrow of the United States government," "promote resentment toward a race or class of people," "are designed primarily for pupils of a particular ethnic group," and/or "advocate ethnic solidarity instead of the treatment of pupils as individuals." I invite you to read the book in question, titled Critical Race Theory: An Introduction, so that you can decide for yourselves whether it qualifies.

In fact, I invite you to take on as your summer reading the astonishingly lengthy list of books that have been removed from the Tucson public school system as part of this wholesale elimination of the Mexican-American studies curriculum. The authors and editors include Isabel Allende, Junot Díaz, Jonathan Kozol, Rudolfo Anaya, bell hooks, Sandra Cisneros, James Baldwin, Howard Zinn, Rodolfo Acuña, Ronald Takaki, Jerome Skolnick and Gloria Anzaldúa. Even Thoreau's *Civil Disobedience* and Shakespeare's *The Tempest* received the hatchet. 15

Trying to explain what was offensive enough to warrant killing the entire curriculum and firing its director, Tucson school board member Michael Hicks stated rather proudly that he was not actually familiar with the curriculum. "I chose not to go to any of their classes," he told Al Madrigal on *The Daily Show*. "Why even go?" In the same interview, he referred to Rosa Parks as "Rosa Clark." 20

The situation in Arizona is not an isolated phenomenon. There has been an unfortunate uptick in academic book bannings and firings, made worse by a nationwide disparagement of teachers, teachers' unions and scholarship itself. Brooke Harris, a teacher at Michigan's Pontiac Academy for Excellence, was summarily fired after asking permission to let her students conduct a fundraiser for Trayvon Martin's 25 family. Working at a charter school, Harris was an at-will employee, and so the superintendent needed little justification for sacking her. According to Harris, "I was told . . . that I'm being paid to teach, not to be an activist." (It is perhaps not accidental that Harris worked in the schools of Pontiac, a city in which nearly every public institution has been taken over by cost-cutting executives working under "emer- 30 gency manager" contracts. There the value of education is measured in purely econometric terms, reduced to a "product," calculated in "opportunity costs.")

The law has taken some startling turns as well. In 2010 the sixth circuit upheld the firing of high school teacher Shelley Evans-Marshall when parents complained about an assignment in which she had asked her students in an upper-level lan- 35 guage arts class to look at the American Library Association's list of "100 Most Frequently Challenged Books" and write an essay about censorship. The complaint against her centered on three specific texts: Hermann Hesse's *Siddhartha*, Harper Lee's *To Kill a Mockingbird* and Ray Bradbury's *Fahrenheit 451*. (She was also alleged, years earlier, to have shown students a PG-13 version of Shake- 40 speare's *Romeo and Juliet*.)

The court found that the content of Evans-Marshall's teachings concerned matters "of political, social or other concern to the community" and that her interest in free expression outweighed certain other interests belonging to the school "as an employer." But, fatally, the court concluded that "government employ- 45 ees . . . are not speaking as citizens for First Amendment purposes." While the sixth circuit allowed that Evans-Marshall may have been treated "shabbily," it still maintained (quoting from another opinion) that "when a teacher teaches, 'the school system does not "regulate" [that] speech as much as it hires that speech. Expression is a teacher's stock in trade, the commodity she sells to her employer 50 in exchange for a salary.'" Thus, the court concluded, it is the "educational institution that has a right to academic freedom, not the individual teacher."

There are a number of factors at play in the current rash of controversies. One is a rather stunning sense of privilege, the confident sense of superiority that allows

55 someone to pass sweeping judgment on a body of work without having done any
study at all. After the *Chronicle of Higher Education* published an item highlighting
the dissertations of five young PhD candidates in African-American studies at
Northwestern University, *Chronicle* blogger Naomi Schaefer Riley wrote that the
mere titles of the dissertations were sufficient cause to eliminate all black studies
60 classes. Riley hadn't read the dissertations; they're not even published yet. When
questioned about this, she argued that as "a journalist . . . it is not my job to read
entire dissertations before I write a 500-word piece about them," adding: "there
are not enough hours in the day or money in the world to get me to read a dissertation on historical black midwifery." Riley tried to justify her view with a cliched,
65 culture-wars-style plaint about the humanities and higher education: "Such is the
state of academic research these days. . . . The publication topics become more
and more irrelevant and partisan. No one reads them." This is not mere arrogance;
it is the same cocooned "white ghetto" narrow-mindedness that allows someone
like Michael Hicks to be in charge of a major American school system yet not know
70 "Rosa Clark's" correct name.

Happily, there is pushback occurring against such anti-intellectualism. One
of the most vibrant examples is a protest group called Librotraficante, or Book
Trafficker. Organised by Tony Diaz, a Houston Community College professor, the
group has been caravanning throughout the south-west holding readings, setting
75 up book clubs, establishing "underground libraries," and dispensing donated
copies of the books that have been removed from Arizona's public school
curriculum.

Source: The Guardian, *May 18, 2012*
http://www.theguardian.com/commentisfree/2012/may/18/anti-intellectualism-us-book-
banning

Discussion/Writing Prompts

1. For Williams, "anti-intellectualism" is fueled by "privilege" and "narrow-
mindedness." How effective would you say her own essay is in redressing this
problem? Does the voice she adopts seem designed to combat "anti-intellectualism"?
If so, how successful is this effort? [Rhetorical Analysis of Voice]

2. Among other things, this essay can be read as a commentary on the lack of serious or
informed discussion in our public culture. How accurate do you find this claim to
be? Like Williams, are you also struck by how substantive issues get discussed? Can
you think of an example that either confirms or refutes this observation? [Personal
Reflection]

3. In reflecting upon the episodes of "anti-intellectualism" she cites here, Williams
speaks of the "stunning sense of privilege" these examples highlight: "[T]he confident
sense of superiority that allows someone to pass sweeping judgment on a body of
work without having done any study at all." Analyze the language Williams uses
here. What do you make of such phrases as "stunning sense of privilege" or

"confident sense of superiority"? What is she using such language to say about this "anti-intellectualism" trend and its root causes? [Close Reading]

4. Williams uses the recent spate of "academic book bannings and firings" across the country to illustrate what she views as a growing trend toward "anti-intellectualism" in America. How effective do you find this rhetorical strategy to be? What aspects of "anti-intellectualism" do these events exemplify? [Analyzing Rhetorical Modes]

5. As the examples here suggest, Williams views the rise of "anti-intellectualism" in American life as a response to the shift toward multiculturalism. What do you think of this thesis? Is there, in your view, a valid connection between the two? Write an essay in which you argue either for or against this key claim. Does the kind of "anti-intellectualism" Williams describes reflect anxieties or hostility toward the idea of multicultural education? How, or how not? [Argument]

6. How do you think Deanna Zandt ("Can't We All Just Get Along?") would respond to Williams' argument? Do you think she would regard the "anti-intellectualism" that Williams profiles here as a contributing factor to the type of "polarization" she describes in her own essay? Why, or why not? [Compare and Contrast]

7. To assess the validity of Williams' argument, undertake some historical research of your own. Choose a moment or example from American history that, in your view, either reinforces or challenges Williams' claim about the "anti-intellectualism" in American life. Research this example, and then write a two-page essay in which you describe this moment fully and also analyze it for what it says about our country's supposedly anti-intellectual roots. [Research]

William J. Astore, "The United States of Euphemism"

When do words mean something other than what they say? To what extent can language obscure or disguise the truth rather than reveal it? Endeavoring to tackle these big questions, William J. Astore asks whether we've grown so accustomed to euphemism that we have lost our capacity, perhaps even our desire, to be told the truth.

"As a country, our eyes glaze over when we see the repetition of terms like 'collateral damage,' an overused military euphemism that obscures the reality of innocents blown to bits or babies buried under rubble."

Judging by the local newspaper that serves the rural area of Pennsylvania where I live, hunters no longer shoot and kill deer: they *harvest* them. "Harvest" is the latest euphemism of choice for killing, and it's applied not just to the culling of the deer herd but also to the killing of bears, bobcats, and other predators.

In his speech on national security before the American Enterprise Institute on May 21st, former Vice President Dick Cheney complained of the "emergence of euphemisms [under the Obama administration] that strive to put an imaginary

distance between the American people and the terrorist enemy." Instead of being properly at war with terrorists and other "killers and would-be mass murderers,"
10   we were now involved, Cheney dismissively noted, in so-called "overseas contingency operations," a catch-all term adopted by the Obama administration in place of the previous administration's "war on terror."

Yet for all of Cheney's posturing about the allegedly milquetoast euphemisms of Obama, he persisted in repeatedly invoking "enhanced interrogation" for meth-
15   ods of torture (such as waterboarding) that have been previously prosecuted as war crimes by the United States.

But the former vice president did put his finger on a problem: Our collective acquiescence in the temporizing—the terrorizing, even—of our language. Mr. Cheney himself continues to stare unblinkingly at euphemisms like "enhanced
20   interrogation methods," which cloak the reality of bodies being slammed against walls and water being poured down people's throats. As a country, our eyes glaze over when we see the repetition of terms like "collateral damage," an overused military euphemism that obscures the reality of innocents blown to bits or babies buried under rubble.

25   Perhaps our temporizing began right after World War II, when the Department of War was folded under and rebranded as the Department of Defense. Coincidentally, just before this occurred, George Orwell penned his classic essay, "The Politics of the English Language" (1946). It remains telling:

> [P]olitical language has to consist largely of euphemism, question-begging and
30   > sheer cloudy vagueness. Defenseless villages are bombarded from the air, the in-
> habitants driven out into the countryside, the cattle machine-gunned, the huts set
> on fire with incendiary bullets: this is called *pacification*. Millions of peasants are
> robbed of their farms and sent trudging along the roads with no more than they can
> carry: this is called *transfer of population* or *rectification of frontiers*. People are im-
35   > prisoned for years without trial, or shot in the back of the neck or sent to die of
> scurvy in Arctic lumber camps: this is called *elimination of unreliable elements*. Such
> phraseology is needed if one wants to name things without calling up mental pic-
> tures of them.

This last point is essential, and it also explains the purpose of the phrase "en-
40   hanced interrogation." After all, how many Americans in 2002 would have favored a "war on terror" if our government plainly admitted it was using torture to terrorize suspects?

As President Obama famously said during the 2008 Presidential Campaign, "Words matter." But, following the lead of the former vice president, Obama also
45   made the political choice of citing "enhanced interrogation techniques" four times in his speech on national security on May 21st, though at first reference he did qualify the phrase. In the same speech, Obama demonstrated his own linguistic dexterity, coining the phrase "prolonged detention" to cloak his proposal of indefinite imprisonment of "enemy combatants" without trial.

Prolonged detention: It sounds quaint, like a few days of after-school punish-   50
ment for misbehaving in class, instead of what it could become—open-ended con-
finement to a gulag.

Of course, we all recognize that we live in an age of public relations, propaganda, and advertising. Post-modernism as well as deconstruction, moreover,
seemingly support the malleability of meaning and the lability of language. Even   55
so, whether you're Dick Cheney or Barack Obama, changing the words does not
change the reality. Instead, our linguistic gymnastics not only tortures our language: It cripples our thinking and even pollutes our souls.

The most blatant historical example of this pollution occurred in Nazi Germany,
as brilliantly exposed by Victor Klemperer in *The Language of the Third Reich*.   60
Klemperer shows, for example, how the word "fanatical" was redefined under Nazi
rule from a pejorative to a desirable trait. This and similar linguistic barbarisms,
Klemperer concluded, acted as "Poison[,] which you drink unawares and which has
its effect."

Let's stop drinking the poison. Let's stop unthinking or dishonest references to   65
"enhanced interrogation" or for that matter to "prolonged detention" and "overseas contingency operations." Let's speak plainly—if we must speak at all—of torture and of killing—whether during hunting season in the forests and fields of
Pennsylvania or during combat in the plains and mountains of Afghanistan.

At least then we won't be hiding behind the false camouflage of euphemisms to   70
justify our blood sports—and our even bloodier wars.

Source: LA Progressive, June 5, 2009
http://www.laprogressive.com/euphemisms-cloak-the-truth-about-torture/

▓ Discussion/Writing Prompts

1. According to Astore, the most potent antidote to the rise of euphemistic language
   in our world is writing that speaks directly and clearly—that means what it says.
   Look over the language Astore uses in his own essay. How many examples can you
   find that fit this definition of clear and direct speech? Can you find examples here
   of language that seems euphemistic? And based on this assessment, how effective
   is Astore's use of language in supporting his larger argument? [Rhetorical Analysis
   of Voice]

2. Think of a personal experience where you resorted to euphemism. What was the
   topic at issue, and who was your audience? Why, under these circumstances, did you
   opt for language that obscured or disguised part of what you were actually thinking,
   feeling, or saying? In retrospect, would use the same language again? Why, or why
   not? [Personal Reflection]

3. Take a closer look at the examples of political euphemism that Astore cites. What
   vision or portrait of US foreign policy do phrases like "collateral damage" or
   "enhanced interrogation" evoke in your mind? In your view, do such phrases serve to

clarify or obscure the truth about these policies? Are there alternative phrases you would substitute for them? If so, what? [Close Reading]

4. Astore concludes his discussion of euphemism with an exhortation:

> Let's stop drinking the poison. Let's stop unthinking or dishonest references to "enhanced interrogation" or for that matter to "prolonged detention" and "over-seas contingency operations." Let's speak plainly—if we must speak at all—of torture and of killing . . .

In a one-page essay, analyze the cause-and-effect claim that underlies Astore's challenge. What difference is he suggesting this sort of change in our public discussion will make? And do you find his use of this rhetorical mode convincing here? Why, or why not? [Analyzing Rhetorical Modes]

5. In presenting his analysis of euphemistic language, Astore quotes President Obama's campaign statement: "Words matter." Choose an issue or controversy whose coverage within the media has, in your view, tended toward the euphemistic. First, identify the issue at hand as well as the specific euphemisms typically used to discuss it. Then, write a one-page essay in which you use the Obama quotation above either to critique or defend this media coverage. In your estimation, are the euphemistic phrases employed here the kind of language that is truly necessary? Or are there other words that would "matter" more? [Argument]

6. How do you think Patricia Williams ("Anti-Intellectualism Is Taking Over the US") would respond to Astore's discussion? In light of the examples she cites in her essay, do you think Williams would consider the practice of "euphemizing" difficult or controversial issues to be "anti-intellectual"? Why, or why not? [Compare and Contrast]

7. Choose a public document or an example of public expressions (e.g., a political speech, the Constitution, a local city ordinance, or a campus announcement), and research the effect its language has had on those to whom it is directed. What is the purpose of this public speech? What goal is it intended to achieve? And to what extent is this goal fulfilled? [Research]

Academic Writing Selections

The rhetorical analysis modeled above doesn't only apply to the types of informal and formal writing found in the real world. It can also serve as an equally useful frame-work for examining the kinds of writing that are often taught within the college classroom. Like their real world counterparts, the authors of these academic selections base their choices about how and what to write on considerations of purpose, audi-ence, argument, voice, and credibility.

The two selections below demonstrate the extent to which academic writing is also shaped by rhetorical concepts. More specifically, these examples highlight the role that considerations about voice play in shaping a writer's choices. Read each selection carefully. Then, answer the questions that follow.

Zora Neale Hurston, "How It Feels to Be Colored Me"

Zora Neale Hurston was an American folklorist, anthropologist, and author, who published four novels and more than 50 short stories, plays, and essays. She is best known for her 1937 novel Their Eyes Were Watching God. *This autobiographical essay tells the story of a young Zora Neale Hurston's growing realization that race serves as the key defining feature of American life—which makes this essay as topical today as when it was first published in 1928.*

I am colored but I offer nothing in the way of extenuating circumstances except the fact that I am the only Negro in the United States whose grandfather on the mother's side was not an Indian chief.

I remember the very day that I became colored. Up to my thirteenth year I lived in the little Negro town of Eatonville, Florida. It is exclusively a colored town. The 5
only white people I knew passed through the town going to or coming from Orlando. The native whites rode dusty horses, the Northern tourists chugged down the sandy village road in automobiles. The town knew the Southerners and never stopped cane chewing when they passed. But the Northerners were something else again. They were peered at cautiously from behind curtains by the timid. 10
The more venturesome would come out on the porch to watch them go past and got just as much pleasure out of the tourists as the tourists got out of the village.

The front porch might seem a daring place for the rest of the town, but it was a gallery seat for me. My favorite place was atop the gatepost. Proscenium box for a born first-nighter. Not only did I enjoy the show, but I didn't mind the actors 15
knowing that I liked it. I usually spoke to them in passing. I'd wave at them and when they returned my salute, I would say something like this: "Howdy-do-well-I-thank-you-where-you-goin'?" Usually automobile or the horse paused at this, and after a queer exchange of compliments, I would probably "go a piece of the way" with them, as we say in farthest Florida. If one of my family happened to come to 20
the front in time to see me, of course negotiations would be rudely broken off. But even so, it is clear that I was the first "welcome-to-our-state" Floridian, and I hope the Miami Chamber of Commerce will please take notice.

During this period, white people differed from colored to me only in that they rode through town and never lived there. They liked to hear me "speak pieces" 25
and sing and wanted to see me dance the parse-me-la, and gave me generously of their small silver for doing these things, which seemed strange to me for I wanted to do them so much that I needed bribing to stop, only they didn't know it. The colored people gave no dimes. They deplored any joyful tendencies in me, but I was their Zora nevertheless. I belonged to them, to the nearby hotels, to the 30
county—everybody's Zora.

But changes came in the family when I was thirteen, and I was sent to school in Jacksonville. I left Eatonville, the town of the oleanders, a Zora. When I disembarked from the river-boat at Jacksonville, she was no more. It seemed that I had suffered a sea change. I was not Zora of Orange County any more, I was now a little colored girl. I found it out in certain ways. In my heart as well as in the mirror, I became a fast brown—warranted not to rub nor run.

But I am not tragically colored. There is no great sorrow dammed up in my soul, nor lurking behind my eyes. I do not mind at all. I do not belong to the sobbing school of Negrohood who hold that nature somehow has given them a lowdown dirty deal and whose feelings are all but about it. Even in the helter-skelter skirmish that is my life, I have seen that the world is to the strong regardless of a little pigmentation more or less. No, I do not weep at the world—I am too busy sharpening my oyster knife.

Someone is always at my elbow reminding me that I am the granddaughter of slaves. It fails to register depression with me. Slavery is sixty years in the past. The operation was successful and the patient is doing well, thank you. The terrible struggle that made me an American out of a potential slave said "On the line!" The Reconstruction said "Get set!" and the generation before said "Go!" I am off to a flying start and I must not halt in the stretch to look behind and weep. Slavery is the price I paid for civilization, and the choice was not with me. It is a bully adventure and worth all that I have paid through my ancestors for it. No one on earth ever had a greater chance for glory. The world to be won and nothing to be lost. It is thrilling to think—to know that for any act of mine, I shall get twice as much praise or twice as much blame. It is quite exciting to hold the center of the national stage, with the spectators not knowing whether to laugh or to weep.

The position of my white neighbor is much more difficult. No brown specter pulls up a chair beside me when I sit down to eat. No dark ghost thrusts its leg against mine in bed. The game of keeping what one has is never so exciting as the game of getting.

I do not always feel colored. Even now I often achieve the unconscious Zora of Eatonville before the Hegira. I feel most colored when I am thrown against a sharp white background.

For instance at Barnard. "Beside the waters of the Hudson" I feel my race. Among the thousand white persons, I am a dark rock surged upon, and overswept, but through it all, I remain myself. When covered by the waters, I am; and the ebb but reveals me again.

Sometimes it is the other way around. A white person is set down in our midst, but the contrast is just as sharp for me. For instance, when I sit in the drafty basement that is The New World Cabaret with a white person, my color comes. We enter chatting about any little nothing that we have in common and are seated by the jazz waiters. In the abrupt way that jazz orchestras have, this one plunges into a number. It loses no time in circumlocutions, but gets right down to business. It constricts the thorax and splits the heart with its tempo and narcotic harmonies. This orchestra grows rambunctious, rears on its hind legs and attacks the tonal veil with primitive fury, rending it, clawing it until it breaks through to the jungle beyond. I follow those heathen—follow them exultingly. I dance wildly inside myself; I yell within, I whoop; I shake my assegai above my head, I hurl it true to the mark yeeeeooww! I am in the jungle and living in the jungle way. My face is painted red and yellow and my body is painted blue, My pulse is throbbing like a war drum. I want to slaughter something— give pain, give death to what, I do not know. But the piece ends. The men of the orchestra wipe their lips and rest their fingers. I creep back slowly to the veneer we call civilization with the last tone and find the white friend sitting motionless in his seat, smoking calmly.

"Good music they have here," he remarks, drumming the table with his fingertips.

Music. The great blobs of purple and red emotion have not touched him. He has only heard what I felt. He is far away and I see him but dimly across the ocean and the continent that have fallen between us. He is so pale with his whiteness then and I am so colored.

At certain times I have no race, I am me. When I set my hat at a certain angle and saunter down Seventh Avenue, Harlem City, feeling as snooty as the lions in front of the Forty-Second Street Library, for instance. So far as my feelings are concerned, Peggy Hopkins Joyce on the Boule Mich with her gorgeous raiment, stately carriage, knees knocking together in a most aristocratic manner, has nothing on me. The cosmic Zora emerges. I belong to no race nor time. I am the eternal feminine with its string of beads.

I have no separate feeling about being an American citizen and colored. I am merely a fragment of the Great Soul that surges within the boundaries. My country, right or wrong.

Sometimes, I feel discriminated against, but it does not make me angry. It merely astonishes me. How can any deny themselves the pleasure of my company? It's beyond me.

But in the main, I feel like a brown bag of miscellany propped against a wall. Against a wall in company with other bags, white, red and yellow. Pour out the contents, and there is discovered a jumble of small things priceless and worthless. A first-water diamond, an empty spool bits of broken glass, lengths of string, a key to a door long since crumbled away, a rusty knife-blade, old shoes saved for a road that never was and never will be, a nail bent under the weight of things too heavy for any nail, a dried flower or two still a little fragrant. In your hand is the brown bag. On the ground before you is the jumble it held—so much like the jumble in the bags could they be emptied that all might be dumped in a single heap and the bags refilled without altering the content of any greatly. A bit of colored glass more or less would not matter. Perhaps that is how the Great Stuffer of Bags filled them in the first place—who knows?

Source: The World Tomorrow, *May 1928*

Discussion/Writing Prompts

1. Much of Hurston's portrait of life in her small southern town revolves around the words and phrases used by her and other members of the community. Why do you think she devotes so much attention to language? What larger point is she trying make by doing so? [Rhetorical Analysis of Voice]

2. Have you ever found yourself in a situation where you felt like an outsider? What did this experience feel like? What were the key differences (e.g., social, economic, or physical) that made you feel set apart from the majority? Did you experience this sense of difference as discrimination? How, or how not? [Personal Reflection]

3. Near the beginning of her essay, Hurston writes: "I remember the very day that I became colored." Reflect on the language Hurston uses to describe this pivotal moment. How do you respond to the idea of "becoming colored"? What larger point about race and racial identity is she trying to make by using this particular phrase? [Close Reading]

4. "I feel most colored," notes Hurston, "when I am thrown against a sharp white background." First, take note the compare-and-contrast strategy at work in this statement. Then, write a short essay in which you analyze how Hurston uses this same rhetorical mode to organize her essay more broadly. To what extent does her examination of racial difference involve an extended comparison and contrast between black and white? And do you find the deployment of this rhetorical mode to be an effective strategy? Why, or why not? [Analyzing Rhetorical Modes]

5. "Sometimes," writes Hurston, "I feel discriminated against, but it does not make me angry. It merely astonishes me. How can any deny themselves the pleasure of my company? It's beyond me." Write a short essay in which you describe and analyze the particular argument about racial discrimination that Hurston is making here. Are you surprised to hear her identify astonishment and not anger as the basis of her reaction to discrimination? Does this reaction challenge any of your assumptions or preconceptions about discrimination? And if so, do you find this to be an effective rhetorical strategy? Why, or why not? [Argument]

6. How do you think Deanna Zandt ("Can't We All Just Get Along?") would respond to Hurston's portrait of early 20th-century race relations? Do you think Zandt would hold up this essay as an historical example of how the divisiveness and "polarization" she decries can be overcome? Why, or why not? [Compare and Contrast]

7. Our political airwaves are filled with public figures inveighing against the evils of discrimination, whether in the classroom, the workplace, or the halls of power. Choose an example of where the public debate over discrimination is currently being waged, and conduct some first-hand research. What specific form of discrimination is at issue? In what setting? And who are those involved in the debate? [Research]

Richard Rodriguez, "Public Language, Private Language"

Language not only lies at the heart of our personal identity, it is also often at the root of our perceived differences from each other. Recounting his own early efforts to navigate two separate languages, Richard Rodriguez, a Mexican-American author and essayist, reflects on the role that words play in both anchoring and altering our understanding of who we are. Rodriguez has long explored the intersections of race, gender, and national identity in American life. His most well-known works include Hunger of Memory: The Education of Richard Rodriguez *(1982).*

Supporters of bilingual education today imply that students like me miss a great deal by not being taught in their family's language. What they seem not to recognize is that, as a socially disadvantaged child, I considered Spanish to be a private language. What I needed to learn in school was that I had the right—and the obligation—to speak the public language of *los gringos*. The odd truth is that my   5
first-grade classmates could have become bilingual, in the conventional sense of that word, more easily than I. Had they been taught (as upper-middle-class children are often taught early) a second language like Spanish or French, they could have regarded it simply as that: another public language. In my case such bilingualism could not have been so quickly achieved. What I did not believe was that I could   10
speak a single public language.

Without question, it would have pleased me to hear my teachers address me in Spanish when I entered the classroom. I would have felt much less afraid. I would have trusted them and responded with ease. But I would have delayed—for how long postponed?—having to learn the language of public society. I would have   15
evaded—and for how long could I have afforded to delay?—learning the great lesson of school, that I had a public identity.

Fortunately, my teachers were unsentimental about their responsibility. What they understood was that I needed to speak a public language. So their voices would search me out, asking me questions. Each time I'd hear them, I'd look up in   20
surprise to see a nun's face frowning at me. I'd mumble, not really meaning to answer. The nun would persist, "Richard, stand up. Don't look at the floor. Speak up. Speak to the entire class, not just to me!" But I couldn't believe that the English language was mine to use. (In part, I did not want to believe it.) I continued to mumble. I resisted the teacher's demands. (Did I somehow suspect that once I   25
learned public language my pleasing family life would be changed?) Silent, waiting for the bell to sound, I remained dazed, diffident, afraid.

Because I wrongly imagined that English was intrinsically a public language and Spanish an intrinsically private one, I easily noted the difference between classroom language and the language of home. At school, words were directed to a general   30
audience of listeners. ("Boys and girls.") Words were meaningfully ordered. And the point was not self-expression alone but to make oneself understood by many

others. The teacher quizzed: "Boys and girls, why do we use that word in this
sentence? Could we think of a better word to use there? Would the sentence
35   change its meaning if the words were differently arranged? And wasn't there a
better way of saying much the same thing?" (I couldn't say. I wouldn't try to say.)

Three months. Five. Half a year passed. Unsmiling, ever watchful, my teachers
noted my silence. They began to connect my behavior with the difficult progress
my older sister and brother were making. Until one Saturday morning three nuns
40   arrived at the house to talk to our parents. Stiffly, they sat on the blue living
room sofa. From the doorway of another room, spying the visitors, I noted the
incongruity—the clash of two worlds, the faces and voices of school intruding
upon the familiar setting of home. I overheard one voice gently wondering, "Do
your children speak only Spanish at home, Mrs. Rodriguez?" While another voice
45   added, "That Richard especially seems so timid and shy."

   That Rich-heard!

   At first, it seemed kind of a game. After dinner each night, the family gathered
to practice "our" English. (It was still then *ingles*, a language foreign to us, so we
felt drawn as strangers to it.) Laughing, we would try to define words we could not
50   pronounce. We played with strange English sounds, often over-anglicizing our pro-
nunciations. And we filled the smiling gaps of our sentences with familiar Spanish
sounds. But that was cheating, somebody shouted. Everyone laughed. In school,
meanwhile, like my brother and sister, I was required to attend a daily tutoring
session. I needed a full year of special attention. I also needed my teachers to keep
55   my attention from straying in class by calling out, *Rich-heard*—their English voices
slowly prying loose my ties to my other name, its three notes, *Ri-car-do*. Most of all
I needed to hear my mother and father speak to me in a moment of seriousness
in broken—suddenly heartbreaking—English. The scene was inevitable: One
Saturday morning I entered the kitchen where my parents were talking in Spanish.
60   I did not realize that they were talking in Spanish however until, at the moment they
saw me, I heard their voices change to speak English. Those gringo sounds they
uttered startled me. Pushed me away. In that moment of trivial misunderstanding
and profound insight, I felt my throat twisted by unsounded grief. I turned quickly
and left the room. But I had no place to escape to with Spanish. (The spell was
65   broken.) My brother and sisters were speaking English in another part of the house.

   Again and again in the days following, increasingly angry, I was obliged to hear
my mother and father: "Speak to us *en ingles*." (Speak.) Only then did I determine
to learn classroom English. Weeks after, it happened: One day in school I raised my
hand to volunteer an answer. I spoke out in a loud voice. And I did not think it re-
70   markable when the entire class understood. That day, I moved very far from the
disadvantaged child I had been only days earlier. The belief, the calming assurance
that I belonged in public, had at last taken hold.

   Shortly after, I stopped hearing the high and loud sounds of *los gringos*. A more
and more confident speaker of English, I didn't trouble to listen to *how* strangers
75   sounded, speaking to me. And there simply were too many English-speaking

people in my day for me to hear American accents anymore. Conversations quickened. Listening to persons who sounded eccentrically pitched voices, I usually noted their sounds for an initial few seconds before I concentrated in *what* they were saying. Conversations became content-full. Transparent. Hearing someone's *tone* of voice—angry or questioning or sarcastic or happy or sad—I didn't distinguish it from the words it expressed. Sound and word were thus tightly wedded. At the end of a day, I was often bemused, always relieved, to realize how "silent," though crowded with words, my day in public had been. (This public silence measured and quickened the change in my life.)

At last, seven years old, I came to believe what had been technically true since my birth: I was an American citizen.

But the special feeling of closeness at home was diminished by then. Gone was the desperate, urgent, intense feeling of being at home; rare was the experience of feeling myself individualized by family intimates. We remained a loving family, but one greatly changed. No longer so close; no longer bound tight by the pleasing and troubling knowledge of our public separateness. Neither my older brother nor sister rushed home after school anymore. Nor did I. When I arrived home there would often be neighborhood kids in the house. Or the house would be empty of sounds.

Following the dramatic Americanization of their children, even my parents grew more publicly confident. Especially my mother. She learned the names of all the people on our block. And she decided we needed to have a telephone installed in the house. My father continued to use the word *gringo*. But it was no longer charged with the old bitterness or distrust. (Stripped of any emotional content, the word simply became a name for those Americans not of Hispanic descent.) Hearing him, sometimes, I wasn't sure if he was pronouncing the Spanish word *gringo* or saying gringo in English.

My mother! My father! After English became my primary language, I no longer knew what words to use in addressing my parents. The old Spanish words (those tender accents of sound) I had used earlier—*mamá* and *papá*—I couldn't use anymore. They would have been too painful reminders of how much had changed in my life. On the other hand, the words I heard neighborhood kids call *their* parents seemed equally unsatisfactory. *Mother* and *Father; Ma, Papa, Pa, Dad, Pop* (how I hated the all-American sound of that last word especially)—all these terms I felt were unsuitable, not really terms of address for *my* parents. As a result, I never used them at home. Whenever I'd speak to my parents, I would try to get their attention with eye contact alone. In public conversations, I'd refer to "my parents" or "my mother and father."

My mother and father, for their part, responded differently, as their children spoke to them less. She grew restless, seemed troubled and anxious at the scarcity of words exchanged in the house. She smiled at small talk. She pried at the edges of my sentences to get me to say something more. (What?) She'd join conversations she overheard, but her intrusions often stopped her children's talking. By

120 contrast, my father seemed reconciled to the new quiet. Though his English improved somewhat, he retired into silence. At dinner he spoke very little. One night his children and even wife helplessly giggled at his garbled English pronunciation of the Catholic Grace before meals. Thereafter he made his wife recite the prayer at the start of each meal, even on formal occasions, when there were guests in the house. Hers became the public voice of the family. On official business, it
125 was she, not my father, one would usually hear on the phone or in stores, talking to strangers. His children grew so accustomed to his silence that, years later, they would speak routinely of his shyness. (My mother would often try to explain: Both his parents died when he was eight. He was raised by an uncle who treated him like little more than a menial servant. He was never encouraged to speak. He grew up
130 alone. A man of few words.) But my father was not shy, I realized, when I'd watch him speaking Spanish with relatives. Using Spanish, he was quickly effusive. Especially when talking with other men, his voice would spark, flicker, flare alive with sounds. In Spanish, he expressed ideas and feelings he rarely revealed in English. With firm Spanish sounds, he conveyed confidence and authority English would
135 never allow him.

      The silence at home, however was finally more than a literal silence. Fewer words passed between parent and child, but more profound was the silence that resulted from my inattention to sounds. At about the time I no longer bothered to listen with care to the sounds of English in public, I grew careless about listening to the
140 sounds family members made when they spoke. Most of the time I heard someone speaking at home and didn't distinguish his sounds from the words people uttered in public. I didn't even pay much attention to my parents' accented and ungrammatical speech. At least not at home. Only when I was with them in public would I grow alert to their accents. Though, even then, their sounds caused me less and
145 less concern. For I was increasingly confident of my own public identity.

      I would have been happier about my public success had I not sometimes recalled what it had been like earlier, when my family had conveyed its intimacy through a set of conveniently private sounds. Sometimes in public, hearing a stranger, I'd hark back to my past. A Mexican farmworker approached me downtown to ask
150 directions to somewhere. "¿Hijito . . . ?" he said. And his voice summoned deep longing. Another time, standing beside my mother in the visiting room of a Carmelite convent, before the dense screen which rendered the nuns shadowy figures, I heard several Spanish-speaking nuns—their busy, singsong overlapping voices—assure us that yes, yes, we were remembered, all our family was remem-
155 bered in their prayers. (Their voices echoed faraway family sounds.) Another day, a dark-faced old woman—her hand light on my shoulder—steadied herself against me as she boarded a bus. She murmured something I couldn't quite comprehend. Her Spanish voice came near, like the face of a never-before-seen relative in the instant before I was kissed. Her voice, like so many of the Spanish voices I'd hear in
160 public, recalled the golden age of my youth. Hearing Spanish then, I continued to be a careful, if sad, listener to sounds. Hearing a Spanish-speaking family walking

behind me, I turned to look. I smiled for an instant before my glance found the Hispanic-looking faces of strangers in the crowd going by.

Today I hear bilingual educators say that children lose a degree of "individuality" by becoming assimilated into public society. (Bilingual schooling was popularized in the seventies, that decade when middle-class ethnics began to resist the process of assimilation—the American melting pot.) But the bilingualists simplistically scorn the value and necessity of assimilation. They do not seem to realize that there are *two* ways a person is individualized. So they do not realize that while one suffers a diminished sense of *private* individuality by becoming assimilated into public society, such assimilation makes possible the achievement of *public* individuality.

The bilingualists insist that a student should be reminded of his difference from others in mass society, his heritage. But they equate more separateness with individuality. The fact is that only in private—with intimates—is separateness from the crowd a prerequisite for individuality. (An intimate draws me apart, tells me that I am unique, unlike all others.) In public, by contrast, full individuality is achieved, paradoxically, by those who are able to consider themselves members of the crowd. Thus it happened for me: Only when I was able to think of myself as an American, no longer an alien in *gringo* society, could I seek the rights and opportunities necessary for full public individuality. The social and political advantages I enjoy as a man result from the day that I came to believe that my name, indeed, is *Rich-heard Road-ree-guess*. It is true that my public society today is often impersonal. (My public society is usually mass society.) Yet despite the anonymity of the crowd and despite the fact that the individuality I achieve in public is often tenuous—*because it depends on my being one in a crowd*—I celebrate the day I acquired my new name. Those middle-class ethnics who scorn assimilation seem to me filled with decadent self-pity, obsessed by the burden of public life. Dangerously, they romanticize public separateness and they trivialize the dilemma of the socially disadvantaged.

My awkward childhood does not prove the necessity of bilingual education. My story discloses instead an essential myth of childhood—inevitable pain. If I rehearse here the changes in my private life after my Americanization, it is finally to emphasize the public gain. The loss implies the gain: The house I returned to each afternoon was quiet. Intimate sounds no longer rushed to the door to greet me. There were other noises inside. The telephone rang. Neighborhood kids ran past the door of the bedroom where I was reading my schoolbooks—covered with shopping-bag paper. Once I learned public language, it would never again be easy for me to hear intimate family voices. More and more of my day was spent hearing words. But that may only be a way of saying that the day I raised my hand in class and spoke loudly to an entire roomful of faces, my childhood started to end.

Source: From Hunger of Memory: The Education of Richard Rodriquez (*Bantam Publishing, 1982*)

Discussion/Writing Prompts

1. As Rodriguez makes clear, learning to cultivate and master the appropriate voice is key to achieving success in the larger, public world. How would you characterize the voice Rodriguez employs in this essay? Does this voice seem appropriate to the subject matter he addresses? Does it help make his essay more successful? Why, or why not? [Rhetorical Analysis of Voice]

2. What experience do you have with learning a second language? Whether in school or at home, how has this experience with bilingualism affected the way you view yourself? Has this change been for the better or for the worse? Why? [Personal Reflection]

3. "I would have been happier about my public success," Rodriguez writes, "had I not sometimes recalled what it had been like earlier, when my family had conveyed its intimacy through a set of conveniently private sounds." What point do you think Rodriguez is trying to make here? What type of loss is he attempting to identify? And what language in particular gives you this impression? [Close Reading]

4. While designed to convey an argument, this essay also tells a story. To what extent do you think the narrative form strengthens Rodriguez's argument? What specific aspects of this narrative do you think are most effective in conveying the larger points Rodriguez is trying to get across? [Analyzing Rhetorical Modes]

5. "The bilingualists," Rodriguez writes, "insist that a student should be reminded of his difference from others in a mass society, his heritage. But they equate his separateness with individuality. The fact is that only in private—with intimates—is separateness from the crowd a prerequisite for individuality." In a two- or three-page essay, discuss the ways this statement can be read as a summation of Rodriguez's main argument. In what ways does his own story of "bilingualism" challenge the equation of "separateness" with "individuality"? At what moments in this story does this critique come across most clearly? [Argument]

6. How do you think William J. Astore ("The United States of Euphemism") would react to Rodriguez's story? Do you think he would be sympathetic to what Rodriguez has to say about the importance of mastering a "public language"? Why, or why not? [Compare and Contrast]

7. The debate over the merits of bilingual education is alive and well today. Conduct some first-hand research into how this debate is currently playing out. Who are the major stakeholders? Over what key questions do they disagree? And which perspective do you find more persuasive? Why? [Research]

Tying It All Together

1. How do you think Brian Moen ("Myth of Objectivity") would react to the discussion of voice and language presented by writers like Patricia Williams ("Anti-Intellectualism Is Taking Over the US") or William J. Astore ("The United States of Euphemism")? Given his own skepticism toward the notion of "objectivity,"

do you think he would be convinced by the argument that style and word choice can affect the "truth" of what we read? Choose one of these other writers, and write a two- or three-page essay analyzing the similarities and differences in the arguments each makes. Does the writer invite us to draw similar conclusions about the possibilities of being truly objective? How, or how not?

2. As Carl Elliot suggests ("The Perfect Voice"), there are any number of ways an accent can define us in the eyes of the general public, shaping both the attitudes we hold toward and the conclusions we draw about each other. Conduct some independent research into this question. First, choose a cultural product (e.g., television show, website, movie, or commercial) that, in your view, showcases a particular accent. Then, describe how this accent is depicted. Who is the speaker? In what setting is the speaker presented? Next, analyze the particular ways this accent is being used to define, label, and/or judge some group or category of people. What assumptions are we encouraged to make? Finally, offer your own assessment of how valid or not you find this depiction to be, and why.

3. As the selections in this chapter make clear, there is a fundamental connection between *voice* and *argument*. Depending on the style we adopt or the language we choose, our readers draw very different conclusions about the larger points we are trying to make. Choose two selections that, in your view, speak to their readers in very different voices, and write a two- or three-page essay in which you identify and compare these differences. How would you characterize the voice that each essay presents? What specific aspects or features make them seem so different from each other? And how do these voices affect or influence the way you respond to each writer's overall argument? Do you find this voice to be an effective vehicle for conveying this argument? Why, or why not?

Using the Steps of Rhetorical Analysis to Write Your Own Academic Essay

The same instruction this chapter presents for analyzing other people's writing can also serve as a guide for undertaking writing of your own. In particular, a number of the steps outlined above provide a useful framework for the kind of writing you are often called upon to do in the classroom. In the same way that these steps teach you to apply the rhetorical concept of voice to what you read, they can also be used to help you better see the role this concept plays in your own essay writing. Take a look at the outline below. Organizing the writing process along the same rhetorical lines modeled above, it provides a map for how to use the concept of voice to organize and create your own academic essay:

- **Step One: Finding the Voice:** What impression of yourself do you want to convey?
- **Step Two: Assessing the Voice:** Why do you want to convey this image? What goal does it help you accomplish?
- **Step Three: Expressing the Voice:** What specific choices do you make to convey this image? What decisions about tone or word choice?

To see how these steps can be put into practice, let's take a look at a specific example. As you read over the essay below, pay attention to the ways that considerations about voice guide the writer's calculations and choices. To assist you in this work, take note of the comments and questions that accompany the essay in the margins. Then, turn your attention to the sample analysis that follows. In what ways does this discussion provide a model for using these three steps to write an academic essay of your own?

Student Essay: Daniel Freeport, "Alternative Versus Conventional Medicine"

In this essay, Daniel Freeport compares alternative and conventional medical approaches.

It is a popular view in today's society that technology can solve all of our problems. Nowhere is this view more prevalent than in the area of modern medicine. Despite the fact that many traditional and/or non-Western approaches to health care have been shown to be highly effective, many Americans continue to hold an extremely negative bias against them, assuming instead that the favor of the newest, the most modern technological advances in medicine must, by definition, be the best. A side-by-side comparison of the two types of approaches, however, reveals that this bias is not justified. While public opinion may run in favor of the modern, a detailed assessment of each shows that both approaches—alternative and conventional—have a lot to offer.

The first key difference between these two types of medical approaches involves the issue of diagnosis. Whereas modern or conventional approaches tend to treat illnesses or disorders as discrete conditions with singular, identifiable causes, alternative approaches stress the importance of diagnosing illness holistically, the result of physiological, psychological, and environmental factors. Each approach has its own advantages. The conventional approach is especially effective in dealing with conditions that stem from acute causes: infections or injuries, for example. In cases like these, a patient could greatly benefit from a diagnostic approach that seeks to address a single, direct cause. In other cases, however, this sort of diagnostic approach can sometimes lead doctors to overlook broader, underlying factors that might be causing a person to feel unwell. If a patient comes to a doctor looking for help with a persistent pain or fatigue, she may be well served by a doctor who diagnoses a single cause and proscribes a single treatment. But this approach might also fail to take into account a wider range of broader factors (e.g., stress, diet, or workplace environment) that might also be contributing to the

Establishing Context

Previewing Argument

First Point of Comparison

5

10

15

20

25

30

35

problem. Because they tend to focus on just such factors, alternative approaches can also be helpful.

Given this difference in diagnosis, it's not surprising that another key difference between conventional and alternative approaches to medicine concerns the issue of treatment. Because conventional medicine often views illness as a discrete condition brought about by a single, discrete cause, its response to illness very often involves a similarly focused and singular treatment: like a pill or a procedure. Because alternative medicine approaches the entire relationship between health and illness in broader, more holistic terms, its approach often proscribes a treatment that encompasses a range of potential solutions: from nutrition to exercise to meditation.

Second Point of Comparison

40

45

A closely related third difference concerns the extent to which conventional medicine relies on chemical drugs and surgical procedures to implement its treatment. Alternative approaches tend to eschew this approach, proscribing instead natural remedies such as herb or vitamins, or traditional healing practices such as acupuncture and massage. Once again, this difference doesn't prove either approach is inherently superior. In fact, what this comparison suggests is that the best approach may well be one that integrates elements of both.

Third Point of Comparison   50

55

While conventional and alternative medicine follow different guidelines and practices for diagnosing and treating disease, a side-by-side comparison suggests that neither one is inherently superior to the other. Each offers approaches that can be useful and effective in different contexts. Conventional medicine is most useful for treating critical or acute conditions, while alternative medicine can be helpful in addressing conditions that stem from a broader range of factors.

Using Conclusion to Reinforce Central Point   60

65

Now, let's see how the rhetorical steps presented above help us understand the choices the writer makes to create this essay:

Step One: *Finding the Voice: What Impression Does the Writer Want to Convey?*

○ While the writer speaks openly about his support for alternative medicine, he also goes to great lengths to stress the advantages of both approaches. Walking readers through a point-by-point comparison, he presents himself as objective, even-handed, and fair.

Step Two: *Assessing the Voice: Is This Style Appropriate to the Occasion?*

o The writer's goal here is less to argue for the superiority of alternative medicine than to challenge the assumption that it is inherently inferior to conventional medicine. In light of this, it is important that the writer present himself as an objective and fair-minded judge. If he were to employ language that betrayed a stronger bias, he would lose some of this authority.

Step Three: *Expressing the Voice: What Specific Elements Best Help Convey the Writer's Style?*

o Throughout the essay, the writer makes rhetorical decisions that reflect his desire to come across as objective and fair. The compare-and-contrast mode is an especially useful vehicle in this regard, allowing the writer to identify the strengths of each respective approach. This same intent is evident in the language the writer uses, which consistently downplays any suggestion of personal bias.

Group Work: Thinking Rhetorically About the Formal Selections

This chapter has given you ample opportunity to analyze voice on your own. Now, let's undertake this same kind of work from a group perspective. Your group should select one of the formal selections above. Prepare for this work by re-reading the selection. Then, with your group, use the outline presented at the beginning of the chapter, *Thinking Rhetorically About Voice*, to analyze the role of voice in this piece. Here is a quick recap of these steps:

- **Step One: Finding the Voice:** What overall impression does the writer convey? What basic style does the writer adopt?
- **Step Two: Assessing the Voice:** Does this style seem appropriate to the occasion? Is it designed to appeal to the writer's target audience? Does it help further the writer's larger goal?
- **Step Three: Expressing the Voice:** What specific elements in the text (e.g., words, phrases, sentences, and paragraphs) best help convey the writer's style?
- **Step Four: Refining the Voice:** What changes in language or organization would help convey the text's style even more effectively?
- **Step Five: Comparing the Voice:** How does the writer's style here compare to other styles that might have been employed?
- **Step Six: Putting It Into Writing:** How do I summarize my findings in writing?

Once you have completed this work, exchange your findings with another group. First, have your group re-read the selection these new findings examine. Then, discuss as a group how helpful you find this analysis. Do you agree with the conclusions about voice this analysis draws? Do you evaluate the role of voice in different or similar ways? Finally, summarize your key findings in a paragraph. Be prepared to share this written assessment with the rest of the class.

Different Goals, Different Voices: Understanding the Connection Between Informal and Formal Writing

Throughout this chapter, we have moved from a focus on informal writing to formal writing. How do these types of writing compare? What are the key similarities and differences in language and tone, form and content, organization and context? And what happens to our understanding of voice when we take these similarities and differences into account?

The activity presented here provides an opportunity to address these questions. First, choose a topic or issue that has been raised by one of the formal selections in this chapter (e.g., accent-reduction programs, anti-intellectualism in public life, or objectivity in the media). Next, choose an informal venue (e.g., blog, Facebook post, tweet, or email), and write about this issue using the conventions of this particular form. Then, choose a formal venue (e.g., journal essay, magazine article, or academic analysis), and write about the same issue using the conventions particular to this form. When you're done, spend a few moments itemizing the specific ways these two writing samples differ and are similar. In what ways did your choice of venue affect the voice you employed? How did this choice of voice influence other rhetorical choices: organization or thesis, purpose or goal?

Connecting Voice to Rhetorical Modes

To better understand how rhetorical considerations about voice relate to rhetorical modes, try the following activity. Choose an example of real world writing from the informal selections in this chapter. First, analyze the particular language or word choice the writer uses to convey the larger point. Next, choose the rhetorical mode (e.g., narration, description, cause and effect, compare and contrast, or definition) for which you think this type of language is best suited. And finally, create an example of this rhetorical mode that employs this particular language.

Speaking for Yourself

Choose two different settings from your own life where you use a different voice. Then, write a two- or three-page essay in which you compare and contrast these two voices. What is each voice like? How, specifically, does each differ from the other? And what is it about each setting that accounts for these differences? Then, in a follow-up paragraph, make an argument for which of these two voices better reflects or expresses the "real you."

9 Credibility

How tall is Mount Everest? What is the population of Zagreb, Croatia? Is global warming a genuine threat? Is vitamin D really good for you? Where is the best place in town to grab a piece of pizza? What will the weather be like tomorrow?

For all the obvious ways these questions differ, they all share one thing in common: Every one of them can be answered by a quick search online. In our digital age, there is no shortage of sites and sources that purport to answer any question we might have. Whether we are looking for a recent movie review or tracking down documents for a US history paper, perusing the latest medical findings about high sodium intake or researching the best way to remove ketchup stains from a rug, we can rest assured there exists some site claiming to have exactly the information we are looking for. But how do we know whether this information is accurate? In a world where our access to countless reams of facts, statistics, and opinions can feel almost limitless, how do we tell the difference between what is true and what is false? At the end of the day, how do we know whom and what to trust?

The situation gets even more complicated when we pause to consider the sheer scope of the questions we turn to our media in the hopes of answering. Some of these searches involve questions that are purely factual: Who was the 23rd president of the United States? How many fluid ounces are there in a gallon? And in cases like these, establishing the validity of a source can be fairly straightforward, answerable by reference to data or statistics that can be objectively verified. In other cases, however, the task of verification gets a bit trickier because the questions at hand are more subjective, pitting opposing claims and competing facts against each other: Is bottled water harmful to the environment? Should all newborns be vaccinated? Even murkier are those questions that don't really have a definitive answer at all, that come down to a question of personal opinion or individual taste: Who is the best professor to take for this course? Where should you go for great Chinese takeout? Whatever the case, though, verifying the validity of what we read requires that we ask some pointed questions: Where does this information come from? Can it be authenticated by other sources? And does this writer seem knowledgeable or trustworthy?

How Do I Make Myself Believable?

The same requirement applies to the writing we do ourselves. As writers, we are constantly called on to negotiate the issue of our own credibility. Whether tweeting our thoughts about a weekend party, blogging about the benefits of organic food, or writing a persuasive essay for a college composition class, we always have to consider which choices are likely to make us most believable. If, for example, we were making an argument about the need for stricter recycling laws, we would probably want to spend a few moments figuring out what, exactly, gives us the authority to speak on this issue. What experience, knowledge, or background qualifies us to offer an opinion on this question? Are the claims we make based on factual evidence? Is our argument supported by reasons that are logical?

To illustrate the importance of credibility, consider the following hypothetical scenario: Imagine you have been assigned the task of researching the environmental effects of the 2010 British Petroleum oil spill in the Gulf of Mexico. From the start, you know this will be no simple task. Ranked as one of the worst environmental catastrophes in recent history, this oil spill has been the subject of literally thousands of investigations, discussions, and critiques. Investigating this issue, therefore, is going to require some tough choices about which of these sources are most believable—and which ones are not.

Imagine, for instance, coming across an account of the spill published by British Petroleum itself, one filled with statistics and statements suggesting that the environmental damage caused by this event is actually quite limited. How do you decide whether to believe this? You might begin by asking yourself questions about context. Does it matter that the information presented comes from British Petroleum? Does this fact suggest any specific interest or bias that might be at work? You might also ask whether this information can be objectively verified by reference to other sources. Drilling down even further, you might even look at *how* this information is being presented. Are there underlying messages about oil drilling, energy consumption, and environmental protection in general that this website is encouraging us to accept? If so, are there other ways to think about these issues that, in your opinion, are equally valid?

It's tempting to conclude that credibility is simply about determining the truth of what we're being told, about separating the right answers from the wrong ones. But as the above example illustrates, the question is actually more complicated. Credibility is less about choosing between a view that is objectively "true" and one that is objectively "false" than it is about understanding the factors that shape and influence *all* viewpoints. Nobody has cornered the market on the truth. We all have biases. The challenge is to figure out what those biases are and to think about the way they influence both what we are told and what we want to say.

How to Analyze Credibility in Real World Writing

To assess the credibility of the writing we come across in the real world, we need a specific set of questions and guidelines. Only with such a framework in hand can we figure out exactly what a writer is asking us to believe and evaluate the basis on which we are supposed to believe it. The outline below provides us with a starting point for accomplishing this goal. Dividing the process of analyzing credibility into a series of discrete steps, it walks us through the process for describing and evaluating the strategies writers use to establish their credibility.

▊ Thinking Rhetorically About Credibility

- **Step One: Identifying Credibility:** What makes the writer qualified to speak on this issue? What knowledge, background, or experience establish the writer's credibility?
- **Step Two: Assessing Credibility:** What makes these qualifications valuable or relevant? How, specifically, do they make the writer's claims more believable?
- **Step Three: Asserting Credibility:** How do these qualifications influence the specific rhetorical choices the writer makes? How are they related to the writer's overall goal, choice of audience, and decisions about language?
- **Step Four: Defending Credibility:** How might you challenge the writer's credibility? What critiques or counterpoints might you offer?
- **Step Five: Rethinking Credibility:** Based on these critiques, how would you go about revising this writing? In what way would such revisions serve to make this writing more credible?
- **Step Six: Putting It Into Writing:** How do I summarize my findings in writing?

To help you master these skills, let's consider a hypothetical example. In the selection below, look at the particular claims the writer makes. Ask yourself: What gives this writer the authority to speak on this issue? What reasoning or evidence does she provide to support this argument? What tone or language does she employ? And do these different choices make this writer more or less believable? Once you've addressed these questions, turn your attention to the sample analysis that follows, and note how each of these steps provides a model for analyzing and evaluating credibility.

Natalie Wu, "Childhood Obesity Is No Laughing Matter"

This blog post by Natalie Wu, a college sophomore, takes a clear stand on the controversial issue of childhood obesity, one of the most urgent and contentious debates in today's society. In doing so, it presents us with an ideal test case for addressing the question of credibility.

Childhood obesity is no joke! If you are a parent or just someone who cares about the welfare of kids, this is a topic you simply cannot ignore. While the representatives of the Big Food Industry want us to believe that there is no health crisis in America, the truth is that we are in the midst of a junk food epidemic in which more and more children are becoming
5   addicted to high-sugar, high-fat, and high-sodium foods. The effect of this epidemic, my friends, is that more and more young people are finding themselves overweight, or even morbidly obese, at younger and younger ages.

       As recent studies by the Centers for Disease Control (CDC) illustrate, American children are getting fatter. According to this data, the percentage of children under 10 who are now
10   classified as "obese" has reached close to 30%. This is a completely unacceptable statistic, and should compel us to take drastic action. The prime culprit behind this statistic is processed foods. If you walk down the average grocery store aisle, you simply cannot avoid

products that contain alarming amounts of processed ingredients. The worst offender among these ingredients is high fructose corn syrup, a processed sweetener that can be found in over 75% of products in a typical grocery store.   15

This fact alone makes clear how difficult it can be for parents to feed their children healthy food. But the situation becomes even more difficult when we take into account the efforts by the Big Food Industry to promote their products as healthy and nutritious when in fact they are not. There is not a single nutritionist who would claim that excessive amounts of sugar, salt or fat are good for you. And yet, if we listened only to the advertis-   20 ers, we might very well be tempted to accept this lie.

▨ Thinking Rhetorically About Credibility: A Step-by-Step Guide

Now, let's see how we can use the steps outlined above to analyze this example in a detailed and comprehensive way:

Step One: *Identifying Credibility: What Makes the Writer Qualified to Speak on This Issue?*

- ○ The writer holds extremely strong views on this subject and gathers a variety of statistics and data to support them. Among them:

  - › A CDC study that identifies "30%" of American children as "obese."

  - › The fact that "75% of products in a typical grocery store" contain high fructose corn syrup.

- ○ These facts seem designed to support the writer's larger points: to provide objective, reliable evidence that reinforces her key claim about the urgent need to address childhood obesity. Filled with scientific-sounding statistics, these data are intended to give the writer's discussion here an additional degree of authority.

- ○ The writer further attempts to support her claims through force of logic: by proposing a causal connection between the widespread presence of "processed foods" on the one hand and the increasing rates of obesity among children on the other. If such a connection does indeed exist, a reader will be far more likely to accept the writer's argument that addressing food production will help solve the obesity problem.

- ○ And finally, the writer attempts to boost her credibility by adopting a tone that underscores the importance and urgency of this issue. We see this most vividly in the writer's opening statement ("Childhood obesity is no joke!") as well as in the outraged tone she strikes throughout the rest of the piece. By speaking in this particular voice, the writer is clearly encouraging his readers to adopt the same attitude: to see this issue as one about which they should feel deep concerns.

Step Two: *Assessing Credibility: What Makes These Qualifications Valuable or Relevant?*

○ Citing academic studies and scientific statistics is a legitimate strategy for establishing the writer's credibility. The larger issue is clearly one that relates to the issue of public health and, as such, touches upon questions related to food science, the food marketplace, and governmental policy regarding food. Given this, it might have been useful for the writer to have included more specific data from nutritionists or food scientists, even though the facts she does provide seem relevant.

Step Three: *Asserting Credibility: How Do These Qualifications Influence the Rhetorical Choices the Writer Makes?*

○ It seems that the writer's belief in the importance of the statistical information she includes is what leads her to adopt the intense rhetorical voice. By repeatedly stressing the urgency of this issue, the writer appears to be looking for a way to reinforce to readers how valuable this information truly is. It's unclear, however, whether this rhetorical style enhances or detracts from the effectiveness of these statistics.

○ A reliance upon statistical information also seems to be part of the writer's strategy for bolstering her own personal authority. At certain points in this piece, the writer uses a statistical finding as an opening for presenting her own views. For example, she cites the CDC data about obesity percentages as a way to transition into her personal belief that the "prime culprit" is "processed foods." The writer, in other words, is careful to bolster her own opinion using the expertise of outside authorities.

Step Four: *Defending Credibility: How Might You Challenge the Writer's Credibility?*

○ The statistical data cited are effective only to the extent that their accuracy can be verified. If they derive from reputable or legitimate sources, they carry a lot weight. Based on how the writer presents this material, however, it's unclear exactly what the sources for many of these facts actually are. She presents her claims about grocery stores or "Big Food" advertising as if they are established facts. Indeed, it almost seems as if the writer is asking her readers to accept these claims based on her personal view rather than some outside authority. "There is not a single nutritionist," the writer declares, suggesting this personal statement alone should be enough to vouch for the accuracy of the information she presents. How would the credibility of this piece seem different if the writer cited the sources from which her information comes?

○ Questions about the accuracy or reliability of the information provided also raise questions about the voice the writer adopts. Does the overly emotional tone make the writer more credible? Or does it reinforce doubts about the legitimacy of what she is saying? It could be argued that the more urgent her tone becomes, the more suspicions about the legitimacy of her claims she raises. If the statistics were convincing enough to speak for themselves, would the writer need to adopt this particular tone? And if she adopted a more low-key or measured voice, would a reader be more likely to accept the information she provides?

Step Five: *Rethinking Credibility: How Would You Go About Revising This Writing?*

° Given that the data cited lack any real context, I would urge the writer to consider providing a fuller description of the particular sources she uses: where they come from, the credentials of those being cited, etc. Doing this would provide readers with a more solid basis for judging the validity of the writer's claims.

° In the same vein, I might also urge the writer to consider employing a different voice in this piece. There seems to be some tension between the objective-sounding data she provides and the subjective, emotional tone she adopts. If she were to address readers in a more restrained and serious tone, one more in keeping with the data, her presentation might be more effective.

Step Six: *Putting It Into Writing: How Do I Summarize My Findings in Writing?*

° The writer raises some important questions about childhood obesity as well as about the general health effects of what we eat. From this perspective, I would say the writer performs a valuable service by encouraging readers to care about this important public issue. When it comes to supporting her claims with solid reasoning and evidence, however, the essay loses much of its effectiveness. Because a great deal of the information the writer cites is presented without any context, it is virtually impossible for a reader to verify its accuracy. As a result, the writer's evidence ends up undermining the very claim it is intended to support.

Informal Writing Selections

Now that you've seen an example of what this kind of work looks like, try putting it into practice yourself. This section brings together a representative sample of the kind of informal writing you might easily come across in your own day-to-day life. Using the format above as your guide, analyze each selection along the same rhetorical lines. How does thinking about credibility help us better understand the other rhetorical features within a given piece of writing: audience, purpose, organization, and voice?

To get started, let's work our way through a sample of what this rhetorical analysis might look like. While reading the selection below, pay close attention to the comments and the questions this sample analysis presents. It is designed as a model for the kind of analysis you will attempt in relation to the other selections included here.

Consumer Reports, "Mercury in Canned Tuna Is Still a Concern"

Consumer Reports is perhaps the nation's preeminent consumer watchdog publication.

Canned tuna, Americans' favorite fish, is the most common source of mercury in our diet. New tests of 42 samples from cans and pouches of tuna bought primarily in the New York metropolitan area and online
5   confirm that white (albacore) tuna usually contains far more mercury than light tuna.

I didn't know tuna was #1 in popularity. This fact makes the information that follows seem even more important. I wonder where the writer got this statistic?

Children and women of childbearing age can easily consume more mercury than the Environmental Protection Agency considers advisable simply by eating one
10   serving of canned white tuna or two servings of light tuna per week. A serving is about 2.5 ounces. Expect a 5-ounce can to contain about 4 ounces of tuna plus liquid.

EPA seems like a reputable source

The heavy metal accumulates in tuna and other fish in an especially toxic form, methyl mercury, which comes
15   from mercury released by coal-fired power plants and other industrial or natural sources, such as volcanoes.

Interesting information.

Fortunately, it's easy to choose lower mercury fish that are also rich in healthful omega-3 fatty acids. That's especially important for women who are pregnant or
20   might become pregnant, nursing mothers, and young children, because fetuses and youngsters seem to face the most risk from methyl mercury's neurotoxic effects.

The writer is really emphasizing the health effects of mercury on pregnant women and young children. I wonder if the health dangers are as pronounced for adults?

Results from our tuna tests, conducted at an outside lab, underscore the longheld concern for those people.
25   We found:

- Every sample contained measurable levels of mercury, ranging from 0.018 to 0.774 parts per million. The Food and Drug Administration can take legal action to pull products containing 1 ppm or more
30   from the market. (It never has, according to an FDA spokesman.) The EPA compiles fish advisories when state and local governments have found high contaminant levels in certain locally caught fish.
- Samples of white tuna had 0.217 to 0.774 ppm of
35   mercury and averaged 0.427 ppm. By eating 2.5 ounces of any of the tested samples, a woman of childbearing age would exceed the daily mercury intake that the EPA considers safe.

- Samples of light tuna had 0.018 to 0.176 ppm and averaged 0.071 ppm. At that average, a woman of childbearing age eating 2.5 ounces would get less than the EPA's limit, but for about half the tested samples, eating 5 ounces would exceed the limit.

40

In 2006 we scrutinized the results of the FDA's tests in 2002 to 2004 of mercury levels in hundreds of samples of canned tuna. The agency's white-tuna samples averaged 0.353 ppm; light tuna, 0.118 ppm. But we found that as much as 6 percent of the FDA's light-tuna samples had at least as much mercury as the average in white tuna—in some cases more than twice as much.

45

These two preceding statistics really enhance the writer's credibility. Everyone has heard of the EPA and the FDA, so there can be few doubts about the veracity of these statistics

50

Given the uncertainties about the impact of occasional fetal exposure to such high levels, we urged the FDA to warn consumers about occasional spikes in mercury levels in canned light tuna. More than four years later, the FDA still hasn't issued such a warning. When we asked why, an FDA spokesman indicated that the agency had already taken the spikes into account when formulating its mercury advice.

Bottom line.

55

This is a really effective way to conclude. The essay presents a lot of dense statistical information, so ending with a straightforward summary leaves the reader with a clear understanding of what is really at stake.

Canned tuna, especially white, tends to be high in mercury, and younger women and children should limit how much they eat. As a precaution, pregnant women should avoid tuna entirely.

60

Source: ConsumerReports.org, January 2011. Copyright 2011 by Consumers Union of U.S., Inc. http://www.consumerreports.org/cro/2012/04/mercury-in-canned-tuna-is-still-a-concern/ index.htm

Step One: *Identifying Credibility: What Makes the Writer Qualified to Speak on This Issue?*

○ Much of the writer's credibility depends upon the authority of the outside sources being cited. Because the writer supports the argument about the dangers of mercury consumption with information from such authorities as the Environmental Protection Agency and the Food and Drug Administration, readers here are far more likely to take the essay's warnings seriously.

○ In addition to the sources themselves, another factor to consider is the sheer volume of information the writer presents. This essay goes much further than simply citing one statistic or a single report. Instead, it devotes an entire paragraph to "the "results of the FDA's tests" documenting mercury levels in canned tuna.

○ And finally, the fact that this information is presented in a magazine such as *Consumer Reports* also serves to reinforce its credibility. *Consumer Reports* is widely recognized as a valuable source for those who wish to learn more about the risks and benefits associated with virtually any product.

Step Two: *Assessing Credibility: What Makes These Qualifications Valuable or Relevant?*

o By citing information generated by the FDA and the EPA, the writer is clearly attempting to link a personal authority to speak on this issue with the authority of these well-regarded agencies. The reader is left with a sense that the views advanced here—about the dangers of mercury in canned tuna—are more than simply those of the writer.

o Aligning with the authority of entities like the FDA and EPA is an important strategy because, as government-sponsored organizations, they carry the reputation of being objective. By association, therefore, the writer's own views come across as less biased, less influenced by personal opinion, than they might otherwise.

Step Three: *Asserting Credibility: How Do These Qualifications Influence the Rhetorical Choices the Writer Makes?*

o Because so much of the argument here depends on the objectivity of the information being presented, the writer goes to great lengths to use language elsewhere in the essay that is similarly unbiased and measured. In fact, the overall voice or tone of the essay is scientific, with the writer frequently conveying the main points through declarations of fact rather than expressions of opinion.

o Even in those few isolated moments where the writer employs a more subjective word choice, it is clear that such language refers back to, and is reinforced by, the more objective statistics. The best example of this is the writer's repeated use of the word "toxic." On the one hand, this is a term clearly intended to convey the writer's personal feeling about how urgent and dangerous the issue of mercury in tuna actually is. On the other hand, it is also a term that has a specific scientific reference, as in "neurotoxin."

Step Four: *Defending Credibility: How Might You Challenge the Writer's Credibility?*

o Because the writer is advancing an essentially medical argument, one challenge to the essay's credibility might take the form of data or testimony provided by medical professionals suggesting that the health effects of mercury are less dire than presented here.

o Also, because this essay focuses primarily on the dangers posed to "pregnant women" and "young children," another potential challenge could focus on the fact that the writer doesn't fully address the reduced danger mercury poses to able-bodied adults. Adding this focus wouldn't necessarily discredit the claims being made here, but it would provide a broader context for assessing the risks of tuna consumption by the general public.

Step Five: *Rethinking Credibility: How Would You Go About Revising This Writing?*

º In response to concerns over the scope of the argument here, the writer could consider broadening the discussion of health effects to include those beyond the groups most threatened. Perhaps this broader discussion could be added to the essay's concluding section, in which the writer lays out "advice" about tuna consumption, supplementing it with additional guidelines for those less directly threatened.

Step Six: *Putting It Into Writing: How Do I Summarize My Findings in Writing?*

º In addressing public anxieties about tuna consumption, this essay does a very responsible job of arguing for reasonable limits and sensible caution. The strength of its recommendations rests with the statistical information the writer brings together. Because this information comes from such widely recognized and respected sources, it lends a degree of authority and objectivity to the writer's own views that might not otherwise have been available.

National Alliance for Public Charter Schools, "Why Charter Schools?"

The National Alliance for Public Charter Schools is a national nonprofit organization committed to advancing the charter school movement.

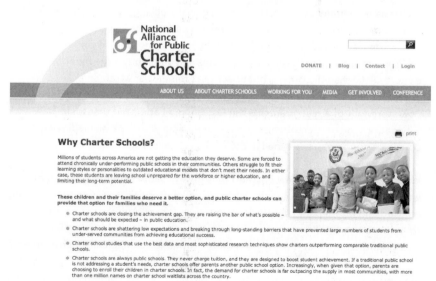

FIGURE 9.3

Source: http://www.publiccharters.org/about-us/

Virginia Heffernan, "Why I'm a Creationist"

Yahoo News is one of the preeminent news aggregators on the Internet.

As a child I fell in love with technology, but I have to admit I never fell in love with science. I kept hoping that messing around with Macs and Atari and eventually the Internet would nudge me closer to caring about the periodic table, Louis Pasteur and the double-blind studies that now seem to stand for science. As it was, I only cared about the double-blind studies that told me what I wanted to hear—that potatoes are good for you or that people of my height are generally happy—and I liked the phrase "double-blind" when it was on my side because it meant "true" and "take that."

I assume that other people love science *and* technology, since the fields are often lumped together, but I rarely meet people like that. Technology people are trippy; our minds are blown by the romance of telecom. At the same time, the people I know who consider themselves scientists by nature seem to be super-skeptical types who can be counted on to denigrate religion, fear climate change and think most people—most Americans—are dopey sheep who believe in angels and know nothing about all the gross carbon they trail, like "Pig-Pen."

I like most people. I don't fear environmental apocalypse. And I don't hate religion. Those scientists no doubt see *me* as a dopey sheep who believes in angels and is carbon-ignorant. I have to say that they may be right.

In the hazy Instagram picture I have in my mind of the mechanisms that animate my ingenious smartphone—a picture that slips in and out of focus, and one I constantly revise—it might as well be angels. At the same time, I have read and heard brilliantly serpentine arguments for and against fracking, not to mention for and against cities and coal and paper (it sidelines carbon and decomposes! it is toxic industrial waste!), and I still don't know right from wrong when it comes to carbon. All I know is one side of these debates seems maybe slightly more bloodthirsty and opportunistic than the other—but now I can't remember which one.

Also, at heart, I am a creationist. There, I said it. At least you, dear readers, won't now storm out of a restaurant like the last person I admitted that to. In New York City saying you're a creationist is like confessing you think Ahmadinejad has a couple of good points. Maybe I'm the only creationist I know.

This is how I came to it. Like many people, I heard no end of Bible stories as a kid, but in the 1970s in New England they always came with the caveat that they were metaphors. So I read the metaphors of Genesis and Exodus and was amused and bugged and uplifted and moved by them. And then I guess I wanted to know the truth of how the world began, so I was handed the Big Bang. That wasn't a metaphor, but it wasn't fact either. It was something called a hypothesis. And it was only a sentence. I was amused and moved, but considerably less amused and moved by the character-free Big Bang story ("something exploded") than by the twisted and picturesque misadventures of Eve and Adam and Cain and Abel and Abraham.

Later I read Thomas Malthus' "Essay on the Principle of Population" and "The 40
Origin of Species" by Charles Darwin, as well as probably a dozen books about
evolution and atheism, from Stephen Jay Gould to Sam Harris.

The Darwin, with good reason, stuck with me. Though it's sometimes poetic,
"The Origin of Species" has an enchantingly arid English tone to it; this somber
tone was part of a deliberate effort to mark it as science and not science fiction— 45
the "Star Trek" of its time. The book also alights on a tautology that, like all tautol-
ogies, is gloriously unimpeachable: Whatever survives survives.

But I still wasn't sure why a book that never directly touches on human evolution,
much less the idea of God, was seen as having unseated the story of creation. In
short, "The Origin of Species" is not its own creation story. And while the fact that 50
it stints on metaphor—so as to avoid being like H.G. Wells—neither is it bedrock
fact. It's another hypothesis.

Cut to now. I still read and read and listen and listen. And I have never found a
more compelling story of our origins than the ones that involve God. The evolutionary psychologists with their just-so stories for everything ("You use a porta- 55
ble Kindle charger because mothers in the primordial forest gathered ginseng")
have become more contradictory than Leviticus. Did you all see that ev-psych
now says it's *women* who are naturally not monogamous, in spite of the same
folks telling us for decades that women are desperate to secure resources for
their kids so they frantically sustain wedlock with a rich silverback who will keep 60
them in cashmere?

Sigh. When a social science, made up entirely of observations and hypotheses,
tells us first that men are polygamous and women homebodies, and *then* that men
are monogamous and women gallivanters—and, what's more builds far-fetched
protocols of dating and courtship and marriage and divorce around these 65
notions—maybe it's time to retire the whole approach.

All the while, the first books of the Bible are still hanging around. I guess I don't
"believe" that the world was created in a few days, but what do I know? Seems as
plausible (to me) as theoretical astrophysics, and it's certainly a livelier tale. As
"Life of Pi" author Yann Martel once put it, summarizing his page-turner novel: "1) 70
Life is a story. 2) You can choose your story. 3) A story with God is the better story."

Source: Yahoo News, July 11, 2013
http://news.yahoo.com/why-im-a-creationist-141907217.html

Houston Chronicle, "On Global Warming, the Science Is Solid"

The Houston Chronicle *is the largest daily circulation newspaper in Texas.
This article appeared in response to the increasing pronouncements of
global warming "skeptics" expressing doubts about the validity of modern
climate change research.*

In recent months, e-mails stolen from the University of East Anglia's Climatic Research Unit in the United Kingdom and errors in one of the Intergovernmental Panel on Climate Change's reports have caused a flurry of questions about the validity of climate change science.

These issues have led several states, including Texas, to challenge the Environmental Protection Agency's finding that heat-trapping gases like carbon dioxide (also known as greenhouse gases) are a threat to human health.

However, Texas' challenge to the EPA's endangerment finding on carbon dioxide contains very little science. Texas Attorney General Greg Abbott admitted that the state did not consult any climate scientists, including the many here in the state, before putting together the challenge to the EPA. Instead, the footnotes in the document reveal that the state relied mainly on British newspaper articles to make its case.

Contrary to what one might read in newspapers, the science of climate change is strong. Our own work and the immense body of independent research conducted around the world leaves no doubt regarding the following key points:

•• The global climate is changing.

A 1.5-degree Fahrenheit increase in global temperature over the past century has been documented by NASA and the National Oceanic and Atmospheric Administration. Numerous lines of physical evidence around the world, from melting ice sheets and rising sea levels to shifting seasons and earlier onset of spring, provide overwhelming independent confirmation of rising temperatures.

Measurements indicate that the first decade of the 2000s was the warmest on record, followed by the 1990s and the 1980s. And despite the cold and snowy winter we've experienced here in Texas, satellite measurements show that, worldwide, January 2010 was one of the hottest months in that record.

•• Human activities produce heat-trapping gases.

Any time we burn a carbon-containing fuel such as coal or natural gas or oil, it releases carbon dioxide into the air. Carbon dioxide can be measured coming out of the tailpipe of our cars or the smokestacks of our factories. Other heat-trapping gases, such as methane and nitrous oxide, are also produced by agriculture and waste disposal. The effect of these gases on heat energy in the atmosphere is well understood, including factors such as the amplification of the warming by increases in humidity.

•• Heat-trapping gases are very likely responsible for most of the warming observed over the past half century.

There is no question that natural causes, such as changes in energy from the sun, natural cycles and volcanoes, continue to affect temperature today. Human activity has also increased the amounts of tiny, light-scattering particles within the atmosphere. But despite years of intensive observations of the Earth system, no one has been able to propose a credible alternative mechanism that can explain the present-day warming without heat-trapping gases produced by human activities.

•• The higher the levels of heat-trapping gases in the atmosphere, the higher the risk of potentially dangerous consequences for humans and our environment.

A recent federal report, "Global Climate Change Impacts in the United States," commissioned in 2008 by the George W. Bush administration, presents a clear picture of how climate change is expected to affect our society, our economy and our natural resources. Rising sea levels threaten our coasts; increasing weather variability, including heat waves, droughts, heavy rainfall events and even winter storms, affect our infrastructure, energy and even our health.

The reality of these key points is not just our opinion. The national academies of science of 32 nations, and every major scientific organization in the United States whose members include climate experts, have issued statements endorsing these points. The entire faculty of the Department of Atmospheric Sciences at Texas A&M as well as the Climate System Science group at the University of Texas have issued their own statements endorsing these views (atmo.tamu.edu/weather-and-climate/climate-change-statement; www.ig.utexas.edu/jsg/css/statement.html). In fact, to the best of our knowledge, there are no climate scientists in Texas who disagree with the mainstream view of climate science.

We are all aware of the news reports describing the stolen e-mails from climate scientists and the errors in the IPCC reports. While aspects of climate change impacts have been overstated, none of the errors or allegations of misbehavior undermine the science behind any of the statements made above. In particular, they do not alter the conclusions that humans have taken over from nature as the dominant influence on our climate.

Source: Houston Chronicle, *March 7, 2010*
http://www.chron.com/opinion/outlook/article/On-global-warming-the-science-is-solid-1623018.php

Robin Warshaw, "Eating Healthfully During Stressful Times"

WebMD is a for-profit organization dedicated to providing up-to-date medical information to the general public.

You just found out that your glowing engine light means another repair bill. That will strain your checking account, which you've already been juggling like a circus performer.

The repair shop vending machine stands nearby, offering sweet, fatty, crunchy and salty snacks. You make your choice, hoping to banish worry with high-calorie help, even though you're not really hungry.

Yet a candy bar or bag of chips gives only a momentary boost to sagging spirits. Refined sugars and starches in most packaged snack foods "make you feel better for a minute, then worse," says Bethany Thayer, MS, RD, director of wellness programs and strategies at the Henry Ford Health System in Detroit and a spokesperson for the American Dietetic Association.

Emotional Eating and Stress Eating

When you feel tense, stress eating or emotional eating seem to be triggered like an automatic response. That's especially so if your body reacts strongly to

15   stress-released hormones. A 2010 study from the University of Michigan showed
      that when levels of the stress hormone cortisol were boosted in healthy, non-
      stressed adults, they ate more snack foods.

          Indeed, stress may increase your desire for doughnuts, ice cream, and other high-
      fat or sugary foods. You also are likely to eat fewer regular meals and fewer vegeta-
20   bles. That may be why you grab a handful of cookies during stressful moments
      instead of healthy snacks such as baby carrots or a few almonds. Not surprising,
      then, that stress eaters gain weight more often than those who aren't stress eaters.

Find New Outlets for Stress

      "Emotional or stress eating soon becomes a habit that changes how you eat regu-
25   larly," Thayer says. Healthy eating and good nutrition disappear as your daily meal
      plan starts looking like the menu for a Cub Scout sleepover.

          "The food drives your behavior and your behavior drives your food choice," says
      Susan Kleiner, PhD, RD, a specialist in nutrition and human performance and author
      of *The Good Mood Diet*. "You are stuck until you put your foot down."

30   You can break the stress eating cycle and enjoy a healthful diet, even if difficult
      times continue, with these effective ideas:

- **Build a good nutritional foundation.** Prepare your brain and body in advance
  and you'll be better able to handle stress when it happens. To keep your emotions in balance, eat regularly during the day, every four or five hours.

35
- **Enjoy complex carbohydrates.** Have oatmeal, raisin bran and other whole-grain
  cereals and breads, as well as brown rice, whole-grain pasta, vegetables, beans,
  fruits, and nonfat milk. These complex carbohydrates help your brain make the
  feel-good chemical serotonin, which counteracts stress, says Thayer. Moderate
  amounts of healthy fats from olives, avocadoes, nuts, seeds, fatty fish, nut but-
40   ters and olive oil also help, adds Kleiner.

- **Recognize what's happening.** When stressful events or thoughts trigger the
  urge to eat, stop and evaluate first. Are you hungry or not? Rate your hunger on
  a scale from 1 to 10. Ask yourself when was the last time you ate, to see if your
  body needs food right now. "Often, negative emotions trigger what feels like
45   hunger but is really just a habitual response to eat to get rid of negative feelings," says Elissa S. Epel, PhD, associate professor of psychiatry at the University
  of California, San Francisco, and a researcher on stress and eating.

- **Try a little mindfulness.** Derail your automatic trip to the cookie jar by becoming more aware of your eating patterns. Mindful eating encourages you to use
50   your senses to choose foods that please you and are nourishing to your body.
  Pay attention to the physical cues of fullness or hunger that your body sends.
  Use these to make decisions about when to begin eating and when to stop.

- **Have a Plan B . . . and C.** The stress-eating urge usually hits suddenly, so keep
  healthy snacks with you wherever you go. Try small packets of nuts or trail mix
55   (without added sweets or salt), apples, or bananas. Those better options will
  help you bypass high-calorie comfort. When possible, Kleiner advises eating

protein and complex carbohydrates together, such as cheese with a slice of whole-grain bread.

- Another great option: a small piece of dark chocolate (72% cocoa is good). "You don't need to eat a ton of it," Kleiner says. 60

- **Fool yourself.** In difficult moments, do you crave crunchy snacks like chips or pretzels? Keep cut-up carrots and celery ready in the refrigerator. Soy chips are also a healthier choice than most fried or baked crunchy snacks.

- **Have a sweet tooth?** Fruit provides natural sweetness that can reduce your urge for high sugar items. 65

- **Out of sight really does help.** If you must keep stress eating temptations like cookies or chips at home for others, store those foods behind larger packages or stacks of dishes. In the freezer, use bags of frozen vegetables to block your view of the ice cream container. When you're commuting to work or running errands, avoid driving past the bakery or fast-food restaurants. 70

- **Call on a substitute.** To make stress eating less automatic, you need to find better ways to deal with everyday hassles and ongoing tensions. Choose a healthy stress-busting alternative such as going for a walk or run, listening to music, calling a friend for a chat, brushing your cat or dog, or just sitting quietly.

Instead of eating, try one of the solutions mentioned above. Add it to your action 75 choices if it works or try a different one next time. By finding healthier alternatives, you'll feel more in control. Then you'll be more prepared for the next step: "You have to figure out what's causing the stress and work to alleviate that," Thayer says.

Source: WebMD.com, June 27, 2011. © 2011 WebMD, LLC.
http://www.webmd.com/parenting/fun-an d-fit-family-11/stress-proof-eating

---

Thinking Rhetorically About Credibility: Expanded Outline

Now that you've gotten some practice with this kind of analysis, choose one of the informal selections included here. Then, use the expanded outline below to work your way through the different goals that underlie and organize this text:

Step One: *Identifying Credibility: What Makes This Writer Qualified to Speak on This Issue?*

º On what basis does the writer claim to speak on this subject? What kinds of expertise does the writer claim? What types of credentials does the writer present?

º Where in the text do you see the clearest proof that this kind of authority is being claimed? Which features (e.g., subject matter, word choice, organization, or tone) would you say best illustrate this?

Step Two: *Assessing Credibility: What Makes These Qualifications Valuable or Relevant?*

º How are the writer's expertise and credentials related to the topic at hand?

○ To what extent does the writer verify this expertise or credentials?

○ What other kinds of expertise or types of credentials might further enhance the writer's credibility?

Step Three: *Asserting Credibility: How Do These Qualifications Influence the Rhetorical Choices the Writer Makes?*

○ How do these qualifications help accomplish the writer's overall goal?

○ How do these qualifications appeal to the writer's target audience?

○ How do these qualifications help convey the writer's main points?

Step Four: Defending Credibility: How Might You Challenge the Writer's Credibility?

○ What forms of expertise or types of qualification does the writer lack?

○ To what extent am I qualified to weigh in on this topic? What are the specific factors (i.e., what knowledge or expertise, what interest or background) that determine my own credibility?

○ How does my own credibility compare to that claimed by this writer? Is either form more legitimate?

Step Five: *Rethinking Credibility: How Would You Go About Revising This Writing?*

○ What information or data would you add to enhance the writer's credibility?

○ What decisions about language or tone would you make to enhance the writer's credibility?

Step Six: *How Do I Put This Into Writing?*

○ How do I summarize my findings in writing?

Formal Writing Selections

While the selections gathered above raise questions about writers' use of evidence, support, and proof, the readings included below examine the issue of credibility from a broader cultural perspective. What are the topics and debates, they ask, that most directly challenge our beliefs about what is right? What are the settings in which we find ourselves most doubtful about the truth of what we're being told?

Looking at a representative range of settings in American life—from school to medicine, celebrity culture to the Web—the essays that follow offer their own answers to these questions. Exploring situations in which there is considerable doubt about what is and is not true, each one presents readers with an opportunity to think more critically about how we define and defend credibility. At the same time, these selections also provide us with another opportunity to analyze the issue of credibility in rhetorical terms. That is, these readings also ask you to think about the role that credibility plays in organizing the writing itself, how a writer's goals and assumptions about credibility shape the other rhetorical choices that get made.

Pamela Rutledge, "#Selfies: Narcissism or Self-Exploration?"

The Web not only gives us countless opportunities to put ourselves on public display, it also provides us with the tools for tailoring this image to our own particular needs. A case in point, notes psychologist Pamela Rutledge, is the "selfie": a picture one takes of oneself and posts online. Sampling some of the most popular "selfie types" in today's culture, Rutledge invites us to reflect on the ways this technology influences—even alters—the ways we view ourselves.

"It's not a big leap to go from a pursuit of self-exploration to the desire for self-portrait."

Selfies are pictures you take of yourself tagged with #selfie or just with #me. They are showing up all across social networks like Facebook or Instagram—often but not exclusively posted by women. As the numbers and frequency of selfies increase, the phenomenon has garnered attention. In our globally connected 24/7 world, anything that gets attention, gets talked about. Some view these self-created self- 5 portraits as proof of cultural—or at least generational— narcissism and moral decline. I, on the other hand, view them as a by-product of technology-enabled self-exploration.

Western civilization has a rich history of self-portraiture that continues to expand with technological innovations. Where once they were the province of the elite 10 either in status or skill, cell phones and Instagram have democratized self-portraiture, making them less precious and more fun. Voila selfies.

Selfies aren't new, in spite of the recent surge. Self-portraits tagged as #selfie began to appear on the photo-sharing site Flickr and on MySpace back in 2004 and the first definition of a "'selfie'" gained entry on UrbanDictionary.com by 2005 15 (albeit spelled "'selfy'"). But camera phones, especially those with front and back lens action, have made taking selfies faster and easier than ever.

Young women are the biggest population of selfie-posters and you know it's going mainstream when marketers jump on the bandwagon. The Fashion Conglomerate Westfield launched a contest called "Selfies Style" soliciting selfies that 20 highlight individual style after research indicated that six out of every ten women used their mobile device to take self-portraits, most of which end up on Facebook.

Humans have long demonstrated an interest in self-exploration. From early Greeks to present day, people have used self-study and self-observation to ex- 25 plore identity and sense of self. Trying to figure out who we are and what we're about is a distinctly human pursuit for almost everyone, whether you are trying to find greater consciousness or figure out what moved you to buy the blue shoes.

30   It's not a big leap to go from a pursuit of self-exploration to the desire for self-portrait. As far back as Ancient Egypt, people of wealth and power have commissioned self-portraits, although less for self-exploration than glorification. Nevertheless, a number of technological breakthroughs throughout history have continued to lower the barriers to the creation and display of self-portraits.

35   We take mirrors for granted, but their invention in the 15th century let artists paint themselves, which some, like Albrecht Durer, did with gusto. The camera in the 1860s launched a new era of selfies, but the technology demanded skill and expense. As the camera evolved, more and increasingly creative versions of self-portraiture appeared. Digital cameras freed portraiture from the cost and time lag of film.

40   Then mobile phones became cameras, too. By 2012, 86% of the population of the US had a cell phone, lagging behind a host of countries like the UK, Italy, Spain and China. You might not always take your camera with you, but you always have your phone. The floodgates were open on our ability to not only document everything at no marginal cost, but share them as well. (Mobile Internet access allows

45   easy real time posting but people can also post to a Facebook page using text messaging.)

Western civilization has a rich history of self-portraiture that expands with technological access. Cell phones and Instagram have democratized self-portraiture, making them less precious and turning them into selfies.

50   In spite of the wealth of negative headlines, there are several reasons for selfies that have nothing to do with narcissism.

- **Selfies facilitate self and identity exploration**. One of the most effective ways to know yourself is to see yourself as others see you. Selfies offer the opportunities to show facets of yourself, such as the arty side, the silly side, or the glamorous side. We learn about people by accumulating information over time. Our understanding of everything, include other people, is a synthesis of all the things we know about them. By offering different aspects through images, we are sharing more of ourselves, becoming more authentic and transparent—things that digital connectivity encourages.

55

- **Selfies can clearly identify a passion or interest that reinforces our social identity**, like the selfies of Japanese teens doing the Kamehameha moves from the popular *Dragon Ball* manga and anime series

60

- **Selfies can be more about the context than the self**, such as an artistic expression of fashion or photographic technique.

- **Selfies can be a transitory question**, such as seeking feedback from a friend— "Do you like this outfit?"

65

- **Selfies are not all about seeking external validation**. People often say that posters of selfies just want approval. We ALL seek approval. Humans are social animals, driven by the need for connection and social validation. We want to be valued, appreciated, and included in the groups that matter to us.

70

- **Selfies have many layers.** As viewers, we are aware that every selfie is self-generated. We also take this into account with every selfie—we inherently look for the sub-text about what is being revealed.

- **Selfies feel more real than traditional portraits.** Selfies are popular with celebrities who cultivate their fans because in their casual rawness, selfies feel more immediate, intimate and personal, enhancing the celebrity's connection to their fans.

75

- **Selfies can be normalizing.** For years, people have been concerned about the amount of images of "'perfect'" women on the Internet. Between profiles pictures and selfies on photo-sharing sites, there are many more photos of "'real'" people images compared to idealized images by thousands. The "ugly selfie" has also emerged in part a response to criticism about narcissism and in part a self-exploration of motive. The push for authenticity has emerged, sometimes through humor as in Reddit's "Pretty Girls Ugly Faces" meme, in which users upload photos of themselves with disgusting faces next to the conventional shot. One artist commented that the ugly selfie challenges her own vanity and puts her personality back into the self-documentation.

80

85

- **Selfies offer users the ability to create a life narrative through images**—silly, ugly, pretty, whatever. Images interact differently with the brain than text. Images encode experience. When we look at old photos, our brains revive the event, allowing us to relive some of the emotions, context and experience. We can look back on our motives and actions and gain insight we couldn't' get in any other way.

90

And maybe it's okay to celebrate yourself along the way. What's your opinion about selfies? Let me know here.

Source: Psychology Today, April 8, 2013. © 2013 Sussex Publishers, LLC. *http://www.psychologytoday.com/blog/positively-media/201304/selfies-narcissism-or-self-exploration*

▌ Discussion/Writing Prompts

1. Rutledge argues that, contrary to public concerns, the increase in self-portraiture online does not represent a shift toward greater "narcissism." How credible do you find this claim? What kind of support does she provide to bolster this claim? Do you find this support credible? How, or how not? [Rhetorical Analysis of Credibility]

2. What do you make of the term "selfie"? What images or associations does it evoke for you? Is it a term you feel comfortable applying to your own acts of self-display online? Why, or why not? [Personal Reflection]

3. "Images," Rutledge declares, "interact differently with the brain than text. Images encode experience." Take a moment to analyze the specific point Rutledge seems to be making here. How does an image "encode experience"? How is this different from

the way a written text captures or records experience? And do you agree with Rutledge that this difference is important? [Close Reading]

4. Rutledge's essay works, in part, as an attempt to challenge the way the term "selfie" is typically defined. How effective do find this effort to be? In your view, does Rutledge succeed in redefining the "selfie"? What alternative definition does she offer? And in your view, is this definition superior to the conventional one? [Analyzing Rhetorical Modes]

5. "Selfies," Rutledge writes, "offer the opportunities to show facets of yourself, such as the arty side, the silly side, or the glamorous side." Write a one-page response in which you analyze and evaluate this particular claim. Do you agree that "selfie" technology provides greater freedom to "show facets" of ourselves? Does such freedom carry any downside? If so, what? [Argument]

6. How do you think Frederic Neuman ("Should You Trust Your Doctor?") would assess the rise of "selfie" culture? Would be more inclined than Rutledge to diagnose the rise of this practice as evidence of "narcissism"? [Compare and Contrast]

7. Research the ways different people use "selfies" to construct images of others. As you sample a range of different "selfies" online, what kinds of images recur most? And how do different people use these images to convey different messages about themselves? [Research]

Frederic Neuman, "Should You Trust Your Doctor?"

Is a doctor's advice always reliable? Is it always safe to assume that the information we hear from representatives of the medical establishment is true? Exploring the ways this phenomenon plays out within the medical profession, Frederic Neuman shares anecdotal evidence suggesting that doctor's assumptions and expectations can sometimes lead to questionable advice.

"We all know stories about doctors who gave their patient a clean bill of health only to see that patient drop dead at their doorstep."

When your life hangs in the balance, you should not trust your doctor. There is too much at stake. If you are a defendant in a criminal trial confronting a life sentence, you should not trust your lawyer either. You need to get involved personally. You need to check on everything that is being done. Consult other doctors. If your problem is legal, consult with other lawyers. For that matter, I don't think you should trust your accountant if there is a lot of money involved—if, for instance, the I.R.S. has attached your bank account and is claiming that you owe them more money than you make in a year. Important matters should not be left entirely in the hands of professionals who work for you. As everyone knows, professionals who are expert—including doctors—have been known to make egregious mistakes, and, in the case of doctors, fatal mistakes.

We all know stories about doctors who gave their patient a clean bill of health only to see that patient drop dead at their doorstep. Of course, this does not mean the doctor made a mistake. People get sick suddenly and unpredictably. But there are also documented accounts of doctors who read an X-ray as normal, when it plainly showed a cancer. I know of a doctor who claimed a patient's eye was diseased, when it was not; and then proceeded to operate on the wrong eye! Luckily the eye he wanted to remove was normal. Over the years I have had a number of malpractice lawyers in my practice, so I have heard numerous stories of this sort—some that would make your hair stand up on end.

But doctors can make a different kind of mistake. What I found strange when I first started running the health anxiety clinics was how many patients had been told they had a fatal disease when they did not! Rather than making the mistake that everyone worries a doctor might make, namely missing the diagnosis of a deadly disease, their doctors worried them unnecessarily by diagnosing deadly diseases that were not present. That happened to me once. I had a swollen leg. Being a health worrier myself at that time, I had already made sure by repeatedly testing myself that I did not have the fatal kidney disease the doctor, when I finally got around to visiting him, informed me blithely that I had. I was able to dismiss his opinion out of hand. But I have had patients who forever after worried about the disease they were told they had.

But we all depend to some extent on doctors—and lawyers and accountants too. Most of them are competent. But it is difficult for a lay person to judge whether a particular practitioner is one of them. I have gone to the same dentist for forty years. I like him. My teeth are in good shape. I have even recommended him to friends. But I really don't know if he is a good dentist. What I would need to know to make that judgment would be how he handled difficult cases—and I don't even know what a difficult case is.

Most of the time we judge these professionals by their reputation. That is the best we can do. We ask a doctor what he thinks of other doctors; but we can be misled sometimes anyway.

When my wife was pregnant for the first time, she complained of a pain in one of her ribs. There was a hard lump there. Being the health worrier I was, I started worrying about malignant bony tumors that are found sometimes at that location. Even my wife was worried a little. I asked a surgical resident, who was a friend, whom *he* would go to see for a consultation if it were his wife. He told me about the surgeon who had the very best reputation at N.Y.U. When this man examined my wife, he went "hmmm." He said he wasn't sure about what this lump was. I asked him about the possibility of it being the bony sarcoma I had fixed on. That tumor was uncommon, he said. He recommended watching it for a while.

When we were walking home, I was fuming. I wasn't a surgeon, but I knew that if it was a possibility she had cancer, we did not want to wait around to see if it got worse! A moment later we happened to walk by the radiologist's office that my wife had gone to in connection with her pregnancy. I suggested stopping in to see him. The radiologist did an X-ray and told us that the lump I was concerned about was the end of her rib. A normal bump on the normal end of a rib. It was unequivocal. He showed it to me on the X-ray. My God, I thought, shouldn't a surgeon with a good reputation by able to decide how to tell a cancer from the normal end of a rib? Why didn't he order an X-ray?

All right. I don't want to overstate this problem. Most doctors I have known—and I have known a lot of them—were competent and responsible. But some surely were not. So, what advice do I give to someone who is looking for a physician?

Look up the doctors in your community. Limit your choices to those who are board-certified. See if they have had particular clinical training and experiences relevant to the sorts of problems you have. Ask other doctors in the community about him/her. Go see the doctor. Does he/she see patients more or less on time—and make a point of being reachable by telephone? Is he/she friendly? Does he/she listen? (good) Is he/she arrogant and unwilling to consider your concerns, however outlandish they may be? (bad) Do records get lost? Does he/she call with laboratory results? Is he/she rude? (very bad, but not uncommon) Does the doctor do tests just to reassure you or because you ask for them? (bad) Does he/she prescribe drugs just because the drug rep left free samples? (I am particularly annoyed by general practitioners who give out anti-depressants carelessly without arranging for proper follow-up.) In the end, it is reasonable to go to a doctor whom you like.

Choosing the right doctor is often put in terms of trust. Can you trust the doctor to do the right thing? Start off with the idea that even very good doctors do the wrong things sometimes. There is so much to know. They may not know as much as someone else—but the good doctors will go out of their way to learn what they may not know. And they will ask for help from other doctors. I would trust some doctors to treat some conditions out of their area of specialization more than I would trust a specialist in that field whom I knew was careless. They can be relied on to approach a medical problem carefully. I cannot describe what goes into having good clinical judgment, but it is a real thing. I am not sure exactly what quality of mind and character it involves. It is a kind of being sensible.

And good doctors care.

I saw one of the many patients who have been told in error that they have hypoglycemia—low blood sugar. Some studies suggest that this diagnosis is made incorrectly about 95% of the time. The symptoms of hypoglycemia seem similar to those of the anxiety disorders, particularly panic disorder, so the two conditions can be confused easily, especially for someone who knows only one and not the other.

This particular patient had been told by a doctor that she had hypoglycemia. She became frightened and carried snacks around with her wherever she went. Given her blood sugar level, I could not understand the doctor's thinking. I called him up and asked him.

"Well, I think there really is something like reactive hypoglycemia," he said, indi- 95
cating that he knew that others did not think so. Reactive hypoglycemia is a pre-
cipitous drop in sugar levels simply as the result of eating. (True hypoglycemia is a
serious condition and can result from acute alcoholic intoxication or endocrine
tumors—or a number of other illnesses.)

"All right," I said. "But her blood sugar is well within the normal range!" 100

"Okay, what do you want me to do? Send her back and I'll tell her she *doesn't*
have hypoglycemia."

I was shocked. Didn't he care one way or the other?

But this doctor sticks out in my mind because he was so unusual.

The real issue is not which doctors can be trusted, but which conditions are such 105
that you can trust any doctor and which conditions are so significant and so difficult to manage that they require going to a particular—especially competent—
physician. You can trust any doctor to treat a sore throat or an ear infection (not
that there are not controversies even in the treatment of these commonplace conditions.) When it comes to replacing your aortic valve to ward off heart failure, you 110
should travel wherever you need to go to see one of the three or four surgeons in
the country who specialize in that operation. This is a commonsense idea.

I have six lawyers in my immediate family, but when someone in the family ran
into a problem with age and sex discrimination, we had to find someone else who
specialized in labor law. 115

Of course, in the end, if you grow dissatisfied with your doctor, you should find
another.

Source: Psychology Today, *June 30, 2013*
http://www.psychologytoday.com/blog/fighting-fear/201306/should-you-trust-your-doctor

▨ Discussion/Writing Prompts

1. Like the physician feedback he discusses, Neuman's essay functions on one level as a
   collection of advice regarding how we all should think about and respond to what
   doctors tell us. How well does this essay work in this regard? Do you find the advice
   Neuman offers—the points he makes, the suggestions he offers—to be credible?
   How, or how not? [Rhetorical Analysis of Credibility]

2. At the most basic level, Neuman's analysis invites us to reconsider the credentials of
   the doctors giving us medical advice. How do you respond to this invitation? Can
   you think of an example or experience from your own life that would seem to
   confirm the validity of Neuman's warning? An example or experiences that would
   seem to challenge it? [Personal Reflection]

3. Put yourself in the position of one of the doctors Neuman references here. In a one-
   page essay, discuss how you would go about redefining the role you play in relation to
   your patients. What, specifically, about the conventional role of "doctor" would you

change? What particular advantages or benefits would these changes bring? [Close Reading]

4. In many ways, Neuman is suggesting that doctors adopt a different rhetorical approach when dealing with patients. What rhetorical mode do you think would be most effective in helping doctors convey advice to their patients? What makes this particular mode preferable to others? [Analyzing Rhetorical Modes]

5. First, take a closer look at the kinds of details about his wife's case that Neuman presents. What stands out to you about them? What message or larger point do these details seem designed to get across? Next, write a two- or three-page essay in which you evaluate the effectiveness of this strategy for presenting Neuman's argument. Is using personal experience in this way an effective tactic? Do you find it persuasive? Why, or why not? [Argument]

6. Pamela Rutledge ("#Selfies: Narcissism or Self-Exploration?") is another writer who explores the issue of trust. How do you think her depiction of the online world compares with Neuman's portrait of doctor/patient relationships? Do these two portraits raise similar questions about whom or what we should believe? [Compare/Contrast]

7. As the above questions suggest, Neuman's essay can be understood as part of a larger public debate over health care in the United States. Choose one example of this larger debate, and research the ways it is waged publicly. What specific issue is being debated? What different groups does it pit against each other, and what are the key differences in each one's point of view? [Research]

Jeff Karon, "A Positive Solution for Plagiarism"

There is a lot of concern over plagiarism among students, but do we have a clear understanding of why this phenomenon is so widespread? Jeff Karon, formerly a visiting instructor at the University of South Florida, offers some novel thoughts about addressing what may stand as the biggest challenge to credibility within higher education. Currently, Jeff Karon is a freelance editing and writing consultant owns an academic tutoring and training service, The Honorable Classroom.

"The solution should be positive; that is, show students how to act as responsible scholars and writers."

We know that students plagiarize. We suppose that plagiarism, as well as academic dishonesty in general, has increased over the past few years, decades, or century—depending on which academic ax we choose to grind.

The caveats are familiar: Perhaps cheating just is easier than it used to be (most 5 honors students who are caught plagiarizing say they did so because it was "easy"). Perhaps we are better at detecting plagiarism because of software such as Google and Turnitin. Or perhaps we forget that every generation, at least since the ancient Romans and Greeks, complains that the next one is composed of lazy, possibly illiterate, youngsters willing to cut ethical corners.

But a good dose of skepticism toward the doomsayers doesn't make the worry go away. For example, a July 21 article in *The Chronicle* on a New York University professor who vowed to stop pursuing plagiarists has drawn 249 comments, several of which were impassioned denunciations of institutional responses to the problem. Dealing with student plagiarism is a nagging, seemingly endless problem for academics, judging from the number of articles, blog posts, and forum discussions on the topic. Indeed, I've contributed to some of those discussions but have yet to find any consensus emerge.

I've organized and participated in conference panels on plagiarism, held workshops for college instructors and schoolteachers on the subject, and for several years have used the methods I'm about to describe. I also began my teaching career with a zero-tolerance policy, which meant that I have been involved in campus judicial proceedings, a step that drains just about everyone touched by the accusation.

But as the Internet has matured, I decided that I did not want to spend time as a cyber-cop. More important, my goal should be to help inculcate honor and integrity rather than build a culture of fear and accusation.

It's easy to find excellent articles and Web sites on dealing with plagiarism. From those sources, we can develop four general guidelines for an effective response:

- The solution should be positive; that is, show students how to act as responsible scholars and writers. The same tone should be reflected in the syllabus. I have seen many syllabi in which the penalties for plagiarism are laid out in excruciating detail, with no positive models or behavior mentioned. Surely by now we know that positive motivation trumps the negative variety.
- It should help students avoid plagiarism rather than focus on our catching it.
- The solution should objectively strengthen both students and teachers.
- It should also make students and teachers feel as though they are stronger.

Those seem to me to be minimal requirements, yet they often are not met in practice. Before laying out a workable solution, let's review some approaches whose weaknesses contribute to the seemingly endless discussions of plagiarism.

Draconian consequences. The instructor who threatens maximum damage if plagiarism is detected usually stakes out the moral high ground. Syllabi and accompanying class discussions list everything that will befall the student, including possible expulsion.

Strength: If applied consistently, without regard for extenuating circumstances, this approach seems to work particularly well for teachers who are both imperious and admired by their students. I knew one colleague, a tenured professor of literature and writing, who threatened to ruin, as nearly as possible, the reputations of offending students. Somehow he still inspired them.

Weakness: Instructors who use this tactic set an adversarial tone at the beginning of a course. Although some can inhabit the Professor Kingsfield character from *The Paper Chase*, many simply come off as nasty or suspicious. And approaching plagiarism this way is dispiriting—it never energizes students or teachers. In the end, it often doesn't prevent enough plagiarism to counter its weaknesses.

Preventive construction. A teacher who is concerned about plagiarism and has read about strategies may attempt to construct every assignment in a way that precludes plagiarism.

Strength: Rethinking assignments—freshening them up—often produces new energy in a course. Those who reflect often on pedagogy will be attracted to this approach.

Weakness: The approach often means devising assignments with a narrow scope. But it's important to train students to explore widely. They need to be able to sift through all sorts of sources, and closely tailored assignments may be too restrictive. Such assignments certainly don't simulate the strengths needed in graduate or professional school. And sooner or later, we either will run out of ideas for assignments or will be lulled into a false sense of security.

Dedicated discussion. Some teachers discuss extensively in class the nature and consequences of plagiarism, believing that such time is well spent.

Strength: Some students may not understand what constitutes plagiarism or its consequences. By discussing it carefully in class, instructors demonstrate an awareness of that problem.

Weakness: Merely talking with students, especially about a critical topic, is a poor way to ensure that they will act correctly. Giving quizzes on the topic is a move in the right direction. But a quiz still encourages passivity. Plagiarism and academic dishonesty are actions taken by people; powerful lessons about it require actions as well.

A workable solution. The first writing assignment I give students in my writing courses involves plagiarism as a topic. I ask them to investigate and read resources on the Web assembled by experts on the subject such as Nick Carbone, a new-media consultant for Bedford/St. Martin's, and Bruce Leland, a professor emeritus at Western Illinois University. I ask students to take notes on the readings, especially on how both authors are unhappy with standard approaches to preventing plagiarism and academic dishonesty. I tell them to pay special attention to Carbone's discussion of Dos and don'ts, a list he developed after deciding that his previous approaches to fighting plagiarism adopted an inappropriate tone, and to Leland's extensive list of resources that instructors can use to deal with plagiarism.

Then I ask students to find a Web site that offers free essays for download. I provide a central source, such as "Cheating 101: Internet Paper Mills," available at www.coastal.edu/library/presentations/mills2.html, though there are many others.

Each student has to download one paper (or as much of one as is permitted by the site) and analyze its strengths and weaknesses. They must bring to class a copy of the paper as well as their notes on their reading, and deliver oral reports.

The idea is for students to read materials written by teachers for teachers, rather than something written just for students. The explicit lesson is for them to learn 95 about plagiarism and academic dishonesty. An implicit lesson is that instructors already are aware of free papers and other Internet dodges. Even if you, as a faculty member, are not particularly computer-savvy, students will assume from this assignment that you understand how to track down plagiarism.

By analyzing these "free essays" before the class, students learn firsthand that 100 the papers available over the Internet often are far inferior to what they could produce on their own. When they occasionally happen on a strong paper, they will remark that it is too good: No professor would believe that such a professionally written piece had come from a student for a course assignment.

You need not guide the students' choices of papers: Their own interests and 105 majors will do that. Through this assignment, they are engaging in research from the first day of the course, and are practicing critical reading. They understand that you will treat them like adults, since you have assigned them to read authoritative, friendly articles from Web sites that speak to adult professionals. And other than require that they concentrate on a paper's strengths and weaknesses, you need 110 not guide the analyses: Students of all writing levels will demonstrate that they can pick apart someone else's work.

You can substitute other Web sites or articles, of course. But you should give students separate credit for their Web-site notes and for their critique of the downloaded paper—both of which should be physical copies. Students who took 115 notes can be distinguished easily from those who did not, which allows you to teach the lesson that strong scholars or professionals take notes. The physical copies also allow you to collect the assignments if you run short on time for the oral reports, though I encourage you to allow everyone to present.

This assignment builds: (1) a direct awareness of plagiarism and its responses; 120 (2) research skills, since students immediately follow and analyze reliable Web sources; and (3) presentation skills, all without creating a hostile or adversarial atmosphere. The assignment can be adapted for large (or online) courses by creating a blog or online discussion area, although nothing beats the in-person connection. (I also ask students to introduce themselves by name every time they present. 125 My philosophy is to maximize what any assignment can achieve.)

I have employed this approach with undergraduate and graduate, traditional and nontraditional students. During the past two semesters, I used it in online classes to great effect. Any method that makes both students and professors feel strong is worth trying. 130

Source: Chronicle of Higher Education, *September 18, 2012*
http://chronicle.com/article/A-Positive-Solution-for/134498/

▪ Discussion/Writing Prompts

1. Karon's essay emphasizes the importance of approaching the issue of plagiarism positively rather than negatively. To what extent does this same idea apply to Karon's own discussion here? Does this essay succeed in encouraging you to approach the issue of plagiarism positively? [Rhetorical Analysis of Credibility]

2. Can you think of a moment in school where you referenced, borrowed, or copied the work of somebody else? As you reflect upon this experience now, do you think it's accurate to characterize it as an act of "plagiarism"? If so, do you think the "solution" Karon proposes would have been helpful? How, or how not [Personal Reflection]

3. At different points in the essay, Karon uses the terms "academic dishonesty" and "plagiarism." How do you understand the relationship between these terms? In your view, are they synonyms? And how does your definition of these terms compare to the ways Karon is defining them? [Close Reading]

4. Can you think of an approach to plagiarism that would serve as an alternative to the one Karon outlines? Do you think the essay would benefit from the inclusion of such a comparison? If so, how? [Analyzing Rhetorical Modes]

5. Karon cites a number of reasons in support of his "solution" to plagiarism:

   "[It] builds: (1) a direct awareness of plagiarism and its responses; (2) research skills, since students immediately follow and analyze reliable Web sources; and (3) presentation skills, all without creating a hostile or adversarial atmosphere."

   Write a two-page essay in which you evaluate the reasoning Karon offers here. Does this reasoning seem logical? Persuasive? Why, or why not? [Argument]

6. Whether it concerns doctors and patients or students and teachers, Karon and Fredric Neuman ("Should You Trust Your Doctor?") are both concerned with how to ensure the credibility of information that gets exchanged between people. In a two- or three-page essay, explore the way these discussions compare. Does Karon's solution to plagiarism echo or parallel Neuman's recommendations to patients in their interactions with doctors? What are the key similarities and differences? [Compare and Contrast]

7. Choose a recent scandal or controversy that involved allegations of plagiarism, and research its specifics. Whom did this scandal involve? How was it uncovered and by whom? And what sort of coverage did it receive once it was exposed? [Research]

Stephanie Pappas, "Oscar Psychology: Why Celebrities Fascinate Us"

Stories about celebrities are a staple of our daily media diet. But can we really explain why this is so? What accounts for our fascination with the lives and loves, the foibles and failures, of famous people? Stephanie Pappas, a senior science writer for LiveScience, delves more deeply into our culture-wide obsession with celebrity. Why are we so hungry for information about the rich and famous? And should such information be believed?

> *"'[P]arasocial' relationships—the psychological term for the kind of one-sided relationships fans have with stars—are easier than ever."*

From the Oscar's red carpet to the tabloids lining supermarket checkout lines, celebrity obsession is everywhere. Even the most casual moviegoer might find him or herself flipping through a slideshow of Academy Award fashion after the big event. So why do we fixate on celebrities?

In most cases, it's perfectly natural. Humans are social creatures, psychologists   5
say, and we evolved—and still live—in an environment where it paid to pay attention to the people at the top. Celebrity fascination may be an outgrowth of this tendency, nourished by the media and technology.

"In our society, celebrities act like a drug," said James Houran, a psychologist at the consulting firm HVS Executive Search who helped create the first question-   10
naire to measure celebrity worship. "They're around us everywhere. They're an easy fix."

The evolution of an Oscar viewer
It's only relatively recently in human history that people have had near-constant access to celebrity news and gossip. But celebrities themselves are nothing new. People have   15
long looked to monarchs for social, and even fashion, cues: The now-ubiquitous white wedding dress caught on after Queen Victoria wore one in 1840.

Even hunter-gatherer societies in which material goods are relatively scarce have status hierarchies, said Daniel Kruger, an evolutionary psychologist at the University of Michigan. Other primate species also keep a close eye on the domi-   20
nant individuals in their groups.

"There's a few different reasons for that," Kruger told LiveScience. "One is just learning what high-status individuals do so you might more effectively become one, and two, it's basically political. Knowing what is going on with high-status individuals, you'd be better able to navigate the social scene."   25

Whether Brad Pitt is on good terms with his ex Jennifer Aniston isn't likely to affect the average person's life one way or another, of course, but the social tendency to care is deeply ingrained, Kruger said.

Twittering stars
Stars and the media exploit this tendency. Celebrities give interviews, share juicy   30
information about their personal lives, and even engage directly with fans on sites such as Twitter. The result is that "parasocial" relationships—the psychological term for the kind of one-sided relationships fans have with stars—are easier than ever.

And reaching stardom seems also to be easier than ever. "You have so many
opportunities for celebrities to develop, because there are so many platforms,"
said Stuart Fischoff, an emeritus professor of media psychology at the University
of California, Los Angeles. "There's this explosion of celebrity possibility."

Much celebrity obsession is intentionally cultivated, Kruger said. Talk show
hosts, for example, try to foster a personal connection with their audience.

"It's savvy marketing," Kruger said.

From fan to fanatic

Most of the time, caring about celebrities is no big deal. Even for some obsessed
fans, celebrity worship can provide a social outlet they wouldn't have otherwise had,
Fischoff told LiveScience. For the seriously shy, celebrity fandom can act as a "psychological prosthesis," he said.

"If they weren't going to be interacting with people otherwise, this makes them
at least have a social relationship they didn't have before," Fischoff said. "So it's
making the best out of a bad deal, psychologically."

There are lines, though. Houran and his colleagues found that it's too simplistic
to divide fans into casual, healthy types and wild-eyed stalkers. In fact, celebrity
worship is a continuum, Houran told LiveScience.

"The bad news is, there's a stalker in all of us," he said.

When celebrity worship goes overboard, it usually starts out benign, Houran
said. People enjoy the escapism of celebrity gossip and bond with others over a
favorite star. Next, there's a shift. The person starts thinking of the celebrity constantly, withdrawing from family and friends. Addictive and compulsive behaviors
come into play.

Finally, a very few people reach what's known as the "borderline pathological"
stage, in which they believe they have a close relationship with their favorite celebrity and take that belief quite seriously. When asked if they'd do something illegal
at the request of their favorite celebrity, these people say "yes."

Personality plays a role in pushing people along the path to celebrity stalker-
hood, Houran said. People who are egocentric or who have personality traits such
as irritability, impulsivity and moodiness are more susceptible. The environment
matters, too. People are more susceptible to over-the-top celebrity worship when
they're in a phase of identity adjustment. If a person is going through a divorce,
loses a job or is having relationship problems, celebrity obsession may be a life raft
they cling to.

This identity factor may be why teenagers are so susceptible to worshipping
Justin Bieber or their favorite sports star. Younger people, who are still establishing their identities, are more susceptible to celebrity obsession, Houran said.

"Celebrity worship, at its heart, seems to fill something in a person's life," he said.
"It gives them a sense of identity, a sense of self. It feeds a psychological need.

Source: Live Science, February 24, 2012
http://www.livescience.com/18649-oscar-psychology-celebrity-worship.html

▊ Discussion/Writing Prompts

1. Pappas shows little hesitation in diagnosing "celebrity worship" as a type of disorder. Does this kind of definitive judgment enhance or detract from the essay's overall credibility? Would Pappas' discussion be more persuasive if it evinced greater sympathy for those who remain fascinated by celebrities? Why, or why not? [Rhetorical Analysis of Credibility]

2. Can you think of an example or experience from your own life where you felt "obsessed" with a particular celebrity? If so, who was it? And how would you describe the experience? As you look back, does your fascination with this star still make sense to you now? [Personal Reflection]

3. Pappas makes a very clear decision to explore the phenomenon of celebrity fandom by using the language of psychological diagnosis. What do you make of this decision? Take a closer look at the particular moments in this piece where Pappas utilizes this sort of language to advance her argument. Does the use of such medical terminology shed light on the root causes of celebrity "fascination"? How, or how not? [Close Reading]

4. Pappas uses the examples of specific stars as evidence to support her larger argument about our culture-wide fascination with celebrities. How do you evaluate this rhetorical strategy? In your view, do the examples included here stand for or exemplify a truly widespread cultural trend? [Analyzing Rhetorical Modes]

5. In a one-page essay, create your own argument on this subject. How do you understand our society's celebration of being famous? Does this emphasis foster attitudes that are helpful or positive? If so, what? Or does this emphasis give rise to actions and attitudes that are counterproductive or harmful? If so, what? [Argument]

6. Both Pappas and Pamela Rutledge ("#Selfies: Narcissism or Self-Exploration?") approach social or cultural practices (i.e., celebrity worship and "selfie" photography) from an overtly medical perspective. How do their respective diagnoses compare? Do you find yourself persuaded by each writer's attempt to cast these cultural issues as "psychological" problems? Do you find one diagnosis more persuasive than the other? [Compare and Contrast]

7. Research the question of celebrity obsession that Pappas examines here. Choose a text (e.g., website, magazine article, or blog) that, in your view, exemplifies what Pappas discusses here. [Research]

Academic Writing Selections

The rhetorical analysis modeled above doesn't only apply to the types of informal and formal writing found in the real world. It can also serve as an equally useful framework for examining the kinds of writing that are often taught within the college classroom. Like their real world counterparts, the authors of these academic selections base their choices about how and what to write on considerations of purpose, audience, argument, voice, and credibility.

The two selections below demonstrate the extent to which academic writing is also shaped by rhetorical concepts. More specifically, these examples highlight the role that considerations about credibility play in shaping a writer's choices. Read each selection carefully. Then, answer the questions that follow.

Shirley Jackson, "The Lottery"

While traditions can valuable, creating a sense of community and belonging among members of a given group, they can also be dangerous, fostering an unthinking acceptance of behaviors and beliefs that cause great harm. It is this darker aspect of tradition that Shirley Jackson explores in her classic short story. Detailing what can happen in a community whose members remain blindly loyal to tradition, Jackson offers a cautionary tale about the destructive power of mass conformity.

The morning of June 27th was clear and sunny, with the fresh warmth of a full-summer day; the flowers were blossoming profusely and the grass was richly green. The people of the village began to gather in the square, between the post office and the bank, around ten o'clock; in some towns there were so many people that the lottery took two days and had to be started on June 20th, but in this village, where there were only about three hundred people, the whole lottery took less than two hours, so it could begin at ten o'clock in the morning and still be through in time to allow the villagers to get home for noon dinner.

The children assembled first, of course. School was recently over for the summer, and the feeling of liberty sat uneasily on most of them; they tended to gather together quietly for a while before they broke into boisterous play, and their talk was still of the classroom and the teacher, of books and reprimands. Bobby Martin had already stuffed his pockets full of stones, and the other boys soon followed his example, selecting the smoothest and roundest stones; Bobby and Harry Jones and Dickie Delacroix—the villagers pronounced this name "Dellacroy"—eventually made a great pile of stones in one corner of the square and guarded it against the raids of the other boys. The girls stood aside, talking among themselves, looking over their shoulders at the boys, and the very small children rolled in the dust or clung to the hands of their older brothers or sisters.

Soon the men began to gather, surveying their own children, speaking of planting and rain, tractors and taxes. They stood together, away from the pile of stones in the corner, and their jokes were quiet and they smiled rather than laughed. The women, wearing faded house dresses and sweaters, came shortly after their menfolk. They greeted one another and exchanged bits of gossip as they went to join their husbands. Soon the women, standing by their husbands, began to call to their children, and the children came reluctantly, having to be called four or five times. Bobby Martin ducked under his mother's grasping hand and ran, laughing, back to the pile of stones. His father spoke up sharply, and Bobby came quickly and took his place between his father and his oldest brother.

The lottery was conducted—as were the square dances, the teen club, the Halloween program—by Mr. Summers, who had time and energy to devote to civic activities. He was a round-faced, jovial man and he ran the coal business, and people were sorry for him, because he had no children and his wife was a scold. When he arrived in the square, carrying the black wooden box, there was a murmur of conversation among the villagers, and he waved and called, "Little late today, folks." The postmaster, Mr. Graves, followed him, carrying a three-legged stool, and the stool was put in the center of the square and Mr. Summers set the black box down on it. The villagers kept their distance, leaving a space between themselves and the stool, and when Mr. Summers said, "Some of you fellows want to give me a hand?" there was a hesitation before two men, Mr. Martin and his oldest son, Baxter, came forward to hold the box steady on the stool while Mr. Summers stirred up the papers inside it.

The original paraphernalia for the lottery had been lost long ago, and the black box now resting on the stool had been put into use even before Old Man Warner, the oldest man in town, was born. Mr. Summers spoke frequently to the villagers about making a new box, but no one liked to upset even as much tradition as was represented by the black box. There was a story that the present box had been made with some pieces of the box that had preceded it, the one that had been constructed when the first people settled down to make a village here. Every year, after the lottery, Mr. Summers began talking again about a new box, but every year the subject was allowed to fade off without anything's being done. The black box grew shabbier each year: by now it was no longer completely black but splintered badly along one side to show the original wood color, and in some places faded or stained.

Mr. Martin and his oldest son, Baxter, held the black box securely on the stool until Mr. Summers had stirred the papers thoroughly with his hand. Because so much of the ritual had been forgotten or discarded, Mr. Summers had been successful in having slips of paper substituted for the chips of wood that had been used for generations. Chips of wood, Mr. Summers had argued, had been all very well when the village was tiny, but now that the population was more than three hundred and likely to keep on growing, it was necessary to use something that would fit more easily into the black box. The night before the lottery, Mr. Summers and Mr. Graves made up the slips of paper and put them in the box, and it was then taken to the safe of Mr. Summers' coal company and locked up until Mr. Summers was ready to take it to the square next morning. The rest of the year, the box was put way, sometimes one place, sometimes another; it had spent one year in Mr. Graves's barn and another year underfoot in the post office, and sometimes it was set on a shelf in the Martin grocery and left there.

There was a great deal of fussing to be done before Mr. Summers declared the
70   lottery open. There were the lists to make up—of heads of families, heads of
households in each family, members of each household in each family. There was
the proper swearing-in of Mr. Summers by the postmaster, as the official of the
lottery; at one time, some people remembered, there had been a recital of some
sort, performed by the official of the lottery, a perfunctory, tuneless chant that had
75   been rattled off duly each year; some people believed that the official of the lottery used to stand just so when he said or sang it, others believed that he was
supposed to walk among the people, but years and years ago this part of the ritual
had been allowed to lapse. There had been, also, a ritual salute, which the official
of the lottery had had to use in addressing each person who came up to draw from
80   the box, but this also had changed with time, until now it was felt necessary only
for the official to speak to each person approaching. Mr. Summers was very good
at all this; in his clean white shirt and blue jeans, with one hand resting carelessly
on the black box, he seemed very proper and important as he talked interminably
to Mr. Graves and the Martins.

85   Just as Mr. Summers finally left off talking and turned to the assembled villagers,
Mrs. Hutchinson came hurriedly along the path to the square, her sweater thrown
over her shoulders, and slid into place in the back of the crowd. "Clean forgot what
day it was," she said to Mrs. Delacroix, who stood next to her, and they both
laughed softly. "Thought my old man was out back stacking wood," Mrs. Hutchinson
90   went on, "and then I looked out the window and the kids was gone, and then I remembered it was the twenty-seventh and came a-running." She dried her hands
on her apron, and Mrs. Delacroix said, "You're in time, though. They're still talking
away up there."

Mrs. Hutchinson craned her neck to see through the crowd and found her
95   husband and children standing near the front. She tapped Mrs. Delacroix on the
arm as a farewell and began to make her way through the crowd. The people separated good-humoredly to let her through: two or three people said, in voices just
loud enough to be heard across the crowd, "Here comes your Missus, Hutchinson," and "Bill, she made it after all." Mrs. Hutchinson reached her husband, and
100   Mr. Summers, who had been waiting, said cheerfully, "Thought we were going to
have to get on without you, Tessie." Mrs. Hutchinson said, grinning, "Wouldn't have
me leave m'dishes in the sink, now, would you, Joe?," and soft laughter ran through
the crowd as the people stirred back into position after Mrs. Hutchinson's arrival.

"Well, now." Mr. Summers said soberly, "guess we better get started, get this
105   over with, so's we can go back to work. Anybody ain't here?"

"Dunbar," several people said. "Dunbar. Dunbar."

Mr. Summers consulted his list. "Clyde Dunbar," he said. "That's right. He's
broke his leg, hasn't he? Who's drawing for him?"

"Me. I guess," a woman said, and Mr. Summers turned to look at her. "Wife
110   draws for her husband." Mr. Summers said, "Don't you have a grown boy to do it
for you, Janey?" Although Mr. Summers and everyone else in the village knew the

answer perfectly well, it was the business of the official of the lottery to ask such questions formally. Mr. Summers waited with an expression of polite interest while Mrs. Dunbar answered.

"Horace's not but sixteen yet," Mrs. Dunbar said regretfully. "Guess I gotta fill in for the old man this year."   115

"Right," Mr. Summers said. He made a note on the list he was holding. Then he asked, "Watson boy drawing this year?"

A tall boy in the crowd raised his hand. "Here," he said. "I'm drawing for my mother and me." He blinked his eyes nervously and ducked his head as several   120 voices in the crowd said things like "Good fellow, Jack." and "Glad to see your mother's got a man to do it."

"Well," Mr. Summers said, "guess that's everyone. Old Man Warner make it?"

"Here," a voice said, and Mr. Summers nodded.

A sudden hush fell on the crowd as Mr. Summers cleared his throat and looked   125 at the list. "All ready?" he called. "Now, I'll read the names—heads of families first—and the men come up and take a paper out of the box. Keep the paper folded in your hand without looking at it until everyone has had a turn. Everything clear?"

The people had done it so many times that they only half listened to the   130 directions: most of them were quiet, wetting their lips, not looking around. Then Mr. Summers raised one hand high and said, "Adams." A man disengaged himself from the crowd and came forward. "Hi. Steve," Mr. Summers said, and Mr. Adams said, "Hi. Joe." They grinned at one another humorlessly and nervously. Then Mr. Adams reached into the black box and took out a folded paper. He held it   135 firmly by one corner as he turned and went hastily back to his place in the crowd, where he stood a little apart from his family, not looking down at his hand.

"Allen," Mr. Summers said. "Anderson. . . . Bentham."

"Seems like there's no time at all between lotteries any more," Mrs. Delacroix said to Mrs. Graves in the back row.   140

"Seems like we got through with the last one only last week."

"Time sure goes fast," Mrs. Graves said.

"Clark. . . . Delacroix"

"There goes my old man," Mrs. Delacroix said. She held her breath while her husband went forward.   145

"Dunbar," Mr. Summers said, and Mrs. Dunbar went steadily to the box while one of the women said, "Go on, Janey," and another said, "There she goes."

"We're next." Mrs. Graves said. She watched while Mr. Graves came around from the side of the box, greeted Mr. Summers gravely and selected a slip of paper from the box. By now, all through the crowd there were men holding the small folded   150 papers in their large hand, turning them over and over nervously Mrs. Dunbar and her two sons stood together, Mrs. Dunbar holding the slip of paper.

"Harburt. . . . Hutchinson."

"Get up there, Bill," Mrs. Hutchinson said, and the people near her laughed.

155   "Jones."

"They do say," Mr. Adams said to Old Man Warner, who stood next to him, "that over in the north village they're talking of giving up the lottery."

Old Man Warner snorted. "Pack of crazy fools," he said. "Listening to the young folks, nothing's good enough for them. Next thing you know, they'll be wanting to
160   go back to living in caves, nobody work any more, live that way for a while. Used to be a saying about 'Lottery in June, corn be heavy soon.' First thing you know, we'd all be eating stewed chickweed and acorns. There's always been a lottery," he added petulantly. "Bad enough to see young Joe Summers up there joking with everybody."

165   "Some places have already quit lotteries," Mrs. Adams said.

"Nothing but trouble in that," Old Man Warner said stoutly. "Pack of young fools."

"Martin." And Bobby Martin watched his father go forward. "Overdyke. . . . Percy."

170   "I wish they'd hurry," Mrs. Dunbar said to her older son. "I wish they'd hurry."

"They're almost through," her son said.

"You get ready to run and tell Dad," Mrs. Dunbar said.

Mr. Summers called his own name and then stepped forward precisely and selected a slip from the box. Then he called, "Warner."

175   "Seventy-seventh year I been in the lottery," Old Man Warner said as he went through the crowd. "Seventy-seventh time."

"Watson." The tall boy came awkwardly through the crowd. Someone said, "Don't be nervous, Jack," and Mr. Summers said, "Take your time, son."

"Zanini."

180   After that, there was a long pause, a breathless pause, until Mr. Summers, holding his slip of paper in the air, said, "All right, fellows." For a minute, no one moved, and then all the slips of paper were opened. Suddenly, all the women began to speak at once, saying, "Who is it?," "Who's got it?," "Is it the Dunbars?," "Is it the Watsons?" Then the voices began to say, "It's Hutchinson. It's Bill," "Bill Hutchinson's got it."

185   "Go tell your father," Mrs. Dunbar said to her older son.

People began to look around to see the Hutchinsons. Bill Hutchinson was standing quiet, staring down at the paper in his hand. Suddenly, Tessie Hutchinson shouted to Mr. Summers. "You didn't give him time enough to take any paper he wanted. I saw you. It wasn't fair!"

190   "Be a good sport, Tessie," Mrs. Delacroix called, and Mrs. Graves said, "All of us took the same chance."

"Shut up, Tessie," Bill Hutchinson said.

"Well, everyone," Mr. Summers said, "that was done pretty fast, and now we've got to be hurrying a little more to get done in time." He consulted his next list.
195   "Bill," he said, "you draw for the Hutchinson family. You got any other households in the Hutchinsons?"

"There's Don and Eva," Mrs. Hutchinson yelled. "Make them take their chance!"

"Daughters draw with their husbands' families, Tessie," Mr. Summers said gently. "You know that as well as anyone else."

"It wasn't fair," Tessie said.   200

"I guess not, Joe," Bill Hutchinson said regretfully. "My daughter draws with her husband's family; that's only fair. And I've got no other family except the kids."

"Then, as far as drawing for families is concerned, it's you," Mr. Summers said in explanation, "and as far as drawing for households is concerned, that's you, too. Right?"   205

"Right," Bill Hutchinson said.

"How many kids, Bill?" Mr. Summers asked formally.

"Three," Bill Hutchinson said. "There's Bill, Jr., and Nancy, and little Dave. And Tessie and me."

"All right, then," Mr. Summers said. "Harry, you got their tickets back?"   210

Mr. Graves nodded and held up the slips of paper. "Put them in the box, then," Mr. Summers directed. "Take Bill's and put it in."

"I think we ought to start over," Mrs. Hutchinson said, as quietly as she could. "I tell you it wasn't fair. You didn't give him time enough to choose. Everybody saw that."

Mr. Graves had selected the five slips and put them in the box, and he dropped   215
all the papers but those onto the ground, where the breeze caught them and lifted them off.

"Listen, everybody," Mrs. Hutchinson was saying to the people around her.

"Ready, Bill?" Mr. Summers asked, and Bill Hutchinson, with one quick glance around at his wife and children, nodded.   220

"Remember," Mr. Summers said, "take the slips and keep them folded until each person has taken one. Harry, you help little Dave." Mr. Graves took the hand of the little boy, who came willingly with him up to the box. "Take a paper out of the box, Davy." Mr. Summers said. Davy put his hand into the box and laughed. "Take just one paper." Mr. Summers said. "Harry, you hold it for him." Mr. Graves took the   225
child's hand and removed the folded paper from the tight fist and held it while little Dave stood next to him and looked up at him wonderingly.

"Nancy next," Mr. Summers said. Nancy was twelve, and her school friends breathed heavily as she went forward switching her skirt, and took a slip daintily from the box. "Bill, Jr.," Mr. Summers said, and Billy, his face red and his feet over-   230
large, near knocked the box over as he got a paper out. "Tessie," Mr. Summers said. She hesitated for a minute, looking around defiantly, and then set her lips and went up to the box. She snatched a paper out and held it behind her.

"Bill," Mr. Summers said, and Bill Hutchinson reached into the box and felt around, bringing his hand out at last with the slip of paper in it.   235

The crowd was quiet. A girl whispered, "I hope it's not Nancy," and the sound of the whisper reached the edges of the crowd.

"It's not the way it used to be," Old Man Warner said clearly. "People ain't the way they used to be."

"All right," Mr. Summers said. "Open the papers. Harry, you open little Dave's."   240

Mr. Graves opened the slip of paper and there was a general sigh through the crowd as he held it up and everyone could see that it was blank. Nancy and Bill, Jr., opened theirs at the same time, and both beamed and laughed, turning around to the crowd and holding their slips of paper above their heads.

245   "Tessie," Mr. Summers said. There was a pause, and then Mr. Summers looked at Bill Hutchinson, and Bill unfolded his paper and showed it. It was blank.

"It's Tessie," Mr. Summers said, and his voice was hushed. "Show us her paper, Bill."

Bill Hutchinson went over to his wife and forced the slip of paper out of her hand. It had a black spot on it, the black spot Mr. Summers had made the night before 250 with the heavy pencil in the coal company office. Bill Hutchinson held it up, and there was a stir in the crowd.

"All right, folks," Mr. Summers said. "Let's finish quickly."

Although the villagers had forgotten the ritual and lost the original black box, they still remembered to use stones. The pile of stones the boys had made earlier 255 was ready; there were stones on the ground with the blowing scraps of paper that had come out of the box. Delacroix selected a stone so large she had to pick it up with both hands and turned to Mrs. Dunbar. "Come on," she said. "Hurry up."

Mr. Dunbar had small stones in both hands, and she said, gasping for breath, "I can't run at all. You'll have to go ahead and I'll catch up with you."

260   The children had stones already. And someone gave little Davy Hutchinson a few pebbles.

Tessie Hutchinson was in the center of a cleared space by now, and she held her hands out desperately as the villagers moved in on her. "It isn't fair," she said. A stone hit her on the side of the head. Old Man Warner was saying, "Come on, 265 come on, everyone." Steve Adams was in the front of the crowd of villagers, with Mrs. Graves beside him.

"It isn't fair, it isn't right," Mrs. Hutchinson screamed, and then they were upon her.
Source: The New Yorker, June 26, 1948, p. 25.

▮ Discussion/Writing Prompts

1. While the portrait of small-town life presented here seems in many ways ordinary and relatable, the brutal behavior of the townspeople themselves is difficult to comprehend. How do you reconcile such opposing facets of the same story? In your view, does the juxtaposition of the mundane and the heinous make the story more or less believable? [Rhetorical Analysis of Credibility]

2. Can you think of a moment in your life where you felt pressured to "go along with the crowd"? If so, what was the context? What specific choice were you confronted with? What type of pressure was brought to compel your conformity? And looking back, what thoughts about this experience do you have now? [Personal Reflection]

3. Take a closer look at the description of the black box in paragraph 5. What aspect of the lottery process do you think this object is intended to symbolize? What kind of commentary or critique is it designed to convey? [Close Reading]

4. Jackson's story offers an ironic example of the rhetorical mode of process. Detailing the specific rules and procedures by which the lottery unfolds, the story uses this mode as a framework for showing how community life should *not* unfold. How effective do you find this rhetorical strategy to be? Does the story succeed in deploying the mode of process writing ironically? [Analyzing Rhetorical Modes]

5. A word that recurs throughout the story is "ritual." To what extent does this term provide a clue about the larger argument this story is making? According to this story, what does "ritual" behavior involve? And what are the particular dangers of adhering to "ritual"? [Argument]

6. Stephanie Pappas ("Oscar Psychology: Why Celebrities Fascinate Us") uses the language of medical diagnosis to analyze the phenomenon of celebrity worship. Do you think the same framework could be applied to Jackson's story? Does her account of "the lottery" offer a diagnosis as well as a description of community life? If so, what kind of diagnosis is this? [Compare and Contrast]

7. Over the years, Jackson's story has been read as an allegory for a number of different historical events—from the Salem witch trials to the McCarthy hearings of the 1950s. Choose a contemporary event for which you think "The Lottery" could be said to serve as an allegory. Then, research this event. In what ways does this event illustrate the dangers of mass conformity? What harmful rituals or practices does this event showcase? And how do these specifics compare with the details in Jackson's story? [Research]

Brent Staples, "Black Men and Public Space"

For all the recent discussion about Americans living in a "postracial" society, many of our society's most entrenched—and pernicious—racial stereotypes persist. And as Brent Staples, an author and editorial writer for The New York Times, *suggests, what makes such stereotypes even more difficult to combat today is the fact that they are enforced in subtle, often unspoken ways. Offering a case in point, Staples examines the complicated and dangerous ways that racial stereotypes affect the way "black men" navigate "public space" itself. This article was first published in* Harper's Magazine *in 1986.*

My first victim was a woman—white, well-dressed, probably in her late twenties. I came upon her late one evening on a deserted street in Hyde Park, a relatively affluent neighborhood in an otherwise mean, impoverished section of Chicago. As I swung onto the avenue behind her, there seemed to be a discreet, uninflammatory distance between us. Not so. She cast back a worried glance. To her, the youngish black man—a broad 6 feet 2 inches with a beard and billowing hair, both hands shoved into the pockets of a bulky military jacket—seemed menacingly close. After a few more quick glimpses, she picked up her pace and was soon running in earnest. Within seconds, she disappeared into a cross street.

5

That was more than a decade ago. I was 22 years old, a graduate student newly arrived at the University of Chicago. It was in the echo of that terrified woman's footfalls that I first began to know the unwieldy inheritance I'd come into—the ability to alter public space in ugly ways. It was clear that she thought herself the quarry of a mugger, a rapist, or worse. Suffering a bout of insomnia, however, I was stalking sleep, not defenseless wayfarers. As a softy who is scarcely able to take a knife to a raw chicken—let alone hold one to a person's throat—I was surprised, embarrassed, and dismayed all at once. Her flight made me feel like an accomplice in tyranny. It also made it clear that I was indistinguishable from the muggers who occasionally seeped into the area from the surrounding ghetto. That first encounter, and those that followed, signified that a vast, unnerving gulf lay between nighttime pedestrians—particularly women—and me. And I soon gathered that being perceived as dangerous is a hazard in itself. I only needed to turn a corner into a dicey situation, or crowd some frightened, armed person in a foyer somewhere, or make an errant move after being pulled over by a policeman. Where fear and weapons meet—and they often do in urban America—there is always the possibility of death.

In that first year, my first away from my hometown, I was to become thoroughly familiar with the language of fear. At dark, shadowy intersections, I could cross in front of a car stopped at a traffic light and elicit the **thunk, thunk, thunk, thunk** of the driver—black, white, male, or female—hammering down the door locks. On less traveled streets after dark, I grew accustomed to but never comfortable with people crossing to the other side of the street rather than pass me. Then there were the standard unpleasantries with policemen, doormen, bouncers, cabdrivers, and others whose business it is to screen out troublesome individuals **before** there is any nastiness.

I moved to New York nearly two years ago and I have remained an avid night walker. In central Manhattan, the near-constant crowd cover minimizes tense one-on-one street encounters. Elsewhere—in SoHo, for example, where sidewalks are narrow and tightly spaced buildings shut out the sky—things can get very taut indeed.

After dark, on the warrenlike streets of Brooklyn where I live, I often see women who fear the worst from me. They seem to have set their faces on neutral, and with their purse straps strung across their chests bandolier-style, they forge ahead as though bracing themselves against being tackled. I understand, of course, that the danger they perceive is not a hallucination. Women are particularly vulnerable to street violence, and young black males are drastically overrepresented among the perpetrators of that violence. Yet these truths are no solace against the kind of alienation that comes of being ever the suspect, a fearsome entity with whom pedestrians avoid making eye contact.

It is not altogether clear to me how I reached the ripe old age of 22 without being conscious of the lethality nighttime pedestrians attributed to me. Perhaps it was because in Chester, Pennsylvania, the small, angry industrial town where I came of age in the 1960s, I was scarcely noticeable against a backdrop of gang warfare, street knifings, and murders. I grew up one of the good boys, had perhaps a half-dozen fist-fights. In retrospect, my shyness of combat has clear sources.

As a boy, I saw countless tough guys locked away; I have since buried several, too. They were babies, really—a teenage cousin, a brother of 22, a childhood friend in his mid-twenties—all gone down in episodes of bravado played out in the streets. I came to doubt the virtues of intimidation early on. I chose, perhaps unconsciously, to remain a shadow—timid, but a survivor.

The fearsomeness mistakenly attributed to me in public places often has a perilous flavor. The most frightening one of these confusions occurred in the late 1970s and early 1980s, when I worked as a journalist in Chicago. One day, rushing into the office of a magazine I was writing for with a deadline story in hand, I was mistaken for a burglar. The office manager called security and, with an ad hoc posse, pursued me through the labyrinthine halls, nearly to my editor's door. I had no way of proving who I was. I could only move briskly toward the company of someone who knew me.

Another time I was on assignment for a local paper and killing time before an interview. I entered a jewelry store on the city's affluent Near North Side. The proprietor excused herself and returned with an enormous red Doberman pinscher straining at the end of a leash. She stood, the dog extended toward me, silent to my questions, her eyes bulging nearly out of her head. I took a cursory look around, nodded, and bade her good night.

Relatively speaking, however, I never fared as badly as another black male journalist. He went to nearby Waukegan, Illinois, a couple of summers ago to work on a story about a murderer who was born there. Mistaking the reporter for the killer, police officers hauled him from his car at gunpoint and but for his press credentials would probably have tried to book him. Black men trade tales like this all the time.

Over the years, I learned to smother the rage I felt at so often being taken for a criminal. Not to do so would surely have led to madness. I now take precautions to make myself less threatening. I move about with care, particularly late in the evening. I give a wide berth to nervous people on subway platforms during the wee hours, particularly when I have exchanged business clothes for jeans. If I happen to be entering a building behind some people who appear skittish, I may walk by, letting them clear the lobby before I return, so as not to seem to be following them. I have been calm and extremely congenial on those rare occasions when I've been pulled over by the police.

And on late evening constitutionals I employ what has proved to be an excellent tension-reducing measure: I whistle melodies from Beethoven and Vivaldi and the more popular classical composers. Even steely New Yorkers hunching toward nighttime destinations seem to relax, and occasionally they even join in the tune. Virtually everybody seems to sense that a mugger wouldn't be warbling bright, sunny selections from Vivaldi's *Four Seasons*. It is my equivalent to the cowbell that hikers wear when they know they are in bear country.

Source: Harper's Magazine, *December 1986*

▪ Discussion/Writing Prompts

1. As Staples himself acknowledges, for those readers who are not black men, the thesis he is advancing might be difficult to believe. How credible do you find his thesis about "black men" and "public space"? Do the examples he cites and the explanation he provides enhance his believability? How, or how not? [Rhetorical Analysis of Credibility]

2. Can you think of a moment when where you found yourself unfairly judged on the basis of your appearance? If so, what options did you have to challenge or alter this perception? How does your experience compare with the ones that Staples describes? What kinds of factors prevent "black men" from challenging or altering the false perception others may have of them? [Personal Reflection]

3. Staples refers to the racial stereotypes with which he has to contend as his "unwieldy inheritance." What do you think he means by this phrase? In what sense is it reasonable to think of such stereotypes as being something that African-American males "inherit"? What sort of commentary about these stereotypes is he using this phrase to make? [Close Reading]

4. To support his argument about "black men" and "public space," Staples recounts a number of stories from his own experience. How effective do you find his use of narration in these instances? Do these stories offer persuasive support for the argument he is advancing? How, or how not? [Analyzing Rhetorical Modes]

5. In Staples' view, the majority of the stereotypes directed against black men involve the perception of criminality. Do you agree? And if so, what do you think accounts for the pervasiveness of this stereotype? [Argument]

6. To what extent does Shirley Jackson's story ("The Lottery") offers a useful framework for understanding Staples' argument? Do you think Staples' would be persuaded by a description of the behavior of fearful whites toward black men as an unthinking "ritual"? Do you think this term is useful? [Compare and Contrast]

7. Research the incarceration rates for black men in the United States. Then, write a three- to five-page essay in which you use Staples' argument as the basis for explaining and understanding these statistics. [Research]

▪ Tying It All Together

1. While they explore different topics, the readings above are all linked by their shared interest in the issue of credibility. In an age where so much information and so many viewpoints can be accessed in so many different ways, how do we know whom and what to believe? Choose three of the above selections. Then, in a three- to five-page essay, describe and analyze the standard of credibility each one examines. What are the standards in these selections for verifying whether something is true? How do these standards compare? And which, in the final analysis, do you find to be most valid? Why?

2. Jeff Karon ("A Positive Solution for Plagiarism") can be viewed as making the case for the role that expertise can play in determining credibility. Write a two-page essay in which you identify and respond to the argument the writer makes about the importance of expertise. How does the writer define what expert knowledge looks like? And how does such knowledge differ from the kinds of knowledge deemed to be more "amateur"? Does this writer argue for the need to place limits around such "expertise"? If so, what and why?

3. One of the principal ways of assessing a text's credibility is to look more closely at *context*: the setting, circumstances, and factors that frame a given piece of writing. Choose one of the selections above, and research the ways that context affects this text's overall credibility. What information can you find about this writer's particular background? About the writer's professional experience or affiliations? What information can you uncover about the source or venue in which this writing appears (e.g., journal or website, popular magazine or academic publication). Who seems to be the target audience? And how do these factors either enhance or inhibit your sense of this text's believability?

Using the Steps of Rhetorical Analysis to Write Your Own Academic Essay

The same instruction this chapter presents for analyzing other people's writing can also serve as a guide for undertaking your own. In particular, a number of the steps outlined above provide a useful framework for kind of writing you are often called upon to do in the classroom. In the same way that these steps teach you to apply the rhetorical concept of credibility to what you read, they can also help you better see the role this concept plays in your own essay writing. Take a look at the outline below. Organizing the writing process along the same rhetorical lines modeled above, it provides a map for how to use the concept of credibility to organize and create your own academic essay:

- **Step One: Identifying Credibility:** What makes you qualified to speak on this issue? What makes these qualifications valuable or relevant?
- **Step Two: Asserting Credibility:** How do these qualifications influence the specific rhetorical choices you make as a writer?
- **Step Three: Defending Credibility:** How might someone challenge your credibility? What responses or counterclaims might a reader present?

To see how these steps can be put into practice, let's take a look at a specific example. As you read over the essay below, pay attention to the ways that considerations about credibility guide the writer's calculations and choices. To assist you in this work, take note of the comments and questions that accompany the essay in the margins. Then, turn your attention to the sample analysis that follows. In what ways does this discussion provide a model for using these three steps to write an academic essay of your own?

Student Essay: Rachel Morton, "How I Learned to Dislike Math"

This essay by Rachel Morton uses the narration mode to make some larger points about the way math often gets taught in elementary school.

As I look back on my earliest years in school, I can honestly say that I didn't start out actively disliking math. In fact, I can vividly recall several moments in my early grade school years actually looking forward to working with numbers.

5 As a third-grader, I remember spending countless hours trying to memorize my multiplication tables, fascinated by the relationship between different numbers this exercise made evident. But somewhere in those elementary school years, my early enthusiasm for math started to fade. While

10 my interest in subjects like reading, writing and art continued unabated, math began to feel more like a rote chore than a genuine interest.

Using personal anecdotes to establish context

Part of this, I think, had to do with the way math was typically taught in school. Where I might complete a writ-

15 ing assignment by composing a creative story or fulfill an art assignment by painting a picture, math assignments invariably took the form of quizzes and tests. Unlike these more creative assignments, math quizzes seem designed to test only my power of memorization. Some of my class-

20 mates loved the certainty such tests provided, the fact that there existed clear right-and-wrong answers, but to me such clarity drained the act of learning of its creative element. Where's the creativity, I wondered, in learning to memorize? What room for personal expression or personal

25 growth did this type of assignment leave.

Using personal narrative to present larger issue

These questions suggest the larger point writer is trying to make

A key turning point occurred in the fourth grade. My teacher, Ms. Schiro, decided that the best way for her students to learn math was for this work to be turned into a class-wide competition. Throughout the year, we were subject to endless

30 contests in which students competed against each other answering a steady stream of math questions from Ms. Schiro in pursuit of a special "prize." "What's the square root of 16?" our teacher would call. "How many times does 7 go into 63?" Rather than inspire me to embrace math, these competitions

35 only confirmed for me what I had already begun to suspect: that learning math was a rigged exercise, in which the ultimate goal was not to think for yourself but to provide the predetermined answer a teacher demanded you to know.

Another personal story

Another key point

Over the course of my fourth grade year, I internalized several messages about math: that thinking for yourself was frowned upon, that the act of learning itself was fundamentally about competing against others, and that memorization and rote recitation were the most important skills. It's not that these kinds of competitions were too hard. They weren't. I was perfectly able to come up with the answers. The problem wasn't what I was expected to do, but why I was expected to do it. These competitions taught me that believe that learning math really isn't about being creative, thinking for yourself, or having fun. And as memorization tests continued to be the norm, my initial indifference bloomed into something bigger and more problematic: an active dislike, even fear, of math.

Using an anecdote to present an overview of the main argument 40

45

50

Even though I am now in college, my dislike of math persists. While it's been years since I participated in my last math competition, the association between math instruction and rote memorization remains strong in my mind. Despite this fact, though, I still harbor fantasies of making math interesting again. I try sometimes to recapture my earliest memories about math, back when I was a small child, before years of elementary schooling stifled my interest. In those moments, what I really hope to recapture is a sense not only that math can be fun, but that my own education—how, what, and why I learn—can truly belong to me.

Conclusion: suggesting how this problem might change

55

60

Now, let's see how the rhetorical steps presented above help us understand the choices the writer makes in this essay:

Step One: *Identifying Credibility: What Makes the Writer Qualified to Speak on This Issue?*

○ The writer bases her entire argument on her own personal experiences in the classroom, using these experiences to illustrate what she feels are the shortcomings in how math typically gets taught.

Step Two: *Asserting Credibility: How Do These Qualifications Influence the Specific Rhetorical Choices the Writer Makes?*

○ The decision to connect her argument to her own personal experience leads the writer to organize her essay as a series of individual stories or narrative anecdotes that illustrate the larger points she is trying to make.

○ This strategy also influences the particular tone the writer adopts. Throughout the essay, she employs informal, conversational language, which succeeds in establishing a closer relationship with her audience.

Step Three: *Defending Credibility: How Might You Challenge the Writer's Credibility?*

○ While the first-person narrative mode the writer employs can be effective, it does raise questions about how typical or representative her own experiences actually are. A reader might well wonder whether the experiences of other students may differ. The writer might have bolstered her credibility by including the voices and stories of other students whose experience confirm her larger point.

Group Work: Thinking Rhetorically About the Formal Selections

This chapter has given you ample opportunity to analyze credibility on an individual basis. Now, let's undertake this same kind of work from a group perspective. In your group, select one of the formal selections above. Prepare for your group work by re-reading the selection. Then, with your group, use the outline presented at the beginning of the chapter, *Thinking Rhetorically About Credibility*, to analyze role that credibility plays in this piece. Here is a quick recap of these steps:

- **Step One: Identifying Credibility:** What makes the writer qualified to speak on this issue?
- **Step Two: Assessing Credibility:** What makes these qualifications valuable or relevant?
- **Step Three: Asserting Credibility:** How do these qualifications influence the specific rhetorical choices the writer makes?
- **Step Four: Defending Credibility:** How might you challenge the writer's credibility?
- **Step Five: Rethinking Credibility:** Based on these critiques, how would you go revising this writing?
- **Step Six: Putting It Into Writing:** How do I summarize my findings in writing?

Once you have completed this work, exchange your findings with another group. First, have your group re-read the selection these new findings examine. Then, discuss as a group how helpful you find this analysis. Do you agree with the conclusions about credibility this analysis draws? Do you evaluate the role of credibility in different or similar ways? Finally, summarize your key findings in a paragraph. Be prepared to share this written assessment with the rest of the class.

Comparing Credibility: Understanding the Connection Between Informal and Formal Writing

Throughout this chapter, we have moved from a focus on informal writing to formal writing. How do these types of writing compare? What are the key similarities and differences in language and tone, form and content, organization and context? And what happens to our understanding of credibility when we take these similarities and differences into account?

The activity presented here provides an opportunity to address these questions. First, choose a topic or issue that has been raised by one of the formal selections in this chapter (e.g., doctor/patient relationships, the rise of the "selfie," or academic plagiarism). Next, choose an informal venue (e.g., blog, Facebook post, tweet, or email), and write about this issue using the conventions of this particular form. Then, choose a formal venue (e.g., journal essay, magazine article, or academic analysis), and write about the same issue using the conventions particular to that form. When you're done, spend a few moments itemizing the specific ways these two writing samples differ and are similar. In what ways did your choice of venue affect the credibility of your discussion?

Connecting Credibility to Rhetorical Modes

To better understand how considerations about credibility relate to the question of rhetorical modes, try the following activity: Choose one of the examples of real world writing from the informal selections above. First, identify the topic this writer raises and the audience the writer seeks to address. Then, focus on the rhetorical mode in the text (e.g., narration, description, cause and effect, compare and contrast, or definition) that you think most helps enhance the writer's credibility. What makes this mode so effective?

Speaking for Yourself

Choose an issue that is currently a topic of public debate. First, figure out what your own personal stand is on this issue. What are your own thoughts or feelings about it? On which side of the debate do you fall? Then, write a two-page essay in which you outline all of the reasons why your viewpoint on this issue is credible. What evidence can you cite, what arguments can you make, that would convince a reader to share your view? When you're done, write a one-page response in which you reflect on the choices you made to enhance your credibility. Why did you choose these arguments? Why this evidence. Are there other forms of support that might also have been effective?

PART THREE
The Research Process

10 Finding and Evaluating Sources

Just like the reading and writing process examined in Part I, conducting research—identifying an issue, locating and evaluating sources with information relevant to this issue, and creating an essay that presents this information in a clear and coherent way—can be approached in rhetorical terms. And as with learning to read and write effectively, research requires that we think about the role played by the core rhetorical concepts of purpose, audience, argument, voice, and credibility. In Part III, we will use these same five terms to create a practical, hands-on guide for undertaking such key research activities as formulating a research topic, creating a research proposal, locating and evaluating research sources, and creating your own research essay.

To begin, let's start with a definition. In the most basic sense, research involves an attempt to uncover additional information about a given subject so that you can understand and argue about it more effectively. Research can take a number of different forms. It can involve examining formal written sources such as books, journals, or articles; it can involve exploring electronic sources like blogs, websites, and online magazines; it can involve conducting first-hand interviews or undertaking field work in the community.

Like other forms of writing, research involves making conscious choices and deliberate decisions about what we want to say and how we want to say it. We conduct research when we want to make clear how our own ideas, claims, and opinions compare to those of others interested in the same topic. We conduct research when we are looking for input and information from others that support our own point of view. We conduct research, in short, to make our own thinking and writing about a given subject more effective.

Thinking Rhetorically About Research

In rhetorical terms, research is about situating our own views in relation to the views of others—and then using those views to supplement, reinforce, and extend our own. The outline below provides a framework for beginning to think about the research process in rhetorical terms. As you make your way through the chapters in Part III, keep in mind the questions presented here. Doing so will help you appreciate the role that rhetorical considerations play in the research process.

- *Purpose*: What is my main objective as a researcher? What issue do I want to examine? What information about this issue do I want to discover and discuss? What types of sources will best help me accomplish this goal?

- *Audience*: What kind of audience am I addressing? What type of reader would be most interested in this issue? What sort of information about this issue would I need to provide to such a reader?
- *Argument*: What is my own point of view on this issue? How does it compare to the viewpoints of others? What larger point am I trying to make about the ways that others view and discuss this issue?
- *Voice*: What style, tone, and/or word choice will best help me present the information about this issue?
- *Credibility*: How credible are the sources I am researching? Are the ideas or information they contain valid?

Generating a Viable Research Topic

Before you can begin actively researching a topic, you first need to figure out exactly what topic you want to research. While this may sound like an easy task, choosing a viable, researchable topic requires some critical thought. And like everything else connected to the research process, this kind of work can be framed in rhetorical terms. The outline below demonstrates how you can use the rhetorical concepts of purpose, audience, argument, and credibility to formulate a viable research topic:

Step One: *Think About Purpose*

  ° What topics do I care about?

  ° What subjects, events, or ideas interest me?

  ° What kinds of topics do I find myself most often discussing with friends, reading about in newspapers and magazines, or linking to online?

Step Two: *Consider the Audience*

  ° What issues or questions does this topic raise?

  ° Who is most interested in discussing or debating them?

  ° What do these discussions and debates look like?

Step Three: *Identify the Argument*

  ° How are these questions or issues arguable?

  ° Over what specific points do people involved in this issue typically disagree?

  ° What is my own view on this issue?

Step Four: *Speculate About Credibility*

  ° Where can I go to find further information about this issue?

  ° What kinds of sources typically contain discussions of this issue?

  ° Which kinds are the most reliable sources of information?

To see how these steps can be put into practice, let's return to the topic we used as an example or model back in Part I: the issue of the minimum wage. Imagine that you wanted to develop your interest in minimum wage work—more specifically, the wages earned by workers on your own college campus—into a viable research topic. To develop this focus into a researchable issue, you could start by using the steps outlined above. Included below is an example of what this kind of rhetorical work might involve:

Step One: *Think About Purpose*

° I care about this topic because it raises questions of economic inequality and basic fairness. In today's society, too many Americans work for wages that are far below what is necessary to maintain a basic standard of living. For this reason, I feel it's important to learn more about the economic challenges faced by the kinds of workers who earn this wage. Only by gaining this kind of perspective will people learn the true scope of this problem.

Step Two: *Consider the Audience*

° In my view, this topic raises important ethical and policy questions that would be of interest both to campus workers and to the college administrators who employ them.

Step Three: *Identify the Argument*

° The ethical question at stake involves the issue of social inequality and basic fairness. Is it right for one group of campus workers to be paid so little relative to what other employees of the college earn? On the policy side, does the current situation warrant a change in such areas as wages or health care coverage for these workers? I can envision a number of different arguments emerging from a fuller discussion of this topic. Through further research, I could see myself deciding to make a claim about the need for the college to change its wage structure for campus workers. Or, I might use this research to argue something more specific about the relationship between campus workers and college administrators.

Step Four: *Speculate About Credibility*

° There are a number of different sources I could explore to conduct this kind of research. I could attempt to gather first-hand information about this issue by interviewing leaders of the campus protests or representatives of the college administration. To put this issue into a wider economic context, I could also gather further information about the larger budget—the revenue and expenses—for the college. To gain a better sense of how the public debate is playing out, I could conduct a search for any articles, editorials, or online posts that address this issue.

Creating a Research Proposal

Once you've established some of the basic boundaries around your topic, the next step is to put together a plan for how you will begin to actually research it. One of the most effective ways to do this is to create a **research proposal**. There are two basic objectives behind a research proposal. The first is to create a plan for how you are going to develop and research your topic: the specific sources you are going to explore, the particular methods you are going to use, and the timeline in which you plan to get this done. The second is to provide an explanation for why you are doing this research in the first place: what you think makes this project significant and what you hope to accomplish through this research. Stated differently: Your proposal is not only where you create a plan for your research argument but also where you make your *own* argument about why this research is useful, important, or necessary. To make this argument successfully, you need to make sure that your research proposal addresses certain key questions:

• What do I already know about this topic? What more do I need to know?
• What do I want others to know about this topic?
• What kinds of sources will help me gain this knowledge?
• Why does this knowledge matter?

To illustrate the form this kind of work might take, let's return to our hypothetical example about campus workers. Having done the initial work of setting boundaries around your topic, you would be ready next to turn your attention to creating a research proposal. As a first step in this process, you could use the questions outlined above as a guide for putting a draft of your proposal together:

What do I already know about this topic? What more do I need to know?
While I'm generally sympathetic to this issue, I have to admit I don't know very much about the specific working conditions for this group of campus employees. On a personal level, I do have some first-hand experience holding down minimum wage jobs myself, and consequently I am aware of the general challenges such low-wages present. My goal is to supplement my own personal knowledge with a more comprehensive and objective set of facts about specific economic challenges faced by these workers: What wages are these workers actually paid? How do these wages compare with the wages paid to workers at comparable colleges? How do these wages relate to the other costs/expenses these colleges confront?

What do I want others to know about this topic?
First and foremost, I want my readers to gain a clearer understanding of the financial and workplace challenges faced by campus workers earning lower wages. To accomplish this goal, I need to make sure my readers are acquainted with the basic facts about such work: their wages, workplace conditions, and major challenges. Armed with this information, I hope, readers will then become more

aware of these challenges and more convinced that something needs to be done to address them.

What kinds of sources will help me gain this knowledge?

Information about the college budget in general, and worker wages in particular, is probably available in online campus documents. Likewise, I should be able to find examples of how this issue is being debated on campus in other campus publications (newspaper editorials, blogs, public statements). Government documents and academic journals might provide a broader picture of the economic situation faced by campus workers nationwide.

Why does this knowledge matter?

This information is important because it provides a necessary context for understanding the true nature of the challenges faced by campus workers. And this knowledge is important because it makes us aware of a key social and economic injustice that needs to be addressed.

Once you've completed this kind of preliminary work, you can then turn your attention to putting together a more formal and developed research proposal. Here is an example of what such a proposal might look like:

Research Proposal Example

Establish Context

Conflicts over wages and work conditions have long been a hallmark of employer/employee relationships. Despite this fact, however, relatively little attention has been paid to the ways these disagreements have increasingly taken place in the world of higher education. On countless universities and college campuses across the country, campus employees (maintenance and janitorial workers, support staff, etc.) have begun to organize in con- 5
certed ways to protest for higher wages and better working conditions. For this research project, I will examine and analyze the way this debate has played out on one college campus. The arguments made by those on both sides of this debate, I believe, are typical of those that characterize the debate nationally. Through an examination of this example, in my view, it is possible to see the key claims and concerns that define both sides of the 10
discussion.

Preview Research Strategies

There are many different facets of this campus debate that I will explore. One involves the claim made by representatives of campus workers concerning the issue of social equality. How do such representatives argue that the wages currently paid to campus workers are unfair? What arguments do campus administrators make in response? A second facet in- 15
volves the economic argument made by these campus representatives. On what basis do they claim that an increase in worker wages is affordable? What economic data do those on the other side of this debate offer in response?

Identify Usable Sources

The cornerstone of my research will consist of the public statements made by representatives of both the campus employees and the college administration. These statements can
be found in a range of sources: articles and editorials in the campus newspaper, statements
and policy positions posted to the college website, and public speeches given on campus. To
supplement these secondary sources, I will conduct first-hand interviews with the princi-
pals involved in this campus debate: leaders of the worker protest and representatives of
the college administration. In addition, I will also attempt to put these arguments into a
broader context by looking at primary sources that provide statistical data about the
wages of campus employees across the country and at secondary sources that present the
views of other worker representatives and administrators on this issue.

Discuss Significance

This project could prove extremely useful for advancing the national conversation about
worker compensation, economic equality, and labor/management relations in the United
States today. Understanding the debate over wages and working conditions on a single
college campus could provide us with a map or blueprint for understanding—or perhaps
even resolving—this debate on a national level.

Create a Timeline
Week 1: *Research proposal due.*

Week 2: *Begin in-depth research of campus debate.*

Week 3: *Complete notes for these sources.*

Week 4: *Review these notes and create a preliminary thesis. Get feedback from
peers and instructors for advice on how to develop this thesis.*

Week 5: *Conduct first-hand interviews. Write up notes for each.*

Week 6: *Complete secondary source research.*

Week 7: *Write first draft of argument.*

Week 8: *Get peer feedback on draft. Conduct additional research.*

Week 9: *Complete second draft.*

Week 10: *Conduct final revisions. Create Works Cited list.*

Using Sources

We conduct research to accomplish a number of different goals. We research to provide
additional information about the topic at hand. We research to compare our views with
the views of others. We research to strengthen or further support the particular claims
we are making. We research to talk back to those with whom we disagree.

The list below provides an overview of the key uses to which research can be put. As you look over this list, think about the types of sources that would best help a writer to achieve each goal.

- *To Provide Further Background or Context on a Subject*: Whenever we write about a topic that is of broader public interest, it can be helpful to include background information that gives our readers a sense of the larger context.
- *To Refine, Reinforce, or Extend Our Own Argument*: Sometimes research can give us different, deeper ways of thinking about the ideas or opinions we are trying to get across.
- *To Provide Evidence or Support for Our Own Point of View*: Much of our research is designed to provide our readers with evidence or proof in support of our claims.
- *To Respond to Those With Whom We Disagree*: Often our research can help us refute claims or counterarguments made by those whose views differ from our own.

Finding Sources

A good deal of the research process revolves around finding and evaluating sources. In a world overflowing with statistics and information, ideas and opinions, claims and counterclaims, it is essential that we learn how to distinguish between sources that are legitimate, accurate, and useful and those that are not. Through the library and the Internet, you can access an enormous number of sources that will help you generate paper topics, gather information, challenge your thinking, and support or refute your opinions.

To help you identify sources that will be most useful to you, it is important to have a clear set of guidelines for how to evaluate them. To get started, let's return one more time to our five key rhetorical terms. As you look over these terms, think about the ways they can help you become a more self-aware and critical researcher.

▓ Thinking Rhetorically About Your Sources

- *Purpose*: What is the main goal or objective behind this source? What is my own goal for how I want to use this source?
- *Audience*: Toward what type of reader does this source seem to be directed? What kind of reader would find this source most useful? What is useful about this source to me?
- *Argument*: How do I evaluate the content of this source? What sort of information does it contain? What message or main point does it attempt to get across? And how does this source help me get across my own point?
- *Voice*: How effectively does this source convey its information or ideas? What type of language does this source use? What specific information does it include?
- *Credibility*: Is this source believable? Is its information accurate? Are its claims legitimate? In what ways does this source enhance your own credibility?

What to Look for

In presenting its examples of real world writing, each of this book's main chapters divides its selections into the two basic categories of formal and informal. Much the same thing can be done when it comes to research. Sources come in a variety of different forms—from scholarly essays and book chapters to popular magazine articles and websites—and can be similarly divided into formal and informal categories. In general, formal sources include scholarly works written by credentialed authors who are experts in their field. They are usually published by academic or other reputable presses, and they present material that is well documented. Informal sources include more mainstream or popular fare (i.e., magazine articles, newspaper stories, and websites) and are written for a more general readership. The list below outlines the most common types of sources in each category:

Formal Sources

- º Journals

- º Academic articles

- º Books and book chapters

Informal Sources

- º Magazines

- º Popular articles

- º Websites

Where to Look for It

For most research projects, the **library** is the starting point for beginning to search for sources. Using the library's resources enables you to find books, journals, and articles as well as access sources through different online databases. To begin your search, log on to your library's home page. This is where you can search for different authors, titles, and subjects. To locate a book, type the title or the author in the appropriate section of the search catalogue; these instructions also apply when searching for a section or chapter within a book. This same approach also works for journal essays or magazine articles you want to locate. For sources such as these, start by entering the author's name or the title of the publication in which the article or essay appears.

   In addition to the home page, you can also utilize the online research databases your library provides. Examples of these include EBSCOhost's Academic Search Elite and Wilson Web's OmniFile Full Text Mega. While they are generally multidisciplinary, these databases allow you to conduct more specialized searches for subjects and titles than those using Google or Yahoo. To search these kinds of databases, start by typing your topic into the search function. The database will then display the relevant books, essays, and articles in a results list.

Beyond these more specialized research databases are a range of popular electronic sources you can access. These include websites, blogs, eBooks, online newspapers and magazines, podcasts, and YouTube videos. The easiest way to begin a search for these types of sources is to access a search engine like Google or Yahoo. Start by typing in your topic. To sample as wide a variety of sources as possible, enter as many terms related to your topic as you can think of. Once you have entered these terms, your search engine will provide you a list of sources along with their URLs (i.e., their website addresses).

Evaluating Sources

In Chapter 9, we looked more closely at what it means to assess and verify the credibility of the writing we either encounter or create in the real world. This question is no less important when it comes to the sources we use in our research. Before we can make a decision about which sources to reference or include, we need to determine whether a source is useful. Does it address questions or issues relevant to our topic? Does it present information that is accurate or viewpoints that seem legitimate? Does the author have the appropriate qualifications or credentials?

Once again, we can begin this process by returning to the same rhetorical terms that have guided our work throughout the book. Take a look at the outline below, and think about how each of these rhetorical terms helps us to evaluate a source's credibility.

Step One: *Analyzing Purpose*

 º What is the text's point of view? What are its main claims, and what support does it provide for them?

 º Who is the publisher? What can you learn about the author?

Step Two: *Analyzing Audience*

 º Who is the intended reader? Is the source intended for a particular type of reader or a universal audience?

 º Would you classify yourself as one of the intended readers?

Step Three: *Analyzing Argument*

 º Does it contain all fact, all opinion, or a mix of both?

 º Does it present information about all sides of its topic?

 º What kind of evidence does it provide in support of its claims?

Step Four: *Analyzing Voice*

 º What sort of language does it use? Does the language suggest a particular bias, or does it present its material in a more neutral or objective tone?

Step Five: *Analyzing Credibility*

   o Is the author a recognized figure in the field?

   o Is the source listed under a reputable domain?

   o Is the source published in a print or online journal that is peer reviewed?

   o Is the source current?

11 Creating and Revising a Research Draft

Organizing Your Research Paper

In the last chapter, you learned the steps necessary to getting the research process underway: how to turn an issue into a viable research topic, how to pose a series of research questions, how to establish a focus for a given topic, and how to formulate a research plan in the form of a written proposal. Once this work is completed, you can begin putting together a first draft of the research essay itself. This is another stage of the research process that can be approached in rhetorical terms: When you make decisions about the kind of source material you want to include in your essay, for example, you are also considering rhetorical issues like *purpose* and *credibility*. When you formulate a plan for how this material is to be organized, you are making calculations about *voice*. When you decide how to integrate your own point of view with the views of others, you are working through the specifics of your own *argument*.

Thinking rhetorically about the drafting stage of the research process requires you to move back and forth between two perspectives: a **macro** perspective that addresses questions about how you want to present the discussion of your topic (What are my main points? How do I organize my material in a logical, effective way?) and a **micro** perspective that focuses on the smaller, individual elements within your essay (What should my introduction look like? Does each paragraph begin with a clear topic sentence? How much information do I need to include from each of my individual sources?). Both perspectives are essential to creating a viable first draft of your research essay, and in this chapter, you will learn the steps necessary to address each. As you work through these steps, you will gain hands-on experience with creating a formal outline for your essay, integrating source information (i.e., quotations, data, and evidence) into your own discussion, and learning how to revise a first draft.

From a broader or macro perspective, the central task in the drafting process involves deciding what types of source material you are going to include in your essay as well as how all of this material will be organized. One of the most useful strategies for accomplishing this goal is to create a **research outline**. The purpose of a research outline is to provide a map of your research paper overall. In more concrete terms, a research outline is a document in which you lay out each of your paper's main sections, describe the specific source information each section will include, and explain how this information relates to the larger argument you are trying to make. Typically, research outlines are structured as a series of headings and subheadings that divide your essay into separate parts: introduction, supporting paragraphs, and conclusion.

Within this general framework, however, there are a number of different ways to organize a research outline. You may, for example, decide to present your main argument up front, using your discussion of source material in the paragraphs that follow to develop and prove it. Conversely, you may decide to foreground your discussion of the source material up front, using it as an introductory frame for presenting your thesis nearer to the end. You might even end up trying several different approaches as you move from an earlier to a later draft.

Here is a quick overview of the forms a research outline can take:

- *Chronological*: organizes source material from most to least recent, or vice versa.
- *Thematic*: organizes source material around a single key idea or issue.
- *Narrative*: organizes source material according to a personal story.
- *Cause and effect*: organizes source material around an argument about the cause or consequences of an issue.
- *Problem solution*: organizes source material in support of a proposal to take action.

To determine which type of research outline is best suited to your topic, let's return to our key rhetorical terms. The steps presented below provide you with a guideline for thinking rhetorically about your research outline:

Step One: *Think About Your Purpose*

○ What larger goal am I trying to accomplish in this essay?

○ What form of organization helps me best achieve this?

Step Two: *Consider Your Audience*

○ What specific audience am I addressing in this essay?

○ What form of organization will best help reach such an audience?

Step Three: *Identify Your Argument*

○ What specific point am I trying to make?

○ How does this point compare to the points raised in other sources?

Step Four: *Construct Your Voice*

○ How should I organize my source material?

○ How do I integrate my own view on this issue with the views of others?

Step Five: *Speculate About Credibility*

○ What sources are most credible?

○ How can I discuss these sources in a way that enhances my own credibility?

To better see how these steps can help you create a research outline, consider the following hypothetical scenario. Imagine that you decided to write a research paper exploring the issue of traumatic brain injury in professional football. And after posing a series of initial research questions, let's say that you narrowed your focus to the recent lawsuit by former NFL players demanding the league compensate them for injuries they suffered while playing. Are these demands valid? Is there a verifiable connection between traumatic brain injury and playing professional football? And if so, what responsibility does the NFL owe to its former players? After conducting extensive research into both primary and secondary sources (e.g., medical, legal, and scientific documents as well as transcripts of interviews with players and NFL officials), let's now imagine you conclude that the players' demands do have merit—that there does exists a solid, verifiable connection between playing professional football and suffering traumatic brain injury. On the basis of this research, you decide to write a research paper arguing that the NFL has an obligation to care for its former players.

First, let's look at how the rhetorical steps modeled above might help you begin putting together a viable research outline:

Step One: *Think About Your Purpose*

- One of my major goals is to provide readers with enough information about traumatic brain injury that they recognize it as a serious problem.

- Another major goal is to help readers understand the responsibility the NFL has in addressing this issue.

Step Two: *Consider Your Audience*

- I am addressing a general audience composed of readers who may or may not follow professional football on a regular basis.

- Because this is not a specialized audience, it is important that my research paper provide a good deal of background information about the issue as well as information about the views of those actively involved in this debate.

Step Three: *Identify Your Argument*

- In the most basic terms, I am trying to make the argument that the National Football League has a responsibility to care for those players who have suffered brain injury playing professional football.

- To support this argument, I want to present convincing evidence about the connection between professional football and traumatic brain injury as well as sources that make a convincing argument about the need for the NFL to take responsibility.

Step Four: *Construct Your Voice*

- ○ To provide the necessary background, it makes sense to start by presenting the scientific evidence establishing the connection between football and traumatic brain injury.

- ○ I will then transition from these sources to those presenting views about the responsibility of the NFL.

Step Five: *Speculate About Credibility*

- ○ The most credible sources for the first section of the paper are those that come from reputable medical and/or scientific organizations.

- ○ The most credible sources for the second section are those that come from representatives most directly involved in the lawsuit over NFL responsibility.

Now, let's take a look at what an example of a research outline for this topic might look like:

Topic: The recent lawsuit between the NFL and a group of retired players over whether the league is responsible for the high incidence of traumatic brain injury among its former players.

Argument: The NFL has a responsibility to care for and compensate those former players suffering from brain disease:

- Because scientific research has uncovered a link between football-related concussions and brain injury.
- Because research reveals that the NFL had prior knowledge of this connection and endeavored to keep it from being made public.
- Because economic research shows that the NFL is one of the most profitable entities in all of American business and can thus easily afford to compensate these former players.

I. Introduction
- Background and History of Brain Injury Debate
- Quick Discussion: Why this issue is important
  - ○ Growing awareness about the dangers of professional football
  - ○ High incidence of brain injuries in former players
  - ○ Emergence of scientific data supporting a connection
- Preview My Argument: The NFL should take responsibility for fixing this problem.

II. First Supporting Point
- Main Idea: How violent professional football is becoming
- Scientific studies showing connection between football and brain injury
- Quote from medical researcher (source 1)
- Examples of former players with brain injuries (source 2)

III. Second Supporting Point
- Main Idea: The NFL's awareness of the problem
- Legal documents showing the league's knowledge of the problem (source 3)
- Quote from NFL lawyer (source 4)

IV. Third Supporting Point
- Main Idea: Representatives of former players making the same allegation
- Testimony from lawyer for retired players (source 5)
- Newspaper op-eds supporting players' claims (sources 6 and 7)

V. Fourth Supporting Point
- Main Idea: The need to protect children
- Need for professional sports to model the right messages for kids
- Need to make football safe at the youth level
- Quote from "Play It Safe" organization (source 8)

VI. Fifth Supporting Point
- Main Idea: How the economics of football prevent progress on this issue
- Annual revenue of the NFL (source 9)
- What compensating retired players would cost (source 10)
- Violence of the sport at the heart of the NFL's popularity

VII. Conclusion
- Restate main argument
- It is the NFL's responsibility to compensate former players
- Strength of scientific evidence
- Issues of fairness
- Sending the right message to kids

Integrating Research Sources

With a completed a research outline in hand, you can then turn your attention to creating a first draft of your research paper, a transition that shifts the focus from the macro to the micro level. Composing a first draft involves making decisions about the specific parts of each source you are going to include and the way you are going to relate this material to your own larger argument. Making these kinds of decisions requires that you take a longer, more critical look at each source you want to include. What makes this source material important? What issue does it address? What information does it contain? And how does this material relate to your argument?

There are three basic strategies for integrating source material into a draft of your essay:

1. *Direct Quotation*: This strategy involves excerpting part or all of the material in a source exactly as it appears. Quoting directly is a useful strategy when the source contains particularly important information or when the person being cited is a recognizable or respected authority on your topic. If you are considering quoting an excerpt directly, make sure you do the following:

- Give the writer credit; make sure you include all necessary bibliographic information.
- Introduce or frame the quote with a comment of your own that establishes the context.
- Follow the quotation with your own discussion of how and why it is significant.
- Copy quotations carefully, reproducing each exactly as it is written.
- Use ellipsis marks if you omit part of the quotation.

Here is an example of a direct quotation based on our hypothetical example:

> In his op-ed, NFL Players Association lawyer William Princeton writes, "It is high time that the NFL owned up to its responsibility for the grievous injuries suffered by countless NFL players. This admission would go a long way toward righting a historic wrong." Princeton's statement offers a succinct summary of the position of those on one side of this debate (4).

2. *Paraphrasing Sources*: Paraphrasing focuses on one part of a source (e.g., a particular idea or a piece of information) and restates this part in the writer's own words. Paraphrasing is an effective strategy when the source itself is complicated, confusing, or otherwise difficult to understand. Paraphrasing is also a handy way for you to demonstrate your own understanding of the source. If you are considering paraphrasing a source, make sure you do the following:

- Identify the source, and comment on its significance.
- Include all relevant information in the quotation.
- Collect the information you need to create an in-text citation.
- State the meaning of the quotation in your own words as objectively as possible.

Here is an example of a paraphrase:

> In his op-ed essay, NFL Players Association lawyer William Princeton urges the NFL to acknowledge responsibility for its injured former players (4).

3. *Summarizing Sources*: Summarizing is where you describe all of the major content within a source using your own words. Unlike paraphrasing, which describes only one piece or part of a larger source, summarizing aims to presents all of a source's major information or key points. It can be a particularly useful strategy for dealing with a source that contains a good deal of information, allowing you to condense this information in a more efficient and succinct way. For this reason, summaries are generally shorter than the source they are summarizing. If you are considering summarizing a source, make sure you do the following:

- Identify the source, and comment on why it is significant.
- Collect all information necessary to create an in-text citation.

• Include only the basic information contained in the source.
• Make sure your summary is shorter than the source you are summarizing.

Here is an example of summarizing:

> In his op-ed, NFL Players Association lawyer William Princeton argues that an NFL admission of responsibility for players' brain injuries would be of historical importance (4).

Obviously, your decision about which of these strategies to employ will depend on the particular goal you are trying to accomplish. If you are using a given source to establish background or context for your discussion, you might choose to paraphrase or summarize its content. If, on the other hand, you want to highlight the particular credentials or individual perspective of a source's author, direct quotation may strike you as a better strategy. Despite these differences, however, there are certain steps you should follow each time you integrate source material into your essay:

• *Present It*: Introduce the source information in some way.
• *Link It*: Show how this source is relevant to the topic at hand.
• *Comment on It*: Make sure you use this source to advance your own argument.
• *Cite It*: Use the appropriate documentation style.

Identifying and Avoiding Plagiarism

Incorporating source material into your research paper can be viewed as engaging in a conversation with those who already care about this topic. It is crucial, therefore, that in making your own research argument, you clearly differentiate between the ideas and information that are yours and the ideas and information that come from others. In practical terms, this means that you need to acknowledge and identify the names of those whose ideas and words you are citing. Failing to acknowledge or credit the work of others is called **plagiarism**. In the most basic sense, plagiarism is using someone else's ideas without acknowledgement in their original—or even altered—form and treating them as your own. As a rule of thumb, make sure that you cite the source for every piece of information in your paper that is not directly your own idea, opinion, or personal observation. Even when done inadvertently plagiarism is a serious offense.

Sometimes it can be difficult to know whether a discussion that includes other peoples' words, ideas, or information is in fact plagiarism. If you find yourself in doubt, you are plagiarizing if:

• You include an exact quotation from someone else without using quotation marks.
• You paraphrase or summarize someone else's words or ideas without citing that person as the source.
• You include information obtained from another source without citing the source.
• You present some else's essay as your own.

Avoiding the pitfall of plagiarism has become even more challenging in today's digital age, as more and more research arguments have begun to incorporate visual and/or multimedia source material. Because many of these sources lack the traditional bibliographic information found in print documents, it is especially important that you acknowledge and credit the person or entity responsible for producing it. As you browse through websites online, for example, make sure you are recording all of the available information about where the source comes from: the website author, the title, the sponsoring organization, and the date. If you are using visual imagery (e.g., a photo, chart, ad, or video) that you have found, make sure to list the Web source information as well as any additional information about where this image may have originally come from. When searching for material online, it's not enough to simply cite the search engine used to find it (e.g., Google). Be sure to find the original source, and list the information about it fully.

Creating Your First Draft

Once you've used your research outline to organize your sources and make some preliminary decisions about what material from these sources you want to include, you are ready to begin writing your first draft. It's important to remember that you are not going to create an entirely finished or polished paper the first time. A first draft, as the term itself makes clear, is your first attempt at organizing all of your source material. As such, you should concentrate on making sure you've included all of the source material you want your paper to contain. As you revise this effort in subsequent drafts, you can work on connecting this material to your own argument.

Student Writing, "Brain Injury and the NFL: Time for a Change"

Using the hypothetical topic of football and traumatic brain injury discussed above, here's an example of what a first draft might look like.

For years, we have heard stories about former pro football players struggling with the effects of Alzheimer's, dementia, and other cognitive disabilities. But it's only recently that new scientific research has begun to *Presenting background information, establishing context*

5   demonstrate a clear connection between the condition of these former players and their careers on the football field. Indeed, a growing number of scientists, activists, and spokespeople are becoming convinced that the violence inherent in modern professional football is

10   the cause behind the rise in traumatic brain injury. Despite this growing belief, the NFL has consistently denied a link between professional football and traumatic injury. And yet, while the league continues to

deny the connection, it's becoming clear that the best
course of action is for the NFL to acknowledge the link
between football and traumatic brain injury, to take responsibility for compensating its former players, and to
institute changes to make the game less violent.

Over the last few years, more and more scientific
research has come to indicate that playing professional football poses significant risk. A study examining the medical histories of 300 former NFL players,
for example, noted "an extremely high incidence of
self-reported problems" among former players and
their caregivers, including "memory loss, dementia,
and suicidal thoughts" (Johnson 34). Similarly, researchers at the Boston University's Center for the
Study of Traumatic Encephalopathy discovered evidence
of degenerative brain disease in autopsies performed
on 19 of the 20 football players they examined (12).
Evidence such as this suggests a strong correlation
between playing professional football and suffering
brain injury.

While the NFL has continued to maintain publicly
that there is no clear connection between professional
football and traumatic brain injury, a set of internal
documents has recently surfaced that appear to indicate the opposite. In fact, the league commissioned
its own study of brain injury 10 years ago, compiling
data about the incidence of such injuries among current players. What this study discovered is alarming.
According to the NFL's own internal study, nearly one-
third of active players suffered an injury to the head or
neck that resulted in temporary loss of cognitive function (Korenki 22). While league officials continue to
deny any responsibility to compensate retired players,
studies like this suggest that league officials understand the degree to which football itself is a cause of
brain injury.

Not surprisingly, the statements made by former
players and their representatives echo the findings of
the NFL's own internal study. In his op-ed essay, NFL
Players Association lawyer William Princeton writes,
"It is high time that the NFL owned up to its responsibility for the grievous injuries suffered by countless
NFL players. This admission would go a long way

15

Previewing argument

Presenting scientific data as   20
first supporting point

25

30

Using primary sources to
present second supporting point   35

40

45

Using secondary source material   50
to present third supporting
point

55

toward righting a historic wrong." Princeton's statement offers a succinct summary of the position of
those on one side of this debate (4).

60   This issue not only affects the welfare of former NFL   *More primary scientific data as*
players, it is also of significance to younger kids. In   *supporting point*
fact, the most recent studies have shown that the most
significant risk of brain injury may exist for those playing football at the youth level. Researchers at Texas

65   A&M University, for example, studied the effect on
high school and middle school football players of
"concussive" and "subconcussive" hits. What they discovered is that these repeated blows to the head con-
stituted a serious threat to the "healthy functioning of

70   the young brain" (15). This kind of research gives credit
to the view espoused by such organizations as Play It
Safe, which urges youth coaches to set strict new limits
around the kind of contact allowable for football players under 17 years of age (3). If kids are just as vulner-

75   able to brain injury as professional players, doesn't the
NFL have a moral obligation to model for such kids a
safe and responsible way to play football?

        Many who oppose the idea of the NFL taking action   *Addressing potential*
on this issue do so on the basis of the claim of its pro-   *counterargument*

80   hibitive cost (Jones, Tsao, and Williams). It is simply too
expensive, they argue, to compensate the number of
players already suffering or expected to suffer in the
future from degenerative brain disease. This argument, however, is belied by evidence of how large and

85   profitable a business the NFL has become. The most
recent statistics identify the total revenue generated
by the NFL to top $1.3 billion annually (NFL 5) an
amount more than adequate to meeting the needs of
its injured players.

90   For all these reasons, it is crucial that the NFL end its   *Recapping main argument*
long-standing silence and act upon the responsibility it
has toward its injured former players. To do so would
not only represent an acknowledgment of the growing
science around traumatic brain injury, it would also con-

95   stitute a significant step forward in the fight for fairness
in the workplace. Not only would the affected athletes
benefit, but so would the millions of football enthusiasts and football participants nationwide, all of whom
look to the NFL as the standard for the sport they love.

Revising Your First Draft

No research paper is going to be ready for final submission after an initial draft. Creating a fully developed and well-organized argument requires that you put your research essay through successive drafts, making additions and changes at each stage. This process is called **revision**. In the most basic sense, revision involves looking at your draft again (i.e. re-visioning) to determine what further work needs to be done to make it better. Revision can take a number of different forms—from adding new sources to amending your main argument to editing for style, grammar, and punctuation. In relation to the draft above, for example, you might begin formulating a revision plan by asking yourself the following questions:

- Is my argument consistent? Am I arguing the same points in the Introduction and the Conclusion?
- Does my discussion progress logically from one point to another?
- Do I present a proper balance between my own views and the views of others I am citing?
- Do my sources reflect an adequate range of views on this topic?
- Do I anticipate and address opposing points of view?
- Do I use clear, straightforward language?
- Do I include the necessary signposts or transitions from one section to another?
- Are there any spelling or punctuation errors?

To see what an example of revision might look like, let's return to our example about football and traumatic brain injury. Look closely at each of the italicized revisions in the essay below. In what ways do they serve to strengthen the presentation, organization, and discussion of the source material in the first draft?

Revision: Student Writing, "Brain Injury and the NFL: Time for a Change"

This revised essay models some of the key changes and additions a writer might consider in moving from a first to a second draft.

For years, *sports media outlets have been filled with stories* about former pro football players struggling with the effects of Alzheimer's, dementia, and other cognitive disabilities. *In the last couple of years, however, this topic has increasingly gained widespread media attention as new scientific research has begun* to demonstrate a clear connection between the condition of these former players and their careers on the football field. *Through the work of organizations like the Center for the Study of Traumatic Brain Encephalopathy at Boston University,* a growing number of

Adding further detail to the context for this topic

5

10

scientists, activists, and spokespeople are becoming
convinced that the violence inherent in modern professional football is the cause behind the rise in trau-
15   matic brain injury.

*And yet, in the face of a growing scientific consensus
around this issue,* the NFL has consistently denied a
link between professional football and traumatic
injury. *On closer inspection, there should be little sur-*
20   *prise that the league would maintain the position. Not*
only does the NFL have a vested financial interest in
protecting itself from compensation claims made by its
former players, it also needs to protect the reputation
of professional football itself, which might be signifi-
25   *cantly harmed by an admission that the sport poses*
real long-term risk to the physical and mental well-
being of its players. And yet, as the scientific evidence
continues to mount, it's becoming clear that the best
(*and perhaps only*) course of action is for the NFL to
30   acknowledge the link between football and traumatic
brain injury, to take responsibility for compensating its
former players, and to institute changes to make the
game less violent.

While some NFL officials continue to question the
35   *validity of the football/brain injury connection,* the sci-
entific research establishing this connection is becom-
ing increasingly clear. The last two years, for example,
has witnessed the publication of no fewer than three
studies, each of which provides compelling evidence
40   *of a connection between professional football and*
traumatic brain injury. Two of these studies, one pub-
lished by the National Institutes of Health (NIH) and
the other by Johns Hopkins University, compile and
analyze data on the injury rates of former professional
45   *football players dating all the way back to the early*
1970s. The NIH study, for example, examined the
medical histories of 300 former NFL players *and* noted
"an extremely high incidence of self-reported problems" among former players and their caregivers, in-
50   cluding "memory loss, dementia, and suicidal thoughts"
(Johnson 34). Similarly, researchers at Boston University's Center for the Study of Traumatic Encephalopathy
discovered evidence of degenerative brain disease in
autopsies performed on 19 of the 20 football players

*Adding reference to a specific
source to establish writer's
authority or ethos from the
outset*

Establishing a clearer transition

*Presenting a more detailed and
complete preview of the overall
argument*

*Creating a topic sentence that
provides a more effective
transition into the main point*

Summarizing source material

Direct quotation

they examined (12). Evidence such as this suggests a
strong correlation between playing professional football and suffering brain injury.

Significantly, these findings were confined to organi-
zations unaffiliated with the NFL. While the league has
continued to maintain publicly that there is no clear
connection between professional football and traumatic brain injury, a set of internal documents has recently surfaced that appear to indicate the opposite.
In fact, the league commissioned its own study of
brain injury 10 years ago, compiling data about the
incidence of such injuries among current players. What
this study discovered is alarming. According to the
NFL's own internal study, nearly one-third of active
players suffered an injury to the head or neck that resulted in temporary loss of cognitive function (Korenki
22). While *such findings are alarming, perhaps the*
most significant fact about this internal study is that
the league attempted to keep them from being dis-
closed to the public for several years. According to a
2013 report by the PBS documentary Frontline, league
officials sought to suppress their own findings about
the dangers of playing football in order to continue de-
nying responsibility to compensate its retired players.

Not surprisingly, the statements made by former
players and their representatives echo the findings of
the NFL's own internal study. In his op-ed essay, NFL
Players Association lawyer William Princeton writes,
"It is high time that the NFL owned up to its responsibility for the grievous injuries suffered by countless
NFL players. This admission would go a long way
toward righting a historic wrong." Princeton's statement offers a succinct summary of the position of
those on one side of this debate (4). *Offering personal*
testimony in support of this same view, retired player Y
discussses the physical and mental challenges he faces
30 years after retiring from the game: "I can't remember things. I can't drive myself. Basically, I can't do
anything anymore."

Personal stories like these give a face to what other-
wise might feel like a strictly scientific debate. They
remind us that the NFL's efforts to deny the scientific
evidence have direct, human consequences. In the

55

Paraphrase

Inserting a topic sentence to
serve as a transition

60

65

70

75

Adding reference to an
additional source

80

Using secondary source
quotations as second
supporting point

85

90

95

face of such moving testimony, it becomes clear that
the scientific debate over football and brain injury is
also an ethical debate, one that raises questions about
the moral responsibility the NFL has to care for the athletes whose sacrifices have done so much to make the
league so profitable.

The moral or ethical implication of this issue becomes
even more apparent when we expand the context to
include not just professional football players but the
thousands who play at the college and youth level as
well. Many of the same studies suggest that brain
injury not only affects the welfare of former NFL players, but may also be a significant risk to those who play
football at a much younger age. In fact, both the NIH
and Boston University studies suggest that the most
significant risk of brain injury may exist for those playing football at the youth level. Researchers at Texas
A&M University, for example, studied the effect on
high school and middle school football players of
"concussive" and "subconcussive" hits. What they discovered is that these repeated blows to the head con-
stituted a serious threat to the "healthy functioning of
the young brain" (15).

This kind of research provides fodder for a growing
number of activist organizations that seek to raise
awareness about the dangers playing football poses to
young kids. Organizations like Play It Safe, which urges
youth coaches to set strict new limits around the kind
of contact allowable for football players under 17 years
of age (3), strengthens the case for those urging the
NFL to take action. While the issue of youth injury may
seem unrelated to the debate over the league's responsibility to its former players, on closer inpection it
becomes clear that the two are linked. Part of the NFL's
appeal depends upon its success in presenting its athletes as role models to young kids. If it turns out that
kids are just as vulnerable to brain injury as professional players, this only increases the obligation of the
league to be as honest and forthright about the threats
that confront its own players.

The obligation the NFL owes to its players is not only
an issue of honesty, it is also an issue of economics.

Adding discussion to show how sources help make the writer's larger argument.

More developed transition sentence

Identifying the specific source

Highlighting this as a separate point in its own pargraph

Anticipating and responding to potential counterargument

Inserting topic sentence to serve as a transition

Some who oppose the idea of the NFL taking action on this issue do so on the basis *of a belief that such an action would simply prove too costly* (Jones, Tsao, and Williams). It is simply too expensive, these critics argue, to compensate the number of players already suffering or expected to suffer in the future from degenerative brain disease. This argument, however, *loses some of its power when considered in light of information about the true financial state of the National Football League. In fact,* the most recent statistics reveal the NFL to be one of the most profitable enterprises in America, generating an annual revenue in 2013 that topped $1.3 billion. *Even by conservative estimates, the league is clearly in a position to weather the financial cost a settlement with its injured former players might incur.*

Whether measured by scientific, economic, or ethical standards, the case for the NFL to do the right thing by its former players is clear. For all the reason cited above, it is crucial that the NFL end its longstanding silence and act upon the responsibility it has toward its injured former players. To do so would not only represent an acknowledgment of the growing science around traumatic brain injury, it would also constitute a significant step forward in the fight for fairness in the workplace. Not only would the affected athletes benefit, but so would the millions of football enthusiasts and football participants nationwide, all of whom look to the NFL as the standard for the sport they love.

Margin annotations:

Addressing potential counterargument (145)

Inserting additional discussion of source (155)

Inserting a topic sentence that previews conclusion to come (160)

Line numbers: 140, 145, 150, 155, 160, 165

Citing and Documenting Sources

Whenever you make reference to material from another source, whether through direct quotation, paraphrase, or summary, you need to provide a citation for this source. There are three main formats for citing sources: the Modern Language Association (MLA), the American Psychological Association (APA), and the Chicago Manual of Style (CMS). Whatever format you follow, there are two, equally important, ways to cite a source: an **in-text citation**, in which the citation is included directly in the essay immediately following the reference, and a **Works Cited** page, where the citation appears on a list at the end of the essay. Included below are guidelines for how to complete both in-text and Works Cited citations, according to the MLA format.

In-Text Citations: MLA Guidelines

On the whole, the MLA system of in-text citation is very simple to understand. The system asks that you show where you originally found a direct quotation or the information for a paraphrase or a summary by inserting a brief, parenthetical citation at the end of the borrowed material in your written text. The typical in-text parenthetical citation contains the author's last name and the page number. However, if you include the author's name in the text, then you do not need to include it in the parenthetical citation. The examples below provide a more detailed picture:

1. *A direct quotation with the author mentioned in the text*: If you introduce the author's name in the body of the text before you quote directly, you do not need to include the name in the parenthetical citation.

    > Although many celebrate the freedom and convenience of social media, Douglass Rushkoff argues that sites like Facebook do "not exist to help us make friends, but to turn our network of connections, brand preferences, and activities over time into money for others" (1).

2. *A direct quotation with the author not mentioned in the text*:

    > Although many celebrate the freedom and convenience of social media, some critics contend that sites like Facebook do "not exist to help us make friends, but to turn our network of connections, brand preferences, and activities over time into money for others" (Rushkoff 1).

3. *A paraphrase or summary with the author mentioned in the text*:

    > According to Douglass Rushkoff, social media are often more interested in making money than in enabling genuine social connection (1).

4. *A paraphrase or summary with the author not mentioned in the text*:

    > In the eyes of some critics, social media are often more interested in making money than in enabling genuine social connection (Rushkoff 1).

In-Text Citation: Electronic Sources

For essays, articles, and book chapters, cite electronic sources in the text just as you would print sources. Introduce the quotation with the author's name, or cite the author's last name (or a short title, if there is no author) with a page or paragraph number in parentheses at the end. If the source has no page or paragraph numbers or if you are citing or quoting from the whole source as a single document, place only the author's name in the parentheses. For websites, in-text citations need to include the name of the website. Included below are more specific examples of in-text citations for electronic sources:

1. *A direct quotation with the author mentioned in the text*:

    > In his online piece "Take America Back," FreedomWorks founder Matt Kibbe makes the argument that the current presidential administration threatens "[t]he very principles that define the uniquely American experiment" (3).

2. *A direct quotation with the author not mentioned in the text*:

> In an online piece, the organization FreedomWorks makes an argument that the current presidential administration threatens "[t]he very principles that define the uniquely American experiment" (Kibbe 3).

3. *A paraphrase or summary with the author mentioned in the text*:

> Writing online, FreedomWorks founder Matt Kibbe argues that the current administration is a threat to democracy (3).

4. *A paraphrase or summary with the author not mentioned in the text*:

> In a recent online piece, the organization FreedomWorks argues that the current administration is a threat to democracy (Kibbe 3).

5. *An in-text citation for a website with no author mentioned*:

> A recent website identifies "canned tuna as the most common source of mercury in our diet" (Consumer Reports).

Works Cited: MLA Guidelines

As noted above, a Works Cited page is a list at the end that includes information about each source referenced or included in the essay. The section below provides examples of the format used to cite each type of source.

PRINT BOOKS

Here are examples of how to cite book sources in MLA format:

1. *A book by one author*:

> Almond, Steve. *Against Football: One Fan's Reluctant Manifesto*. New York: Melville House, 2014. Print.

2. *A book by two or three authors*:

> Blanco, William T., and David Canon. *American Politics Today*. New York: Norton, 2013. Print.

3. *An edited collection of articles or an anthology*:

> Andersen, Margaret, and Patricia Hill Collins, eds. *Race, Class, Gender: An Anthology*. New York: Cengage, 2012. Print.

4. *An article in an edited collection or an anthology*:

> McIntosh, Peggy. "White Privilege: Unpacking the Invisible Knapsack." *Race, Class, Gender: An Anthology*. Eds. Margaret Andersen and Patricia Hill Collins. New York: Cengage, 2012. 13–37. Print.

PRINT ARTICLES

Here are examples of how to cite other print sources in MLA format:

1. *An article from a magazine*:

   Nussbaum, Emily. "Demographic Art." *New Yorker* 15 Sept. 2014: 72–81. Print.

2. *An article from a newspaper*:

   Hakim, Danny. "Google Faces Backlash in Europe on US Dominance." *New York Times* 9 September 2014: A1+. Print.

3. *An article in a periodical with no author listed*:

   "Two Premiers and a Reunion." *New Yorker* 9 Sept. 2014: 10. Print.

4. *An article in a journal*:

   Ferris, Dana R. "'English Only' and Multilingualism in Composition Studies." *College English* 77.1 (2014): 73–83. Print.

ELECTRONIC SOURCES

Here are examples of how to cite electronic sources in MLA format. Note that MLA no longer requires that the URL information be included in the citation.

1. *A document from a website*:

   Foster, Jan. "Challenges in Clinical Nurse Special Education and Practice." *Online Journal of Issues in Nursing* 9.3 (2014). American Nurses Association, 2014. Web. 20 June 2014. http://www.nursingworld.org/MainMenuCategories/ANAMarketplace/ANAPeriodicals/OJIN.aspx.

2. *An online book*:

   Melville Lee, W.L. *A History of Police in England*. London: Kessinger, 2007. *Project Gutenberg*. Project Gutenberg Online Book Catalog, 2014. Web. 31 Mar. 2014.

3. *An article in an online newspaper*:

   Phillip, Abby. "Take a Seat: You May Be Able to Reverse the Damage to Your Health." *Washington Post*. Washington Post, 8 September 2014. Web. 10 September 2014.

4. *An article in an online magazine*:

   Finley, Klint. "Ex-Googler Shares His Big Data Secrets With the Masses." *Wired* September 2014. CondéNet. Web. 10 Sept. 2014.

5. *An article in an online scholarly journal*:

   McClintock, Elizabeth Aura. "Beauty and Status: The Illusion of Exchange in Partner Selection." *American Sociological Review* 79.4 (2014): 575–604. Web. 12 Sept. 2014.

Credits

Introduction

Ashlyn Archer, et al. Letter to the Editor, *The DePauw*, April 13, 2010. Reprinted by permission of *The DePauw*.

Chapter 1

Planet Green Recycle, "The Bike Revolution," on *The Official Planet Green Recycle Blog*, Reprinted by permission.

Reprinted by permission of Arne Hückelheim.

Excerpt from Editorial, "To Eliminate Fraternity Hazing, Pledging Must End," *The Cornell Daily Sun*, November 29, 2012. Reprinted by permission of *The Cornell Daily Sun*.

Joel Pett, *The Lexington Herald-Leader*. Provided by Cartoon Arts International/The New York Times Syndicate.

Sherry Turkle, "The Flight from Conversation," *The New York Times*, April 21, 2012. Reprinted by permission of *The New York Times*.

Chapter 2

Editorial Staff. "A Big Change, But Not the End," *The Spectator*, September 16, 2013. Reprinted with permission.

Chapter 4

Suleika Jaouad, "Life, Interrupted: Five Days of Chemo," *The New York Times*, August 30, 2012. Reprinted by permission of *The New York Times*.

Sheryl Sandberg, "Introduction: Internalizing the Revolution," from *Lean In: Women, Work, and the Will to Lead* (New York: Knopf, 2013), 3–11.

Anon, "More Lessons About Charter Schools" op-ed, *The New York Times*, February 1, 2013. Reprinted by permission of *The New York Times*.

Anon, "I am an Undocumented Immigrant at Stanford University," *The Guardian*, May 16, 2013. Copyright Guardian News & Media Ltd, 2013.

Julia Angwin, "Why I'm Unfriending You on Facebook," JuliaAngwin.com, February 12, 2013. Reprinted with permission.

Leah Koenig, "The Classy Dive: The Dos and Don'ts of Dumpster Diving," Mother Nature Network, January 5, 2010. Copyright © 2010 MNN Holdings, LLC. Reprinted with permission.

Beth Teitell, "Why Do We Loathe Mullets?" *Boston Globe*, July 15, 2010. Reprinted by permission of the author.

Lawrence Gostin, "Banning Large Sodas Is Legal and Smart," CNN.com, March 13, 2013. © 2013 Cable News Network, Inc. Used by permission.

Chapter 5

Courtney Wittmann, "Best Warriors Highlight Army Strong Values," Army Live, October 20, 2010. Used by permission.

Matt Kibbe, "Take America Back," *FreedomWorks*. Reprinted by permission of FreedomWorks.

Andy Reynolds, "Voto Aqui." *Getty Image 82600554*, Andy Reynolds/Taxi/Getty Images.

Alicia Criado, "After Waiting 13 Years, My Family Reunited," National Council of La Raza, *May 16, 2013*. © 2013 by the National Council of La Raza. All rights reserved.

Jamie Kelley, "The Steroid Problem, and How to Fix It," Sports Illustrated Kids, SIKids.com, September 19, 2012. Reprinted by permission of the author.

Bryan Johnson, "Make State-Church Separation Absolute," *FreeThought Today*, December 2012. Reprinted by permission of the author.

José Cruz, "College Affordability: Damned If You Go, Damned If You Don't?" *The Huffington Post*, January 20, 2012. Reprinted by permission of the author.

Sherry Turkle, "The Flight From Conversation," *The New York Times*, April 21, 2012. Reprinted by permission of *The New York Times*.

Douglas Rushkoff, "Why I'm Quitting Facebook," CNN, February 25, 2013. Reproduced by permission of Cable News Network, Inc.

Shankar Vedantam, "Partisanship Is the New Racism," *Slate*, January 24, 2011. © 2011 The Slate Group, used by permission.

Mario Tama/Getty Images News/ Getty Images.

F. Diane Barth, "Why Women Fear Envy and Why We Don't Need To," *Psychology Today*, July 17, 2013. Copyright © 2013 Sussex Publishers, LLC, used with permission.

Tillie Olsen, "I Stand Here Ironing." from *Tell Me a Riddle, Requa I, and Other Works* by Tillie Olsen. (Lincoln: University of Nebraska Press, 1961). © 1989 by Tillie Olsen, reprinted by permission of the publisher.

Stephen King, "Why We Crave Horror Movies." in *Models for Writers, Short Essays for Composition,* by Alfred Rosa. (Boston: Bedford/St. Martins, 2004), 460–463. Originally published in *Playboy*. Reprinted with permission.

Chapter 6

Dani DiPirro, excerpt from "Get Happier (.com)!" from PositivelyPresent.com, September 23, 2009. © Dani DiPirro/PositivelyPresent.com, reprinted with permission.

"Why Fitness Matters," Reprinted with permission. *http://www.girlshealth.gov/fitness/whygetfit*

Justin Bilicki, "We Are Destroying the Earth" cartoon, 2012. Union of Concerned Scientists, used with permission.

Peter Hakim and Cameron Combs, "Why the US Should Legalize Marijuana," *The Miami Herald*, January 26, 2014. Reprinted by permission of *The Miami Herald*.

"Kate and William Bring Home Royal Baby Boy," CNN.com, July 23, 2013. © 2013 Cable News Network, Inc., used by permission.

Michael Solís, "Social Media: Obstacle to Friendship/Love." from *The Huffington Post*, August 26, 2013. Reprinted by permission of the author.

Christopher Calabrese and Matthew Harwood, "Destroying the Right to be Left Alone." © 2013 American Civil Liberties Union, used by permission. Originally published at TomDispatch.com, September 22, 2013.

Allison Brennan, "Microtargeting: How Campaigns Know You Better Than You Know Yourself," CNN.com, November 5, 2012. © 2012 Cable News Network, Inc., used by permission.

Photo reproduced by permission from Getty Images, Digital Vision/Photodisc.

Daniel Solove, "Why Privacy Matters, Even When You Have 'Nothing to Hide'" from *Nothing to Hide: The False Tradeoff Between Privacy and Security*, by Daniel J. Solove. (New Haven, CT: Yale University Press, 2011), 21–32. Reprinted by permission of the publisher.

Photo reproduced by permission from Getty Images, Tim Robberts/Digital Vision/ Getty Images.

Jim Taylor, "Popular Culture: Reality TV is NOT Reality," *Psychology Today*, January 31, 2011. Copyright © 2011 Sussex Publishers, LLC.

George Orwell, "Shooting an Elephant" from *A Collection of Essays by George Orwell* (Boston: Houghton Mifflin Harcourt). Copyright 1950 by Sonia Brownell Orwell and renewed 1978 by Sonia Pitt-Rivers. Reprinted by permission of the publisher.

Jhumpa Lahiri, "Rice." *The New Yorker*, November 23, 2009. Copyright © 2009 by Jhumpa Lahiri. Reprinted by permission of William Morris Endeavor Entertainment, LLC as agent for the author.

Chapter 7

Adam Copeland, excerpts from "I Will Pray on National Day of Prayer but NOT Because Congress Told Me To," A Wee Blether blog, May 6, 2010. © 2010 Adam Copeland. Reprinted by permission of the author.

Kristi Myllenbeck, "You're Vegan, We Get It," *The Spartan Daily*, October 10, 2013. Copyright 2013 by The Spartan Daily. Reprinted by permission of *The Spartan Daily* at San Jose State University.

Post from "Should the Pledge of Allegiance Be Said in Schools?" Debate.org, 2013, reprinted by permission of Juggle, LLC.

Getty Image 80466899, Design Pics/Chris Knorr/Design Pics/Getty Images

Amanda Hall, "College Affordability and the Growing Cost of Education," Rock the Vote blog, August 29, 2013. Reprinted by permission of the author.

John Darkow, "Student Loan Debt" cartoon, *Columbia Daily Tribune*, October 28, 2011. Reprinted by permission of Cagle Cartoons.

Penny Lee, "The Problem with a $15 Minimum Wage," US News.com, September 4, 2013. Reprinted with permission of U.S. News & World Report LP.

Myisha Cherry, "Twitter Trolls and the Refusal to Be Silenced." *The Huffington Post*, August 6, 2013. Reprinted by permission of the author.

Lisa Bonos, "The Art of the Digital Breakup," *The Washington Post, August 23, 2012.* Reproduced with permission of Washington Post Co. via Copyright Clearance Center.

Geoffrey Nunberg, "Swearing: A Long and #%@&$ History," *Fresh Air*, July 11, 2012. Reprinted by permission. Fresh Air is produced by WHYY, Inc. and distributed by NPR.

Bonnie Erbe, "As Religious Affiliation Declines, What's the Impact?" *Long Island Newsday*, December 26, 2012. Reprinted by permission of Scripps Howard News Service.

E.J. Dionne, "Will We Keep Hating Government?" *Truthdig.com, May 6, 2010.* Appeared originally in *The Washington Post* titled "Can We Reverse the Tide on Government Distrust?" Reproduced with permission of Washington Post Co. via Copyright Clearance Center, © 2010.

Courtesy archives.gov

Courtesy teachingamericanhistory.org

Chapter 8

Hailey Yook, "Positive Stereotypes Are Hurtful, Too," *The Daily Californian*, March 10, 2014. Copyright © 2014 *The Daily Californian*, the Independent Berkeley Student Publishing Co., Inc. Reprinted with permission.

"Ah, To Be Young, Rich, White, Male, College-Educated, Straight, and in Love," *The Onion,* October 23, 2013. Copyright © 2013, by Onion, Inc., reprinted with permission.

Adrian Rodriguez, "Body Art Stereotypes Misrepresent Tattoo and Piercing Culture." *Golden Gate Xpress*, May 11, 2013. © 2013 by Adrian Rodriquez, reprinted by permission of the author.

Chapter 9

Index